LITERATURE, LAW, AND RHETORICAL
PERFORMANCE IN THE ANTICOLONIAL
ATLANTIC

Literature, Law, and Rhetorical Performance in the Anticolonial Atlantic

ANNE W. GULICK

The Ohio State University Press • Columbus

Copyright © 2016 by The Ohio State University.
All rights reserved.

Library of Congress Cataloging-in-Publication Data

Names: Gulick, Anne W., author.
Title: Literature, law, and rhetorical performance in the anticolonial Atlantic / Anne W. Gulick.
Description: Columbus : The Ohio State University Press, [2016] | "2016" | Includes bibliographical references and index.
Identifiers: LCCN 2015040582| ISBN 9780814213025 (cloth ; alk. paper) | ISBN 0814213022 (cloth ; alk. paper)
Subjects: LCSH: African literature (English)—20th century—History and criticism. | Caribbean literature (English)—20th century—History and criticism. | Postcolonialism in literature.
Classification: LCC PN51 .G84 2016 | DDC 809/.8896—dc23
LC record available at http://lccn.loc.gov/2015040582

Cover design by Authorsupport.com
Text design by Juliet Williams
Type set in Adobe Minion Pro
Printed by Thomson-Shore, Inc.

♾ The paper used in this publication meets the minimum requirements of the American National Standard for Information Sciences—Permanence of Paper for Printed Library Materials. ANSI Z39.48-1992.

9 8 7 6 5 4 3 2 1

FOR PHIL AND OSCAR

CONTENTS

	Acknowledgments	ix
	Introduction	1
1	Black Nation Time: Haiti's Textual Foundations and Generic Novelty in the Age of Revolution	16
2	The Romance of Prodigal Literacy: C. L. R. James's Histories of Rhetorical Revolution in the Black Atlantic	48
3	Declaring Negritude: The Universal Declaration of Human Rights and Aimé Césaire's *Cahier d'un retour au pays natal*	77
4	If You Could Make the Laws: Popular Authorship and the South African Freedom Charter	121
5	Novel Constitutions: The Genres of African Decolonization	146
6	The Right to Opacity: Ngũgĩ, Glissant, and Radical Multilingualism	188
	Coda	220
	Notes	227
	Works Cited	237
	Index	249

ACKNOWLEDGMENTS

THE INSTITUTIONAL, INTELLECTUAL, and personal support that made this book possible is difficult to account for in words. I am grateful for the funding I received from Duke University's Kenan Institute for Ethics as well as a William Preston Few fellowship. A grant from the Critical U.S. Studies Program made possible my participation at the Futures of American Studies Institute at Dartmouth College in 2007, where I received invaluable feedback on what became chapter 6. At the University of South Carolina, a Provost's Office Humanities Grant provided vital funds for writing time and travel. I want to express my gratitude to the staff of Perkins and Bostock Libraries at Duke, as well as the University of South Carolina's Thomas Cooper Library, Interlibrary Loan department, and PASCAL. Staff at Wits University's Historical Papers and the South Africa History Archive were unbelievably accommodating and helpful during my week and a half in Johannesburg in October 2011.

I know few academics who look back on their graduate school experience with as much fondness as do I and many of the other members of my cohort from the Duke English Department and Literature Program. I am forever indebted to the wisdom and kindness of Ian Baucom and Ranjanna Khanna, both extraordinary mentors as well as scholars. Srinivas Aravamudan and Michael Valdez Moses watched my writing and thinking mature throughout my studies, and remained generous and helpful even as the project changed shape and direction over time. Over lunch one day in the fall of 2003, Priscilla Wald sat down to talk with me about a paper I wanted to write about the Haitian Constitution; many lunches, coffees, walks, and hallway chats later, the paper evolved into this book manuscript. I am unspeakably lucky to have met and worked with her, and I aspire to her passionate, loyal, and rigorous brand of mentorship and scholarship. Former Dukies Monique Allewaert, Fiona Barnett Hollianna Bryan, Andrew Burkett, KC Clemens, Joseph Fitzpatrick, Monica Gerlach, Alexis Pauline Gumbs, Nathan Hensley, Matthew Irvin, Shannon Kelley, Madhumita Lahiri, Erin Gentry Lamb, Stacy Lavin, Russ Leo, Kathleen McClancy, John Miles, Vin Nardizzi, Tami Navarro, Eden Osucha, Britt Rusert, Philip Steer, John Tangney, and Cord Whitaker exemplify the kind of intellectual generosity to which I aspire, and all played a role in helping me conceive of this project in its earliest stages. I am grateful to Lesley Curtis for sharing her expertise on Haitian revolutionary history and literature, as well as some much-needed translation assistance (though all errors in the final manuscript are entirely mine). Hillary Eklund and Nihad Farooq helped me grow as a writer with their astute, insightful out-of-field feedback, and their friendship has nourished me in more ways than I can enumerate over the past thirteen years. The brilliant Allison Dushane has been among my most faithful friends, intellectual interlocutors, and commiserators since I first bought her friendship with a batch of molasses cookies in 2002. Sarah Lincoln's and Erin Fehskens' sharp eyes, meticulous comments, and unflagging encouragement have seen this project through to the very end.

My lucky streak has continued at the University of South Carolina English Department, which over the past seven years has provided a dynamic, collegial, and exceptionally supportive environment for teaching and research. Chairs Bill Rivers and Nina Levine have been my champions since the very beginning. Greg Forter's mentorship has kept me focused, confident, and passionate during this very long process; he is an intellectual inspiration, and I am proud to call him a friend. Elise Blackwell, Debra Rae Cohen, Susan Courtney, Cynthia Davis, Erik Doxtader, Jeanne Garane, David Miller, Tara Powell, and Qiana Whitted exemplify the intellectual generosity of the humanities programs here at (the other) USC, and have offered considerable sage advice during my years on the tenure track. Writing group members Kate Adams, Holly Crocker, and Tony Jarrells offered invaluable feedback on the project in its early stages. Brian Glavey, Catherine Keyser, Sara Schwebel, and Gretchen Woertendyke have read nearly every page of this manuscript multiple times. Without their friendship and support this book would not exist.

Beyond Duke and South Carolina, I am grateful to a host of other people who helped bring this project to fruition. Undergraduate studies with David Armitage, Robert Ferguson, Julie Stone Peters, Edward Said, and Deborah Elise White at Columbia University, and with Ato Quayson at the University of Cambridge, were formative in ways I was unaware of at the time. I thank David Lloyd for making possible my participation on an American Studies Association Convention panel in 2007 that opened up a number of new doors for me intellectually; Elizabeth Maddock Dillon for her insightful comments on an early iteration of chapter 6; and my anonymous readers at *American Literature* for the thoughtful and thorough feedback they gave a first-time author. Conference conversations with Mara de Gennaro and Alexandra Schultheis Moore have provided much intellectual stimulation, and helped me think through many of the major claims of my argument. I am very grateful for the patience and consistent support of Lindsay Martin at The Ohio State University Press. The unbelievably generous feedback from my manuscript's two outside readers, Michael Malouf and Samantha Pinto, helped me write the book I really wanted to write; my gratitude for their time and energy knows no bounds.

My thanks to the publishers who have given permission for me to reprint work that has appeared in print previously. Small portions of chapter 1 originally appeared as an article titled "We Are Not the People: The 1805 Haitian Constitution's Challenge to Political Legibility in the Age of Revolution" in a special issue of *American Literature* 78.4 (December 2006): 799–820, edited by Kathryn McKee and Annette Trefzer. Portions of chapter 2 are reprinted from "Declaring Differently: C. L. R. James, International Law, and Mid-Twentieth Century Internationalisms," in Peter D. O'Neill and David Lloyd, eds., *The Black and Green Atlantic: Cross-Currents of the African and Irish Diasporas* (Palgrave Macmillan, 2009). Reproduced with permission of Palgrave Macmillan.

This project has required sacrifice and patience on the part of my friends and family. I had only to do the work; they had to watch me do it, at times put their own needs aside while waiting for me to come up for air, and help me find a way back from the highs and lows, often daily, that were part of the writing process. My parents, Nancy Smith and Robert Gulick, spent years tolerating a daughter who read her way through meals, argued and pontificated in excess, and demanded, also in excess, their encouragement, faith, and love—all of which she got. Since Sara Arnold, my stepmother, came into my life, she has offered much of the same with kindness and generosity. I have a wise and faithful sister, Ellie Willman, whose ambition, energy, and wisdom has given me the confidence to aim high in life. All of these people have stood by me throughout unreturned phone calls, overdue visits, and a career that has taken me far from my New England home. For that unfailing support I offer my deepest thanks.

I'm not sure what Phil Schneider thought he was getting into when he asked me to a concert in 2004. Not, I suspect, the eleven years he would spend patiently waiting for a single intellectual project to come to fruition. Not the three years he would spend providing solo entertainment to a newborn-turned-toddler while I worked on manuscript revisions. And not the heroic role he would play in the very final days of my revisions by tracking down one last rogue citation and thus expediting the project's completion by several days. The love, faith, patience, and care that Phil has offered me during these years is unquantifiable and unrepayable. I am happily in his debt for good.

Introduction

THIS BOOK TRACES a long history of fierce, creative, and distinctly literary responses to a North Atlantic legal imagination in the work of anticolonial African and Caribbean writers. From Haiti's early-nineteenth-century founding texts to late-twentieth-century postcolonial language manifestoes, these texts undertake subversive experiments with First World state and international legal forms.

In the wake of decolonization—beginning with the independence of the Atlantic world's first black nation-state in 1804 and continuing through the dissolution of Europe's overseas empires in the wake of World War II—First World political texts and institutions have provided inspiration for anticolonial thinkers while simultaneously proving to be powerful tools for the perpetuation of empire in a postcolonial era. Colonized peoples, who for centuries had served as legal objects and subjects, now gained widespread recognition as legitimate *authors* of international and state law. Yet the legal texts and institutions that helped grant decolonized nations their political autonomy were usually crafted by a small elite in conjunction with the country's former rulers, and often did little to reconfigure colonial economic and political power relations. Law has served both emancipatory and oppressive functions in Africa and the Caribbean, offering newly independent states and their citizens the means of asserting political legibility while also reinforcing colonial structures of rule and fostering new forms of economic and political dependency in a decolonized, but hardly postcolonial, world.

Jean-Jacques Dessalines, C. L. R. James, Aimé Césaire, the organizers of South Africa's Congress of the People Campaign, Ngũgĩ wa Thiong'o, and Édouard Glissant confront these paradoxes of law as an institutional reality and imaginative project in revolutionary modernity. Across a wide range of genres—literary, legal, and otherwise—their work draws on the cosmopolitan aspirations and the emancipatory potential of the Western juridico-political declaration, while also exposing First World law's complicity with imperial rule. Critically engaging the experimental forms through which a modern international community came into being, these writers have asked, and sought new answers to, the question: Who gets to "write" the law, and under what circumstances? Their work constitutes a provocative anticolonial Atlantic tradition of rhetorical performance, a tradition whose critical comment on a Western juridico-political imagination has vital implications for our not-quite-postcolonial present.

ANTICOLONIAL ROMANCE, RHETORICAL PERFORMANCE, AND POSTCOLONIAL "SUCCESS" NARRATIVES

In *Literature, Law, and Rhetorical Performance in the Anticolonial Atlantic* I read comparatively across a broad range of aspirational, future-oriented, often utopian works of African and Caribbean anticolonialism. These texts audaciously envision and attempt to enact new political identities that were well beyond the realm of possibility in a colonial/imperial imagination. They thus lend credence to David Scott's proposal in *Conscripts of Modernity* that romance is the "mode of emplotment" best suited to anticolonialism, a movement which, he explains, produces "narratives of overcoming, often narratives of vindication; they have tended to enact a distinctive rhythm and pacing, a distinctive direction, and to tell stories of salvation and redemption. They have largely depended upon a certain (utopian) horizon toward which the emancipationist history is imagined to be moving" (7–8). Romance signals an expectation on the part of colonized peoples that their struggle for freedom will end in success—that a liberatory postcolonial future is nigh, and that the path to that future entails committed, organized resistance. Romance, as configured by Scott, points to the ambition and audacity of anticolonialism as an imaginative project—a project whose scope certainly encompassed the pressing goal of political independence for colonized peoples in the mid-twentieth century, but for which liberation also had psychic and ontological dimensions.

"Romance" also has a second, more specific resonance in my study. The anticolonial writers to whom I attend make strategic use of what I am calling a romance of rhetorical performance—the fiction of reproducing the conditions of a live, declarative speech-act in textual form. They are what J. L. Austin, in his 1962 *How to Do Things with Words,* identifies as illocutionary acts—utterances, either oral or written, that *do* something through the act of saying something. These texts are imagined, and often seem to imagine themselves, as events in time. They self-consciously strive to imitate—and, indeed, even stand in for—live declarative performances; they aim to simultaneously name, instantiate, and legitimize new postcolonial political communities on the basis of their own authority alone. I argue that this romance of rhetorical performance is fundamental to the anticolonial project; it is also, more broadly, fundamental to revolutionary modernity, in which the written juridico-political declaration has served a privileged genre of articulating political legibility. Revolutions, Hannah Arendt observes at the outset of her study of the French and North American revolutions of the late eighteenth century, "are the only political events which confront us directly with the problem of beginning" (*On Revolution* 21). Revolution marks the suspension of an existing legal order, a temporality in which the founding violence of a new political authority becomes possible. And in the revolutionary North Atlantic world of the late eighteenth century, written declarations served as a means of confronting this problem of founding authority in spectacular fashion. Documents such as the U.S. Declaration of Independence and the French *Déclaration des droits de l'homme et du citoyen* are rhetorically risky texts, asserting the existence of a political order that has yet to take shape while also asserting their own authority to declare a new political order into existence in the first place.

Tasked with the burden of endowing political legibility upon communities whose humanity was at best ignored and more often actively denied by the architects of North Atlantic juridico-political modernity, anticolonial writers have radically appropriated and transformed these newly emergent declarative genres of First World law. Their rendering of legibility, visibility, and authority to black subjects within the postcolonial political communities they envision takes place at the level of content—through, for example, the 1805 Haitian Constitution's explicit insistences on blackness as a *qualification* for national citizenship rather than as the basis for its exclusion. But their more radical disruption to a First World juridico-political imagination takes place at the level of form. Caribbean and African anticolonial declarations are characterized by an intense preoccupation with the precarity and radical potential of the declaration's association with live performance. Public oath-takings, community meetings, and declarations made by charismatic leaders to crowds of revolutionary masses often appear as prominent contexts for (or narrated events within) these documents. They seek to answer the question of how to instantiate a truly postcolonial political community in real time but also in perpetua; they aim to bridge what Jacques Derrida identifies as the unbridgeable gap between the constative and the performative, the "are" and the "ought to be" of the declaration of independence,[1] in order to usher in a postcolonial future that remains powerfully connected to its revolutionary anticolonial past.

Of course, there is nothing inherently liberatory about anticolonial revolution or its forms of articulation. Revolutionary declarations are also acts of force through which the legitimacy of the old political order is decimated and claims for a new one are made; indeed, as Derrida argues in a later essay, the force of law and the performance of that force through language are always one and the same. Law is not merely a "docile instrument" of force but also "a performative and therefore interpretive violence" ("Force of Law" 241). The revolutionary declaration not only provides the language through which to render legible a new political order but also serves as a means of obfuscating the inherent instability and illegitimacy of that order. Declaring independence or human rights—in writing or out loud—does not guarantee that independence will be achieved, nor that human rights will be protected. For Arendt, post-Revolutionary France offers an especially devastating example of revolutionary constituting gone wrong; its 1791 constitution "remained a piece of paper, of more interest to the learned and the experts than to the people. Its authority was shattered even more before it went into effect, and it was followed in quick succession by one constitution after another until, in an avalanche of constitutions lasting deep into our own century, the very notion of constitution disintegrated beyond recognition" (*On Revolution* 125). At first glance, the history of decolonization seems to tell a similar story: early independence constitutions (from Haiti in 1805 up through the first decades of African postcolonialism) tended to alienate the general population from participation in the process of lawmaking and constituting and was characterized by rapid constitutional turnover and periods of emergency suspension. Postcolonial states have proved largely incapable of combating the continuation of imperial rule by other means—the transformation of a colonized elite into a neocolonial ruling class with no interest in the redistribution of economic or political power in postcolonial society; aggressive efforts by Western governments, businesses, and financial institutions to undermine attempts to nationalize industry and natural resources; and the imposition of a draconian debt structure on the countries of the Global South. Indeed, law—both state and international—has often facilitated these very betrayals of the anticolonial vision in the years and decades following independence. Late-twentieth-century African and Caribbean constitutional history seems to serve as ready proof of the widespread failure of the romantic aspirations of the anticolonial project.

It is my sense that the field of postcolonial studies has tended to overemphasize this narrative of the failures of the anticolonial project at the expense of more closely examining the implications of its various kinds of successes. Certainly the reality of decolonization and independence fell short of the emancipatory dreams of anticolonialism in many ways; and certainly, anticolonial-turned-post-independence writers of the 1960s and '70s registered this situation in their work, realizing, as Neil Lazarus puts it in his 1990 *Resistance in Postcolonial African Fiction*, "that something had gone terribly wrong" with the national liberation project in the years following decolonization (18). There is nothing wrong, on its own, with this pointing out the disappointments and even disasters experienced by African, Caribbean, and Asian countries in the late twentieth century. The problem, as Lazarus himself asserts twenty years later in his 2011 *Postcolonial Unconscious*, is that this narrative has become an automatic and shorthand account of how postcolonial studies frames the relationship between the anticolonial past and the post-independence present. The institutionalization of postcolonial studies within the Western academy was predicated on the "decisive defeat of liberationist ideologies" (9), a ready and uncritical acceptance of the untenability of the anticolonial project after decolonization. The resulting perspective on this literary-historical period has been clumsy and stultifying: "Scholars in the field have evidently not known how—other than through . . . wholesale repudiation—to account for the setbacks and defeats of the post-independence years, and more particularly for the stupefying violence and criminality of postcolonial governance" (69). Overstating the extent, the finality, and most importantly the implications of the failures of anticolonialism for the late twentieth and early twenty-first centuries has had negative consequences—including, Ania Loomba argues, the creation of some uncomfortable overlap with contemporary neoliberal narratives that justify the perpetuation of an unequal geopolitical order in which the Global North remains the winner.[2] And disenchantment with national liberation movements, nationalism, and the nation-state as a unit of meaningful political articulation give way to an uncritical celebration of globalization, hybridity, and postcolonialism as a discursive condition rather than material history. As Benita Parry has noted, the field of postcolonial studies has depoliticized and dehistoricized by quietly but deliberately distancing itself from anticolonial critique (6–7). This failure to interrogate what we mean by anticolonialism's "failure" is particularly unfortunate given the ways in which postcolonialism seems to be losing traction as a necessary critical term in the early twenty-first century, overshadowed by a new emphasis on globalization, empire as a networked entirely de-territorialized entity, and the degradation of the nation-state as the site of meaningful politics.[3] Our postcolonial present calls for *more* engagement with the anticolonial past, not less. As Jennifer Wenzel observed in her 2007 contribution to an MLA roundtable on the state of the field of postcolonial theory in the new century, "If the era of postcolonial studies is over, it ends just when the need for historically informed critiques of imperialism could not be more urgent" (Yaeger 634). And as Lazarus insists, a richer and more complex account of the post-independence era is all the more essential given the ways in which post-9/11 geopolitics "have demonstrably rejoined the twenty-first century to a long and as yet unbroken history, wrongly supposed by postcolonial theory to have come to a close *circa* 1975" (*Postcolonial Unconscious* 15).

Literature, Law, and Rhetorical Performance in the Anticolonial Atlantic thus argues for the centrality of anticolonial critique to postcolonial studies by attending to the geohistorical and rhetorical specificity of the anticolonial archive. If revolutionary rhetorical performance is precarious, it is also potentially innovative and creative, enriching their audiences' imaginations with novel visions of what political community and justice might look like. In this book, I resist the assumption that the "success" or "failure" of any given text is dictated by whether the exact vision that text charts for the postcolonial future came to pass as anticipated. Many of the texts I explore contain utopian aspirations that do not materialize according to their authors' exact expectations or desires. But their capacity to disrupt predominant ways of thinking and talking about political community is not limited to authorial intent. I read anticolonial literature (broadly construed to include texts that do not readily qualify as "literary") not teleologically—that is, directed at a single, zero-sum postcolonial future that either is or is not brought about—but rather constellationally, as a collection of disruptions to the *form* of a First World juridico-political imagination, disruptions that continue to take place in the so-called postcolonial era. The African and Caribbean declarative texts I examine are "successful" in the sense that they reconfigure the contours of a liberatory juridico-political imagination for the Global South. They challenge the racism that is inherent in the exclusionary terms of authorship and authority that underlie First World law. They propose alternative ways of conceiving of representation, participation, and political belonging in a postcolonial world yet to come. And they suggest unusual and unexpected uses for the quasi-legal discourses of human rights and humanitarianism that dominate a Western imagination of the Global South in the twenty-first century—discourses that have radical potential, though they have often been deployed in the service of empire in the post-independence era.

THE ANTICOLONIAL BLACK ATLANTIC

My use of the term "black Atlantic," and my conception of the Atlantic as a geohistorical framework for the textual traditions I explore in this book require some explanation, as in some important respects they work against the grain of much of the scholarship that makes use of these same concepts. The Atlantic is a privileged space in the history of the development of the genres of First World juridico-political modernity—the revolutionary declarations of the late eighteenth century, and then, in the mid-twentieth century, the charters and declarations through which postwar international institutions and legal norms came into being. The title of the Atlantic Charter, the Allied Powers' first articulation of a post–World War II international community, indicates the extent to which the (North) Atlantic would serve as the stage for the conception and creation of postwar international institutions as well as their founding texts. These juridico-political documents of course circulated more widely, and twentieth-century internationalisms were meant to aspire to global inclusivity and avoid privileging one region over others. Nonetheless, the distinctly Atlantic history of Western modernity—with its origins in European overseas exploration, colonial occupation, trade in human cargo, and imperialism—continues to exert pressure on our "globalized" present in any number of ways.

This European and North American genealogy of juridico-political modernity has always coexisted and interacted with what Paul Gilroy has famously identified as a black Atlantic counterculture, one that confronted and challenged Enlightenment thought's long-standing complicity with the "racial terror of colonialism and slavery" that it helped to perpetuate (*Black Atlantic* 39). Gilroy's 1990 *Black Atlantic* and its nuanced assessment of the terms under which black writers and artists engage Western philosophical traditions is fundamental to how I approach the work of African and Caribbean writers. And like most postcolonial scholarship produced in the wake of Gilroy's study, my work is informed by his insight that the magnitude of this "counterculture of modernity" only comes into full view through the transnational, transregional, geohistorical scope of Atlantic space. Gilroy's is a "transversal" reading practice, one that remains responsive and responsible to the historical violence through which black Atlantic culture is linked, while also recognizing the ways in which those links demand comparative analysis in excess of traditional national and regional frames.[4] *Literature, Law, and Rhetorical Performance in the Anticolonial Atlantic* aspires to an equally reflective and capacious comparative methodology.

Beyond those two crucial insights, however, the "black Atlantic" I have in mind in this book departs from Gilroy's model in two key senses. First and foremost, I attend to geographical contexts that Gilroy's study—which focuses almost exclusively on African diasporics living in the Global North—sidelines and even ignores.[5] Here I seek to de-exceptionalize Africa in a black Atlantic critical frame, identifying and comparatively exploring experimental appropriations of the declarative forms that emerge from African and Caribbean contexts. Further, the anticolonial Atlantic world that I explore in this book is characterized less exclusively by its melancholic relationship with the slave trade and slavery (though certainly that experience is integral to the historical imaginations of many of the writers I discuss) and more by active networks of resistance that prompt solidarities—both real and imagined—across regional and linguistic boundaries. Brent Hayes Edwards's privileging of internationalist networks of exchange over more passive versions of diasporic cultural formation is thus especially useful to me in thinking through the paradoxical, uneven, and aesthetically complex means by which black intellectuals have attempted to imagine political solidarities. In *The Practice of Diaspora*, Edwards's critical mapping of mid-twentieth-century cultural *and* political forms of black transnationalism across Africa and the Americas leads to his crucial insight that "the cultures of black internationalism can be seen only *in translation*" (7)—that is, as aspiring to solidarity but consistently encountering the problem of how to translate across contexts that are differentiated by nation, region, language, genre, and gender. While working with a different (if occasionally overlapping) archive, *Literature, Law, and Rhetorical Performance* takes inspiration from Edwards's insights about the connections between seemingly nation- or race-based conceptions of political community and black internationalisms, as well as his identification of imperfection, failure, and mistranslation as constitutive *and productive* parts of a twentieth-century black political imagination.

A black internationalist critical framework also helps explain how and why the African contexts to which I attend in this study call for an especially expansive and flexible, and occasionally counterintuitive, conception of "Atlantic" space. Incorporating both Africa and anticolonial history into a black Atlantic critical framework raises questions about the meaning and utility of that framework's geographical scope: anticolonial projects took place across the continent in the mid-twentieth century, and they did so as part of transnational, transregional, and transoceanic networks of exchange. As Edwards and other scholars, such as Cedric Robinson, have shown, transatlantic routes of discursive and material exchange are and always have been constitutive of black internationalism. Caribbean and African liberation movements have long been in conversation, and attuned to the historical confluences of colonial occupation and exploitation of black labor. The Caribbean texts, writers, and historical circumstances to which I attend in the book are easy to place within black internationalist, anticolonial, and Gilroyian black Atlantic critical frames all at once. And writers such as James and Fanon, whose political involvement with African decolonization was central and explicit in their work, offer up one important model for understanding the intellectual and political borrowings that take place across African and Caribbean contexts. Moreover, South Africa, the site of creation for the 1955 Freedom Charter, which I discuss in my fourth chapter, boasts not only a geographically obvious connection to the Atlantic but also a well-established history of transatlantic cultural and political exchange with other colonial and postcolonial locales.[6] However, the same cannot be said for Algeria and Kenya, whose decolonization struggles I attend to in chapter 5, and which have no straightforward ties to the history of transatlantic slavery that grounds the black Atlantic of Gilroy's study. In this chapter, as with the other portions of the book that attend to African contexts, my primary interest lies with the strong imaginative, discursive, and political ties between Africa and other parts of the Atlantic world. Ngũgĩ wa Thiong'o's intellectual biography, and the transatlantic exchanges that have been constitutive of his life and writing career, elucidate the importance of these ties. No writers were more central to his aesthetic and political development, in the 1960s, than George Lamming and Frantz Fanon; and from early on, he would seek to draw connections in his critical writing between the settler colonialism that took place in Kenya and the other forms of racial exploitation facilitated by colonial rule in other parts of the world. Moreover, after his arrest and imprisonment by the Moi government for his subversive populist community theater work in the late 1970s, Ngũgĩ left Kenya and spent the next thirty years of his career living mainly in the United States and England, thus joining a new generation of African diasporics whose journeys abroad were spurred by an entirely different set of historical conditions for which Gilroy's conceptual framework offers no explanation.[7] I thus have no qualms about identifying Ngũgĩ, in particular, as a black Atlantic anticolonial intellectual, one whose work points to the necessity of incorporating multiple diasporic experiences, as well as a rich and complex history of transnational political and aesthetic experimentation, into that critical framework.

LAW AND LITERATURE IN POSTCOLONIAL CONTEXTS

Literature, Law, and Rhetorical Performance in the Anticolonial Atlantic draws on a rich and growing body of contemporary multidisciplinary scholarship that has interrogated the relationship between law and postcoloniality. I am first and foremost indebted to the insights of legal theorists and historians who, against the backdrop of a proliferation of popular and scholarly depictions of late-twentieth-century international institutions as triumphs of a new era of global cooperation guided by a collective belief in human rights, have exposed the long-standing complicities between international law and empire. In his 2005 *Imperialism, Sovereignty and International Law*, Antony Anghie has made a compelling case for locating international law's origins in the earliest years of colonial exploration and encounter, identifying in Francisco Vitoria's sixteenth-century lectures on the legal basis for Spain's authority over (and seizure of land and resources from) the Saracen Indians a "dynamic of difference" (4) between civilized and uncivilized peoples of the world. This dynamic, Anghie argues, persists across four and a half centuries of colonial and imperial rule, and continues to be integral to the institutional and philosophical underpinnings of international law, under new rubrics, in an early-twenty-first-century global order. Revisionist histories of international law such as Anghie's inform my own critical perspective throughout the book.[8] More importantly, they register for contemporary scholarship many of the insights about the entanglements of a global legal order with the needs of empire that, as I will show, anticolonial writers began articulating much earlier. Anghie's "dynamic of difference," for instance, translates seamlessly into what Aimé Césaire, in his 1950 *Discours sur le colonialisme*, calls a "geographical curse" (34)—a global civilizational imperative that has justified colonial rule in flexible but remarkably consistent ways over time, and that, importantly, has proved capable of accommodating not only pre-twentieth-century theories of scientific racism but also later revisions of those theories that replace culture with biology as the basis for constructing a hierarchy between the Global North and the Global South.

Within this body of postcolonial legal scholarship, human rights and humanitarian law have garnered particular attention. As ideological concepts and as concrete areas of international legal practice, both are often figured as antidotes to empire, entities that provide badly needed advocacy to peoples of the Global South and speak truth to power within the international community. But, as David Kennedy observes, well-intentioned international humanitarian lawyers find themselves confronted by a political economy in which those goals are easily co-opted by the interests of First World states. Further, as Samuel Moyn has argued, Cold War politics and post-Cold War neoliberalism have been constitutive to the development of a contemporary international human rights regime. The institutions, discourses, and norms that emanate from contemporary international law do not exist in a privileged outside sphere; they do not enjoy immunity from the exploitative structures inherent in a contemporary global neoliberal political economy that actively perpetuates the "dynamic of difference" between the North and the South.[9]

Given the prominence of international institutions in the political and economic constitution of the postcolonial world, especially in the late twentieth and early twenty-first centuries,[10] it is not surprising that when postcolonial literary critics became interested in the intersections of literature and law, they focused their attention almost exclusively on *international* law. In *Human Rights, Inc.* (2006), the study that opened the floodgates for this now well-established subfield, Joseph Slaughter posits human rights law and the postcolonial bildungsroman as "mutually enabling fictions" whose "cooperative social work" constitutes "a network of conceptual, lexical, and grammatical intersections within the larger discourse of human development and emancipation" (8). In our effort to recognize the problems with human rights law, Slaughter insists, we must do more than simply declare the concept's bankruptcy, bemoan the co-option by First World imperial interests of its utopian vision for global justice, and identify the limits of its professed universalism. Postcolonial literature, he argues, does not merely speak truth to law's power. It is only through a cross-disciplinary critical approach that the shared imaginative stakes of literature *and* law come into view, and through which we can "learn to recognize not only our structural complicity in an international system that extends and denies human rights differentially, but also the triumphalist cosmopolitan pretensions and privileges of our humanitarian reading practices that can exacerbate the divisions between the incorporated and the disenfranchised that both we and these novels presumably aspire to remedy" (326). My book is palpably indebted to Slaughter's vital insights about literature and law as mutually constitutive fields in the postcolonial world, and how reading comparatively between literary and legal archives thus serves as a powerful interpretive tool for postcolonial studies.[11]

Literature, Law, and Rhetorical Performance situates international law as one among many juridico-political archives with relevance to African and Caribbean postcolonies. I am firmly in the camp of postcolonial scholars who contend that the nation-state still matters as a unit of analysis. If indeed the nation-state is "on its last legs" (Appadurai 19), then those last legs strike me as still quite sturdy. Thus while U.S.-based Critical Race Theory does not figure explicitly in my argument, its insights have provided crucial theoretical inspiration for my project. Just as postcolonial legal scholars have debunked the myth of law's transcendence of the realities of race and empire that constitute our contemporary geopolitical order, Critical Race Theory has helped interrogate assumptions about the race-blindness of U.S. law, from its constitutional origins up through contemporary issues such as affirmative action and the right to privacy.[12] These incisive critical treatments of law at the level of the *nation-state* have been essential to the scope and argument of this book, for, as discussed above, I am convinced that national and international frames of reference for anticolonial responses to a First World juridico-political imagination are inextricable from one another. The extraordinary intervention of Haiti's 1805 Constitution into the early-nineteenth-century Atlantic world, for example, really only makes sense in light of its stark contrast to the U.S. Constitution's inscription-through-erasure of race into the country's founding law.

This dual focus on national and international legal imaginations leads me to different conclusions from those of other postcolonial literary critics about the capacity of anti- and postcolonial texts to formulate strategic, critically astute, and formally innovative responses to law. While in *Human Rights Inc.* Slaughter attends exclusively to "reformist" strains of law and literature, and to First World legal texts, I explore documents that claim more radical agendas and actively articulate alternatives to the formal and ideological norms of juridico-political legibility. For example, chapter 5 attends to Africa's first wave of independence constitutions, which have been largely neglected by postcolonial studies and long dismissed as disappointing documents inadequate to the work of ushering in a new and truly liberatory postcolonial political order. I argue that despite their significant shortcomings, including their short-lived legal currency, these constitutions warrant recognition as rich sites of formal experimentation and political innovation.

Decolonization marks the point at which law is no longer authored exclusively by the West. And while postcolonial legal texts and discourses failed to fully instantiate the kinds of postcolonial communities to which national liberation struggles aspired, many of them nonetheless *reflect* those aspirations, seeking new strategies through which to give life to anticolonial idealism in a postcolonial legal order. Moreover, anticolonial writing that seems to have little (good) to say about the new "postcolonial" juridico-political order is in fact actively engaged in rethinking the grounds on which a more just, emancipatory order might be created well after the advent of political independence. The era of decolonization and national liberation has come and gone, but this archive of resistant black Atlantic declarative interventions can—and should—inform our understanding of what it means to imagine alternative possibilities for law and political belonging in a twenty-first century in which postcolonialism remains largely an elusive ideal.

CHAPTER DESCRIPTIONS

The book begins with an examination of how Haiti's founding documents appropriate and subversively transform the North Atlantic world's brand-new genres of juridico-political expression, the declaration of independence, the rights declaration, and the written state constitution. Haiti's founding texts foreground the paradoxes of representation, performativity, and revolutionary temporality that underlie the French and North American versions of these new forms. Jean-Jacques Dessalines's fiery 1804 Declaration of Independence severed the new black nation-state's ties to France, but it also signaled a rejection of North Atlantic form, charting an alternative set of generic conventions for the declaration of independence to those established in North America in 1776. Proclaiming the end of slavery on the island and declaring all citizens of the new nation-state "black"—including a handful of Haitians of European descent—the 1805 Constitution went on to make manifest the paradoxes of racial exploitation and political belonging that were silenced in canonical French and North American revolutionary writing. By critically refashioning the quintessential genres of a North Atlantic juridico-political imagination, these texts articulate transformative alternatives for what legal authorship and authority might look like not just for Haiti, but also for a *postcolonial* international community.

The Haitian Revolution became a crucial historical touchstone for mid-twentieth-century anticolonial thinkers from the anglophone and francophone Caribbean. If Haiti's founding texts are the first instance of the anticolonial black Atlantic "writing back" to First World law and its forms, then C. L. R. James, I argue in chapter 2, is the first anticolonial thinker to theorize the romance of rhetorical performance as a central, strategic component of revolt in the black Atlantic world. In the multiple histories of black revolt that he published—and republished—over the course of his long career, James is fascinated by moments of felicitous connection and exchange between revolutionary black leaders and "the people" whose revolutionary will they aspire to voice; in his histories these are the moments through which revolution has been *authored* in the black Atlantic world, from the days of Toussaint L'Ouverture up through Julius Nyerere's 1974 Arusha Declaration. Liberation, for James, is never separable from the strategically necessary and productive—if also problematic—work of performance as a means of instantiating new political community. And it is this inseparability that offers up hope for the future in these histories, even in the wake of the disappointments of decolonization.

Aimé Césaire's critical engagement with declarative form takes place contemporaneously with James's—and contemporaneously with the decade during which the Universal Declaration of Human Rights was being conceived, drafted, and ratified, and gaining discursive weight. Chapter 3 reads Césaire's epic-length poem, *Cahier d'un retour au pays natal* (*Notebook of a Return to the Native Land*), as staging a critical engagement with the Universal Declaration. The romance of universal authorship that underpins the Declaration depends on its skillful elision of the authority of the international body charged with drafting the text and the global community of subjects of human rights that the text sought to bring into existence. Césaire's poem, in contrast, interrogates the ethical and political stakes of speaking for an oppressed population in a voice that claims universal authority. Saturated by a series of speech acts proclaiming independence and personhood, the *Cahier* seeks a declarative form that encapsulates an anti-imperial ethics and politics—a form uniquely suited to the colonized world on the cusp of anticolonial revolution.

The second half of the book shifts focus to African texts and contexts in order to explore the ways in which African writers are engaged with the romance of revolutionary performance in the late twentieth century. Chapter 4 reads South Africa's 1955 Freedom Charter as a radical instance of reimagining the possibilities for political authorship under the unique conditions of southern Africa's "colonialism of a special type." Like Haiti's founding documents, the Charter is at least as radical in its form as in its content, drawing inspiration from international law but transforming some of its key midcentury genres—and provocatively staging what it would look like to insist that the democratic ideals at the core of the Atlantic Charter be applied to Africa's oldest settler colony. The grassroots campaign that led to the creation and ratification of the Freedom Charter was a novel experiment in mass authorship; and the final version of this declarative text puts forth a decidedly localized conception of human rights and political belonging that stands in stark contrast to First World institutions' abstract universalism.

My investigation of the Freedom Charter's radical populism gives way, in chapter 5, to a broader exploration of the diversity of genres of African anticolonialism in the 1960s. Here I define decolonization as a process characterized by multiple, sometimes incommensurate and antagonistic, attempts to constitute the postcolony through rhetorical performance. Reading comparatively among decolonization's myriad forms of constitutive expression—including independence-era state constitutions, "Mau Mau" loyalty oaths, Frantz Fanon's *The Wretched of the Earth*, and Ngũgĩ wa Thiong'o's quintessential novel of decolonization, *A Grain of Wheat*—I move beyond interpretive approaches that frame this historical moment in terms of anticolonialism's "success" or "failure." Instead I insist on the imaginative and political complexities inherent in mid-twentieth-century literary and legal articulations of African postcolonial community.

Finally, I turn to the decades during which postcolonial theory became established as a field—and anticolonial thought got repackaged under that rubric as an important piece of postcolonial history. In a comparative transatlantic examination of two prominent late-twentieth-century "postcolonial" writers who due to geographic and linguistic difference had no contact with one each other during their careers, chapter 6 examines what happens to anticolonial declarative performance in an era in which anticolonial revolution is supposed to be an anachronism. Critical essays on the politics of postcolonial language by Ngũgĩ and Édouard Glissant appropriate the rhetorical strategies of an ever more prominent discourse of universal human rights in order to interrogate the stakes of linguistic diversity for postcolonial politics. But in doing so, these essays also critically comment on the possibilities—and limitations—of human rights discourse for the not-quite-postcolonial world. Like their midcentury anticolonial predecessors, Ngũgĩ and Glissant seek to articulate an alternative to First World internationalism, one that counters the logic of a form of globalization organized around empire with a radical multilingualism grounded in a definitively anticolonial politics and aesthetics.

CHAPTER 1

Black Nation Time

*Haiti's Textual Foundations and Generic
Novelty in the Age of Revolution*

THE LONG TWENTIETH CENTURY of black Atlantic radical anticolonialism dates back to 1791, the year of the slave revolt in the French Antillean colony of Saint-Domingue that would quickly transform into a revolution—the first and only revolution in the Atlantic world to simultaneously overthrow both European colonialism and plantation slavery. It has become commonplace to describe the Haitian Revolution as both the ultimate provocation to and ultimate fulfillment of North Atlantic Enlightenment ideals. As C. L. R. James wrote in 1938, the slaves of Saint-Domingue recreated the French Revolution "in their own image," seeing its motto—liberty, equality, fraternity—through to its logical and radical conclusion for a people thrust into modernity through Europe's exploitation and dispossession (*Black Jacobins* 81). France's 1789 *Déclaration des droits de l'homme et du citoyen* marked the rhetorical origins of a modern philosophy of universal human rights; Haiti's revolution challenged this philosophy to make good on its pretensions to universality by insisting on its application to the regions of the world that had suffered some of modernity's greatest human rights abuses.[1] Building on James's now classic account of the Revolution, as well as Paul Gilroy's conception of the black Atlantic as a "counterculture of modernity," a wave of recent multidisciplinary scholarship has begun to come to terms with how Haiti's origins reshape our conceptions of Enlightenment, modern revolution, and the universality of the democratic ideals whose articulation we are accustomed to attributing to the Age of Revolution.² "If we live in a world in which democracy is meant to exclude no one," Laurent Dubois observes, "it is in no small part because of the actions of those slaves in Saint-Domingue who insisted that human rights were theirs too" (3).

Perhaps nowhere is Haiti's anticolonial provocation to North Atlantic revolutionary thought more palpable than in its 1804 Declaration of Independence and 1805 Constitution, the documents through which the country formalized its separation from France and sovereignty as a nation-state. These founding texts radically redefine the nascent genres of the declaration of independence and the written state constitution, as they had been conceived and constructed in the Global North just years earlier. Haiti occasioned the black Atlantic world's first rhetorical performance of statehood by adapting those novel forms of juridico-political expression to the needs and goals of a country whose future as a modern nation-state would be explicitly informed by its inhabitants' heritage as slaves rather than as slave-owners. While contemporaneous North Atlantic revolutionary declarations erased the reality and philosophical implications of racial exploitation from their professions of the rights of man and the ordering of the modern nation-state, Haiti's founding documents made slavery, anticolonial revolution, and racial identity central components of the country's postcolonial national identity.

The Haitian Declaration of Independence and 1805 Constitution are subversive and provocative assertions of postcolonial nationhood, texts that seek to render the new black republic politically legible to a hostile international community as well as to the country's own citizens. Their anticolonial vision is far-reaching and threatening, a precursor to Frantz Fanon's insights about the psychic violence of colonial racism—and his insistence on physical and epistemological violence as necessary components of redressing that damage. Scholars such as Sibylle Fischer and Deborah Jenson have already begun the work of elucidating the postcolonial stakes of Haiti's revolutionary founding documents. Building on their insights, I contend that these texts' most profound disruption to a North Atlantic political imaginary, with its ties to the institutions of plantation slavery and colonial structures of authority, takes place at the level of form. Critically appraising the relationship between political authority's enactment as live performance and its enshrinement in a written text, they expose the limitations of representation as conceived in North Atlantic revolutionary thought. Haiti's radical refashioning of the Age of Revolution's quintessential genres of juridico-political expression puts forth an alternative vision of the meaning of legal authorship and authority not just for Haiti but also for the postcolonial international community yet to come.

GENERIC NOVELTY AND TEXTUAL PERFORMANCE IN THE NORTH ATLANTIC AGE OF REVOLUTION

> The question was not whether, by a declaration of independence, we should make ourselves what we are not; but whether we should declare a fact which already exists.
>
> —Thomas Jefferson, "Notes of Proceedings in the Continental Congress"

The quintessential documents of the North Atlantic Age of Revolution—the 1776 U.S. Declaration of Independence, the 1787 U.S. Constitution, and the 1789 French *Déclaration des droits de l'homme et du citoyen*—inaugurated three new genres of modern juridico-political expression. While both "declaration" and "constitution" were potent concepts with long lineages in Western political thought well before the end of the eighteenth century, it was during this period that these terms came to apply to distinct textual genres.[3] "Rising" during the same years as the English novel (Watt), these new genres were integral to the creation of the imagined community of the modern nation-state—as well as to the no less imaginative project of constructing a transatlantic international community.

The declaration of independence, the declaration of rights, and the written state constitution are discrete genres, each with its own conventions and functions. But here I point to their shared origins in order to explain the way in which all three of them are distinctly *declarative* genres: they are genres for which the project of declaring a new political order into existence is both their foremost aspiration and their central paradox. They signal a new way, in the late eighteenth century, of thinking about the authorship and authority of modern political community. As Jefferson insisted, the most remarkable innovation of the American Revolution was its audacious self-authorization; the Declaration of Independence did not create but rather confirmed the existence of a new and distinct political order in North America. Yet that political order urgently needed to be declared in textual form—not only to Britain and the residents of its North American colonies, but to the transatlantic international community that it would help to constitute in the late eighteenth century (Armitage). The juridico-political genres that emerge from the revolutionary North Atlantic world perform stunning rhetorical feats, with tremendous consequences for how political belonging would be expressed textually for the next two centuries.[4]

Two late-twentieth-century theoretical accounts of the political and aesthetic novelty of the North Atlantic's genres of revolution help elucidate the context within which Haiti's texts proved so disruptive. The central insight of Hannah Arendt's *On Revolution* is that revolutionary founding texts locate the source of their claims to authority in their own performative iteration. And Jacques Derrida's explorations of the relationship between founding law and founding violence share Arendt's fascination with performativity, but more skeptically assess the distance between the textual performance of statehood and the violence that founds and preserves a new political order. As products of the Age of Revolution, Haiti's founding texts carry out the kind of radical experimentation with performing political novelty that Arendt describes; but they also exhibit a heightened critical awareness of the relationship between the performance of nationhood and the violences (of revolution and of slavery) out of which such a performance emerges.

Appearing just a few years after the publication of J. L. Austin's *How to Do Things with Words, On Revolution* shares speech-act theory's preoccupation with linguistic performativity—with the connection between language's potential to do and its potential to say. For Arendt, the dazzling accomplishment of the U.S. Declaration of Independence is that in it "we are confronted with one of the rare moments in history when the power of action is great enough to erect its own monument" (*On Revolution* 130). As the originator of a new genre of political expression, the Declaration is an event as well as a text; its claim to political authority derives not from its philosophical or ideological scope but rather from its appearance at a distinct time and place. The kind of political community created through modern revolution cannot seek legitimation from extrapolitical sources such as God or tradition. Instead, its authorization relies on "the world-building capacity of man," or in other words "the human faculty of making promises ... which, in the realm of politics, may well be the highest human faculty" (180). A stunningly successful textual instantiation of a collective promise, the Declaration was the speech act that in Arendt's words "would provide the sole source of authority from which the Constitution, not as an act of constituting government but as the law of the land, derives its own legitimacy; for the Constitution itself, in its preamble as well as in its amendments which form the Bill of Rights, is singularly silent on the question of ultimate authority" (193–94). The founding legal document of the United States, in other words, is legitimized entirely by another rhetorical performance—albeit an extraordinarily successful one. The "perfect way for action to appear in words" (130), Arendt's ideal revolutionary text is a tangible expression of the collective work of promise-making and community creation that took place in North America in the eighteenth century. Its rhetorical success depends less on its content than on its ability to persuade its reader that that content—the thing that it declares to be true—was true all along.

Real revolution and real constitution-making, in Arendt's account, are historical rarities; hers is an argument against what she perceives as the overuse and *mis*use of the term "revolution" in her own historical moment, as well as a call to rediscover the origins of this phenomenon in order to reinvigorate its potential for twentieth-century political thought. Revolutionaries in Arendt's own time were finding more inspiration in the French model, whereas France, in Arendt's view, had made the fatal mistake of aiming to solve a social rather than a political problem—to eradicate inequality rather than to instantiate freedom. Doomed from the start as a consequence of its impossible goal, the French Revolution failed to found a new lasting political order. The constitutional chaos that ensued in France in the 1790s serves, for Arendt, as evidence of this failure; reduced to a mere "piece of paper" (125), the original 1791 Constitution soon found itself buried beneath an "avalanche of constitutions," each one weakened not only by the tumultuous political circumstances out of which it emerged but also, more simply, by this excess of texts, none strong enough to do their intended job. Arendt's problematic antipathy toward "the social question" and France aside,[5] her description of the tragedy of the country's first revolutionary constitution points to her more general anxiety about the relationship between the specifically *textual* nature of founding law and the authority it seeks to claim. Deprived of the necessary force of law—the power to put an end to revolutionary violence and replace it with a new political order—France's constitution is disenchanted; it says without doing; it is a failed speech-act. This, Arendt contends in *On Revolution,* has been the fate of the many revolutions that have proliferated in her own lifetime—social struggles that, neglecting to focus on political freedom, have obscured the much more difficult and important work that modern revolution—at least as envisioned by the founding fathers of the United States in the late eighteenth century—was meant to do.[6]

Derrida shares Arendt's fascination with the performative work of founding texts—but argues for the inseparability of rhetorical enactments of political community from the (decidedly non-rhetorical) "constative" force through which that community derives its legitimacy. In "Declarations of Independence" Derrida interrogates the paradoxical nature of the U.S. Declaration's final signature, which is at once performative and institutionalizing, and serves both as sign and as effacement of the process through which the text was created. Within the "chain of . . . representatives of representatives" that the 1776 Declaration embodies and enacts, Derrida observes a supreme indeterminacy that characterizes the basic conditions of its existence: "One cannot decide—and that's the interesting thing, the coup of force of such a declarative act—whether independence is stated or produced by this utterance" (9).

Like Arendt, Derrida points to the playful paradox of the Declaration's dual task of saying and doing. But whereas Arendt insists that the text manages to eschew extrapolitical authority altogether, Derrida argues that that authority is still present, located at the intersection of the uneasy negotiation of two verb tenses in the preamble, "are"—the constative—and "ought to be"—the prescriptive. His is a far more skeptical assessment of the U.S. text's romance of political novelty. The constative function of this text, its assertion of what *is*, carries with it the force of law, a force that originated not in rhetorical action but instead in the lawmaking violence of revolutionary war that will become the law-preserving violence of the state, enshrined in its constitution. "Violence is not exterior to the order of law," Derrida insists in a later essay; "It threatens law from within law" ("Force of Law" 268). Derrida identifies the paradox of law's creation through declaration, the inseparability of its performance from the violence through which law is made and preserved. "A 'successful' revolution, the 'successful' foundation of a state (in somewhat the same sense that one speaks of a 'felicitous performative speech act') will produce after the fact [*après coup*] what it was destined *in advance* to produce, namely, proper interpretative models to read in return, to give sense, necessity and above all legitimacy to the violence that has produced, among others, the interpretative model in question, that is, the discourse of its self legitimation" (270).

Arendt's insistence on the exclusion of violence from the realm of the political means that she cannot (and will not) come to terms with how racial violence factors into these revolutionary contexts. It also means that she cannot even begin to confront the complexities of anticolonial revolution in her own lifetime. A Derridean reading, in contrast, insists on the inextricability of language and violence. That insight has much to offer an investigation of what happens, in the Atlantic world of the early nineteenth century, when a political text attempts to acknowledge the way in which law—even law that on the surface seems to promise peace, democracy, equality, rights—works entirely copacetically alongside and *with* the inherently violent and racialized institutions of slavery and colonialism.

HAITI AND THE ROMANCE OF BLACK POLITICAL COMMUNITY

I began this chapter by invoking a stark contrast between Haiti's revolution and the revolutions that took place in the United States and France in the late eighteenth century. It was precisely this contrast between disparate Atlantic modernities—and the spectacular fashion in which Haiti overthrew both slavery and colonialism at such an early date—that so inspired mid-twentieth-century anticolonial thinkers, particularly those who hailed from the Caribbean. Yet this contrast also threatens to romanticize the liberatory aspects of Haiti's revolution, reducing to binary terms an enormously complex series of conflicts among multiple constituencies in France's biggest sugar colony during the final decade of the 1700s. In the early years of political turmoil on Saint-Domingue, the only group advocating political independence from France was the planter class, which was fearful of the concessions the metropole would make to slaves as well as free people of color in the colony. Free blacks and mixed-race residents of the island, meanwhile, did not consistently see their interests (i.e., increased political rights and socioeconomic privilege within colonial society) as aligned with those of the revolting slaves. Toussaint's 1801 draft constitution for Saint-Domingue stopped short of declaring independence; more importantly, its land policies were decidedly colonialist, intended to keep the plantation system more or less intact, maintain the property rights of French residents, and severely limit former slaves' access to political and economic power (Fick 206–8). The Revolution only became explicitly anticolonial in its aims after Toussaint's death in 1802, and after Dessalines joined forces with Alexandre Pétion, leader of the island's "mulatto" troops, to defeat Napoleon.[7] The solidarity that formed in the early nineteenth century among the various nonwhite constituencies—ex-slaves, free blacks, mixed-race colonial subjects—was new, and it was tenuous. Further, the new nation-state that came into being under Dessalines was not a democracy; the rights of man were applied differently to men and women in the 1805 Constitution; and race, skin color, and pre-revolutionary social status would continue to structure life in the new postcolony.

I approach my analysis of the performance of Haitian nationhood staged in the Declaration of Independence and 1805 Constitution with an awareness of these historical complexities. These founding texts critically rewrite the script for the relationship between race and law in the revolutionary Atlantic world; but they do so by relying heavily on what Miranda Joseph calls a "romance of community"—a fiction of unity that depends upon the repression of internal fissures and a disavowal of the exclusions that help create the possibility of these documents' existence. Dessalines's articulation of Haitian nationhood in the early nineteenth century was grounded in a romance of blackness as a legible and legitimate political identity. As a former field slave, Dessalines had enjoyed none of the relative status and educational privilege to which Toussaint, as a house slave, had had access; his French was rudimentary, and he was even rumored to have been born in Africa.[8] His anti-Western, antiwhite, authentically Afro-Caribbean identity claims were certainly performances, but they were incredibly potent performances in the years leading up to Haitian independence. They were crucial to his ability to collapse what were originally two separate revolutionary narratives of abolition and anticolonialism into a single narrative of Haitian nation-formation. Under Dessalines, and through the founding texts that he authorized and authored, Haiti became now both postcolonial and "black."

My reading of Haiti's declarative founding documents thus takes this romance of black, anticolonial nationhood quite seriously—not toward the goal of uncritically celebrating or perpetuating it, but instead as a means of elucidating how it made use of some basic and important elements of black Atlantic rewritings of a First World political imagination in the early nineteenth century. These are elements that will reappear in later-twentieth-century versions of anticolonialism. To the best of my knowledge, none of the twentieth-century writers I discuss further along in the book have much direct knowledge of or interest in Haiti's founding texts. Even Césaire and James, two of the midcentury anticolonial intellectuals who were most invested in exploring the historical and philosophical importance of Haiti's past for their Caribbean present, have nothing to say about Dessalines's Declaration of Independence or the country's early constitutions. Nonetheless, the audacious experimentation with and provocative reimagining of political authorship that take place in these texts indicate just how important it has always been for black Atlantic anticolonialism to confront, appropriate, and try to transform the conventions of First World law.

THE 1804 DECLARATION OF INDEPENDENCE

The Haitian Declaration of Independence had one, and only one, generic predecessor in 1804: the 1776 U.S. Declaration. There was no way for the drafters of the Haitian text not to engage this earlier text; there was no other such document for Haiti to borrow from, rebel against, or "write back" to. Like its model, the Haitian Declaration explores what it means to declare a "people" into existence; to represent that people on paper; and to assert the legitimacy of this new political community, born of revolution, into the future as well as in the present. And in the most basic terms, the Haitian text accomplishes roughly the same goal as the U.S. Declaration: it severs political ties between the colonized and the colonizer, asserting the existence and legitimacy of a new postcolony, a nation whose claims to legitimacy are rooted in a shared experience of political oppression and a collective (military) response thereto. But declaring a nation-state of ex-slaves into existence presents some notable additional complications for which the North American text offers no precedent. Like the U.S. Declaration, the Haitian text addresses itself to an Atlantic international community; but for Haiti to assert political equality with the other states within that community is a much more fraught and audacious undertaking than was the claim to political autonomy made by the North American colonies twenty-seven years earlier. Haiti was saddled with the added responsibility of demonstrating the personhood of the island's nonwhite inhabitants in addition to endowing those inhabitants with a specifically national collective identity. In this sense, this Declaration of Independence is also, tacitly, a declaration of rights—a document charged with extending the rights of man to people of African descent. The Haitian text is anything but a reprise of the U.S. Declaration that served as its generic model. Just as Haiti's revolution called for a reappraisal of the concept of revolution itself, one that would account for its response to racialized violence and exploitation, so the Haitian Declaration of Independence demands a rethinking of the meaning of this quintessential revolutionary rhetorical form. The Haitian text reconfigures the grounds upon which a political community claims the authority to declare itself into existence in Atlantic modernity.

A declaration of independence appears amid the tumult and upheaval of revolutionary time, in which the political order that preceded revolution has been shattered but in which no new political order has been established. The unique predicament that declarations of independence face is how to instantiate that present in writing—how to distill the performance of revolutionary authority into textual form in a way that convinces its readers that the gap between text and performance is insignificant, if not nonexistent. The U.S. Declaration of Independence and the French *Déclaration des droits de l'homme et du citoyen* seek to solve this problem through recourse to the language of natural rights, language which transforms a legal fiction into a statement of the obvious: North Americans are asserting truths that are held to be self-evident; the French National Assembly's document serves as a *reminder* of rights with which all men and citizens are already endowed. In the face of a hostile, slave-owning international community, the Declaration authored by Dessalines cannot and does not rely on natural rights theory. Instead, departing drastically from those models, the Haitian text manages its revolutionary temporality by identifying two key sources for its authority: blood-spilling and oath-taking. Dessalines rejected the first version of an independence declaration that was drafted for him because, too closely resembling the North American version, it did not exude the requisite "heat and energy" suited to the circumstances of Haiti's intervention into the revolutionary Atlantic world (qtd. in Dubois 298). The final text of the 1804 Haitian Declaration, purportedly drafted by Louis Boisrond-Tonnerre,[9] corrects that earlier version's shortcomings in full. Boisrond-Tonnerre famously described his approach to writing Haiti's first official statement of national sovereignty in vividly corporeal terms: "To draw up the act of independence we need the skin of a white man for parchment, his skull for an inkwell, his blood for ink, and a bayonet for a pen" (qtd. in Geggus, *Haitian Revolutionary Studies* 208). Declaring Haitian independence, for this writer/secretary, is not merely a matter of listing grievances, depicting the betrayal of a long-standing kinship between a people and its ruler, and justifying a political break from that ruler on those grounds (the key components of the U.S. Declaration). Rather, it entails an act of cannibalistic textualization, an incorporation of the necessary violence of the revolution—the dismembering of the Frenchman—into the material form of the text. What Doris Garraway identifies as the Haitian Declaration's "negative universalism" requires the construction of a nationalism that is structured explicitly around the exclusion of France and that consequently also stages a rejection of the abstract figure of the rights-bearing individual from French revolutionary rhetoric (*Tree of Liberty* 79). Boisrond-Tonnerre's Frenchman is reduced to the sum of the parts of his mutilated body, which, as the inverse of universal abstraction, renders Haiti's history as a slave colony constitutive of its future as a nation; Haiti's independence has been "consacrée par le sang du peuple de cette Isle" ["consecrated by the blood of the people of this island" (translation mine)]. The state of war out of which Haiti emerged did not begin in 1791; the founding violence of the Haitian nation consists of the centuries-old violence of Atlantic slavery as well as the slaves' resistance to it. And it is because of this much longer, deeper conflict between master and slave that the Haitian Declaration makes what David Armitage identifies as its greatest departure, at the level of content, from its U.S. model (115): "Paix à nos voisins, mais anathème au nom français, haine éternelle à la france: voilà notre cri" ("Haitian Declaration of Independence") ["Peace to our neighbors; but let this be our cry: 'Anathema to the French name! Eternal hatred of France!'"]. This is a declaration of war, written and disseminated fourteen years after the fighting broke out—though certainly not before revolutionary violence had come to an end on the island. In the months following the creation and publication of the Declaration of Independence, Dessalines would work to finalize the eradication of the presence of French bodies on Haitian soil by means of a series of massacres that would horrify the white Atlantic world and confirm the text's insistence on a continued antagonism with France.

Thus, on one hand the Declaration seems to be merely a textual precursor to the real work of Haitian state-making, which takes place through (violent) actions, not words. But the opening lines of the text reveal that violence cannot alone do the important work of ensuring the survival of Haitian independence:

> Ce n'est pas assez d'avoir expulsé de votre pays les barbares qui l'ont ensanglanté depuis deux siècles; ce n'est pas assez d'avoir mis un frein aux factions toujours renaissantes qui se jouaient tour-à-tour du fantôme de liberté que la france exposait à vos yeux; il faut par un dernier acte d'autorité nationale, assurer à jamais l'empire de la liberté dans le pays qui nous a vu naître; il faut ravir au gouvernement inhumain qui tient depuis long-tems nos esprits dans la torpeur la plus humiliante, tout espoir de nous réasservir; il faut enfin vivre indépendans ou mourir. ("Haitian Declaration of Independence")

> It is not enough to have expelled the barbarians who have bloodied our land for two centuries; it is not enough to have restrained those ever-evolving factions that one after another mocked the specter of liberty that France dangled before you. We must, with one last act of national authority, forever ensure liberty's reign in the country of our birth; we must take any hope of re-enslaving us away from the inhumane government that for so long kept us in the most humiliating stagnation. In the end we must live independent or die. (Dubois and Garrigus 188)

Even as the French themselves disappear from the island, Dessalines explains, Frenchness threatens to survive as a powerful and dangerous discursive force in the postcolony. Haiti's real antagonist, in 1804, is not a French army infringing on national territory, but rather a multifaceted two-hundred-year history of French cultural hegemony—an imprint that has the power to to undercut the formation of a new, postcolonial national consciousness:

> Tout y retrace le souvenir des cruautés de ce peuple barbare; nos lois, nos mœurs, nos villes, tout encore porte l'empreinte française; que dis-je, il existe des français dans notre Isle, et vous vous croyez libres et indépendans de cette République qui a combattu toutes les nations, il est vrai; mais qui n'a jamais vaincu celles qui ont voulu être libres. ("Haitian Declaration of Independence")

> Everything revives the memories of the cruelties of this barbarous people: our laws, our habits, our towns, everything still carries the stamp of the French. Indeed! There are still French in our island, and you believe yourself free and independent of that republic, which, it is true, has fought all the nations, but which has never defeated those who wanted to be free. (Dubois and Garrigus 188–89)

The challenge Haiti faces in the present is an anticolonial challenge of the sort that Frantz Fanon would describe 150 years later in *The Wretched of the*

Earth. Even as the opening words of this Declaration name the French as "les barbares qui l'ont ensanglanté depuis deux siècles," the text as a whole makes relatively few references to the institution of slavery. As Jenson notes, "liberty" and "independence" most likely connoted political independence rather than emancipation from slavery for Dessalines by this time (85). And political independence, as distinct from emancipation, calls for the creation of a new political consciousness, one that will bring about Haiti's psychic liberation in the nation-state to come. Blocking the formation of this consciousness is not a military but—to borrow Chris Bongie's term—a *scribal* force, a French "imprint" that encompasses colonialism's legal, cultural, and discursive violence.

One means of erasing the "empreinte française" from Haitian shores was through a reclamation of an alternative historical genealogy for modern Haiti, an assertion of solidarity with the island's precolonial inhabitants—the most obvious example of which is the country's new name. Borrowing from a Taino-Arawak term believed to mean "rugged" or "mountainous" (Geggus, *Haitian Revolutionary Studies* 207), "Haiti" indigenizes the new postcolony to the Americas—and simultaneously casts Frenchness as foreign. In another striking rhetorical move for which the U.S. Declaration provides no parallel, the Haitian text invokes Saint-Domingue's exterminated native population as a model of anticolonial heroism for the modern state:

> Marchons sur d'autres traces, imitons ces peuples qui, portant leurs sollicitudes jusques sur l'avenir et appréhendant de laisser à la postérité l'exemple de la lâcheté, ont préférés être exterminés que rayés du nombre des peuples libres. ("Haitian Declaration of Independence")
>
> Let us walk down another path; let us imitate those people who, extending their concern into the future and dreading to leave an example of cowardice for posterity, preferred to be exterminated rather than lose their place as one of the world's free peoples. (Dubois and Garrigus 190)

The exterminated native Americans serve here as models of bravery and intractability, a sublime kind of freedom that ultimately found victory in death rather than compromise.[10] The Haitians to whom Dessalines speaks are "Citoyens Indigènes," nativized through an affective affinity to an island population that valiantly confronted the French at an earlier historical moment.

Haiti's new name is, however, only the first step toward eradicating France's formidable discursive imprint. After years of war, Haiti now faces a final battle of institutionally sanctioned words and beliefs: "Victimes pendant quatorze ans de notre crédulité et de notre indulgence; vaincus, non par des armées françaises, mais par la pipeuse éloquence des proclamations de leurs agens; quand nous lasserons-nous de respirer le même air qu'eux?" ["Victims of our [own] credulity and indulgence for fourteen years; defeated not by French armies, but by the pathetic eloquence of their agents' proclamations; when will we tire of breathing the air that they breathe?" (Dubois and Garrigus 189)]. By waging a protest against the power of other proclamations *within* a proclamation, the document renders explicit its project of declaring independence from North Atlantic textual forms. Haiti needs its own, indigenized form of an official speech-act in order to rid itself of "le nom français" which still looms large in the nation's self-image.

Political declarations, not troops, are Haiti's most dangerous and active oppressors as of 1804. This is the reason for the text's second major departure from its North Atlantic models: its presentation as a singular performance of oath-taking, set on a specific day in a specific place and enacted by a discrete group of individuals tasked with representing a national will. Dessalines is the speaking voice and performing body in charge of this performance:

> Citoyens, mes Compatriotes, j'ai rassemblé dans ce jour solemnel ces militaires courageux, qui, à la veille de recueillir les derniers soupirs de la liberté, ont prodigué leur sang pour la sauver; ces Généraux qui ont guidé vos efforts contre la tyrannie, n'ont point encore assez fait pour votre Bonheur.... Le nom français lugubre encore nos contrées.

> Citizens, my countrymen, on this solemn day I have brought together those courageous soldiers who, as liberty lay dying, spilled their blood to save it; these generals who have guided your efforts against tyranny have not yet done enough for your happiness; the French name still haunts our land. (Dubois and Garrigus 188)

In contrast to the U.S. Declaration, this text is not voiced by a ubiquitous national "We," nor does it resort to the disembodied third-person voice of the French *Déclaration des droits de l'homme et du citoyen*; instead the Haitian text presents itself first and foremost as the transcript of a speech. The effects of Dessalines's foregrounding of his own individual voice here are twofold. On one hand, doing so draws attention to his distance from the citizens he addresses; by announcing that he speaks *to* (as well as on behalf of) the "long-suffering people of Haiti," he reminds his audiences—all of them—that the Haitian people themselves speak only indirectly in this founding document. On the other hand, in foregrounding the Declaration as a singular, embodied performance, he once again deliberately eschews the abstraction upon which the U.S. text relies. There is an intimacy to this moment of direct exchange between leader and citizens, both of whom are being initiated into those roles through this rhetorical performance. While the U.S. Declaration presents itself as a public address to a general international audience, the Haitian Declaration is an intimate, live performance, a speech delivered in front of a crowd at Gonaïves at a specific moment in time. Though, as Jenson notes, Dessalines and his government certainly did have international audiences in mind as they drafted and disseminated this and other independence-era proclamations (132–33), it is important that this text requires foreign and domestic readers alike to engage with the scene (whether real or imagined) of its original iteration. They must, in other words, imagine themselves as live witnesses to a revolutionary rhetorical event.

This is a rhetorical event that calls for a brand-new beginning, one that Dessalines cannot enact alone. The Declaration concludes with a call for its various audiences to participate directly in the performance of Haitian political authority:

Généraux, et vous Chefs, réunis ici près de moi pour le bonheur de notre pays, le jour est arrivé, ce jour qui doit éterniser notre gloire, notre indépendance.

S'il pouvait exister parmi nous un cœur tiède, qu'il s'éloigne et tremble de prononcer le serment qui doit nous unir.

Jurons à l'univers entier, à la postérité, à nous-mêmes de renoncer à jamais à la france, et de mourir plutôt que de vivre sous sa domination.

De combattre jusqu'au dernier soupir pour l'indépendance de notre pays.

Et toi, peuple trop long-tems infortuné, témoin du serment que nous prononçons, souviens toi que c'est sur ta constance et ton courage que j'ai compté quand je me suis lancé dans la carrière de la liberté pour y combattre le despotisme et la tyrannie contre lesquels tu luttais depuis quatorze ans; rappelle-toi que j'ai tout sacrifié pour voler à ta défense, parens, enfans, fortune, et que maintenant je ne suis riche que de ta liberté; que mon nom est devenu en horreur à tous les peuples qui veulent l'esclavage, et que les despotes et les tyrans ne le prononcent qu'en maudissant le jour qui m'a vu naître; et si jamais tu refusais ou recevais en murmurant les lois que le génie qui veille à tes destins me dictera pour ton bonheur, tu mériterais le sort des peuples ingrats.

Mais loin de moi cette affreuse idée; tu seras le soutien de la liberté que tu chéris, l'appui du Chef qui te commande.

Prête donc entre ses mains le serment de vivre libre et indépendant, et de préférer la mort à tout ce qui tendrait à te remettre sous le joug. Jure enfin, de poursuivre à jamais les traîtres et les ennemis de ton indépendance. ("Haitian Declaration of Independence")

Generals and you, leaders, collected here close to me for the good of our land, the day has come, the day which must make our glory, our independence, eternal.

If there could exist among us a lukewarm heart, let him distance himself and tremble to take the oath which must unite us. Let us vow to ourselves, to posterity, to the entire universe, to forever renounce France, and to die rather than live under its domination; to fight until our last breath for the independence of our country.

And you, a people so long without good fortune, witness to the oath we take, remember that I counted on your constancy and courage when I threw myself into the career of liberty to fight the despotism and tyranny you had struggled against for fourteen years. Remember that I sacrificed everything to rally to your defense; family, children, fortune, and now I am rich only with your liberty; my name has become a horror to all those who want slavery. Despots and tyrants curse the day that I was born. If ever you refused or grumbled while receiving those laws that the spirit guarding your fate dictates to me for your own good, you would deserve the fate of an ungrateful people. But I reject that awful idea; you will sustain the liberty that you cherish and support the leader who commands you. Therefore, vow before me to live free and independent and to prefer death to anything that will try to place you back in chains. Swear, finally, to pursue forever the traitors and enemies of your independence. (Dubois and Garrigus 190–91)

One hundred fifty years later, Frantz Fanon would articulate the central conundrum of decolonization: what sustains the sense of common purpose and community after the period of anticolonial warfare has come to a close? What prevents the old order from reasserting its authority in the postcolony, undoing the work of revolution and undermining the solidarity from which colonized subjects derived the strength to overthrow their oppressors in the first place? The Haitian Declaration exhibits a Fanonian anxiety with the possibility of revolutionary failure, and its response is to resist identifying an endpoint for that period, and indeed to fold anticolonial revolution into the practice of imagining and narrating the present of the new nation-state. In contrast to the U.S. Declaration, this text does not culminate in a definitive declarative performance. Instead, it ends with a series of orders for declarative performances that have yet to take place. The text serves to elicit more declarations in the future—speech acts that will continue the work of instantiating postcolonial independence well after the founding text as rhetorical event has concluded. The formation of political community in the Haitian Declaration is a creative, performative, and ongoing activity—one that exceeds the space and time of the text, and that transfers iterative power from Dessalines onto the people themselves. In this sense the Declaration is meant to mark a beginning of the cultivation of a citizenry's sense of collective identity rather than a one-time iteration of an identity that already exists.

And yet this Declaration is not, in fact, the first rhetorical iteration of Haiti's independence; another speech act precedes it. Prior to 2010, the original, official copy of the Declaration—the one that was originally printed and disseminated by the government—was thought to be lost. The versions that were in circulation before 2010 present it as a stand-alone text, prefaced only by various editors' framing comments.[11] In April 2010 Julia Gaffield discovered an original copy of the Declaration in the British National Archives, one that had traveled first to Jamaica in the hands of a colonial officer, Edward Corbet, who presented it to the Governor of Jamaica ("Duke Graduate Student"). This original version of the Declaration was accompanied by Corbet's note to the Governor, but also by a two-page preface that was printed with the text itself. This preface, which had not been read alongside the Declaration since 1805, narrates yet another rhetorical event that preceded the delivery of the Declaration itself by just a few hours, and positions the text in an even more extensive chain of live performances of fidelity to the new nation.

> Aujourd'hui premier Janvier, mil huit cent quatre, le Général en Chef de l'armée Indigène, accompagné des Généraux, Chefs de l'armée, convoqués à l'effet de prendre les mesures qui doivent tendre au bonheur du pays.
>
> Après avoir fait connaître aux Généraux assemblés, ses véritables intentions, d'assurer à jamais aux Indigènes d'Hayti, un Gouvernement stable, objet de sa plus vive sollicitude; ce qu'il a fait par un discours qui tend à faire connaître aux Puissances Etrangères, la résolution de rendre le pays indépendant, et de jouir d'une liberté consacrée par le sang du people de cette Isle; et après avoir recueilli les avis, a demandé que chacun des Généraux assemblés prononçât le serment de renoncer à jamais à la France, de mourir plutôt que de vivre sous sa domination, et de combattre jusqu'au dernier soupir pour l'indépendance.
>
> Les Généraux, pénétrés de ces principes sacrés, après avoir donné d'une voix unanime leur adhésion au projet bien manifesté d'indépendance, ont tous juré *à la postérité, à l'univers entier, de renoncer à jamais à la France, et de mourir plutôt que de vivre sous sa domination.*
>
> Fait aux Gonaïves, ce 1er Janvier 1804 et le 1er jour de l'indépendance d'Hayti. ("Haitian Declaration of Independence")

> Today, the first of January, 1804, the General in Chief of the Native Army, accompanied by his generals, chiefs of the army, convened in order to take measures necessary for the welfare of the country.
>
> Having established the assembled Generals' true intentions to secure forever for the natives of Haiti a stable government as the object of their warmest solicitude; this they have done in words that foreign powers will come to know, the resolution to render the country independent, and to enjoy a liberty consecrated by the blood of the people of this island; and after having gathered these opinions, the General in Chief has demanded of each of his assembled generals that they speak an oath forever renouncing France, to die before living under her domination, and to fight to the last breath for independence.
>
> The Generals, penetrated by these sacred principles, having given in a unanimous voice their loyalty to this well-manifested project of independence, have all sworn *in posterity, universally, to renounce forever France, and to die before living under her domination.*
>
> Enacted in Gonaïves on this first of January and the first day of Haiti's independence. (translation mine)

In this version of the text, Dessalines's speech is preceded by a report of a *previous* performance of collective loyalty. The past tense of these opening paragraphs contrasts to the immediacy of the present tense of the declaration that follows, and as a consequence this preface introduces and sharpens the reader's focus on the Declaration's placement in time: even the date of its performance and ratification can be split into a recent past and an immediate present. The prefatory oath competes with the Declaration itself by introducing another speech act into the mix, a speech act that had to happen *in advance of* the one that Dessalines's public proclamation calls for. The preface thus creates a doubling effect in this founding text of Haiti; the "real" declaration, the official declaration of independence itself, is haunted by a declaration that already happened, a shadow declaration that indeed seems to be the source of authorization for the main event.

The italicized oath taken by Dessalines's generals reappears in the text of the Declaration proper, as its culmination, the "dernier acte d'autorité nationale" that must be (but has not yet been) completed in order to "assurer à jamais l'empire de la liberté dans le pays qui nous a vu naître." Dessalines draws his audience's attention to the presence of the generals on the scene, who, along with Dessalines himself, "nous vous devons la dernière preuve de notre dévouement" ["offer you the ultimate proof of our devotion"]. Dessalines's final solicitation to the people of Haiti to take this oath themselves takes on a new set of meanings when read alongside—and more importantly, *after*—this preface. The oath is a speech act that occurs both in advance of the event of the Declaration, by the generals, and as a result of the Declaration, by the people. It functions as a strategy for rooting the Declaration in a specific moment, endowing the text with an immediacy associated with oral performance, and thus grappling with the impossibility of distilling a live performance into textual form. The oath links together past and future through a fantastical present evoked by the document itself.

In both the Haitian and U.S. declarations of independence, there is a calculus of past, present, and future in which reference to the new nation's past necessitates the present declaration, promise, or compact in order to secure a particular vision of the future (a future in line with a vision established by that same past). For Haiti, however, the past that the Declaration recalls is not a prehistoric natural law, but instead a decidedly modern history of racial violence that continues to shape power and authority across the present-day Atlantic world. To the North Atlantic world in 1804, there was nothing self-evident about the claims to natural rights and self-rule that the slaves, ex-slaves, and descendants of slaves had been making on Saint-Domingue during the previous decade. Natural rights was not a comfortable tautology to which the drafters of Haiti's founding documents could resort in order to convince readers of these texts' authority. Instead national sovereignty, in this document, finds its justification amid a chain of verbal promises.

THE 1805 HAITIAN CONSTITUTION

Haiti's first postcolonial constitution made its appearance seventeen months after Dessalines declared independence in Gonaïves. In the interim, Dessalines had made two moves that marked the end of the war and established Haiti's independence in spectacular terms. In February 1804—just as the news and the text of the Declaration were beginning to circulate abroad—he ordered the massacre of all remaining whites on the island. Largely unassuaged by his reassurances that this action was a just and even relatively measured response to a long legacy of French acts of barbarism against Haitians, the outside world viewed it instead as an indiscriminate program of violence against all whites.[12] In October of that same year, and as a consequence of the rumor that Napoleon was about to do the same, Dessalines had himself crowned emperor of Haiti. Written and ratified just a few months later, the 1805 *Constitution Impériale d'Haïti* registers both of these events. Naming Dessalines emperor for life and endowing the executive with nearly total governmental control, the text brings the country's revolutionary period to a close and establishes an autocratic new regime that guarantees racial equality and permanently outlaws slavery, while offering no provisions for popular sovereignty. The 1805 Constitution transforms the Declaration of Independence's aspirational claims about nationhood into a much more constrained narrative of statehood and order.

Critical commentary on Haiti's early experiments in constitutionalism has tended to focus on the extent to which Dessalines—as well as Toussaint before him and Henri Christophe a year later—drew heavily on France's revolutionary constitutions as models. Sibylle Fischer notes, for instance, that Toussaint's 1801 draft constitution of the colony of Saint-Domingue borrowed from the French constitutions of 1791 and 1793—but, crucially, declined to contain the all-important guarantees against slavery and racial exploitation within a bill of rights; "once the elimination of racial subordination is at the center of the foundational agenda of the state," rather than itemized in a list of (potentially contingent) rights, "neither customary distinctions between 'the social' and 'the political' nor clear-cut distinctions between liberty and equality are persuasive" (265). Dessalines's 1805 Constitution differs dramatically from Toussaint's text in many respects, but follows suit when it comes to rendering freedom and racial equality as the key organic components of the political community to come. Yet just as the vast majority of scholarship on the Haitian Revolution to date has remained focused on its relationship with the French Revolution, with little discussion of its possible connections to and borrowings from North American revolutionary activity, so does Fischer not consider the ways in which Dessalines's constitution might also be in conversation with the U.S. Constitution. The importance of the U.S. text as a model for Haiti's first constitution has received little scholarly attention—even though it was the one and only other properly "postcolonial" constitution in existence as of 1805. Along with the 1776 Declaration of Independence, this document provides the first Haitian government with a model for how to translate political independence from a program of military action into an institutional, territorial, and social reality. The Haitian Constitution is in fact in conversation with *multiple* constitutional models. Indeed, to the extent that Hannah Arendt's classification of the different aims and orientations of French and North American constitutionalism is valid, we might say that one of this text's most notable provocations to the genre of the modern constitution is its borrowing from both of these constitutional traditions at once.

The U.S. Constitution originated a brand-new juridico-political genre, one that wedded the legitimacy of national sovereignty to its articulation in textual form. Before the late eighteenth century, Bernard Bailyn explains, the word "constitution" denoted "not, as we would have it, a written document or even an unwritten but deliberately contrived design of government and a specification of rights beyond the power of ordinary legislation to alter" but instead "the constituted—that is, existing—arrangement of governmental institutions, laws, and customs together with the principles and goals that animated them" (67–68). Company charters and the Mayflower Compact set a precedent for conceiving of a written basis for the organization of government and its institutions, but the U.S. Constitution—together with the state constitutions that preceded it—nonetheless introduced something new, a textual genre that signified statehood. The printedness of the constitution was integral to its generic identity; after a decade of extralegal violence inflicted from both the government and the people, textuality, Michael Warner argues, served to legitimize "the legality of law" in North America (98). "The presence of the people to themselves was for [the North American constitutionalists] not legitimate enough precisely because it was recognized as the *source* of legitimacy. As source, or sovereign, it was by definition not legally constrained" (103–4). Live performance, in contrast, threatened to be *too* authentic, too closely conjoined to the force behind law rather than to law itself.

> What was needed for legitimacy, the Americans came to believe, was the derivative afterward of writing rather than the speech of the people. By articulating a nonempirical agency to replace empirical realizations of the people, writing became the hinge between a delegitimizing revolutionary politics and a nonrevolutionary, already legal signification of the people; it masked the contradiction between the two. (104)

The legal constitution of the United States depended on a masquerade, a textual elision of the incommensurability of revolutionary and post-revolutionary time. Its distillation of "the people" into a textual sign rather than an active political force was countered, in turn, by the document's appearance in print. The printedness of the Constitution transformed constituting (back) into a process of ongoing interpretation and debate rather than merely a matter of legal codification. In the preamble to the U.S. text, Warner claims, "the reading citizen interpellates himself—even herself—into the juridical order precisely at its foundation" (111).

The U.S. model thus provided Haiti with inspiration on two fronts. It was a postcolonial constitution, an example of what it looked like to found statehood in an ex-colony; and as the first ever *written* constitution it attested to the new, high stakes that modernity would place on the textualization of law. Yet just as he had done with the Declaration of Independence, Dessalines did not borrow uncritically from this North American model in constructing this text; he also sought to lay down some distance from it and appropriate it to better suit Haiti's needs. A crucial component of Dessalines's claim to have "avenged America," after all, was the Revolution's eradication of slavery from Haitian shores—an event for which there was no precedent elsewhere in the New World (Dessalines). In the U.S. Constitution, race makes its appearance only obliquely, in moments such as the "three-fifths clause" of Article I that acknowledge and legitimize the practice of slavery without ever using the words "black" or "slave." Blackness is written into the U.S. Constitution primarily by being written out.[13] The "people" included *within* the scope of the Haitian Constitution is precisely the population that the U.S. Constitution excludes from its scope.

Moreover, Haiti's politics of textuality and representation differed dramatically from U.S. contexts in the early nineteenth century. The vast majority of Haitian citizens-to-be could not read or write in, and did not even speak, French; Dessalines himself relied heavily on a host of secretaries due to his own limited proficiency in written French. Nonetheless, French was the language in which the Constitution was written and published. In Warner's assessment, the popular legitimacy of the U.S. Constitution derived largely from its circulation in print, which allowed "the reading citizen" to access and claim hermeneutic ownership over the text. But such a model translates imperfectly to a country in which only a small minority could have read the founding document. As Joan Dayan notes, the elitism not only of the French language but more importantly of the discursive contexts for the creation of Haiti's official founding text undercuts their emancipatory potential (4). Yet rather than just acknowledge that the experience of the majority of Haiti's citizenry had little to do with the creation of its early constitution(s), I want to consider how this experiential gap contributes to the 1805 text's very different staging of the relationship between representation, textual form, and the performative instantiation of a new nation-state. Haiti's first constitution refutes the distance that Warner identifies between live performance and the "legalization of law" in the case of the U.S. text. That refutation indicates that we need to think differently about the meaning of a written state constitution in a country in which it makes little sense to define literacy in terms of print culture, and in which the abolition of slavery and racial equality are the cornerstones of how a constitution legitimizes the basis for its existence.

The opening words of the U.S. Constitution announce a definitive and tight representational relationship between the authors of the document in the narrowest sense—the men sitting around a table in the middle of a hot Philadelphia summer—and the "people," the population that will claim citizenship in the nation-state that the text is helping to usher into existence. The magic of the phrase "We the People" lies in the elision not only of the constative and the performative tasks of the text, but also of the story of the representative relationship between the document's immediate authors and the citizenry on whose behalf those authors are speaking (and writing). The preamble to the Haitian Constitution undercuts the inevitability and sanctity of the representational relationship the earlier model sets up. The Haitian text's "We" is a somewhat less self-evident democratic hero of the narrative, and "the People" of the new nation are not so closely linked to this hero on the page.

> Au palais impérial de Dessalines, le 20 mai 1805, an II:
> Nous, H. Christophe, Clerveaux, Vernet, Gabart, Pétion, Geffrard, Toussaint-Brave, Raphaël, Lalondrie, Romain, Capois, Magny, Cangé, Daut, Magloire Ambroise, Yayou, Jean-Louis François, Gérin, Férou, Bazelais, Martial Besse,
> Tant en notre nom particulier qu'en celui du peuple d'Haïti, qui nous a légalement constitués les organes fidèles et les interprètes de sa volonté . . . (Janvier 30)

> At the imperial palace of Dessalines, 10 May 1805, Year Two:
> We, H. Christophe, Clerveaux, Vernet, Gabart, Pétion, Geffrard, Toussaint-Brave, Raphaël, Lalondridie, Romain, Capois, Magny, Cangé, Daut, Magloire Ambroise, Yayou, Jean-Louis François, Gérin, Férou, Bazelais, Martial Besse,
> As much in our particular name as in that of the people of Haiti, who have legally constituted us the faithful organs and the interpreters of their will . . .

This "We" first narrowly denotes a named group of authors, revolutionaries née national leaders, who claim legitimate solidarity with the Haitian people at large but exist, at least for purposes of constitution-making, at a distance from that people. Gone, in these opening lines, is the illusion of the people as authors; gone as well is any mystification of the *representational* relationship through which this text has come into existence. With this extensively drawn syntactical distinction between the named signatories of the Constitution and the newly created Haitian citizenry, the text sets up a formidable challenge for itself: how to establish a unity among these different constituencies, the speakers and the spoken-for, that will ground its legitimacy in some kind of popular sovereignty. The Declaration of Independence also foregrounded the different actors in the construction of Haitian nationhood—the leader, the elite, the populace—but did so in order to orchestrate their coming together by way of a unifying oath of allegiance and solidarity. In contrast, the opening lines of the Constitution expose the lack of connectivity among these separate constituencies, and especially the distance of "the people" from the exchange between Dessalines and his secretaries that this document records.

The second part of the preamble goes on to signal a number of different possible relationships between the names at the top of the page (two of which belong to future presidents of the country) and the rest of the nation. "We" refers, at different points in a lengthy set of clauses, to all of the following: an entity distinct from but involved with "the people of Haiti"; the victims of nature's past neglect; the possessors of expressive hearts; companions to those who hold the "general will"; and, finally, the group with the capacity to make direct contact with the state's executive power, who await the completion of this foundational text. It is difficult to pin down a single referent for the Constitution's opening pronoun anywhere in these opening paragraphs. At no point does any one of these descriptors of "we" present itself as the most accurate, inclusive, or important relationship of speaker and spoken-for. Instead, readers are offered a set of options that conflict, that overlap, and that can be put together in any number of different ways as well as in accordance with multiple philosophical traditions. Choosing one option appears to be less important than knowing how many different possibilities exist.

Where and how, then, does the Constitution establish the right of its named signatories to speak on behalf of the people? This constitution does not establish a democracy; the stakes of drawing this connection are therefore not the same as they are in the U.S. Constitution, or in the revolutionary French constitutions of the early 1790s.[14] Yet the drafters do take great pains to establish themselves as legitimate representatives of the Haitian citizenry; this document aims to prove the existence of such a relationship rather than being able to assume it as a given at the outset. The "We" with which the preamble begins derives its authority from a confluence of natural and historical forces that are unique to this particular nation-state-in-the-making:

> En présence de l'Etre-suprême, devant qui les mortels sont égaux, et qui n'a répandu tant d'espèces de créatures différentes sur la surface du globe qu'aux fins de manifester sa gloire et sa puissance par la diversité de ses œuvres;
>
> En face de la nature entière, dont nous avons été si injustement et depuis si longtemps considérés comme les enfants repoussés . . . (Janvier 30)

> In the presence of the Supreme Being, before whom all mortals are equal, and who only spread so many different species of creatures over the surface of the globe after manifesting his glory and his power through the diversity of his works;

In the face of nature in its entirety, by whom we have been so unjustly and for so long considered outcast children . . .

The Constitution here echoes the preamble of the French *Déclaration des droits de l'homme et du citoyen* and its invocation of a Rousseauian Supreme Being,[15] but also alters that phrasing, first by attributing to this not-quite-secular entity the central principle of human equality, and then by locating vindication from an oppressive past in nature. The preamble asserts a universal unity, *through which* the Haitian people's common history as unjust "outcasts" from that unity can be articulated. The *Être suprême* unites Haitians positively; but nature, caught up in this sentence with chance and maybe even fate, has united Haitians negatively, for all are victims of its past neglect. But for their permanent spectral presence in the name "Haiti," the Taino-Arawaks—the original anticolonial heroes of the Declaration of Independence—make no appearance in this text. In their place is the historical experience shared by the island's current inhabitants, a common background of alienation and oppression that provides the basis for unity in this modern postcolonial nation-state.

After the preamble, the text's most famous articles offer further justification for the basis of national unity through an audacious reconfiguring of the meaning of blackness. Articles 12 through 14 reinforce the friend/enemy lines between Haiti and France drawn in the Declaration, but provocatively code these lines through skin color, turning the logic of nineteenth-century racial ideology on its head:

> Art. 12—Aucun blanc, quelle que soit sa nation, ne mettra le pied sur ce territoire, à titre de maitre ou de propriétaire et ne pourra à l'avenir y acquérir aucune propriété.
>
> Art. 13—L'article précédent ne pourra produire aucun effet tant à l'égard des femmes blanches qui sont naturalisées haïtiennes par le gouvernement qu'à l'égard des enfants nés ou à naitre d'elles. Sont compris dans les dispositions du présent article, les Allemands et Polonais naturalisés par le gouvernement.
>
> Art. 14—Toute acception de couleur parmi les enfants d'une seule et même famille, dont le chef de l'Etat est le père, devant nécessairement cesser, les Haïtiens ne seront désormais connus que sous la dénomination génériques de noirs. (Janvier 32)

> 12. No white, whatever his nationality, shall put his foot on this territory with the title of master or proprietor, neither shall he in the future acquire any property therein.

> 13. The preceding article cannot in the smallest degree affect white women who have been naturalized Haitians by the government, nor does it extend to children already born, or to be born of these women. The Germans and Polish naturalized by government are also included in the provisions of the present article.
>
> 14. All preference based on color among the children of one and the same family, within which the head of state is the father, having necessarily to cease, the Haitians shall henceforth be known only under the generic appellation of blacks.

This three-part negotiation of Haitian citizenship first transforms whiteness from the only legible political identity to the only identity that will henceforth be *illegible* to the new nation-state. In essentially outlining the Revolution's terms of surrender for France, Article 12 establishes Haiti's national boundaries as a contrast in color: whiteness, a concept developed and deployed by the French, now denotes enemy status, the outcome of colonialism and slavery's mutual defeat.[16] The qualifications put forth in Article 13 reinforce the politicized nature of the Constitution's redefinition of "white" by citing exceptions—mothers of Haitians, as well as German and Polish soldiers who defected from Napoleon's troops—that dissociate the language of skin color from the color of Haitian skin. These groups, however, are not merely exceptions to a general rule; they also support what for the new citizenry was already a long-standing reality of racial hybridity, evidenced in Saint-Domingue's sizeable "mulatto" class. Once whiteness correlates exclusively with foreignness, blackness is free, in Article 14, to offer Haitians a common basis for citizenship and unification more powerful than societal divisions based on education, economic power, and even skin color. As Fischer notes, it is the narrative progression of these articles through which their subversion of North Atlantic conceptions of national identity are fully revealed (234). Cumulatively, Articles 12 through 14 announce that Haiti, perceived already by the rest of the world as black, has the same claim to political legibility as the French Republic or the United States of America—not in spite of, or even without reference to, but *because* of its blackness. Merely changing or erasing the descriptive language of race and skin color cannot counteract its potency; this constitution methodically exposes the political constructedness of these concepts in order to then pull them apart and dissolve their efficacy. Moreover, it is this process of exposure and dissolution—not the equation of blackness with citizenship on its own—that makes these articles, and the text as a whole, most subversive. In the U.S. Constitution, race and slavery occupy a space of uneasy, and almost unspoken, compromise. In contrast to the silences legitimized by the

North American model, the Haitian Constitution brings these historical conditions to the fore.

"Calling all Haitians 'black,'" Fischer observes, "is clearly a political act, or what legal scholars would call 'expressive lawmaking'" (234). Another present-day term for the work accomplished in Articles 12 through 14 of this early-nineteenth-century text is strategic essentialism. And while Aimé Césaire and other black anticolonialists of the mid-twentieth century never made reference to Dessalines's constitution, these articles read like a prescient template for the reclamation of blackness that was at the heart of the negritude movement. Blackness is declared politically legible in this 1805 text, without qualification and, importantly, as a resistant identity, one that creates national solidarity by defining whiteness as foreignness.

Yet this explosion of nineteenth-century racial categories is only the first of two varieties of strategic essentialism at work in the Constitution. This text's radical recoding of race as the basis for citizenship depends on the fact that it also puts forth a detailed prescription for how gender, family relations, and heredity will participate in constructing the new nation. In newly postcolonial Haiti, the meaning of lineage through reproduction was formed in part by the particular demographic history of colonial Saint-Domingue. Article 13's provisions for "white women who have been naturalized Haitians by the government" pertained to a small group of French widows that Dessalines had placed under his protection during the massacres (Dubois 300). But it also has implications for the politics of race and reproduction in postcolonial Haiti: if (some) white women and their children (of whatever color) are exempt from the correlation of whiteness with foreignness, but if Haitian national identity is still ultimately a black identity, no such ambiguity surrounds *male* national identity; Article 14 only culminates in a proclamation of blackness as politically legible after framing this claim to citizenship within the structure of a male-headed family. Whiteness—even French whiteness—can be forgiven the mother of a Haitian child; the "generic appellation of blacks" established through Articles 12 through 14 is not possible unless Haiti itself can be conceived of as a single family. Articles 9 and 10 have already coded national and family duties as one and the same by stipulating that "No one is worthy of being Haitian if he is not a good father, a good son, a good husband, and especially a good soldier," and denying "fathers and mothers ... the right to disinherit their children" (Janvier 31). Women—tacitly excluded from all types of civic participation outlined in Article 9—nonetheless play a crucial role in managing the Haitian national bloodline. Thus in these articles women are caught up in the metonym both as an unraced, monolithic group and as undifferentiated (and unindividuated) mothers and wives, articles of property belonging to nuclear families as well as to the larger family that is the state. The text exposes but also tries to work through its own confusions regarding the nation's inequities of color and class; no such ambivalence presents when it comes to defining property rights and national identity through gender and family relations. The Constitution's essentializing of gender is no less strategic than its essentializing of blackness and whiteness. But the results here are conservative and hegemonic.

The Constitution thus contains a number of different arguments about the source of national unity—shared historical experience, blackness as an oppositional identity, gender and reproductive roles that manage social relations in the new nation. But the more immediate source of the connection between "We" and "the People" derives from an event that took place well before the Constitution itself was written. Below the list of names with which the preamble begins, the authors of the text explain that the people of Haiti "*have* legally constituted us the faithful organs and the interpreters of their will." Like the Declaration of Independence, the Constitution shores up its authority from another, earlier contractual event. Unlike the Declaration, however, the Constitution assigns that earlier event a kind of authority that it cannot really have had. What does it mean for the preamble to assert that an act of legal constitution has already taken place—before the ratification of the actual Constitution? Not only political community and national identity but law itself transcends the text that is supposed to found it! This peculiar phrasing recalls the revolutionary constitution-making explored by Arendt and Derrida: the problem of how to assert legal authority when there is no legal structure in place—when, in fact, the new "authorities" have up to this point been preoccupied with dismantling the existing legal structure. On one hand, no piece of paper alone should be able to embody the (revolutionary) force behind the new law. On the other hand, the crux of the written state constitution's authority lies in the perception, at least, of its *separation* of force and law, of the existence of a subtle but crucial distance between constitution through revolutionary action and constitution through textualization. The Haitian Constitution's claim that legal constitution has preceded law's codification in writing collapses that distance.

The paradox of law's constative and performative properties may be an inherent feature of all constitutions, but this text's insistence on its revolutionary authority has a particular strategic value for the Dessalinean government in 1805, particularly in terms of how this text would be read and received abroad. In the wake of the North American and French revolutions, the political legitimacy of revolution and constitution-making had precedent in the North Atlantic world by the early nineteenth century—but its application to one of Europe's most lucrative sugar colonies was a far more fraught question for obvious reasons. Denied official recognition by the international community, the "legality" of Haiti remained nebulous for decades after the French had left the island. The word "legally" in this preamble allows the Dessalinean government to remind a skeptical international audience that the military and rhetorical events of the Haitian Revolution—its successful ousting of French colonialism and its declaration of independence—find justification in an already-existent template for the dissolution of an unjust regime and its replacement, through revolutionary action, with a new one. Insofar as any revolution can claim legitimacy, Haiti's can. But in sending this message, in insisting on not just the legitimacy but the *legality* of the people's already-existent compact with the drafters of the Constitution, the drafters undertake a more ambitious task. This text argues that there is something inherently legal about the Haitian people endowing their own representatives, rather than France, with the authority to constitute them on paper. But in order for that argument to work, *law* must be redefined; its origins must be relocated not only in the text at hand, but also in the popular force that authorized the creation of the text.

Like the Declaration of Independence, the 1805 Constitution presents itself as part of a chain of rhetorical performances; the authority of this text depends on an event of constituting that has already taken place. Also like the Declaration, the Constitution is itself a kind of performance: the presentation of the document by the secretaries to Dessalines for his imperial signature. The secretaries

> Déclarons que la teneur de la présente Constitution est l'expression libre, spontanée et invariable de nos cœurs et de la volonté générale de nos concitoyens;
> La soumettons à a sanction de Sa Majesté l'Empereur Jacques Dessalines, notre libérateur, pour recevoir sa prompte et entière exécution. (Janvier 31)

> Declare that the content of the present Constitution is the free, spontaneous and invariable expression of our hearts and of the general will of our fellow-citizens;
> and Submit it for the sanction of His Majesty the Emperor Jacques Dessalines, our liberator, to receive its prompt and entire execution.

The expressive hearts of a band of writers/leaders have come together with the general will of a much vaster community in order to compose the text that follows. In a significant departure from the U.S. Constitution, these concluding words of the preamble identify the act of formal constitution as a *closed* and *live* transaction between a small coterie of representatives and the emperor. If the text remains vague as to the nature of the event through which the people "legally constituted" the signatories as "the faithful organs and interpreters of our will," it is quite specific about the moment of textual presentation that marks the triumphant conclusion of the new nation-state's constituting process. The Constitution's identity as a written text takes on a significance that departs from Warner's assessment of textuality in the early United States: the Constitution here becomes a material object as much as a living document, a gift to the emperor at the end of a long, laborious process of constitution-*making*. Textuality matters because it makes possible the Constitution's materiality.

There is a finality to the preamble's staging of this presentation of the Constitution: Dessalines, who was the fiery speaker in the Declaration of Independence, is here a more shadowy presence, a sovereign whose signature will enact the law on the page. Yet in another sense the specificity of this exchange suggests that the work of constituting Haiti has only just begun. The 1805 Constitution identifies Dessalines as emperor, and, in Article 26, gives him the power to name his own successor. The text is thus not only an imperial constitution; it is a specifically Dessalinean imperial constitution, and, as such, it comes with an expiration date. Unlike the U.S. Constitution, this text is not meant to last in perpetuity. Its most important provisions—such as Article 2's assertion that "L'esclavage est à jamais aboli" ["Slavery is abolished forever"] (Janvier 31)—will perhaps, in the not so distant future, no longer be in danger of being reversed or overturned; but they may still need to be reiterated in a new text at a later date, just as the rights of man were reiterated in the new constitutions that came after France's original Constitution of 1791. The 1805 Constitution was not meant to outlast the lifespan of the country's revolutionary leader-turned-emperor.

OF COURSE, DESSALINES did not anticipate that his life—and the legal currency of his constitution—would come to an end in the following year! A civil war, fomented by the former *anciens libres* of Saint-Domingue who were disgruntled with Dessalines's land redistribution policies, led to the emperor's assassination in October 1806; Henri Christophe and Alexandre Pétion wrote new constitutions for the two separate northern and southern Haitian nations that uneasily coexisted for the next fourteen years; and neither those texts nor any of the nearly thirty separate constitutions that held legal currency from the early nineteenth century to the early twenty-first century would replicate the provocative strategic essentialism and preoccupation with performativity that are so prominent in Dessalines's text. The 1805 Constitution is ephemeral and anomalous in Haitian, and in black Atlantic, history. If Hannah Arendt had spent any time contemplating Haiti's founding documents in her study of modern revolution, she would no doubt have interpreted the country's tumultuous constitutional history as proof of the country's failure as a political community, rooted in its revolution's reproduction and in fact expansion of the unanswerable "social" questions that underpinned the French Revolution a decade earlier.

But as Sibylle Fischer explains, it is precisely because of the way in which Haiti exposed the inextricability of the "social" from the realm of the political that Arendt could *not* talk about this black Atlantic revolution in her work. "Considering slavery as a political issue makes her recoil," Fischer notes, and so she simply does not do it; in *On Revolution* "slaves vanish, first literally, through the institution that cloaks them with invisibility, and then conceptually, in the abyss between the social and the political. Revolutionary antislavery is a contradiction in terms. Haiti becomes unthinkable" (9). To render Haiti once again thinkable is thus to call into question not only Arendt's problematic dichotomization of the social and the political—already the subject of much criticism[17]—but also, more broadly, our assumptions about the kind of work we expect the founding texts of new political communities to do. What if we did not equate constitutional ephemerality with political failure? By asking this question I am not arguing in favor of a romanticized rereading of Haitian history that ignores the political instability and economic devastation experienced by the country over the past two hundred years—though certainly it is impossible to talk about the more dismal aspects of Haiti's past and present without accounting for factors such as the West's deliberate isolation of the country in the international community in the nineteenth century, France's demands that Haiti pay reparations for the economic losses suffered by former white planters, two twentieth-century U.S. occupations, and a global financial system that has subjected Haiti along with the rest of the "developing" world to debilitating debt programs in recent decades. Haiti's pairing of "social" and political revolutionary aims contributed to the country's post-independence instability insofar as this pairing was profoundly threatening to the institutions of colonialism and slavery in which the North Atlantic's political economy was grounded in the early nineteenth century. To assign blame for this history to the decisions, actions, and words of Haiti's revolutionary leadership—to suggest, for instance, that the Revolution "failed" because Toussaint was too conflicted, or Dessalines too bloodthirsty, or the legal structure put in place by the first constitution too weak—is to commit a glaring logical fallacy and affirm a pessimism about Haitian history with unpleasant political consequences in the twenty-first century.

Writers with more sympathetic orientations toward Haiti's anomalous and extraordinary history have had other reasons for affording scant attention to the country's founding documents. During the same years that Hannah Arendt was rendering Haiti unthinkable in her work, black internationalists such as C. L. R. James and Aimé Césaire were busy carving out a central role for Haiti's revolutionary past in their own writings, developing an alternative and radically disruptive model of modernity in which anticolonialism and antiracism would be the constitutive ethical components. Yet if these writers had read Haiti's founding texts at all, they most likely would have deemed them irrelevant, end products rather than constitutive events of the revolutionary process, and plagued by the same problems that would later loom large for late-twentieth-century postcolonies: a disconnect from the popular consciousness of a national citizenry that had little to do with the creation of these documents and that would not have even been able to read them. In the next two chapters I examine how James's and Césaire's work does, in fact, engage with and even help shape a mid-twentieth-century juridico-political imagination, putting forth an alternative way of thinking about the foundations of political authority at a moment in which decolonization and dramatic changes in international law are giving those questions new urgency. But it is notable and telling that for the most capacious and insightful anticolonial thinkers of the mid-twentieth century, the legal foundations of the Atlantic world's first black postcolony were of little interest.

If black internationalists simply ignored Haiti's juridico-political origins, late-twentieth-century postcolonial scholarship has been quite explicit about the problems with placing too much emphasis on a juridico-political archive that was so detached from the work of revolution on the ground. Carolyn Fick, ironically echoing Dessalines's own description of and language in the Declaration, cautions that since slaves inscribed themselves into the revolutionary process "by fire and blood and by the sacrifice of their own lives" rather than with pen and paper, written records—and definitions of literacy that privilege those records' authority—are of limited historiographical use (9). In a similar vein, Joan Dayan notes that "no declaration of independence, whether spoken or written in French or Haitian Creole, could sever the bonds between the former colony and its 'Mother Country'" (4). There are good reasons not to place too much weight on Haiti's official documents; doing so risks replicating a colonialist knowledge system in which the privilege of records created in writing by oligarchs goes unquestioned, and other ways of coming to terms with the disruption of Haiti remain obscured.

And yet these complications of literacy and political privilege are hardly unique to Haiti in the Age of Revolution, even if race and the social structures of Caribbean sugar plantation slavery did intensify the stakes of having access to written and spoken French, and even if Creole and Vodou change the discursive and imaginative tapestry of revolutionary slave culture. Overstating the irrelevance of Haiti's founding texts comes with its own set of problems, for there is much to be said about the fact that this black Atlantic revolution was preoccupied with the same questions about the political architecture of modernity that were so central to the revolutions taking place further north. If Haiti's revolution is the original event in the history of modern anticolonialism, then it is worth scrutinizing its quest for the forms in which to render the postcolony politically legible, both internally and for a broader international community. In acknowledging their own temporal situatedness, exposing and foregrounding the paradoxes of authority and representation that underlie their existence, and self-consciously staging a disruption to a North Atlantic audience, Haiti's founding texts offer up possibilities for a distinctly anticolonial and black Atlantic way of conceiving of law in revolutionary modernity. The political lessons of these texts are not restricted to the question of whether they "succeeded" or not as juridico-political documents, though the fact that the 1805 Constitution held legal currency for a while—that it was a "felicitous" textualized speech-act, even if only for a short time—is a crucial part of the story. Instead, they raise questions about some of our most basic assumptions about what law, especially law enshrined in written texts, can do. Put differently: they produce a postcolonial black Atlantic critical literacy of law. And as such, they offer up some insight as to how we might read anticolonial writings from the mid-twentieth century as participating in that same project.

CHAPTER 2

The Romance of Prodigal Literacy
C. L. R. James's Histories of Rhetorical Revolution in the Black Atlantic

CHAPTER 1 DEMONSTRATED how a distinctly black Atlantic form of rhetorical performance served as a tool, in Haiti's founding texts, for critically engaging and radically reinventing newly emergent First World genres of revolution. Here I shift focus from that early-nineteenth-century moment of the anticolonial revolution through which Haiti was constituted to the mid-twentieth century and the years leading up to the decolonization of much of Africa and the Caribbean. In this chapter and the next, I also turn away from an examination of texts with an explicit connection to law in favor of exploring the way in which the work of two of the most prolific and prominent mid-twentieth-century theorists of anticolonial revolution challenges a modern juridico-political imaginary in other genres and by other means. Here I attend to the work of C. L. R. James, the Trinidadian intellectual whose work contains anticolonialism's most sustained and compelling theorization of rhetorical performance. James rarely engages directly with First World law's texts or institutions in his work; from his earliest encounters with Marx, Lenin, and Trotsky in the 1930s, he placed little faith in the ability of organizations such as the League of Nations or the UN to address the racial and economic violence carried out by empire and capitalism, the political and economic structures these institutions were of course designed to uphold.[1] Instead, he was deeply invested in imagining alternative modes of political organization and participation, and how new political communities might form and assert their authority through revolutionary means. As Richard King observes, James shared with Hannah Arendt a preoccupation with "the return of political activity and, by extension, political freedom to the tradition of democratic politics, once Western but now global in reach" ("The Odd Couple" 110). James was interested in radically new forms of liberatory political life for a post-imperial, post-capitalist future, forms for which he found inspiration in the black Atlantic world's long history of revolt and resistance.

A historian and theorist rather than a statesman or fighter, James preferred to engage with anticolonial revolution through critique. While he may have briefly contemplated joining a Pan-African brigade to fight with Ethiopia after Mussolini's 1935 invasion (Høgsbjerg 97), he never took up arms in any of the midcentury national liberation movements unfolding all around him. As Grant Farred explains, "It is as commentator, in the role of revealing and unpacking the codes for those not directly party to the event, that James thrives, not as participant" (142). And yet James is actually the first of several anticolonial intellectuals I discuss in this book whose work reveals how difficult it is to differentiate between commentary and participation, between historical analysis and declarative event. One of James's most remarkable traits as a historian, David Scott argues, is his recognition of history-writing itself as a means of radical world-historical intervention. *The Black Jacobins*, James's groundbreaking historical account of the Haitian Revolution and by far his most renowned historical work, is nothing less than "an exercise in writing a history of the present" (Scott 57), "a *revolutionary* history" that both attends to a moment of radical geopolitical transformation in the black Atlantic world and makes a revolutionary intervention into its own transformative historical moment (58). *The Black Jacobins* theorizes anticolonial rhetorical performance but also constitutes such a performance in its own right, conceiving of discursive activity as at least as important to the revolutionary cause as armed struggle and military prowess.

At the narrative core of this text, as well as James's other histories of black revolt, is a romance of revolutionary rhetorical performance. James is fascinated by moments of felicitous connection and exchange between anticolonial leaders and "the people" whose revolutionary will they aspire to voice—transformative moments in which black revolutionary authorship is both created and authorized. In identifying romance as a productive and persistent mode of engagement in James's histories of black revolt, I draw on but also come to different conclusions from those of Scott, who, following Hayden White, argues that at a pivotal moment in James's career—1963—tragedy replaces romance as this author's chosen "mode of emplotment" for the story he tells about colonialism, anticolonial resistance, and postcolonial disillusionment (134). In Scott's account, the proof of this shift lies in the second edition of *The Black Jacobins,* published in 1963 and containing a discrete but dramatic set of revisions to the original through which James recasts Toussaint in tragic terms. My reading of James's work troubles Scott's insistence on 1963 as a historical and conceptual rupture point in James's work in two ways. First, I note that even as early as 1938 James's casting of the anticolonial struggle in romantic terms was riddled with ambivalence. Second, I argue that James does not abandon romance in the later decades of his career. It is important that while the original 1938 version of *The Black Jacobins*—written during the earliest years of his philosophical engagement with Marxism and his political involvement with Pan-Africanism—marks James's first and most sustained engagement with revolutionary romance, it is certainly not the last; romance pervades *all* of his accounts of black revolution, from *A History of Negro Revolt* (also published in 1938) to his 1977 *Nkrumah and the Ghana Revolution.* That is, this mode of emplotment re-emerges as a crucial conceptual tool in James's work well past the heyday of decolonization, and well after Africa and the Caribbean had entered into the so-called postcolonial era of the late twentieth century. Even as he confronts what Scott dubs "the bleak ruins of our postcolonial present" (45) in the 1960s and 1970s, James continues to write, revise, publish, and republish histories of anticolonial revolt—and to suggest that this historical trajectory had not yet come to an end. The romance lives on, in part through the act of republication, but most importantly through his continued investment in the possibilities enabled by acts of rhetorical performance through which novel forms of political community come into existence.

James's faith in the revolutionary possibilities of anticolonial speech-acts is enabled in no small part by his own class and gender affiliations. A powerful orator, James is also captivated throughout his career by the figure of the speaker-hero, the revolutionary leader whose organic connection to the people he corrals is affirmed and solidified through heroic public rhetorical performances. Consuelo Springfield writes: "As a man of the people, a product of the politics of colonialization in the Third World, James demands that the orator not preach to an audience nor plan to lead it but that he work consistently **with** his audience. The great speaker is one who understands and articulates the desires of the people in their own terms" (90). But as many critics have noted, James and his speaker-heroes are exceptional in terms of their class privilege and their levels of access to the Western canon.[2] These figures are also, not incidentally, all male. The revolutionary heroism they epitomize is predicated on a conception of a male-dominated public sphere that excludes the experiences, participation, and voices of women. The theory of rhetorical performance that emerges from his writings on black revolution is thus profoundly gendered. As Belinda Edmondson argues, James's "emphasis on one central, masterful personality in an otherwise Marxist account of revolution makes sense only if we understand it to be a particularly West Indian, particularly middle-class and male version of revolutionary discourse" (106). And as Hazel Carby observes, this classed and gendered discourse in turn enables the romance, so important to James as well as other black male intellectuals, of perfect communication and representational harmony between the revolutionary hero and the masses, who are often depicted in far more passive, feminized terms (116). The elitism inherent in James's affinity for structuring his histories around biographical profiles of exceptional male historical actors means that the erasure of women is both symptomatic and constitutive of this writer's more general limitations as a historian of revolution from below. Recent feminist scholarship has aptly demonstrated the ways in which the history and conceptual contours of black internationalism are very different when imagined, experienced, and critiqued by women.[3]

I point to these problems of class, gender, and romanticization in the male-authored black Atlantic anticolonial imagination in order to be as clear and specific as possible about what I hope to accomplish by exploring James's engagement with the romance of revolutionary speaker-heroes and their rhetorical performances. Without wishing to ignore the very real limitations of James's ability to think through the gender and class dynamics of his conception of revolution, solidary, and political community, I propose that his use of romance was not entirely oblivious to the representational problems that accompany this mode of emplotment. On numerous occasions, and importantly well before 1963, his writing does express a fair amount of ambivalence about the romance of revolutionary heroism and the limits of his own imagination to place and tell the story of non-elite historical actors. His famous explication of Toussaint L'Ouverture's writing in the original edition of *The Black Jacobins* works hard to justify the kind of authority this anticolonial speaker-hero claims over the masses for whom he speaks. In other texts this anxious ambivalence is even more pronounced, as James's reliance on revolutionary heroism as a central narrative structure coexists uneasily with a desire to write history from below without quite knowing how to do so. In reading James as a strategic and critical romantic, I draw inspiration from Michelle Stephens's account of the ways in which his gender politics change and become more inclusive in his later writings on Melville and the United States—of how we might read, in his preference for federation rather than revolution as a model for transnational solidarity, "the beginnings of a gendered critique of the gendered politics of black transnationalism and pathways toward envisioning an equal role and place for the woman of color in a black masculine global imaginary" (212). James's ambivalence about the revolutionary heroism that played so central a role in his historical imagination, an ambivalence that was in place well before the advent of decolonization and its aftermath, presents a similar interpretive possibility: a way of reading this writer's investment in romance as always already aware of the limitations of that narrative strategy—but still unwilling to disavow its uses and possibilities. Despite its problems, James's romance of anticolonial revolutionary rhetorical performance is both self-aware and productive; his deployment of this mode of emplotment well after the early 1960s is not merely a sign of anachronistic or naively utopian thinking in a less idealistic time.

Taking the limitations of James's theorization of resistance and community as a given, I interrogate what his work can offer twenty-first-century theorists of anti- and postcolonialism who do not share or wish to replicate his blind spots. James sees modern revolution as a historical phenomenon whose uniqueness lies in its enabling of a kind of ultimate political creativity, its opportunity for the total reconfiguration of political authority for which we may not even yet have the language. Revolution is an ineffable utopian future for which the past gives us only imperfect examples. Consequently the speaker-heroes and rhetorical performances that populate James's histories of black revolution are best understood as crucial narrative devices, the flawed but nonetheless vital tools through which James can narrate black Atlantic anticolonialism as a movement that has been underway since the late eighteenth century and that remains alive and well even in the postcolonial present.

TOUSSAINT L'OUVERTURE, ANTICOLONIAL SPEAKER-HERO

By the time the first edition of *The Black Jacobins* appeared in print in September 1938, James's anticolonial politics were well established. Christian Høgsbjerg notes that even before Mussolini's 1935 invasion of Ethiopia, James had begun to move away from the faith in Britain's Labour Party and parliamentary solutions to colonial problems that had informed his 1932 *Case for West Indian Federation*; as early as 1933, for instance, he had voiced criticism of the European "civilizing mission" as justification for the colonial government's brutal displacement and economic exploitation of African natives in the settler colony of Kenya (57–58). During his 1934 trip to Paris, where he conducted much of the research for *The Black Jacobins* but also met prominent figures in the emergent francophone negritude movement and witnessed dramatic worker protests across the city, he was a committed black internationalist who had placed his faith in revolutionary action toward national liberation rather than reform within the colonial system. Preceding the publication of *The Black Jacobins* by four months, *A History of Negro Revolt* laid out James's vision for the African revolution yet to come—a vision that was also intrinsic to his political organizing throughout the mid- and late 1930s. Along with George Padmore, James galvanized and organized England's Pan-African movement around anticolonial goals at a time when, Høgsbjerg observes, "the notion of decolonization in Africa . . . was quite unthinkable" in British public discourse across the political spectrum (201).

And yet in many ways the Toussaint L'Ouverture that James depicts in *The Black Jacobins* seems out of step with these anticolonial commitments. Primarily interested in securing France's permanent abolition of slavery in Saint-Domingue, Toussaint never prioritized political independence for the colony; moreover, his plan for a post-revolutionary Saint-Domingue as outlined in his 1801 draft constitution would have kept the island's plantation economy, as well as much of the economic power and privilege of the white planter (*béké*) class, intact. As I discussed in my first chapter, the more ostensibly "anticolonial" phase of the Haitian Revolution began only after Toussaint's death, with Dessalines, Christophe, and Pétion's united offensive against Napoleon's troops and the ousting of the island's French population. Yet these final years of the Revolution are sidelined in *The Black Jacobins,* the bulk of which is devoted to chronicling Toussaint's career as a revolutionary leader in the last decade of the eighteenth century rather than the first years of the nineteenth.

In order to understand what was nonetheless anticolonial about Toussaint for James, we need to recognize that James's anticolonialism was never narrowly focused on the achievement of juridico-political independence; instead his project was always directed toward a much more fundamental shift in the black world's political consciousness, one for which the severing of political ties with Europe was only the beginning. For James, Toussaint's most profoundly anticolonial challenge to the French Empire in the late 1700s was first and foremost a discursive challenge. *The Black Jacobins* credits Toussaint as a military strategist and tracks his accomplishments as a leader of an army of ex-slaves in great detail. Yet the moments that establish the real source of James's esteem for this historical figure are those in which he quotes and explicates his writing. James reads Toussaint's most famous text, his 1791 letter to the French Directory in which he solicits France's aid in staving off the *békés*' renewed efforts to reimpose slavery on the island, as a stunning performance of political legibility, an anticolonial declaration that leaves no doubt as to the authority of Saint-Domingue's slaves to stake a claim to the rights of man so recently realized in textual form by the French Assembly. Evincing his own immersion in a Western rhetorical tradition and an especially strong affection for Edmund Burke's "world of breathtaking oratory" (Springfield 87), James quotes and praises Toussaint's appeal to French political and philosophical ideals in order to expose their perversion in the hands of the ruthless colonists:

> France will not revoke her principles, she will not withdraw from us the greatest of her benefits. She will protect us against all our enemies; she will not permit her sublime morality to be perverted, those principles which do her most honour to be destroyed, her most beautiful achievements to be degraded, and her Decree of 16 Pluviôse which so honours humanity to be revoked. *But if, to re-establish slavery in San Domingo, this was done, then I declare to you it would be to attempt the impossible: we have known how to face dangers to obtain our liberty, we shall know how to brave death to maintain it.* (*Black Jacobins* 196–97)

Toussaint's letter draws heavily on the rhetorical tools of late-eighteenth-century French declarative texts. The French imperial nation-state that he addresses is in danger of betraying its own revolutionary "principles" and "achievements," those enshrined not only in the 1796 abolition decree but also in the *Déclaration des droits de l'homme*. In fact, Toussaint alleges that should France's "sublime morality . . . be perverted," the legitimacy of her sovereignty in Saint-Domingue would fall apart. Here, then, is Toussaint's version of an anticolonial declaration, or in Laura Winkiel's assessment, a manifesto that "announces the birth and transformation of a new society by imagining the present as *already* moving, working, and fighting to realize a radically novel future" (27). Echoing not only France's own rhetoric of Enlightenment-era humanism but also the U.S. Declaration of Independence, Toussaint's letter identifies war as the necessary, though tragic, outcome of the metropole's failure to live up to its own legal-moral principles.

What a contrast between this letter and Dessalines's 1804 Declaration of Independence, which eschews all professions of affection for France and French ideals, calling instead for Haitians to jettison that affection from their hearts and minds in order to cultivate a postcolonial national consciousness! James elucidates how Toussaint stages his challenge to France, in a language that France understands all too well—that of a Western Enlightenment tradition into which Toussaint inserts his own voice. He does not merely gain admission to a Western canon of revolutionary political discourse; he reinvents that canon.

> Pericles on Democracy, Paine on the Rights of Man, the Declaration of Independence, the Communist Manifesto, these are some of the political documents which, whatever the wisdom or weaknesses of their analysis, have moved men and will always move them, for the writers, some of them in spite of themselves, strike chords and awaken aspirations that sleep in the hearts of the majority in every age. But Pericles, Tom Paine, Jefferson, Marx and Engels, were men of a liberal education, formed in the traditions of ethics, philosophy and history. Toussaint was a slave, not six years out of slavery, bearing alone the unaccustomed burden of war and government, dictating his thoughts in the crude words of a broken dialect, written and rewritten by his secretaries until their devotion and his will had hammered them into adequate shape. Superficial people have read his career in terms of personal ambition. This letter is their answer. Personal ambition he had. But he accomplished what he did because, superbly gifted, he incarnated the determination of his people never, never to be slaves again. (*Black Jacobins* 198)

The distinguished roll call that opens James's analysis here is most extraordinary in its collapsing of dramatic opposites: ancients and moderns, to start, but then also Jefferson and Marx, on the basis not of the ideological traditions they helped to create, but of the common tradition in which they were trained, the "liberal education." Comparisons to these luminaries of Western political thought—and specifically to several declarative texts within that tradition—legitimize and canonize Toussaint's words, and in so doing, situate him as a world-historical revolutionary. The only basis for the Haitian General's absence from this list of political thinkers/declarers, James argues, is that he lacked a formal education; yet his letter, stylistically on par with texts such as the Declaration of Independence and the Communist Manifesto, compensates for that lack, and indeed only heightens the sense of Toussaint's exceptional intellectual and rhetorical abilities.

James insists on Toussaint's claim to membership in a community of world-historical men of letters, a heretofore all-white, all-European group within which Toussaint's affiliation is as disruptive as it is just. But in his reading of this letter—and in the rest of this text—James also has to cast Toussaint as an organic intellectual, someone whose words express a popular will in a way that this European roster did not and could not. Toussaint's encounter with North Atlantic revolutionary thought (and his anticipation of Marx and Engels' contributions thereto) is informed by his own very recent experience of slavery—an experience he shares with the people for whom he speaks. That experience grounds his authority, but it also renders his status as an author uncertain and in need of a certain amount of defense and justification.

> Soldier and administrator above all, yet his declaration is a masterpiece of prose excelled by no other writer of the revolution. Leader of a backward and ignorant mass, he was yet in the forefront of the great historical movement of his time. The blacks were taking their part in the destruction of European feudalism begun by the French Revolution, and liberty and equality, the slogans of the revolution meant far more to them than to any Frenchman. That was why in the hour of danger Toussaint, uninstructed as he was, could find the language and accent of Diderot, Rousseau, and Raynal, of Mirabeau, Robespierre, and Danton. And in one respect he excelled them all. For even these masters of the spoken and written word, owing to the class complications of their society, too often had to pause, to hesitate, to hesitate, to qualify. Toussaint could defend the freedom of the blacks without reservation, and this gave to his declaration a strength and a single-mindedness rare in the great documents of the time. The French bourgeoisie could not understand it. Rivers of blood were to flow before they understood that elevated as was his tone Toussaint had written neither bombast nor rhetoric but the simple and sober truth. (198)

Even as he praises Toussaint's rhetorical skill, James attributes his exceptionality as a leader to natural ability and not, as is the case in earlier chapters of *The Black Jacobins,* to his privileged access to formal education as a former house slave.[4] Both Toussaint and the "backward and ignorant mass" for whom he speaks make more of French revolutionary rhetoric than do the French themselves; Toussaint's unique gift is his ability to turn that instinct for liberty and equality into textual form—to "find the language and accent" of these world-historical revolutionary ideals. Toussaint requires an entire team of secretaries to help him say what he has to say in this letter; the aesthetics of his declaration, the style and the word choice and the rhetorical flourishes, are not entirely his own.[5] But his reliance on editors does not weaken his claims to authorship; rather in James's reading this textual feature bolsters the sense of Toussaint as the conveyor of a collective consciousness. When his secretaries polish his French for export across the Atlantic, the text they translate is co-authored by the enslaved residents of Saint-Domingue, the people whose experience is just as closely connected to the world-historical ideals of the Enlightenment as is Toussaint's.

Toussaint's most important revolutionary gift, in James's analysis, is that of prodigal literacy. The 1794 letter is a text that moves men: it strikes chords, awakens aspirations, prompts readers to undertake radical acts. Toussaint's distinction in a (heretofore) Western and white canon of revolutionary political thought is his extra-institutional and relatively unconscious achievement of "a strength and single-mindedness rare in the great documents of the time" (198). That distinction is a direct consequence of the fact that Toussaint is not merely a faithful representative of the Saint-Dominguean masses, but rather an instrument through which the masses' consciousness itself gains a voice. Prodigal literacy emerges as a result of widespread denial of access to formal education, text-based literacy, and Western cultural privilege. It is *because* Toussaint and the slaves have been similarly silenced that he is able to speak for them in this letter. It is this intimate connection between them—what Paul Miller identifies as Toussaint's synthesis of leaders and masses in James's text (1078)—that forms the basis of Toussaint's authority and authorship.

Prodigal literacy is the definitive mark of genius of many of the revolutionary heroes James chronicles in *A History of Negro Revolt*, wherein a more diverse and dispersed group of black revolutionaries seize and redefine political legibility and belonging for the Atlantic world's victims of racial exploitation. The leaders James treats in this text are described as great orators, capable of rousing their audiences to momentous revolutionary action. But *Negro Revolt* takes things one step further, because in this study the audiences these rhetorical heroes address are not colonial officials, as was the case with Toussaint's letter, but rather slaves and workers. These prodigals are the erstwhile lumpenproletariat in the process of discovering their own collective identity and power. Clements Kadalie, founder of South Africa's Industrial and Commercial Workers' Union, is described by James as "an orator, tall, with a splendid voice," who "used to arouse the Bantu workers to great heights of enthusiasm" with his speeches (*History of Negro Revolt* 61). And whereas *The Black Jacobins* draws sharp distinctions between Toussaint's intellectual chops and the much more pragmatic (and brutal) actions of his successors, Dessalines and Christophe, in his very compressed account of the Haitian Revolution that appears in the first chapter of *Negro Revolt* he instead foregrounds what all three of these leaders have in common with the rest of Saint-Domingue's black population:

> These slaves, lacking education, half-savage, and degraded in their slavery as only centuries of slavery can degrade, achieved a liberality in social aspiration and an elevation of political thought equivalent to anything similar

that took place in France ... Christophe and Dessalines, who shared the leadership with Toussaint, were quite illiterate, slaves sprung from the ranks. But they and their fellow officers not only acted but spoke and dictated like highly-trained modern revolutionaries. (17–18)

The diminutive language in which James here describes the "half-savage" future citizenry of Haiti underscores the almost miraculous anomaly of the Revolution itself, as well as the rhetorical prowess of its leaders. Haiti's revolutionary actors, elite and non-elite, lay claim to (and thereby transform the meaning of) Enlightenment modernity by rendering themselves legible through speech as well as action. And conversely, modern revolution comes to structure the meaning of literacy: Toussaint, Christophe, and Dessalines all tap into the spirit of republicanism, which no longer belongs to France exclusively but rather floats freely around the Atlantic, making itself manifest in new and more radical ways as it travels south.

A History of Negro Revolt illustrates just how hard James was working, as early as the 1930s, to think past the top-down, elite model of revolutionary history upon which he was also heavily dependent. In this text James subordinates revolutionary heroism, and biographical narrative more generally, to the task of establishing *patterns* of revolt across the African and African diasporic world. There is a concerted effort to foreground the role of the exploited peoples of the black Atlantic in the making of history. It is by no means an entirely successful effort, as evidenced by the prominent role that revolutionary leadership continues to play in the narrative thread of the text as well as his diminutive depictions of the black masses as "half-savage," "backward," and "ignorant." My point here is not that James, in the late 1930s, was a brilliant theorist of mass participation in revolution—he was not—but rather that *Negro Revolt* and *The Black Jacobins* show evidence of his own dissatisfaction with himself as a historian in this respect. Even as early as 1938, James was aware of the limitations of a narrative of revolution that fetishized the words and actions of revolutionary leadership. He was, in other words, conflicted about the work that he himself was doing as a historical actor whose action was the (re)writing of history. In all of the passages from this text that I have discussed here, it is possible to read James attempting to legitimize the authority *he* has conferred upon revolutionary leadership by claiming that this legitimization was originally enacted by the people.

James's tacit antidote to his own tendency to narrate from above rather than below lies in his theorization of the mechanism through which heroes such as Toussaint have been authorized by "the people." This mechanism has to do with the temporal immediacy of the hero's rhetorical performance.

Recall that for James the difference between Toussaint and Enlightenment intellectuals such as Diderot and Robespierre is that "even these masters of the spoken and written word, owing to the class complications of their society, too often had to pause, to hesitate, to qualify. Toussaint could defend the freedom of the blacks without reservation, and this gave to his declaration a strength and a single-mindedness rare in the great documents of the time" (*Black Jacobins* 198). What is absent from Toussaint's writing—despite his host of editors, on hand to polish his imperfect French, and more importantly despite his distance from the majority of Saint-Domingue's ex-slaves—is any hesitancy, any *temporal* lag between himself and those whom he represents. In doing away with this lag, the plague of his European counterparts, Toussaint achieves, in James's view, the pinnacle of stylistic success: he writes "the simple and somber truth" and avoids the fallacious distraction of "bombast" and "rhetoric." James's concept of effective political language is romantic, but it is also Romantic, in the sense that, as Angela Esterhammer has demonstrated, the precarious performativity of the declarative speech-act was central to British and German Romantic philosophy in the late eighteenth and early nineteenth centuries. Toussaint, as cast by James, is fully part of that tradition.

James thus locates Toussaint within two distinct forms of intellectual and political solidarity. One is a solidarity with other world-revolutionary thinkers and actors, that quasi-universal circle of Western luminaries to whom James compares him. The other is a solidarity with the slave revolutionaries of Saint-Domingue. In a sense it is much easier for James to establish the first of these; his own affinity with Western intellectual traditions mirrors Toussaint's. But that tradition also threatens to alienate him, and Toussaint, from the people with whom he aspires to claim a common historical experience and set of revolutionary goals. James spends much of *The Black Jacobins* narrating Toussaint's exceptionality, and this exceptionality makes it hard to then claim that Toussaint is a legitimate *representative* as well as leader of his people. James's solution to this problem is to abandon the concept of representation with that of incarnation. Toussaint's authority depends on his ability to justly and genuinely speak on behalf of the subaltern population of Saint-Domingue. But the language in which James describes this representational capacity is important: Toussaint "*incarnated* the determination of his people never, never to be slaves again" (emphasis mine). Incarnation, the transformation of spirit into flesh, replaces rational or mathematical relationality with intuitive, imaginative affinity and miraculous, spontaneous connectivity. Incarnation as a mechanism through which Toussaint's representational authority gains legitimacy is on one hand closely in line with James's association of his protagonist with European Romanticism's theory of language and performance. On the other hand, it is also a way to establish Toussaint's legitimacy to speak on behalf of a population whose means of authorizing him as their representative was at best limited. Incarnation, I discuss below, also emerges as a key term in James's 1963 repositioning of *The Black Jacobins* in the wake of the decolonization of the anglophone Caribbean. The term comes to signify not only the miraculous mechanism of revolutionary repetition but also a principle of historical reappearance, the means by which the past asserts its own claims on the revolutionary struggles of the present. It is important, then, that James makes use of this word so early on in his writing—well before decolonization and its early disappointments could have begun to shape his thinking about the historical interconnectivity of black revolutionary rhetorical and political events.

NEGRITUDE AND REVOLUTIONARY REAPPEARANCE IN THE 1960S

The first edition of *The Black Jacobins* was written and published before World War II, the onset of the Cold War, and the acceleration of national liberation movements in Asia, Africa, and the Caribbean that would culminate in decolonization in the 1960s and 1970s. In the anglophone Caribbean, decolonization quickly resulted in a failed attempt at a West Indian Federation, a body meant to secure a modicum of collective political and economic power on the world stage for the region's former British colonies; James, like many other Caribbean intellectuals, was feeling the sting of the Federation's defeat in the early 1960s. Between 1938 and 1963, James would also experience a number of major changes in his personal professional life: in 1938 he would leave England for the United States, where he would first work closely with American Trotskyist organizations before branching off to form his own political program, the Johnson-Forest Tendency, an anti-statist, anti-bureaucratic socialist vision centered around the practices of everyday life and the transformation of human consciousness (Bogues, *Caliban's Freedom* 100); arrested by the McCarthy-era FBI, detained on Ellis Island, and deported for subversive activities, he would return to London and then finally to Trinidad; and by the early 1960s he had parted ways with two anticolonial leaders turned postcolonial statesmen, fellow Trinidadian Eric Williams and Ghana's Kwame Nkrumah. The second edition of *The Black Jacobins* registers both James's own intellectual growth and the historical transformations that prompted that growth during the twenty-five years since the publication of the original text.

The most dramatic change James made to the 1963 text was his inclusion of a new afterword. As David Scott has argued, the second edition's appendix invites

James's readers to think comparatively not only between 1963 and 1791 but also between 1963 and 1938. If Africa served as the most urgent political context for the 1938 version of this text, then in the appendix James reframes the story of Haiti's revolutionary past in relation to the Caribbean's not-quite-revolutionary present. This reframing is enacted first and most explicitly in the essay's title—"From Toussaint L'Ouverture to Fidel Castro"—which sutures together two revolutionary Caribbean figures from different historical moments and, importantly, from different imperial lineages and linguistic traditions. In the wake of the collapse of the West Indian Federation, this comparative gesture intimates the author's persistent faith in the possibilities for political solidarity across the fragmented region. At the outset of the essay, James is incredibly precise in his delineation of the particular *kind* of interconnectivity he envisions between Toussaint and Fidel, as well as within the more expansive Caribbean revolutionary genealogy that these two leaders metonymically bracket:

> Toussaint L'Ouverture is not here linked to Fidel Castro because both led revolutions in the West Indies. Nor is the link a convenient or journalistic demarcation of historical time. What took place in French San Domingo in 1792–1804 reappeared in Cuba in 1958. (*Black Jacobins* 391)

James here rejects analogy as a tool of historical linkage, and replaces it with the more abstract and evocative concept of reappearance. Toussaint and Fidel, Haiti and Cuba, 1794 and 1959, are joined to one another not merely through a pattern that the historian can seek out and identify, but rather by the advent of an uncanny return that takes even the astute critical observer by surprise. Cuba does not simply serve as another example of "what took place" on another island on another historical occasion; rather, these two revolutionary moments are part of a continuous narrative whole that operates by a logic that remains somewhat opaque. Haiti and Cuba's revolutionary moments are linked not primarily through their content but through their ability to demand a certain kind of recognition when they appear. While the preceding 370 pages of *The Black Jacobins* aimed to demystify the events on Saint-Domingue in the 1790s and early 1800s with the hindsight of historical perspective and narrative representation, James's diction at the outset of this appendix reinstates a sense of the unknowable that is not specific to the 1790s but instead characteristic of a revolutionary impulse that crosses all kinds of spatial and temporal boundaries in West Indian history. Just as incarnation provided James with a somewhat mystical alternative to the rationality of representation in the original text of *The Black Jacobins*, reappearance serves in the appendix as a means of historical narration that foregrounds revolutionary patterns. Indebted to

Trotsky's concept of permanent revolution, the vision of historical movement that James's words point to here insists on continuity amid change, a romance of revolutionary recurrence across black modernity's long history.

James delineates the significance of the historical reappearance of *The Black Jacobins* by way of another black internationalist text that has also done its fair share of reappearing as of 1963: Aimé Césaire's *Cahier d'un retour au pays natal,* published in three separate editions in 1939, 1947, and 1956. James's reading of Césaire's poem serves as the centerpiece of the appendix, the focal point for this essay's theorization of black revolutionary history. With the hindsight of twenty-five years, James reflects on the unconscious intellectual and political affinity between himself and Césaire: "*Cahier* appeared in 1938 in Paris. A year before that *The Black Jacobins* had appeared in London" (*Black Jacobins* 402). The first edition of *The Black Jacobins* emerged as part of the "inherent movement" of an inevitable "Caribbean quest for national identity" (391), a quest in which Césaire's writing was also participating during the same time frame. James starts echoing the language of Césaire's poem in the appendix well before he explicitly introduces the text. His bold assertion about the origins of Caribbean national consciousness—"West Indians first became aware of themselves as a people in the Haitian Revolution" (391)—alludes to the *Cahier*'s description of "Haiti, where negritude rose for the first time," as does his later identification of negritude as a guiding historical concept for Haitian resistance to U.S. occupation in the earlier part of the century: "The Haitians did not know it as Negritude" (394). Similarly, and around the same time, Marcus Garvey "did not know the word Negritude" when he built up his transnational movement, "but he knew the thing" (397). Following Césaire, then, James differentiates between negritude as a historical phenomenon, the revolutionary undercurrent that pervades black Atlantic history in its entirety, and the moment in which Césaire intervened in that history by making negritude manifest in language in his poem. Citing T. S. Eliot's conceptualization of incarnation in *The Dry Salvages,* James glosses negritude as an "impossible union / Of spheres of existence" in which "the past and future / Are conquered, and reconciled" (402). James figures negritude as a dormant ghost that radical Caribbean thinkers and actors have been conjuring forth, often without knowing it, since the very beginning of colonial modernity. Negritude serves as the connective thread between Haiti's slaves and Garveyites—but also between James and Césaire, who, without any knowledge of one another, wrote the first versions of their masterpieces at the same time. The historical confluence of *The Black Jacobins* and the *Cahier,* each composed in the late 1930s and revisited amid the political turbulence of subsequent decades, epitomizes James's romance of revolutionary rhetorical performance.

But what are the stakes of insisting on the continued relevance of this romance for James in 1963, when the meanings associated with anticolonial revolution—and the negritude movement itself—are quite different from what they were in the 1930s? By 1963, after all, negritude had fallen out of fashion with many anti- and postcolonial intellectuals, its associations with surrealist aesthetics having given way—especially in African contexts—to not-so-strategic essentialism, and having been cynically co-opted by newly emergent African states as a conservative tool of social control. James's reading of a triumphant passage toward the end of Césaire's poem answers this question:

> for it is not true that the work of man
> is finished
> that man has nothing more to do in the
> world but be a parasite in the world
> that all we now need is to keep in step
> with the world
> but the work of man is only just beginning
> and it remains to man to conquer all
> the violence entrenched in the recesses
> of his passion
> and no race possesses the monopoly of beauty,
> of intelligence, of force, and there
> is a place for all at the rendezvous
> of victory . . .

Here is the centre of Césaire's poem. By neglecting it, Africans and the sympathetic of other races utter loud hurrahs that drown out common sense and reason. The work of man is not finished. Therefore the future of the African is not to continue not discovering anything. The monopoly of beauty, of intelligence, of force, is possessed by no race, certainly not by those who possess Negritude. Negritude is what one race brings to the common rendezvous where all will strive for the new world of the poet's vision. The vision of the poet is not economics or politics, it is poetic, *sui generis,* true unto itself and needing no other truth. But it would be the most vulgar racism not to see here a poetic incarnation of Marx's famous sentence, "The real history of humanity will begin." (401)

The first sentences of this explication indicate that something has recently gone wrong with the projects of Pan-Africanism and anticolonialism: "loud hurrahs," a cacophony of noise without speech, threaten to take the place of "common sense and reason" in the present of the essay. Whatever decolonization has achieved thus far, it has not brought about the beginning of the real history of humanity; the post-revolutionary future that negritude anticipated has not yet come to pass. Yet James ultimately reasserts a continuity between past and present through this reading; by reproducing this passage from the *Cahier* within his own text, by reading that poem for the present moment, he reasserts that the work of (Césairean) negritude is itself not yet finished—at the very moment in which other African and Caribbean writers were beginning to announce negritude's conceptual bankruptcy. The *Cahier* transcends its original historical moment of iteration because it is poetry, and it is as poetry that this text is connected to the broader ongoing historical process of black Atlantic revolution. *The Black Jacobins,* while written in prose, participates in that process on the same terms: it is a rhetorical intervention into revolutionary history. Césaire puts forth a powerful revolutionary voice capable of drowning out a hapless and hopeless post-decolonization cacophony. But importantly the poetry also insists that the revolution that gave this voice its power is not yet over: both the *Cahier* and *The Black Jacobins* make rhetorical interventions into history both in their original moment of appearance in the late 1930s *and* in the midst of decolonization in the 1960s—James through republication, Césaire through James's citation of him in this appendix. The *re*appearance of these two texts in the not-quite-postcolonial present does not constitute a ritualistic recitation of earlier speech-acts but rather a set of brand-new rhetorical performances, set to make manifest the revolutionary creativity of the black Atlantic world amid new historical contexts.

After 1963 James reflects on the historicity of his own histories of black revolt on several occasions, not least in a series of lectures on *The Black Jacobins* at the Institute of the Black World in 1971 (published in *Small Axe* in 2000). Here James identifies aspects of the original text that he would change were he to rewrite it in the present; notably, he anticipates one of the most prominent and trenchant critiques of the text from the late twentieth and early twenty-first centuries when he indicates that a (hypothetical) revised version would attend to, and where possible give voice to, the slaves themselves, the Revolution's non-elite actors whose experiences are overshadowed by Toussaint and other revolutionary leaders in the 1938 text. But for my purposes the most intriguing moment in these lectures is the one in which James reflects on the question of what it means for him (and his audience) to revisit his masterpiece—and to consider what it would mean to rewrite it—at a distance of thirty-three years from its original moment of publication, and at a markedly different moment in the history of twentieth-century black liberation movements.

I refer you ... to the introduction, the first introduction [to the 1938 edition], where I say: "This book is the history of a *revolution* and written under different circumstances it would have been a different but not necessarily a better book" [p. xi]. And I would write today a different book, and I wouldn't like to say it would be a better book (although I think it would be), but it would be a book more suited to 1971 and the particular period in which we live. ("Lectures" 100)

James here reminds his audience that even at the very beginning of his career, *The Black Jacobins* was not just a story *of* a revolution; it was also a story written *during* what James anticipated, in 1938, as the beginning of a revolutionary movement across the black Atlantic world. The banal claim that *The Black Jacobins* would look different, not necessarily better or worse, if crafted at another historical moment is far less interesting than the fact that James leads up to this observation by quoting himself from 1938. There is nothing new, he implies, about the question of how context informs the performance of historical narrative; he has been thinking historically about the act of historical writing for a long time. To (re)read *The Black Jacobins* in the 1970s is to occupy a very different problem-space from the one within which he wrote the book in the 1930s; but the 1938 James, newly immersed in Marxist theory and in Trotsky's and Michelet's histories of the Russian and French revolutions, had already grasped the implications of this difference for the kind of authority his historical account of the Haitian Revolution could claim. A new, rewritten *Black Jacobins* might, James parenthetically concedes, be "better," especially if it relied less heavily on colonial sources and more so on those that would focus instead on the words and thoughts of the masses. But rather than rethinking the content of his first and most famous revolutionary history of the black world, he draws attention to the distance that separates himself and his audience from the moment(s) of the text's appearance.

Thus while James's 1963 revisions to and reframing of *The Black Jacobins* certainly resituate the text within changed historical circumstances, there were also significant stakes attached to the mere act of republication—of making the original text reappear at a different moment in the black Atlantic's revolutionary history. Republication is, in and of itself, a form of historical intervention. The second edition circulated much more widely than the original, and this was the edition that gained particular traction as a key text of Pan-African thought; Stuart Hall recalls that "although of course I knew of its existence" beforehand, "I'm pretty certain I didn't read [*The Black Jacobins*] until the paperback publication of 1963, and so far as I remember it wasn't prominent in public discussion. So for me, and for many others, it was in fact a text of the sixties" (Hall and Schwarz 22). But if it was a text of the sixties, it was one that required its readers to engage with their own relationship not only to the past of the Haitian Revolution, but also to the prewar, black-internationalist past in which James wrote the first edition. The publication and *re*publication history of *The Black Jacobins* tells its own tale about how the anticolonial past reappears in the (equivocally) postcolonial present—and with what consequences.

This story proves even richer when we consider that James keeps writing, revising, and republishing his histories of black revolt well after 1963. Rather than reading the appendix as the swan song of James's engagement with the romance of anticolonial rhetorical performance, we can instead identify it as the first of several reiterations of that romance in the 1960s and 1970s. Others included *A History of Pan-African Revolt* (1969), the new edition of *A History of Negro Revolt* that included a new epilogue; *Nkrumah and the Ghana Revolution* (1977), containing James's collected writings on Ghanaian and African anticolonial movements from the 1950s onward; and *At the Rendezvous of Victory* (1984), the final collection of essays, articles, and speeches in which James's writings on black revolution feature prominently. James does indeed have a different kind of story to tell about black Atlantic revolution after 1960. But the reiteration, republication, and recirculation of his earlier work during this time suggests that there is also an important story here about his sense of continuity, both within his own intellectual life and in history. Closely interconnected not only thematically but also through citation—each post-1960 text reproduces language from one or more of its predecessors—these later versions of black revolutionary history attest to the persistence of James's engagement with a single, if not static, historical argument over the course of forty years. The "postcolonial present" with which James is confronted in the 1960s prompts him to adjust and renarrate rather than abandon his earlier historical and political vision.

This work of renarration has consequences for how we understand James's other form of writerly self-consciousness—his conception of the historian as historical actor, the doubling of his role with that of revolutionary heroes such as Toussaint. These texts' republication of these texts function as performative interventions into history, occasions on which James demands of his readers that they consider not only the historical distance that separates them from the moment of the texts' original publication, but also the demands that that earlier moment might exert on them in the present. Like communism for Marx and Engels, and like negritude for Césaire, Jamesian black revolution has a relentless historical durability. Republication is a kind of manifestation, a refusal to be confined to the past, even in the face of "the bleak ruins of our postcolonial present." As rhetorical performances James's post-1963 histories require James's readers to imagine postcoloniality through the critical lens of anticolonialism. This chapter concludes with a discussion of how such a performance takes place most sustainedly in James's final full-length study of revolution in the black Atlantic world, *Nkrumah and the Ghana Revolution*.

NKRUMAH, NYERERE, AND JAMES'S POSTCOLONIAL RELOCATION OF RHETORICAL ROMANCE

James's final full-length history of black revolt appeared in 1977—twenty years after Ghana gained political independence from Great Britain, fourteen years after Kwame Nkrumah had broken off contact with James, and eleven years after a coup had removed Nkrumah from power. *Nkrumah and the Ghana Revolution* was published in only one edition, and does not announce itself as preoccupied with the problems of revolutionary continuity that James dealt with quite explicitly in 1963. But in *Nkrumah* James's reader encounters a notably multilayered text, one in which the story of Ghana's liberation struggle gives way midway through to questions about what it means to write that story in the aftermath of decolonization. James wrote part 1 (which makes up approximately two-thirds of the final manuscript) in the late 1950s—that is, a few years before he wrote the revised sections for the second edition of *The Black Jacobins*. These years afforded James his first opportunity to narrate the event that in 1938 he could only imagine and anticipate: Africa's entrance onto the scene of world-historical revolution. Ghana was the first African nation to gain independence from Britain, and it did so in dramatic terms that would, James predicted shortly thereafter, set the pattern for the rest of the continent. *Nkrumah* is thus a "history of the present" in ways that James's other full-length histories of black revolution are not: it is a historical account that attends exclusively to events that took place during James's own lifetime, and whose immediate consequences were still unfolding while James wrote. Moreover, this history centers around a revolutionary hero with whom James was well acquainted; he met, and mentored, Nkrumah in New York in the 1940s, and kept in close contact with him until the early 1960s. *Nkrumah* is written with a unique energy and intimacy that reflects the author's personal and historical proximity to the story he tells.

Part 2 of *Nkrumah* replicates *The Black Jacobins*'s preoccupation with the figure of the lone revolutionary speaker-hero, one whose relationship to "the people" is constituted and legitimized through a series of rhetorical feats. The first of these was Nkrumah's 1943 proposal to create a new constitutional agenda for Ghana, one that would—in contrast to the wishes of the colonial government—seek input and participation from more than just the colony's elite native class of chiefs and merchants in drawing up a plan for the transition to self-government. In his narration of Nkrumah's actions James highlights the swiftness with which this leader spurred the nationalist party to action: "written if we want to press the matter on the very day he presented it," the resultant constitutional plan was "*the* document of revolution," a radical response to the failure of colonial legal architecture that owed its existence to Nkrumah's ability to rouse its authors into action on the spot (*Nkrumah* 47). This revolutionary moment is one of performance, not of composition—of live exchange, not the belabored and bureaucratic process of drafting, revision, and ratification that characterized colonial administrators' approach to authoring constitutional documents during these same years. Speed and immediacy characterize Nkrumah's populist politics in the 1950s in James's account; this is how and why the circulation of nationalist periodicals, to which Nkrumah was a regular contributor, took effect.

> Copies passed from hand to hand at increasing prices. They spread all over the country, one African reading aloud to a circle of those who could not read ... The style was an immense, uninhibited vigour, and reminds one of nothing so much as the Leveller pamphleteers, with the same rapidity, the same singlemindedness which saw in the cause the truth, the whole truth and nothing but the truth; the same mercilessness in denunciation, both general and particular, especially particular. On the one side was the scrupulous calculation of illiteracy percentages; on the other the creation of organizations and instruments for the national dissemination of information and ideas among all sections of the population. (89)

England's seventeenth-century Levellers, Janet Lyon notes, radically transformed "legalistic, vatic, analytical, and imperative" forms of writing (16–17), replacing the humility embedded in the genre of the petition with "the confident 'we' of a new civic voice making demands," "a new kind of political subject—'a citizen'—through declarative performance" (21). Such performativity is clearly central to the kind of work James sees Nkrumah's pamphlets undertaking in the early 1950s. Nkrumah's words, in James's account, claim authority on two levels, both content—the "truth"—and form—the fluidity with which the revolutionary message circulates among a population long presumed to lack a unified political voice. As with Toussaint's letter to France, Nkrumah's pamphlets expose the falseness of colonial definitions of literacy. "To an intellectual in a highly developed country," James asserts, "an article in a newspaper is just another article ... working people do not read that way unless they are, as a few of them undoubtedly are, highly politicised. With the ordinary working man a good article in the paper, a pamphlet, is an event of some significance in his intellectual life. Workers think over it, pass it around, they remember it, they check events by it and it by events" (*Nkrumah* 122). Pamphlets, circulating freely and intensely among the general population, transform Nkrumah into a revolutionary leader through the creation of a newly politicized reading public—a political community formed, as theorized by Benedict Anderson, through the shared experience of reading. Literacy here is reimagined not as the exclusive province of those who know how to read print, but more broadly as a literacy of the revolution—a literacy tied to rhetorical acts that educate and foster unity as they are performed.

The Nkrumah James describes in these early chapters is a Nkrumah whose political genius, and claims to anticolonial heroism, are tied to his ability to create a new citizenry through a transformation of public consciousness that takes place through various kinds of rhetorical action. For James, the most notable occasion of Nkrumah's legitimization as revolutionary leader occurred not on the battlefield—nor even through direct engagement with colonial authorities of any sort—but rather during a famous public speech he gave in 1947, by the end of which his political destiny was sealed.

> During the speech which launched the Convention People's Party, before sixty thousand people in the Arena, he asked them if he should break away from any faltering leadership and throw in his lot with the chiefs and the people for full self-government now. The question was not in the least rhetorical. The issue was whether the party should go ahead in defiance of the leaders of the United Gold Coast Convention and so take the serious step of splitting the national front. Nkrumah notes: "The unanimous shout of approval from that packed Arena was all that I needed to give me my final spur. I was at that moment confident that whatever happened, I had the full support of the people." It is rare to find anywhere in the history of revolutions, particularly after the event, this meticulous registration of the distinct stages by which the people mould the perspectives and will of the leader. Although he is writing many years after, he seems here as elsewhere, to remember the emotional reactions of his audiences as if they were outstanding historical events. Perhaps they were something like that to him. (102)

Nowhere in this volume are James's romantic inclinations clearer than in this description of the legitimization of this anticolonial leader by "the people" as a result of that leader's rhetorical prowess. The ultimate creativity and unpredictability of the Ghana Revolution derives, in this account, from Nkrumah's ability to create a new political community out of the heretofore disenfranchised masses, who are called to consciousness through this singular public oratorical performance. As in *The Black Jacobins*, the dramatization of this moment of miraculous synthesis requires certain narrative erasures: the masses themselves—whom James insists are the true protagonists of this story—remain voiceless. In *Nkrumah* James does offer some reflection on the difficulty he faces in narrating what he claims was a people's revolution from above: "at moments like these what the crowd is really thinking and the motives of its actions are profoundly difficult to recapture after the actions have taken place" (44). As a Marxist historian, however, James sees himself as in a position to make a good faith effort at addressing this dilemma. Revolutionary theory both explains why it is so difficult to access history from below, and helps the historian identify and interpret mass consciousness from an outside perspective:

> The fundamental difficulty is that only after a revolution or at a certain definite stage in it, as for example in the 1951 elections on the Gold Coast, is one able to estimate what the people were like before the revolution began. The people themselves do not know. The process of the revolution is essentially the process of the people finding themselves. (50)

The event of Nkrumah's 1947 speech is extraordinary not just because of the way in which it transforms its speaker into a legitimate leader, but also because of the unlikelihood of this moment's appearance in the historical record. The problem, of course, is that James's source material is Nkrumah's own recollection of the speech in his autobiography. James provides an earnest justification for this; the anticolonialist's "unselfconscious" narrative powerfully refutes colonial accounts of the Ghana revolution as a "striking episode in the history of backward Africa upon which we must look with, at most, benevolence" (106). In the absence of other sources, he suggests, Nkrumah's words are the closest the historian can come to accessing the true story of revolution on the Gold Coast. James's ruminations on the speechlessness of Ghana's subalterns signal at least some awareness of his own historiographical limitations in the late 1960s, but do little to temper the romantic tendencies of his portrayal of early-career Nkrumah.

However, when we read these passages in the context of their final published form, the meaning if not the substance of those romantic tendencies changes significantly. In 1977, twenty years after Ghanaian independence, *Nkrumah* demands that its readers recognize and critically consider their own historical distance from not only the historical moment being narrated—in the earlier chapters, the 1940s—but also the historical moment in which those events were narrated—that is, the late 1950s and on into the 1960s. Packaged and published in the late 1970s, the romance of Nkrumah's speaker-heroism must be read through a new lens. A collection of short writings from the 1960s, part 2 brings James's historical narrative of the events leading up to Ghana's 1957 independence to an abrupt close. The (relatively) triumphant story of the anticolonial struggle gives way to a much more troubled, and much less coherently presented, portrait of the first decade of Ghanaian independence—and the swift and disappointing deterioration of James's relationship with its president. *Nkrumah* begins with a passionate account of the acts of rhetorical heroism through which Ghana staged its revolutionary struggle; it ends with a fragmented story about the aftermath of that struggle, and more specifically a set of reflections on the role of the intellectual under these new historical circumstances.

Part 2 also marks the first and only occasion in his book-length accounts of revolution in the black Atlantic world on which James inserts himself into the story he tells; the letters, speeches, and essays that appear in the final chapters of *Nkrumah* depict James himself attempting, unsuccessfully, to counsel the Ghanaian president, and coming to terms with his disappointment in the way in which the early years of the nation's long-awaited postcolonial future were unfolding. The text's introduction—the only part James actually wrote as late as the 1970s—historicizes the contents of the volume, and foregrounds James's role in the story. On the very first page he identifies the origins of the text as the result of his "long conversations with Nkrumah" in 1957 (7), and again upon his second trip to Ghana in 1960. *Nkrumah* is not James's first published work that contains an important autobiographical component; his 1963 *Beyond a Boundary*, for instance, is what Grant Farred calls a "reconfigured autobiography" (138), one in which James situates himself as a marginal participant in, and commentator on, a political history of cricket, Trinidad's radical vernacular colonial battleground. But *Nkrumah* is the first revolutionary history in which he self-identifies as a participant, and in the introduction to the text he takes the opportunity to justify the autobiographical component of this narrative by pointing to its ambitious generic affiliations:

> Beginning with Kierkegaard and Nietzsche and reaching a completion in Sartre, modern philosophy expresses its modernity by assuming the form of a personal response to extreme situations, and is no less philosophical for that. I record here a sequence of political responses to an extreme political situation, the African situation, as it has developed during the last thirty years. (23)

Neither autobiography nor history, but rather political philosophy, *Nkrumah* derives its authority as a "response" to a world-historical revolutionary drama whose unfolding felicitously coincided with the author's own intellectual maturity in the 1950s and '60s. James is implicated in this story in a way that he never was with that of Haiti and Toussaint, or with any of the other revolutionary movements, save perhaps Trinidadian independence, that he has chronicled in his other histories.[6] While always sympathetic to Toussaint, James narrated that figure's virtues and flaws with an analytic omniscience afforded by historical distance. In *Nkrumah*, the author and his readers are quite differently implicated in the story of twentieth-century Ghana. Part 2 lays bare the challenges of telling a revolutionary history of the present *in* the present. Here, and with no additional commentary or framing, James tells the story of his own involvement with Ghana and his relationship with its president. The tonal shift that takes place across a series of letters James wrote to Nkrumah in 1962 and 1963 registers Nkrumah's transformation in James's eyes from the heroic figure of revolution to a postcolonial leader whose moral authority is far more compromised. In the second letter in this series, James expresses dismay at the president's autocratic and baldly self-serving dismissal of Ghana's Chief Justice after an unfavorable ruling; when Nkrumah did not write him back, he published the letter in the *Trinidad Evening News*. Reappearing in print in *Nkrumah* fourteen years later, these letters become source materials from which readers can discern the dissolution of Ghana's stable, revolutionary narrative in the post-independence period. They also signal Nkrumah's dramatic and disgraced exit from the narrative whose title bears his name. Part 1 is densely populated by Nkrumah's own words; James quotes him regularly and at length. In part 2, James instead quotes himself; his letters to Nkrumah stand in place of the president's own voice.

Nkrumah is a palimpsestic text, an extreme example of James's tendency, in all of his later histories of black revolution, to repeat and reproduce parts of his earlier accounts. Part 1 of *Nkrumah* is somewhat exceptional since the bulk of it was written but never published several years prior to 1977; but the text announces the gap between the composition and the publication of the narrative of Ghana's anticolonial period. Part of the process of reading through the volume is registering the eclecticism of its components—including the appearance of some recycled writings alongside newer material. Portions of James's reading of Césaire's *Cahier* from the 1963 appendix to *The Black Jacobins* appear in the introduction, for example. But perhaps the most revealing textual reappearance in this volume is that its final pages overlap with the final pages of the epilogue of James's 1969 *A History of Pan-African Revolt*— an epilogue that provided a condensed "update" to the original 1938 *History of*

Negro Revolt, surveying the three decades of black revolutionary history that had transpired in the interim, and closing with an account of Julius Nyerere's early tenure as president of Tanzania. In reproducing the story of Nyerere in the final pages of *Nkrumah,* James replicates the optimism of the conclusion of *Pan-African Revolt.* Both texts close with an acknowledgment of the rapid devolution of the black world's populist anticolonial struggles into neocolonial dictatorships and disastrous economic and social realities in the 1960s. Yet despite these catastrophic aftereffects of colonialism and decolonization, both texts also resist a pessimistic assessment of Africa's anticolonial past and postcolonial future. Nyerere's Tanzania gives James cause for celebration and hope in 1969. And appearing at the end of *Nkrumah,* this case study provides a redemptive antidote to the disappointing demise of the leadership abilities of Ghana's own first president.

James locates postcolonial optimism in Tanzania's recent history by finally turning away from individual biography as a primary mode of narrating radical political innovation. The true protagonist of the last chapter of *Pan-African Revolt* is not Nyerere himself but rather the texts that he authors—the most important of which is the 1967 Arusha Declaration, Tanzania's famed statement of an egalitarian, socialist program committed to democratic principles of civil and political rights. James was certainly not alone in identifying the Arusha Declaration as the textual instantiation of the most promising radical experiment in postcolonial African socialism at the time, but the kind of authority he assigns to this text at the end of *Nkrumah* is striking: the Declaration serves as proof of Tanzania's role as "one of the foremost political phenomena of the twentieth century," the harbinger of a "new stage of political thought" which is uniquely (pan-)African (*Pan-African Revolt* 117). Quoting the text at great length, James praises its equation of true political leadership with democratic power-sharing, its mandate that the government itself be composed of workers and peasants (132). In providing a roadmap for economic restructuring, the Arusha Declaration reconfigures political authority for postcolonial Tanzania—which is to say that the authors of the postcolonial community yet to come will be the Tanzanian people, not Nyerere.

Nyerere is the first and only truly *post*colonial leader/intellectual that James examines in all of his histories of black revolution. And in in his treatment of this figure he finally altogether abandons his long-standing proclivity to biography and the individual revolutionary hero in favor of drawing out the heroism that is intrinsic to the revolutionary *text.* Nyerere is James's model postcolonial intellectual—to borrow Grant Farred's term, a vernacular intellectual—whose ability to develop novel political categories for postcolonial Africa is both a natural consequence of his connection to the people of Tanzania and prodigal, a result of his personal gifts as a leader and speaker. But here, these gifts are deployed in the service of creating the legal basis for a radically postcolonial infrastructure for the country. James structures his praise for Nyerere around his iteration of a program of secondary education, and in his commentary evokes that same international literary genealogy of revolutionary thought that in earlier works made room for, and was redefined by, Haiti's ex-slaves:

> The simplicity with which Dr. Nyerere states what his government proposes to do disguises the fact that not in Plato or Aristotle, Rousseau or Karl Marx will you find such radical, such revolutionary departures from the established educational order. (133)

Like Toussaint, Nyerere does European political philosophy one better by refusing any separation between revolutionary action and the revolution's philosophical underpinnings. Moreover, Nyerere's perspicacious recognition of the need for an organic connection between the state and the people is revolutionary both because of its Africanness and because of its clear connection to revolution as a world-historical phenomenon. "In a conversation with Dr. Nyerere," James recounts, "the present writer (having previously read his writings) drew his attention to [a] particular passage from Lenin" in which Lenin stresses the importance of revolution from below. "The African leader said that he did not know it—he had arrived at his conclusion by himself and with his people" (143). Nyerere is prodigally literate—an intuitor of the fundamentals of world revolution whose own thought and action offers proof of the truly global nature of that historical process. But his prodigal literacy is made manifest in his authoring of Tanzania's postcolonial legal instruments. Toussaint's corrective to revolutionary rhetoric was spontaneity; Nyerere's is simplicity, which we might interpret as an authorial self-effacement that redirects his audience's attention to the text on its own terms. Dismissive and disdainful of African states whose leaders claim allegiance to socialism but steer clear of articulating a specific program for ensuring social and economic equality, James identifies a truer, better version of African socialism in Nyerere's writing. Nyerere's is a stylistic achievement, but for James it is also an achievement of wedding language to action, meaning to purpose.

The account of Nyerere that concludes *Nkrumah* (and, before it, *Pan-African Revolt*) is compressed and brief; while Nyerere certainly joins the long list of heroic revolutionary figures that James has named and celebrated over time, this epilogue marks a shift away from James's traditional preoccupation with biographical narrative. He seems to have escaped or surpassed his need to focus so extensively on the lone individual hero of black Atlantic revolution. This change has much to do with his effort to come to terms with the post-decolonization landscape in which *Pan-African Revolt* and *Nkrumah* appear. Ousted from power over a decade before this volume was published, Nkrumah himself has no place in the conclusion of a narrative whose title bears his name. Neither, it seems, does Ghana; the chapters of part 2 of *Nkrumah* gradually shift in focus from Ghanaian politics and Ghanaian audiences to issues that pertain to Africa—and the postcolonial black world—more generally. "To overthrow a discredited régime is a great achievement," James writes in a brief prefatory paragraph to the final chapter. "However, what is now needed is the creation of a new régime" (*Nkrumah* 214), or in other words, Nyerere's Tanzania. If part 2 of *Nkrumah* began by confronting the fall of an anticolonial hero, then it ends with a revival of the anti-/postcolonial dream that that hero epitomized—but heroism now resides not in an individual leader's rhetorical talent so much as in the juridico-political texts that such a leader is able to bring into being. At the end of *Nkrumah,* the romance of anticolonial speaker-heroism has transformed into a romance of postcolonial law.

IN HIS 1984 *At the Rendezvous of Victory,* one of his final collections of essays, James would once again cite Aimé Césaire. In a post-Grenada moment, *Rendezvous* contains essays written from 1931 through 1976 and invites readers to think transhistorically across the anticolonial and postcolonial periods of the mid- and late twentieth century, which, of course, correspond to the time frame of James's own intellectual career. The epigraph for this collection, as well as the title, come from the section of the *Cahier* that James had cited thirty years earlier in his appendix to the second edition of *The Black Jacobins*:

> . . . For it is not true that the work of man is finished
> that we have nothing more to do
> but be parasites in the world
> that all we need do now is keep in step with the world.
> The work of man is only just beginning
> and it remains to conquer
> all the violence entrenched
> in the recesses of his passion.
> No race holds the monopoly of beauty, of intelligence, of strength
> and there is a place for all at the rendezvous of victory . . .
> (*Rendezvous* vi)

This portion of the *Cahier* provides James with a powerful articulation of a rejection of narrative finitude, a refusal to accept the terms under which the humanist project, as defined by Europe, has claimed a kind of completion in the late twentieth century. It evokes Fanon's assertion, in *The Wretched of the Earth*, that decolonization will bring about the creation of a brand-new man. Its appearance in this 1984 volume—after the era of decolonization, and after Grenada's unsuccessful revolution, often identified as the tragic capstone of the anticolonial era[7]—speaks to James's own intellectual optimism, as well as to his deep attachment to the black internationalism of an earlier historical moment. It also indicates that James saw his own life as a public intellectual as following the same pattern as the black radical history he had devoted so much of his career to studying and narrating. Finally, his inclusion of Césaire's poetry reinforces his argument that the negritudean undercurrent of revolt that connects Toussaint L'Ouverture to Julius Nyerere has proved resistant to narrative finitude over time. Despite all evidence to the contrary, the black internationalist liberation project and its redefinition of humanism are, in James's assessment, ongoing in the final decades of the twentieth century.

Despite James's deep devotion to his francophone contemporary, he and Césaire had very little contact with one another during their lifetimes. They are not the only pair of anticolonial writers I explore in this study whose politics and interests overlap in intriguing and important ways but who remained relatively isolated from one another, in no small part because of the way in which linguistic difference has continued to isolate anti- and postcolonial thinkers throughout the twentieth century. (Ngũgĩ wa Thiong'o and Édouard Glissant are another notable example, and in my final chapter I seek to remedy the dearth of comparative critical treatments of these two writers in postcolonial scholarship.) Like James, I am interested in the critical possibilities that emerge from bringing together disparate figures of black Atlantic anticolonialism whose projects map onto one another's in sometimes surprising ways. The bases on which I draw my connections are not identical to James's. But the reason I begin my exploration of twentieth-century black Atlantic anticolonialism with this writer's work is that the romance of rhetorical performance—as well as the paradoxes and problems with that romance—that are so integral to his political vision also appear in a broad range of Caribbean and African texts and contexts in the late twentieth century. The question facing all of the writers I examine in the remaining chapters of this book is how to declare political community into existence when the existing language and imaginative scope for political belonging, as laid out by First World texts and institutions, does not allow for the possibility of emancipatory postcoloniality at all.

CHAPTER 3

Declaring Negritude

*The Universal Declaration of Human Rights and
Aimé Césaire's* Cahier d'un retour au pays natal

IN 1947, a multinational group of lawyers, philosophers, and dignitaries was midway through its process of drafting the Universal Declaration of Human Rights, which was ratified by the General Assembly in the following year. Also in 1947, the Martinican writer Aimé Césaire published the second of what would be three editions of his epic-length poem, *Cahier d'un retour au pays natal* [*Notebook/Journal of a Return to My Native Land*]. These were the inaugural texts of two new internationalisms that came into existence contemporaneously, but also largely separately, in the 1940s: a universal human rights movement with close affiliations with international law, and the negritude movement, spearheaded by Césaire along with other francophone Caribbean and African writers that harnessed the power of avant-garde aesthetics to celebrate blackness in defiance of colonial racism. Both of these projects sought to speak truth to power—from a position of relative powerlessness—at the outset of the Cold War and the reconfiguration of global economic and political structures for the late twentieth century.

Despite their contemporaneity, the *Cahier* and the Universal Declaration were products of geographies, institutions, and discursive contexts that remained tellingly disconnected from one another in the mid-twentieth century. In fact, as Samuel Moyn has argued, it is important to recognize just how *little* contact there was between anticolonialism and human rights in the 1940s. In carefully excluding peoples' right to self-determination from its scope, the drafters of the Universal Declaration—none of whom were, or consulted, colonial subjects—steered clear of addressing the most obvious goal of anticolonial movements in the wake of World War II: national liberation. Thus Moyn explains that "human rights entered global rhetoric in a kind of hydraulic relationship with self-determination: to the extent the one appeared, and progressed, the other declined, or even disappeared" (88).[1] In the 1940s anticolonialism and human rights were internationalisms with missions that were not only entirely separate from each other but indeed working at cross-purposes.

And yet these two ideologically and strategically disparate midcentury movements—one literary and black Atlantic, one affiliated with the nascent institutions of First World law—inhabited what David Scott calls a common problem-space, "an ensemble of questions and answers around which a horizon of identifiable stakes (conceptual as well as ideological-political stakes) hangs" (*Conscripts* 4). Negritudean anticolonialism and universal human rights were the products of intensive formal experimentation, one whose parallels with the generic and philosophical innovations of the Age of Revolution are striking. The foundational texts of both movements sought out, and in fact sought to create, new declarative forms up to the challenge of putting forth radically new visions of global justice for a new world order. Césaire's poem and the Universal Declaration pose and confront a common set of questions about new ways of imagining universal ethics and political community for the late twentieth century—and arrive at very different conclusions.

Midcentury anticolonial critique, I am suggesting, challenged not only the authority of colonial regimes but also a North Atlantic internationalist and universalist imagination that manifested in the human rights project taking shape through the United Nations—an imagination that would play a vital role in the translation of nineteenth- and early-twentieth-century European imperial rule into the "imperial internationalism" of the late-twentieth-century new world order.[2] Saturated by a series of real and imagined speech-acts of independence and personhood, the *Cahier* interrogates the fantasies of abstract representation, institutional authority, and universal applicability that underlie the Universal Declaration. Drawing on the conventions and the subversive possibilities of the modernist manifesto, Césaire conceives of the declaration as an inherently ethical act, a risky but vital performance of transnational and transhistorical solidarity meant ultimately to cede the speaker/author's authority to the new collectivity that it brought into being in the first place. Just as Haiti's founding texts stage a critical disruption to the nascent North Atlantic genres of modern political community, so Césaire's poem offers up a very different version of what a declarative assertion of transnational justice might look like—and whose interests it might serve. Césaire's poem functions as a radical supplement to the Universal Declaration, a necessary mode of imagining—and performatively iterating—global justice through an engaged internationalist politics at the moment of the birth of a universal human rights movement riddled with conservative and depoliticizing tendencies (often despite the desires and intentions of its proponents). Many critical studies of the *Cahier* have illuminated this poem's thematic and formal exploration of the radical potential of the speech act, of the possibilities for the reinvention of the colonized subject—and the colonized nation—through rhetorical performance.[3] I build on this scholarship to argue that this pivotal feature of the poem signals Césaire's engagement with other midcentury contexts in which the declaration came to serve as a potent mode of articulating new concepts of justice, law, and political belonging. At the same moment in which the First World was developing a renewed faith in the declaration as a means of putting forth universal prescriptions for human rights and global justice, the *Cahier* scrutinizes the declarative text's ability to claim universal authority.

This chapter shifts the book's focus for the first time to an author and a text that are readily identifiable as "literary." It is my contention that the literary comes to play a vital role in anticolonial thought in the mid-twentieth century, first as a mode of critiquing the colonial past and present, and second as a means of articulating visions of the postcolonial future on the horizon. Indeed, we might observe that there is an inverse relationship between anticolonial writers' embrace of what Raphael Dalleo calls the "ideology of the literary" (97) and the increasingly programmatic and instrumental goals of national liberation movements the closer they got to political independence. As decolonization (as well as post–World War II reconfigurations of colonial authority such as departmentalization) became a reality, literature increasingly became a means through which dissent, critique, and radical visions for the future could still be voiced even as postcolonial forms of governance restricted the scope and ambition of the anticolonial project as that project was enlisted in the service of official state nationalism. Yet as the cases of Haiti's founding texts and James's historical writings have shown, literary strategies are fundamental to anticolonialism's critical revaluation of First World juridico-political expression across a wide range of genres, and they are part and parcel of these texts' revolutionary identity. Revolution is the creation of a space and time outside the law in which law itself gets reimagined. The act of declaring a new political community into existence—of claiming the authority to do so while simultaneously enacting that authority in a textual performance—has an important aesthetic dimension. Literature is thus best understood not as a space of escape or retreat for anticolonial writers but rather as one of vital political engagement.

This is certainly true in the case of Aimé Césaire. I am unpersuaded by accounts of Aimé Césaire's literary career that see it as divorced from or at odds with his political thought and action. A poet and statesman throughout his adult life, Césaire was highly attuned to points of overlap and convergence between literary and legal approaches to the question of what it means to be human in a not-yet-postcolonial world. He shared with many of the drafters of the Universal Declaration a commitment to humanism and even some form of universalism, though he demanded that both of these philosophical principles be radically rethought outside the oppressively exclusionary parameters of Eurocentrism. While he rarely made explicit reference to human rights in his work, it is impossible for me to imagine that this Martinican poet-politician was unaware of or insensitive to the discourse of universal human rights that was emerging during the most prolific and innovative years of his writing career. I open my reading of the *Cahier* with a brief discussion of how we might understand Césaire's negotiation of his political and literary work—and of how the title of the poem evokes an important Enlightenment-era legal tradition, suggesting that the text does in fact invite readers to contemplate the relationship between literature and law in ways that critics have not previously addressed.[4]

More broadly, however, my reading of the *Cahier* aims to illuminate how the poem occupies the same problem-space as the Universal Declaration—how it raises questions about form, authority, and history that overlap with (or, in some important ways, starkly contrast with) the concerns of the UN-sponsored text. The *Cahier* is an anticolonial reappraisal of the internationalism of First World international law and its pretensions to global justice in the mid-twentieth century. But such a reading demands a recognition of the capaciousness of the imaginative ambition of midcentury anticolonialism. If we define anticolonialism narrowly, as a program designed solely to win political independence for the colonized world, then this project and that of human rights appear, indeed, to have no meaningful connection to one another. But such a definition does not do justice to Césaire, or to the other anticolonial figures I discuss in later chapters. The negritude movement was not primarily concerned with national self-determination; it was profoundly anticolonial, however, in its challenge to colonialism's discursive and psychic authority in the black Atlantic world. That challenge, I argue, took place by way of an interrogation of the notions of universality and authority that underlie First World juridico-political documents such as the Universal Declaration of Human Rights. The truly postcolonial world yet to come requires new declarative forms through which to be imagined and voiced. The *Cahier* is not a declaration of rights per se. But we might identify it as a manifesto of a postcoloniality yet to come, a new global order under which rights, political belonging, and community will have to be radically redefined by the wretched of the earth.

EXTRALEGALITY, GLOBAL AUTHORITY, AND THE UNIVERSAL DECLARATION OF HUMAN RIGHTS

The mid-twentieth century was a radically transformative period for international law, characterized by intense experimentation with new doctrines, institutional structures, and textual forms. In fact, as Nathaniel Berman argues, we might do well to describe midcentury international legal thought as modernist: both it and aesthetic high modernism, he contends, can be read as "an overlapping series of responses to a common cultural situation" (352), characterized by crises of representation, the question of how to give voice to "primitive" cultural or political energies, a high degree of technical innovation, and the juxtaposition of elements that were seen as incompatible under traditional aesthetic or legal systems (354, 362). Translating this claim using Scott's terminology, we might posit that international law and modernist art inhabited a common problem-space in the mid-twentieth century, one that sought new forms through which to accommodate the imaginative, aesthetic, and political demands of the present.

Berman's identification of parallels between midcentury law and aesthetics is a useful lens through which to investigate the experiments with form, language, and conceptions of authorship through which the Universal Declaration of Human Rights came into being in the 1940s. Key to the story of the text's origins—its drafting, revision, and ratification under the auspices of UN internationalism—is the development of a peculiar relationship between the Declaration's claims to *authority* and the way in which its drafters conceived of themselves as *authors*. As the UN Commission on Human Rights began to think of this text as having universal rather than international applicability and resonance, the committee members' sense of their role as authors changed as well. By 1948 universal human rights, enshrined in the Declaration and officially ratified by the UN, was a fantasy of collective, borderless authorial participation—of a kind of global authorship that sanctioned the text's claims to universal authority. This fantasy masked the far more specific and confined institutional and geopolitical that governed the text's creation. The genre of the declaration, with its liminal relationship to law—and, consequently, its claims to more than "just" legal authority—enabled this fantasy. Like the North Atlantic revolutionary genres that made their first appearance in the late 1700s, the Universal Declaration signaled a transformative moment in geopolitics that called for the creation of equally transformative genres. And like those earlier declarative texts, the Universal Declaration put forth its radical and utopian political vision while ignoring the complications of colonialism and racial exploitation that were constitutive of the authoring and authorization of this text.

"Human rights" gained discursive and institutional prominence for the first time in the 1940s; the term made a notable appearance in Franklin Delano Roosevelt's 1941 "Four Freedoms" speech and provided moral gravitas to the preamble of the UN Charter just a few years later. As a component of the UN's mission, however, human rights played a decidedly minor role. In fact, human rights was not only peripheral but arguably antithetical to the organization's goal of shoring up political and economic security among its founding member states. Many attendees at the inaugural San Francisco conference, Mark Mazower notes, "saw its universalizing rhetoric of freedom and rights as all too partial—a veil masking the consolidation of a great power directorate that was not as different from the Axis powers, in its imperious attitude to how the world's weak and poor should be governed, as it should have been" (7). Samuel Moyn observes that pressure to mention human rights in the Charter at all—even "as a negligible line buried in the proposal for an Economic and Social Council and without any serious meaning" (56)—had come not from the major postwar power but rather from smaller member states, newly formed NGOs, and individuals with no affiliation to the UN. During and after World War II, the adoption of human rights by international institutions "reflected a need for public acceptance and legitimacy, as part of the rhetorical drive to distinguish the organization from prior instances of great power balance. It was a narrow portal to offer morality to enter the world, and a far cry from a utopian multilateralism based on human rights" (59).

The United States in particular was anxious to contain and co-opt a newly emergent human rights agenda, working hard as early as 1945 to ensure that the UN Charter would not commit its member states to adopting specific human-rights-related measures (Normand and Zaidi 131). And yet these efforts indicate just how much radical potential such an agenda seemed to hold—and even threaten—at that time. Despite the fact that the Commission on Human Rights (CHR) could claim little power within the UN, its members took their task very seriously; and because of its relative powerlessness, the Commission was in fact aptly positioned to speak truth to power within the organization. The Commission saw itself as counterbalancing the goals of global security and the sanctity of national sovereignty which were at the heart of the UN's mission, and refuting early-twentieth-century legal positivism with a moral doctrine that had universal applicability (Glendon 176). Setting aside (at least initially) the limitations of what the UN's most powerful member states would ultimately agree to ratify, the CHR began by thinking broadly and idealistically about how to articulate the nature and scope of human rights in the space of an official text.

The UN Charter did not specifically call for a particular kind of document—or, indeed, for any document at all—that would define and delineate the "fundamental human rights" invoked in only vague terms in its preamble. It did, however, charge the Economic and Social Council with establishing the Commission, and in 1946 that Commission met for the first time in the form of an eight-member Nuclear Committee with Eleanor Roosevelt as its chair. The Nuclear Committee quickly expanded into a group of eighteen, all state delegates; John Humphrey, of the UN Secretariat, also participated in nearly every meeting. Over the course of a thirty-two-month drafting process, all fifty-eight UN member states—as well as a number of NGOs—had the opportunity to make recommendations to the Commission. The UN ratified the final version of the Universal Declaration on December 10, 1948, one day after it ratified the Convention for the Prevention and Punishment of the Crime of Genocide. The drafting process was characterized by personality-driven meetings and debates; an earnest effort at maintaining geographical and cultural diversity that was nonetheless frequently undercut by Cold War politics, and the predominance of Western and Western-educated delegates on the Commission; the United States' overarching control over the contents and capabilities of the document; and a central, ongoing tension over what kind of authority the completed text would be able to claim within and beyond the UN.

While much of the commentary and critical debate over the Universal Declaration of the past sixty-five years has revolved around the meaning of "human rights," those two words were the least controversial component of the document's title during the CHR's drafting process.[5] There was nothing inevitable about the Commission's choice to present the UN General Assembly with a text titled a Declaration; it was not until a year into the drafting process that Commission members stopped referring to the text they were creating as a Bill. And it was not until October 1948 that "Universal" replaced "International" as the first word of the working title of the document. Both of these changes were deliberate and controversial, and both had consequences for the kind of authority the document would be able to claim upon ratification.

One of the central tensions within the final text of the Universal Declaration—as well as of the drafting process—stems from the fact that it is meant to serve on one hand as a prominent instrument of international law, and on the other hand as an explicitly extralegal document, one whose function was finally put forth as eminently literary and pedagogical. The most contentious debate within the CHR centered around the question of whether the document it produced would be legally binding, or whether it would be an early instance of "soft law," a text with commonly agreed-upon moral principles intended to inform international and domestic law but without any mechanisms for compulsion or implementation. A legally binding document would have taken the form of a convention, a kind of text that, Johannes Morsink explains, is "far more difficult to write because it is far more detailed than a declaration of general principles. It needs to be done by experts in international law and takes a long time to write. Also, the states that sign a convention or covenant commit themselves to tell 'the authorities' how they have implemented the terms of the covenant in their own domestic legal systems." In contrast, a declaration is "a relatively simple matter. The parties need to agree on the principles to be proclaimed and then proclaim them . . . The truth is that nations can walk away from a declaration far more easily than from a signed covenant" (15). As of the mid-twentieth century, the declaration was among the weakest possible instruments of international law.[6]

Despite the strong desire of a majority of the Commission members to present the UN General Assembly with a legally binding covenant, this dream was more or less doomed from the start; the United States and the Soviet Union never had plans to sign such a document.[7] More than any other issue of contention among the drafters of the Universal Declaration, it was the debate over implementation that most baldly exposed the extent to which the interests of the world's emergent superpowers governed the shape and scope of the final text. Small nations, including the UK, vehemently dismissed the type of document endorsed by the United States and the Soviet Union as mere propaganda. The Commission's decision in June 1948 to work on two separate documents—a declaration and a covenant—simultaneously, and to temporarily table the question of implementation, "taken solely at the insistence of the CHR's two most powerful members against the wishes of nearly every other delegation, was highly unpopular among human rights advocates and the public at large" (Normand and Zaidi 171). The fact that the group did not actually give up hope of presenting the General Assembly with a covenant until quite close to the end of the process speaks to just how fraught the issue of legal authority was for the drafters—and just how ambitious many Commission members' dreams for this text were, in contrast to the realpolitik of the UN at large.

Relinquishing the goal of producing a text with legal authority, however, also made it possible for the drafters to claim other kinds of authority for the text. Charged with inspiring and educating the public rather than with binding states to uphold and enforce its contents, the Declaration was less obliged to tread softly around the sovereignty of UN member states; nor did it need to confine its scope to the peoples of those member states. The Commission's replacement of "international" with "universal" in the document's title signaled a shift in focus from the more contained and pragmatic contours of the international community involved in drafting the text to the world at large to whom the text was meant to apply. The title change was prompted by the removal, close to the end of the drafting process, of an article guaranteeing the cultural rights of minorities from the text of the Declaration; Émile Saint-Lot, the Haitian delegate, bargained for this change in order to stress the Declaration's applicability to *all* groups, even if unspecified as such. Morsink sums up the Commission's replacement of "international" with "universal" as "a shift of attention away from the authors of the Delegation . . . to the addressees of the document" (33). I would phrase the shift a bit differently, as a dissociation of the exclusivity of the individual writers of the text from the inclusivity of the people to whom the text would apply. In other words, in keeping with the drafters' belief that the rights they were including were inherent and universal, not positively acquired, one would have no need for direct experience with this text in order to be spoken *of, for,* and *to.* An international declaration would privilege the contained international community whose members had had some sort of direct say in the creation of this document; a universal declaration would, in contrast, stress the *global* community to (and for) which that declaration was meant to speak. In making this titular change, the CHR took on metonymic responsibilities, representing the interests of humanity as a whole.

The success of this transformation depended on the drafters adopting an audaciously ambitious conception of their role as authors. With the Universal Declaration, René Cassin proclaimed to the General Assembly in 1948, "something new ha[d] entered the world" because this was "the first document about moral value adopted by an assembly of the human community" (qtd. in Morsink 33). Cassin's romanticization, his implication that the CHR counts as an "assembly of the human community" rather than an assembly within a much more exclusively constructed international institution, is precisely the sleight of hand that the Universal Declaration itself aspires to pull off—an elision of the political constituency involved in authoring the Declaration and the unorganized, undifferentiated, global population that the text declares as its subject. This conception of collective authorship allowed the CHR to see itself as writing a universal declaration, one that manages at once to meet the needs and bear the stamp of an international bureaucracy and to convincingly proclaim a moral imperative with global applicability.

The Universal Declaration ultimately deflects attention away from its creators and on to the subjects of human rights. But it also grounds its authority in the fact that it puts forth few, if any, truly original ideas. When John Humphrey submitted his "draft outline" of an International Bill of Rights to the Commission in June 1947, it was accompanied by over four hundred pages of source material including a number of state constitutions as well as bills of rights by organizations such as the American Law Institute and the Inter-American Juridical Committee (Morsink 6). Members of the CHR did not necessarily think of themselves as original authors, and instead saw their task as one of researching, collecting, distilling, and canonizing a set of already-existent—if not yet declared—tenets on the meaning of human rights. In his 1986 autobiography, Humphrey reflects the importance of the collective accomplishments of the Commission rather than the contributions of its individual members:

> The Universal Declaration of Human Rights has no father in the sense that Jefferson was the father of the American Declaration of Independence. Very many people . . . contributed to the final result. It is indeed this very anonymity which gives the Declaration some of its great prestige and authority. (43)

Humphrey here takes issue specifically with a widespread perception that René Cassin was the architect in chief of the Declaration; in doing so, however, he equates anonymity with a lack of paternity in order to reframe the meaning of the document, at forty years' distance, according to what he identifies as its true original spirit. What paternal anonymity makes possible, in Humphrey's assessment, is the introduction of principles of compilation, editorial decision-making, and anthologizing that go hand in hand with the success of a text intended to establish juridical and moral norms on a global scale. Deflecting attention from himself and his colleagues as *authors* of the Declaration enables an expanded understanding of this text's *authority*. This is the Enlightenment-era dream of the encyclopedia reconfigured for a mid-twentieth-century knowledge project: universality finds its legitimation in global erudition.

Accordingly, once the draft text had been transformed from an International Bill to a Universal Declaration, the Commission began to root its authority in morality and pedagogy rather than in law. This shift had already begun in June 1947, with Cassin's drafting of a rhetorically powerful preamble that explicitly cited the horrors of the world wars and stressed the UN's role as a promoter (rather than enforcer) of human rights.[8] While the turn away from implementation disappointed many of the delegates, it also made it possible for the Commission to draft, submit, and ratify a document that conceived of human rights quite broadly—including economic and social rights as well as the more familiar set of civil and political rights for which eighteenth-century revolutionary declaration provided clear precursors (Normand and Zaidi 173). The General Assembly would not have voted in favor of the rights to social security, employment, leisure time, social welfare, and education proclaimed in Articles 22 through 26 had these articles bound member states to implementation measures, but as moral precepts and pedagogical tools they proved less objectionable.[9]

The Universal Declaration's pedagogical function is inextricably linked to its claims to universality. The text, as well as the broader universal human rights movement it helped inaugurate, were imagined to be profoundly populist in spirit, a "vision," to borrow Paul Gordon Lauren's term, shared by its proponents with evangelical energy. The text itself establishes human rights as an essential component of human development in Article 26:

> Education shall be directed to the full development of the human personality and to the strengthening of respect for human rights and fundamental freedoms. It shall promote understanding, tolerance and friendship among all nations, racial or religious groups, and shall further the activities of the United Nations for the maintenance of peace. (UN General Assembly Art. 26)

Perhaps the most explicit textual example of what Joseph Slaughter identifies as the tautological nature of contemporary human rights discourse, Article 26 asserts that everyone has the right to be educated . . . about human rights![10] To reach its full potential—to transform from a "discourse in waiting" (Slaughter 84) to an ideal finally and fully realized—the Universal Declaration must be disseminated, read, and taken to heart by *everyone*; the entire "human community" to whom the articles of the text apply must itself become universally human rights literate. In the months surrounding the General Assembly's ratification of the Declaration, Eleanor Roosevelt articulated the significance of the text in precisely these terms. The CHR, she wrote, had "been of outstanding value in setting before men's eyes the ideals which they must strive to reach" (558). But the work of reaching those ideals remained to be done: the Universal Declaration, she explains, must be made "a living document, something that is not just words on paper but something which we really strive to bring to the lives of all people, all people everywhere in the world" (559). Roosevelt imagines the spirit of human rights as transcending not only the letter of the (quasi-)law but all political and geographical strictures. Precisely because it has not yet been realized, human rights is a pedagogical project;

and precisely because it is pedagogical, human rights both exceeds and aims to obscure the (localizable, historicizable) internationalism out of which it was created in order to profess a truly universal ethics.

The Declaration's claim to universal authority—both through and despite its much more narrowly international conditions of author*ship*—was a powerful fiction, and has remained so in many subsequent narratives of the history of the text and its role in late-twentieth-century human rights movements.[11] But, of course, this fiction depended on certain elisions and silences on the part of the drafters—particularly when it came to how issues such as colonialism, imperialism, and long global histories of racial exploitation might trouble this claim. The CHR, Morsink notes, "had an unwritten rule that delegates were not supposed to refer to 'violations' in various countries. Such allegations would lead to all sorts of ad hominem arguments and block the goal of writing a declaration acceptable to all the delegations" (32). The UK participated entirely comfortably in the drafting process—and even came to be seen as a champion of the interests of smaller nations—because the UN Charter's creation of a Trusteeship Council effectively nullified any real objections to Britain's colonial holdings and practices (Normand and Zaidi 134). As Mark Mazower has pointed out, there was no perceived incompatibility—at least among Britons—between the existence of the British Empire and the dream of a more effective postwar version of the League of Nations designed as the bulwark of an "imperial internationalism" that would secure peace among Western nations precisely by keeping global imperial structures more or less intact. The fact that Jan Smuts, one of the architects of South Africa's apartheid regime, drafted the preamble to the UN Charter is a testament to the extent to which older strains of imperial thought played a crucial role in the organization's ideological origins (62). Nor did the new international order threaten to impose much scrutiny or pressure on the United States' own version of apartheid: even before the CHR had begun its work, the UN had stonewalled two 1946 petitions submitted on behalf of African Americans, one by the National Negro Congress, and one by W. E. B. Du Bois for the NAACP, which identified Jim Crow as a human rights violation.[12] Neither U.S. segregation nor European colonialism came up with frequency in the CHR's drafting meetings, and occasional accusations of Western powers' hypocrisy regarding their own records of human rights violations were interpreted as defensive attacks from countries with poor human rights records of their own (in particular, the Soviet Union, Saudi Arabia, and South Africa).[13] The CHR also failed to take advantage of one prime opportunity to incorporate a wider set of perspectives into the Declaration when it all but completely ignored the results of a 1947 UNESCO report, which had surveyed political, literary, and philosophical figureheads around the world in order to establish human rights as inherent in and indigenous to all of the world's cultures and nations. Irked by UNESCO's failure to communicate and coordinate with CHR in conducting the survey, CHR members "did their utmost to ignore and bury" its contents, voting against passing the report on to the General Assembly and making no reference to it as the drafting process progressed (Normand and Zaidi 183).

Most importantly, however, from the very beginning the CHR assiduously avoided dealing with the realities of colonialism that shaped the power dynamics of the drafting process. Or, more to the point, the Commission *did* deal with the problem of colonialism by successfully containing it and preventing it from raising thorny and contentious questions for the next two years. Britain and France drew clear lines between their championing of a new international human rights regime in the UN and their quashing of "civil disturbances" and "insurgencies" within their colonial territories (Klose 123). Within the eighteen-member Commission, India served as the only nonwhite country to have undertaken and triumphed in anticolonial struggle against a European imperial power.[14] Colonized peoples were represented only by proxy on the CHR. Moreover, while the preamble of the Declaration acknowledges that under extreme circumstances man can "be compelled to have recourse, as a last resort, to rebellion against tyranny and oppression," the text makes no mention of rebellion or self-determination as a right.[15]

The CHR's silence on the subject of colonialism, and the lack of direct representation of colonized subjects on the committee, indicates the issue's inflammatory potential, not its irrelevance. My claim here, moreover, is that this silence and the Universal Declaration's fantasy of universal authority is also a fantasy of universal authorship. In positing a universal and indeed global scope for the Declaration, the CHR figures colonized peoples, and more broadly the Global South, as the grammatical and political subjects of human rights. Costas Douzinas cites the consequences of this kind of figuration in late-twentieth and early-twenty-first-century discourses of human rights and humanitarianism: the present-day victims of human rights violations are very rarely "us." "The premise and appeal of humanitarianism is distance and alienation. We must participate in campaigns and fine-tune our morality because we, Western liberals, have *not* suffered in the past, because we cannot share the torments of those unfortunate and exotic parts of the world now. Because we have always been human, we must now extend our generosity to those less than human" (*Human Rights and Empire* 74–75). This, for Douzinas and others, is the story of human rights and postcolonialism in late modernity: human rights and humanitarianism serve primarily as vital mechanisms of empire. They are the next generation of the nineteenth-century civilizing mission, reconfigured for a new late-twentieth-century global order. The Universal Declaration initially became "universal" through the efforts of small nations, such as Haiti, to ensure that cultural minorities the world over would not be excluded from this document's scope. But global inclusion and applicability became the means of perpetuating the divide between the West and the Rest, the creators/authors of a global civil society and those who are governed/authored by that society.[16]

The other contemporary story about human rights and postcolonialism, however, is a story about the ways in which anti- and postcolonial movements have made use of human rights discourse toward emancipatory ends in the late twentieth century, when it came to serve as a powerful tool of (at least a certain kind of) resistance from below. Beginning as early as 1950, as Third World delegates developed more of a presence in the UN, human rights gradually became a Third World project, closely linked in its early years to arguments in favor of a UN-sanctioned right to self-determination.[17] Since the 1970s, activism from the Global South has forced the UN and other international institutions to address a wider range of issues under the rubric of human rights and development, two projects which have, during this same time period, become increasingly interconnected.[18]

Conceived and written in an altogether different context, by a poet who had nothing to do with the formation of the institutions of a postwar new world order, Césaire's *Cahier d'un retour au pays natal* registers both of these futures of human rights in the postcolonial world. The poem is trenchantly critical of universality and of grandiose, imperial assertions of representational authority. However, it also recognizes and embraces the liberatory potential contained in the act of declaring a new ethical vision for the future, one that—like the Universal Declaration of Human Rights—sees a need for much more than *just* the constitution of new political bodies in order to right the wrongs of the past. The *Cahier* anticipates the future of human rights both as a radical tool of Third World resistance and as a tool of empire, whose form as well as content must be approached critically.

AIMÉ CÉSAIRE'S LITERARY ANTICOLONIALISM

In a 1967 interview with René Depestre, Césaire recalls his earliest experiments with poetic form in the late 1930s—and provocatively relates that the first version of what would become his masterpiece, the *Cahier d'un retour au pays natal*, owed its origins to a moment of deep frustration with verse form:

> If *Return to My Native Land* took the form of a prose poem, it was truly by chance. Even though I wanted to break with French literary traditions, I did not actually free myself from them until the moment I decided to turn my back on poetry. In fact, you could say that I became a poet by renouncing poetry. Do you see what I mean? Poetry was for me the only way to break the stranglehold the accepted French form held on me. (*Discourse* 82)

The image that Césaire here constructs of himself in the late 1930s is that of a revolutionary in the most literal sense: turning away from poetry only to *re*turn to it as a tradition remade in his own text, the writer began his literary career by breaking the laws of genre and writing them anew from scratch. The poem that Césaire published in 1939—a poem which would be heavily revised for two subsequent editions in 1947 and 1956—was meant to disentangle poetry from its Frenchness, and from French poetry's tradition of exoticizing and romanticizing non-European landscapes. Even if Césaire did ultimately return to poetry—if we, along with the author, retrospectively accept "poem" as an appropriate generic descriptor of the text we now read—then what kind of poem is it? What form did Césaire turn *to* during his escape from poetic form in the 1930s?

This experience of generic flux that Césaire recalled for Depestre in 1967 speaks to a more general fluidity in this writer's work among disparate modes of thought and expression, and more specifically between the literary and political projects in which he was involved throughout his adult life. In his seven-decade literary career he would demonstrate extraordinary generic versatility, authoring plays, poems, histories, and hybrid works such as his *Discourse on Colonialism* which are difficult to classify under conventional generic categories; but Césaire was also professionally versatile, elected mayor of Fort-de-France and delegate to the French National Assembly in 1946, and holding political office nearly continuously for the next fifty-five years. When critics have attempted to parse the relationship between Césaire's political and literary work, many have done so by contrasting the pragmatism of his career as a statesman with the idealism that characterizes his poetry, drama, and literary essays.[19] Such accounts tend to interpret his (in)famous vote for the Lamine Guèye Act of 1946, the law that conferred departmental status on Martinique, Guadeloupe, and Réunion, as a sign of the dwindling of his anticolonial commitments as a legislator, a point past which those commitments would only survive in his art. In 1946 departmentalization offered the formerly colonial subjects of the French Antilles full incorporation into the French body politic, including economic equality with France's mainland departments. It quickly became clear that departmentalization would instead offer the former colonies a kind of "fake economic assimilation" coupled with a renewed (though hardly new) imperative toward *cultural* assimilation with the metropole—a new form of colonial domination under another name (Hale and Véron 55). Critics of departmentalization cast Césaire's support for it as evidence of his abandonment of the project of national liberation, and as an enabling of the cultural and economic alienation that would plague the French Antilles throughout the rest of the twentieth century and into the twenty-first.[20]

Such accounts tend to assume a fundamental disjuncture between Césaire's literary and political careers, and read his creative work—especially post-1960—as a response to the political disillusionments of decolonization, which left little room for the aspirational aspects of his earlier anticolonialism. The problem with such a critique is that it relies on a fairly narrow conception of anticolonialism as aimed exclusively at the successful attainment of national liberation. In doing so it does not acknowledge the extent to which Césaire's thinking about departmentalization was shaped by a much broader understanding of the world-system that was coming into existence in the 1940s. European imperialism may have been coming to an end in the wake of World War II, but empire, as Michael Hardt and Antonio Negri have argued, was alive and well—and visible in the Caribbean in the form of a number of occupations by the United States as well as the U.S.-led international political and financial institutions put in place during this time that would, in subsequent decades, exert tremendous control over the economies of nominally independent Third World nation-states.[21] "American domination," Césaire observed in the final pages of his 1950 *Discourse on Colonialism,* is "the only domination from which one never recovers" (77). Departmentalization offered a chance to shield Martinique from U.S. empire, and thus Césaire's support of the new law, Nick Nesbitt argues, might in fact be best understood as a form of dissidence rather than a turn toward a more conservative and resigned political agenda.[22] Césaire's vote was strategic and pragmatic, and it did not achieve what he had hoped for, as he would spend subsequent decades fighting hard against an increasingly conservative National Assembly intent on curtailing the overseas departments' social and economic self-sufficiency. But to interpret this vote as simply in conflict with Césaire's literary anticolonialism is to ignore the geopolitical contexts in which he cast it.

To better understand the continuity between Césaire's political and literary work, we need a more capacious definition of anticolonialism—one that does not hinge on the "success" or "failure" of the achievement of political independence but instead indicates a critical stance toward empire in all of its historical manifestations. Anticolonialism's end goal is what Raphael Dalleo describes as postcoloniality, "understood not as the end of foreign domination or even a partial freedom still haunted by the colonial past but as a new form of hegemony born of the decline of the modern colonial system in order to manage the successes of decolonization. There is no law of history that has predetermined how these shifts from one period to another would occur; the interaction of resistance movements with systems of control have dictated the forms of freedom and domination that have emerged" (13). This book similarly presses for an understanding of anticolonialism that recognizes political independence as just one component of a much larger project of reimagining the world in postcolonial terms. Both departmentalization in Martinique and decolonization elsewhere in the Atlantic world revealed the shortcomings of political independence *on its own* as the end goal of anticolonialism. As Gary Wilder has recently argued, Césaire's capacious thinking about the possibilities for a postcolonial new world order in the 1940s meant that he never felt trapped in a narrow understanding of national self-determination as the only desirable outcome of an anticolonial politics: "Rather than ask why this incendiary anticolonial poet 'failed' to demand independence, perhaps we should ask why he regarded departmentalization as a creative anticolonial act" (*Freedom Time* 21).

This broad conception of Césaire's anticolonial vision of postcoloniality is key to accounting for the declarative work of his *Cahier d'un retour au pays natal*, a creative anticolonial *literary* act that was staged during the same years as Martinique's transformation into a department of France. The poem was published in three separate editions, in 1939, 1947, and 1956; as A. James Arnold has shown, the final version is palimpsestic, containing but also obscuring a diverse range of aesthetic and political contexts with which Césaire engaged during the 1930s, 1940s, and 1950s.[23] In the seventeen-year period during which Césaire twice returned to and revised the *Cahier,* he met André Breton and engaged with European surrealism; traveled to Haiti and deepened his knowledge of African-influenced cultural practices in the Caribbean, such as vodou; joined and quit the French Communist Party; and saw anticolonial politics across Asia, Africa, and the Caribbean begin to transform into concrete plans for decolonization. Of course, the years between 1939 and 1956 were also marked by World War II, the creation of the Bretton Woods Institutions and the United Nations, the onset of the Cold War, and the ratification of the Universal Declaration of Human Rights. The new aesthetic influences as well as political contexts that Césaire encountered during this period constituted the raw materials of a utopian political vision, invested in national liberation but also in conceiving, in the broadest possible terms, of the global ethical conditions under which postcoloniality would one day be able to take root.

Here lies the common ground between Césairean negritude and universal human rights. Both are projects that insist on articulating the ethical dimensions of a new global order. Césaire's version of this articulation, however, refuses to erase the ongoing effects of the colonial past from its scope. Césairean negritude instead insists on a conception of global justice that accounts for that past and the ways in which its violence has been constitutive of Western modernity. In the *Cahier*, such a conception necessitates first a critical reappraisal of representation, including an interrogation of the relationship between political and aesthetic representation; an insistence on the situated solidarities enabled by internationalism rather than easy assertions of abstract universalism; and a reworking of the relationship between the spheres of literary and legal expression through an engagement with socialist and avant-garde traditions of the manifesto. Like the drafters of the UN text, Césaire was focused on the more fundamental questions of the stakes of what it meant to author and iterate a "declaration" with universal pretensions than he was on the question of what "human rights" meant. Put differently, he recognized that the meaning of "human rights" would depend on the declarative form in which that concept was expressed and the universal authority the declarative form helped to legitimize. Césaire's poem is at once a declaration and a meditation on what it means to declare—and more specifically, on the ethics of representation that accompany the act of declaring. In its experimentation with and intermixing of literary *and* political forms of expression, the *Cahier* seeks to forge a mode of articulating an alternative internationalism in which the most basic premises of aesthetic and legal representational authority must be completely rethought.

THE GENERIC AMBIGUITY that Césaire claims characterized his poem's origins is reflected in the first word of its title. What kind of text is a "cahier"? English translators' diverse approaches to this word give some indication of just how wide-ranging its significations are. The gloss for "Cahier" in the first English translation of the poem in 1947, by Émile Snyder, was "Memorandum"; subsequent English editions translated by John Berger and Anna Bostock in 1969 and 1970 left the first word of the title out entirely, presenting the text simply as *Return to My Native Land*; Clayton Eshleman and Annette Smith's 1983 version, which has become the standard English translation of the title, called the poem a "Notebook" for the first time.[24] "Notebook" accommodates the eclectic nature of the *Cahier*, its shifts from verse to prose, the fragmented, nonsequential character of its stanzas, and the cohabitation of a narrative centered around the spiritual journey of a first-person protagonist with myriad fantastical passages that reflect the poet's commitment to "the image, the revolutionary image, the distant image, the image that overthrows all the laws of thought" (*Lyric and Dramatic Poetry* li). This gloss also intimates that Césaire's speaker enjoys the kind of freedom that comes with writing for an audience of one, with no clear intent to circulate the contents more widely. It is in this spirit that the poem strays from formal strictures, weaves capriciously between prose and verse form, maintains an unfinished, fragmented quality, and, indeed, admits no necessary obligation to legibility or transparency, a point that the poet-narrator drives home with this defiant pronouncement: "Whoever would not understand me would not understand the roar of a tiger" (*Notebook* 12).

But "cahier" also has other, older significations which push in the opposite direction of the introspective and semiprivate connotations of "notebook." These significations open up very different possibilities for how we make sense of the revolutionary generic novelty of the poem, and also complicate our sense of the poem's speaker as a private, introspective individual by generically situating him as a potential political representative—a speaker who declares a collective self into existence over the course of 173 stanzas. Before the nineteenth century, "cahier" referred primarily not to the introspective and private spaces of writing that we might associate with a notebook but instead to a genre that was decidedly public and performative. France's *cahiers de doléances* were the documents in which delegates to the Estates General presented grievances of the people of France to the King. In 1789, when Louis XVI convened the Estates General for the first time in 175 years, the *cahiers* provided a comprehensive and detailed picture of the concerns of all three estates in the period directly preceding the outbreak of the Revolution. Local *baillages* met to draft the *cahiers* that would express regional concerns in a text that was explicitly intended to represent the voice of local constituents, most of whom could participate fairly directly in the drafting process. The role of the delegate who transported the *baillage*'s *cahier* to the Estates General was precisely *not* that of the writer; he did not bear the responsibility of representing his local constituency in his capacity as an individual but instead was responsible for transporting that constituency's own words and voice to the legislative assembly. Paul Friedland explains the distinctly nonrepresentative nature of the relationship between the text and its handlers: "In theory, at least, there was a perfect transparency between the deputies and those they represented, and between the *cahiers* and the grievances of the people, such that it could be said that through the body of the Estates General all the people of France met with their king" (35). The key to this transparency lay in the capacity of the text of the *cahier* to truthfully present the local voice: "Above all, it was the *quality* of the *cahier* and not the *quantity* of deputies that would speak on behalf of those in the region" (36). Referred to as "le testament de l'ancienne société française, l'expression suprême et ses désirs, la manifestation authentique de ses volontés" by Tocqueville (qtd. in Soboul et al. 175), the *cahiers* could lay claim to some measure of genuine collective authorship. Grounded in the idea of the tangible, local voice that could participate in a larger political collectivity on its own terms—that is, without giving way to abstraction, and the supposition of accurate representation by a delegate whose own voice would be meant to stand in for the local—the *cahiers de doléances* provide a notable contrast to the models of political representation that would emerge in texts such as the U.S. Declaration of Independence and the French *Déclaration des droits de l'homme et du citoyen* in the years to follow—texts which asserted "a moral right to represent the nontangible, abstract will of public opinion" (Friedland 57). To link Césaire's poem to this earlier form of "cahier" is thus to link it to a form of political writing that prefigures revolution and that speaks truth to power in a voice that claims a different mode of representational authority from that of the two most famous political declarations of the Enlightenment. Such a reading of the first word of Césaire's title situates the poem in a long tradition of (French) revolutionary protest—and as a type of document within that tradition that imagines representative authority differently from how it comes to be conceived in the texts of North Atlantic representative democracies.

If the poem's title tacitly suggests an affiliation with performative revolutionary political writing, the text of the poem does so much less subtly: the *Cahier* both reflects on what it means to declare a new self into existence (thereby foregrounding the ethical challenges of claiming representational authority), and performatively experiments with mergings of the individual and collective self, the "I" and the "We." Saturated with both actual and imagined speech-acts, the poem begins with a kind of declaration of independence: the poet-protagonist evicts his colonial interlocutor with a forceful "Va-t'en" (Irele 1) / "Beat it" (Césaire, *Notebook* 1). This speech act of anticolonial resistance seems to work; the colonizer, at least, is never again directly addressed in the poem. But the speaker then turns to face the landscape that the colonizer has fled—a diseased, impoverished, and "sinisterly stranded" Antilles in which other voices besides the speaker's own gradually emerge.

> And in this inert town, this squalling throng so astonishingly detoured from its cry as this town has been from its movement, from its meaning, not even worried, detoured from its true cry, the only cry you would have wanted to hear because you feel it alone belongs to this town; because you feel it lives in it in some deep refuge and pride in this inert town, this throng detoured

from [à côté de] its cry of hunger, of poverty, of revolt, of hatred, this throng so strangely chattering and mute. (2–3)

The poet-protagonist's singular, authoritative "Beat it" contrasts starkly with the "strangely chattering and mute" noise of the Martinican morne that he hears once he has redirected his focus. Through a detour—a concept that Césaire's one-time student, Édouard Glissant, would borrow decades later for an updated and more elaborate theorization of Martinique's political and cultural inertia—the town surveyed by the poet-protagonist has been reduced to a "throng," a babbling mass, estranged from its "true cry" of agony and anger. What has been lost to this town is not speech in particular, but simply a cry—the capacity to register, vocally, an injury, a use of voice that is entirely absorbed in responding to the violence to which it has been subjected.

The contrast between the simple, absolute command with which the poem began and the tortuous struggle of verbal/vocal expression in the morne means that when the poet-protagonist steps back onto the scene as a (potential) speaker, his own capabilities of expression have been altered: the problem with which he must contend is the problem of how to learn to begin to speak all over again, this time in some kind of relation to and with the "squalling throng" and its efforts to bring forth a "true cry." The opening speech-act turns out to be something of a false start, a red herring: saying "Beat it" to the figures of colonial authorities was easy; finding out what kind of speech is possible in the context of the Antillean morne on its own is not. The town that the protagonist encounters "crawls on its hands without the slightest desire to drill the sky with a stature of protest" (9).

In order to reactivate this desire and return the throng to its "movement" and "meaning," the protagonist of Césaire's poem must reassess his own relationship to language. His opening speech-act creates a newfound freedom: once he has kicked his interlocutor out of the Antillean landscape, Natalie Melas notes, the voice of the poem "can, in principle, say anything at all, let loose all its hope and all its recriminations, for there will be no consequences" (575). The speaker accordingly begins fantasizing about new forms of speech acts now available to him:

> I would rediscover the secret of great communications and great combustions. I would say storm. I would say river. I would say tornado. I would say leaf. I would say tree. I would be drenched by all rains, moistened by all dews. I would roll like frenetic blood on the slow current of the eye of words turned into mad horses into fresh children into clots into curfew into vestiges of temples into precious stones remote enough to discourage miners.

Whoever would not understand me would not understand any better the roaring of a tiger. (12)

The transformations imagined in this passage depend on the utterance of single words, all tied to natural forces and elements as well as movements, "great combustions," and the rolling of blood. The stakes of the power of *saying* that the speaker imagines for himself (a power which is tellingly tied to the power of rediscovery) become clear in the final sentence: he longs for an ultimate challenge to comprehension, the creation of a language that would eschew misinterpretation not because of its transparency but because of its power. Yet unlike the poem's opening "Beat it," these speech acts are only imagined, not executed. Further, these fantasies of speaking get extended, shortly thereafter, into fantasies of *speaking for*.

I would go to this land of mine and I would say to it: "Embrace me without fear . . . And if all I can do is speak, it is for you I shall speak."

And again I would say:
"My mouth shall be the mouth of those calamities that have no mouth, my voice the freedom of those who break down in the prison holes of despair."
And on the way I would say to myself:
"And above all, my body as well as my soul, beware of assuming the sterile attitude of the spectator, for life is not a spectacle, a sea of miseries is not a proscenium, a man screaming is not a dancing bear." (13–14)

The poet's ousting of the colonizer was a lone act of verbal resistance; it may have been effectual, but it left the speaker dependent on a dialogue with a now-absent interlocutor—and aware of but alienated from the anguished cry of the throng. After imagining a new kind of authority for himself—the power to name—he then attempts to combat his alienation from the throng by imagining himself in possession of representative authority. In relinquishing his speech and his mouth to the ailing homeland, the poet assigns himself a dual role as hero and lyricist; he presents the potential of his voice as a form of devotional heroism, a gift accorded the homeland that springs from a place of love. Speech is devalued in the poet's humble address—it is all the protagonist can do—but it is also the best he has to offer, a replacement for something else, for the "bloodthirsty burst" of protest and revolt that has been both repressed and forgotten. Embodiment underlies the speaker's concept of representation here: the mouth that substitutes for the silenced mouth recalls and seeks to remedy the corporeal violence of silencing depicted a few stanzas earlier. Like the *cahiers de doléances,* the speaker's (imagined) words resist representative abstraction, as well as "the sterile gaze of the spectator"; part of the process of envisioning himself as a representative entails being cognizant of the potential dangers of that role.

Critics have praised this cautionary turn at the end of this stanza, and more generally the poet-protagonist's progression over the course of the poem "beyond a desire to speak for others" (Rabbitt 43) toward "the violent demystification of his desired sense of heroism as a savior of his race who is somehow untainted by the ideology of white supremacy; that is, the one who would speak for, rather than with, the oppressed" (Garraway, "What Is Mine" 80). Césaire's healthy skepticism regarding his speaker's representative capacities showcases the subtlety and anti-essentialist thrust of his conception of negritude. But while the poem's fantasy of representative authority certainly needs to be—and is, in the text—complicated and questioned, I would also caution against losing sight of just how important the *presentation* of that declarative fantasy is at this point in the poem. Its productive value lies in its articulation of the poet's desire to collapse his own identity into a collective; it is a profession of love; of a willingness to let his own voice, and the body that houses that voice, serve as a prosthesis; of overcoming the colonized intellectual's class estrangement; of an openness to the possibility of letting the first-person singular become subsumed within the auspices of a collective "We."

And, indeed, the first occurrence of the first-person plural appears shortly after this dream of collective synthesis—and after the text's first iteration of the word "negritude." Césaire's collective subject follows the same aspirational pattern as did the lone protagonist, initially imagining but not actually performing a series of naming speech-acts: "We would tell. Would sing. Would howl / Full voice, ample voice, you would be our wealth, our spear pointed" (17). The colonial interlocutor reappears here, but this time gets *re*placed as well as *dis*placed: "Because we hate you and your reason, we claim kinship with dementia praecox with the flaming madness of persistent cannibalism" (17–18). The "we" forms an alliance with anti-reason, with a negritudean "madness that remembers" (18), in contrast to a rationality that has systematically forgotten the slave trade and the slave plantation. Yet these lines importantly do not mark a stable or definitive transition in the poem from the first-person singular to the plural; rather, Césaire will continue to shift back and forth between the two throughout. The poem's central rhetorical question—"Who and what are we?" is answered with a return to the singular voice:

> From staring too long at trees I have become a tree and my long tree feet
> have dug in the ground large venom sacs high cities of bone
> from brooding too long on the Congo
> I have become a Congo resounding with forests and rivers
> where the whip cracks like a great banner
> the banner of a prophet
> where the water goes
> likouala-likouala
> where the angerbolt hurls its greenish axe forcing the boars of putrefaction
> to the lovely wild edge of the nostrils.
> (18–19)

In the *Cahier*, Gregson Davis has shown, "négritude is not to be regarded as a state, but an activity—an activity of self-exploration, of 'delving' into the psychosocial unconscious. Négritude is nothing less than the ongoing process itself, the subterranean interior journey" (*Aimé Césaire* 50–51). Césaire's replacement of *being* with *doing*, and of "we" with "I," illuminate the text's resistance to temporal fixity, corruptively ubiquitous collective identities, and—at the level of poetic grammar—the tyranny of parallel structure. The "I" flows through a steady stream of identities in this stanza; even "Congo" signifies multiply, first as a geographically located river and then as a snake (or spiritual entity that encompasses both river and snake) that rejects spatial fixity. Fabulous metamorphosis disrupts the stability of "I" and "We" as categories of identity.

The last instance in which "We" appears as a grammatical subject occurs toward the end of the poem, and in some measure provides a more direct response to the question of who and what "we" are.

> And we are standing now, my country and I, hair in the wind, my hand puny in its enormous fist and now the strength is not in us but above us, in a voice that drills the night and the hearing like the penetrance of an apocalyptic wasp. And the voice complains that for centuries Europe has force-fed us with lies and bloated us with pestilence,
>> for it is not true that the work of man is done
>> that we have no business being on earth
>> that we parasite the world
>> that it is enough for us to heel to the world whereas the work of man has only begun
>> and man still must overcome all the interdictions wedged in the recesses of his fervor

and no race has a monopoly on beauty, on intelligence, on strength
and there is room for everyone at the convocation of conquest and we
know now that the sun turns around our earth lighting the parcel des-
ignated by our will alone and that every star falls from sky to earth at
our omnipotent command. (44)

This is perhaps the closest Césaire comes to articulating collectivity in positive, and relatively static, terms—the "we" is *standing* at the beginning of
this stanza. But the omnipotence and omnipresence of that speaking voice is
quickly undercut by the existence of another voice "above us," one that now
speaks on behalf of the "we," asserting its legitimacy in a deracialized cos-
mos. And just as the supremacy of the first-person plural is displaced by other
voices, so is the spatial and temporal firmness of its standing: "the work of
man has only begun." Identity can be proclaimed only provisionally, only for
a moment, before it dissolves back into the flow of humanity.

And yet that moment of proclamation is nonetheless crucial, unskippable;
it is an act of beginning, the importance of which the speaker reflects on much
earlier along in the poem. The question of what it means to begin emerges at
the tail end of an early confrontation between the plural and singular voice.

we sing of venomous flowers flaring in fury-filled prairies; the skies of love
cut with bloodclots; the epileptic mornings; the white blaze of abyssal sands,
the sinking of flotsam in nights electrified with feline smells.

What can I do? [*Qu'y puis-je?*]

One must begin somewhere. [*Il faut bien commencer.*]

Begin what? [*Commencer quoi?*]

The only thing in the world worth beginning [*La seule chose au monde qu'il
vaille la peine de commencer*]:

The End of the world of course [*La Fin du monde parbleu*]. (*Cahier* 12)

The first stanza once again features a bold "we," a powerful voice certain enough of its identity and purpose to enact, through communal song,
an apocalyptic natural disaster and its aftereffects, "the sinking of flotsam
in nights electrified with feline smells." After the break the poem's language
decompresses from a prose paragraph saturated with fantastic, ornate imagery

to a fragmentary, simple, monologic call-and-response sequence. If the song sung by the collective voice just above this question has unbridled power to create total destruction, "the End of the world," then the necessary work of beginning that the poet-narrator takes up is a solitary project, and in some sense an impossible one: to begin is to claim the authority that makes a beginning, but where does that authority come from, how does it get claimed, and, finally, how does this power to begin necessitate the ultimate ending? This conundrum is tied to another: what does it mean for Césaire to foreground this question of beginning at the narrative midpoint of a poem whose linear starting point is the end of daybreak? The problem never quite gets resolved, but only posed and then deferred in the text; "the End of the world of course" to which we return at the end of this stanza is still very much in process, and, moreover, in confusing and collapsing the distinction between beginning and ending, refuses to engage with the desire behind the original question.

Beginning is an act of magic, an audacious and aspirational leap of faith through which new authority takes effect in language. The *Cahier* marks a revolutionary beginning, an act of self-authorization that Césaire dramatizes midway through as parthogenesis.

> I am forcing the vitelline membrane that separates me from myself
>
> I am forcing the great waters which girdle me with blood
>
> I and I alone
> make contact with the latest anguish
> I and oh, only I
> secure through a straw
> the first drops of virginal milk!
> (24)

The poet-protagonist here brings himself into being, situating himself both inside and outside the creative act—imminent and external all at once, and suggesting that the present must understand its debt to the past in a new way. If birth can take place without the participation of a mother, if the self is accountable to nothing beyond itself for existence, then what Césaire cut loose is the role of inheritance and history in the self's constitution. Abiola Irele notes that the birthing imagery in these lines locates ancestry elsewhere, as the birthing fluid "recollect[s] . . . the forced voyage of the poet's ancestors across the ocean and their subsequent ordeal under slavery" (91). Even the boldest statements about self-creation in this poem contend with the indelible past in one way or another. But it is worth noting that the past appears in this passage as oceanic fluid, as the stream that ushers the poet into (re)birth, and *not* as the womb or the birth canal. In other words, while ancestry, heritage, and history accompany the poet in this self-birthing process, the poet is solely in control of the process itself; whatever obligation he has to this past, it is of a different nature than filial piety. The ocean, as other moments in the poem make clear, is also a grave, and its ghostly inhabitants are in a somewhat separate category from the ancestors who completed the journey across the Middle Passage: these are the ancestors who in fact did not survive to become biological ancestors. Lineage has an organic, ancestral component in the *Cahier,* but, freed from the figure of the parent, the poet-protagonist can consider new ways to think about how to hold himself accountable to the future.

Yet the imagery also alludes to a fantasy of parthogenesis that links the passage back to European island romance, and as such threatens to pull the consciousness of the poet-narrator back into the realm of spectacle. Prospero's wife, as Stephen Orgel's reading has shown, is perhaps never more of an absent presence in Shakespeare's *The Tempest* as when Prospero narrates his own arrival on the island as a form of self-birthing. Nearly three decades after beginning work on the *Cahier,* Césaire would make his own contribution to the rich legacy of Caribbean writers' adaptations of this early modern European drama; Césaire's *Une Tempête* features a recalcitrant Caliban resonant of Black Power, a Caliban who abandons a befuddled, impotent Prospero to languish in the decay of a former colonial regime at the end of the play. Yet in the *Cahier,* the first-person protagonist much more closely resembles Prospero, the ultimate symbol, in late-twentieth-century Caribbean literary contexts, of colonial authority. In Orgel's explication, Prospero's self-birth is a spectacular testament to the character's intellectual and creative sovereignty:

> Power, as Prospero presents it in the play, is not inherited but self-created: it is magic, or 'art,' an extension of mental power and self-knowledge, and the authority that legitimises it derives from heaven—*Fortune* and *Destiny* are the terms used in the play. It is Caliban who derives his claim to the island from inheritance, from his mother. (8)

Heaven, fortune, and destiny are not among the *Cahier*'s key terms, but there is perhaps no better word than magic to describe the poet-narrator's acquisition of self-knowledge—and with self-knowledge, authority—that begins to unfold about a third of the way through the poem. Verging into sardonic parody, Césaire's poet-narrator indulges in a fantasy of total power that may also be a fantasy of *too much* power, too much autonomy, the replication of a sovereign "I" that abandons the obligations and debts that accompany inheritance and suffocates the collective voice. Once again, fantasy, in the *Cahier*, is a crucial but risky activity. For all the declarative work this poem does, it also consistently and consciously raises questions about the ethical implications of that work—the possibilities but also the perils of claiming the authority to represent.

INTERNATIONALISM AND UNIVERSALISM

After his ejection of the colonizer in the poem's opening stanza, Césaire's protagonist turns to the unequivocally Martinican morne, a landscape with geographical and autobiographical specificity. It is through his engagement with that landscape that he begins to reflect on the problem of how (and whether) to speak on behalf of others. The *Cahier* cannot declare what it wants to declare without beginning locally, and reconfiguring a landscape long exoticized and romanticized in colonial prose. But the poem is also crucially a product of Césaire's internationalist vision for negritude, one that grew out of his encounters and collaborations with Senghor, Damas, and other African and Antillean immigrants in Paris in the 1930s. Moreover, Césaire purportedly began work on the *Cahier* while doubly "abroad" from his own native land: in 1936, on the invitation of his Yugoslavian friend, Petar Guberina, he left Paris and traveled to Martinska, an island in the Aegean Sea. The island reminded him of Martinique, and he wrote the first draft of the *Cahier* during that visit (xvii). The poem is thus a product of Césaire's own earliest experiences with international travel and transnational comparison.

The world described and imagined by the *Cahier* bears witness to Bruce Robbins's claim that "any given version of internationalism turns out to be local and conjectural"—that there are "many versions" of internationalism, "and they are all imperfect" (7). Césaire's is a world of multiple internationalisms, of a plurality of discursive solidarities that challenge the hegemonic and oppressive internationalism of First World legal, economic, and cultural systems. These are the basic building blocks of the poem's political vision, the collective identity and program of collective action that the poet-protagonist both envisions and seeks to instantiate through language. The pluralism of Césaire's conception of solidarity gets articulated most clearly and insistently in the first two-thirds of the poem; it is a conception that captures the liberatory desires that would, a year before the publication of the final version of the *Cahier*, be articulated on a grander scale at the Bandung Conference, and it is a conception that remains committed to protecting the particularity of negritude even as it also constellates negritude beyond that particularity. Diasporic scatteredness and hermetic circularity collide fabulously in the poem's celebration of "those whose survival travels in the germination of grass" alongside a more general cry: "Eia perfect circle of the world, enclosed concordance!" (36).

Black internationalisms such as negritude are different from other midcentury internationalisms in at least one important respect. Communism, surrealism, international human rights law, and other cosmopolitan projects originating in the Global North presuppose the existence of—and therefore aim to exceed or transcend—the nation-state. But the Atlantic slave trade, colonialism, and imperialism made such a presupposition nonsensical for Africa and its diaspora; these were the very conditions that had systematically deprived Africa and the Caribbean of nation-state-hood (Edwards 24). Black internationalism is therefore a kind of internationalism that never takes for granted the nation-state and its affordance of important forms of political legibility. Yet for the same reasons, black internationalism also holds up the *concept* of the nation-state, in its North Atlantic forms, to a high degree of scrutiny. Black Atlantic anticolonialism encompasses what Michelle Stephens identifies as "the contradiction between specific notions of racial nationalism—based in ideals of national sovereignty and imperial civilization, the ship of state itself—and the openness of the alternative routes that ship has taken in its quest for racial freedom" (39).

As we have seen, the Universal Declaration of Human Rights conflates internationalism with universalism; the drafters and the text itself obscure the discretely international circumstances of its creation (within the UN, in the hands of a small and quite Western and Westernized committee) in order to present it as a universal text, written not only for but in some sense *by* the human community writ large. Such deracinated, dehistoricized universalism is precisely the kind of universalism with which Césaire would take issue in his 1956 letter of resignation from the French Communist Party. Césaire's *Lettre à Maurice Thorez* contains a lucid analysis of the party's failure to account for the crucial difference of colonialism to the experience of African and Caribbean countries, a failure which serves as Césaire's explanation for why the party itself is inherently incapable of remedying the problem. After identifying the "embarrassment" of communism in its present forms, the majority of Césaire's letter works to build a case for the singularity of colonized African and African diasporic peoples, and for the incommensurability of their voice with the platforms of the French and Soviet Communist parties at this point in time. In his final paragraphs, he articulates his decision to quit the Party as a philosophical intervention—one that incorporates his observations of how race and colonialism refigure Marxist questions and problems, but also one that steps back and considers the possibilities for thinking about transnational (or even global) movements alongside a theory of critically inflected universalism.

> Provincialisme? Non pas. Je ne m'enterre pas dans un particularisme étroit. Mais je ne veux pas non plus me perdre dans un universalisme décharné. Il y a deux manières de se perdre: par ségrégation murée dans le particulier ou par dilution dans l'«universel».
>
> Ma conception de l'universel est celle d'un universel riche de tout le particulier, riche de tous les particuliers, approfondissement et coexistence de tous les particuliers. (*Lettre* 15)
>
> Provincialism? Certainly not. I do not bury myself in a narrow particularism. But neither do I want to lose myself in a detached universalism. There are two ways in which to lose oneself: by walled segregation in the particular or by dilution into the "universal."
>
> My conception of the universal is that of a universal rich in all of the particular, rich in all particulars, and profoundly coexistent with all particulars.

Césaire's *Lettre* reveals the impoverished nature of communist "universalism," its failure to account for—and celebrate—difference in an attempt to maintain orthodoxy and centralized aesthetic, philosophical, and political authority. Césaire is unwilling to altogether renounce the concept of universalism; but we might rephrase his "universalism in all its particulars" as more of an internationalism, a movement, a spirit, and—to borrow once again from Robbins—a "feeling" that derives its potency from the fact that it is situated in a particular space and time. If the Universal Declaration masks its internationalism under professions of universal applicability, then the *Cahier* does the opposite: Césaire's universalism is much harder to detect, until the final pages of the poem, beneath a number of iterations of his nuanced and capacious internationalist imagination. Césaire's is an internationalism based on discursive solidarity and subversive reconceptions of a global geography; its impulse toward universalism, with which the poem closes, asserts human unity based not on revolutionary action but instead on something that approximates a human rights ethic, one that situates negritude within a more generalized and transcendent cosmology and sacrifices (or at least seems to sacrifice) the historical specificity around which its internationalist identity is constructed.

As a diasporic internationalism, Césairean negritude is ultimately concerned with affiliations among people rather than spaces. But in the *Cahier* those affiliations can be neither recognized nor developed without a reconceptualization of geographical space, a remapping of the world. While relegated to the position of a bitter and despairing spectator in the opening stanzas of the poem, Césaire's poet-protagonist strives to reclaim a positive identity for his "country" and its inhabitants by asserting the authority to reinvent geography itself:

> I have no right to measure life by my sooty finger span; to reduce myself to this little ellipsoidal nothing trembling four fingers above the line, I a man, so to overturn creation that I include myself between latitude and longitude! (*Notebook* 14)

Self-inclusion, in this formulation, entails claiming the geographer's tools as his own, the creation of "my special geography [*mon originale géographie*] too; the world map made for my own use, not tinted with the arbitrary colors of scholars, but with the geometry of my spilled blood" (43). The maps drawn up by the inventors of powder and compass need to be discarded in favor of a new geography of the globe, one that will render visible the spatial and historical contours of a diasporic community.

To some extent, Césaire's new geography of negritude is a black Atlantic geography, one in which the historical triangulation of Europe, Africa, and the Americas collides with the speaker's (and poet's) present. But it also resists assigning spatial and relational fixity to these continents; recall the way in which elsewhere in the poem Césaire transforms the Congo from its static, passive existence as an African river to a slithering, living entity that eschews geographical fixity. Even the transatlantic connections which are so often invoked as the very crux of negritudean identity, those between Africa and its diaspora, are, on closer examination, less central or determinant than they at first appear. Africa enters the poet-protagonist's consciousness through a language of racial ancestry: "Tepid dawn of ancestral heat and fear I now tremble with the collective trembling that our docile blood sings in the madrepore" (32); "my country is the 'lance of light' of my Bambara ancestors" (44). But the collectivity at the heart of the poem shares the historical memory of the Middle Passage: "We the vomit of slave ships / We the venery of the Calabars" (28). Negritude, for Césaire, is first and foremost a diasporic identity, one that excludes contemporary Africans whose ancestors did not experience the slave-ship hold and its "enchained curses, the gasps of the dying, the noise of someone thrown into the sea" (28).

At other points in the text, the *Cahier* does make powerful claims for solidarity among present-day Africa and the diaspora. But those claims coincide with moments in which the poem asserts an internationalism that exceeds both the space of the black Atlantic and African bloodlines. These solidarities are established in the first half of the poem, and take the form of lists of historically specific names. The first such list posits a series of imaginative identifications in a passage that leads up to the poet-protagonist's aspirations of representational authority:

> To go away.
> As there are hyena-men and panther-men, I would be a jew-man
> a Kaffir-man
> a Hindu-man-from-Calcutta
> a Harlem-man-who-doesn't-vote
> (11)

The departure the poet-protagonist contemplates here facilitates—or, more precisely, *would* facilitate—any number of identifications between the protagonist and other racially degraded figures. The "Kaffir-man," the "Hindu-man-from-Calcutta," and the "Harlem-man-who-doesn't-vote" provide the basis for the speaker's inclusion of his own racially constructed identity into a larger world of such identities, and at the same time (implicitly) threaten to dissolve the specificity of his experiential identity. Reductive and derogatory labels are ironically reappropriated as the basis for a new form of internationalist solidarity; as Mara de Gennaro explains, Césaire here "denaturaliz[es] racist and culturally elitist concepts and practices constructed in colonialist discourse as inevitable ... by appealing to a supracultural state of commonality and interconnectedness that, in his view, transcends cultural particularities, including, and especially, the fictive idealism of the West" (61). This "supracultural state" is constellative; there is no central point from which all other points become intelligible. Conversely, *any* point from within this schema can shed light on its interconnectedness with all others. Racism, this stanza reveals, is an experience that not only is not unique to blacks but that in fact provides the basis for solidarity among blacks and other racially oppressed groups.

Césaire further complicates the poem's Atlanticism in the presentation of his next list, in which he constellates five cities within the speaker's radically redrawn global geography: "And I say to myself Bordeaux and Nantes and Liverpool and New York and San Francisco / not an inch of this world devoid of my fingerprint" (15). The first four cities in this short catalog frame a circum-Atlantic space whose unity could derive from the financial and cultural networks of the Atlantic slave trade and its contemporary legacies; San Francisco, however, conspicuously disrupts that geographical frame. Césaire's naming of this Pacific city in the *Cahier* has prompted relatively little critical commentary; the most extensive gloss I have come across is Irele's comment that San Francisco and New York denote "cities whose development was largely due to the exploitation of cheap labor, especially that of black workers" (72). Césaire's inclusion of a West Coast U.S. city in this list certainly serves as a reminder that racism against blacks was not exclusive to the South. Yet Irele's gloss seems so intent on connecting San Francisco to a history of black exploitation that it fails to explore the significance of this location to the poem's conception of a plurality of global histories of racial exploitation and colonial and imperial control. More than any other U.S. city, San Francisco is known as the port of arrival for East Asian immigrants to the Americas, and more broadly is associated with the economic exploitation of East Asian workers in the nineteenth-century construction of the Transcontinental Railroad. Césaire's San Francisco reference may signal the reach of the Atlantic diaspora beyond the shores of the Atlantic, but it also brings to mind the existence of analogous diasporic populations that bear the mark of the poet-protagonist's "fingerprint": other transnational throngs whose experience with capitalist and imperialist forms of violence lays the groundwork for comparison, mutual recognition, and perhaps even political solidarity with black internationalism.

These moments of global comparative identification in the *Cahier* indicate a conceptual approach to internationalism that resembles what Michael Malouf, drawing on Nancy Fraser, identifies as discursive solidarity. Malouf demonstrates how "Caribbean cosmopolitanism" constructed by figures such as Marcus Garvey, Claude McKay, and Derek Walcott forms by way of "detours through other nationalisms" (14); McKay, for example, "does not 'use' Irish nationalism so much as he dialogues with it, in Fraser's sense, as part of a process of developing an alternative political vocabulary" (85). The multiplicity of political identities (not all of which are nationalist) in the *Cahier* are similarly situated by Césaire as in dialogue—able to recognize, interact with, and inform one another once the oppressive geography of European imperialism has been thrown out. But this dialogical multiplicity emerges from a poem that also baldly poses the question, midway through, "Who and what are we?" (*Notebook* 18). The poet-protagonist himself announces the difficulty of asserting any of these identities as stable and fixed. Through the *Cahier*'s ever-widening geographical scope, Césaire maps a plurality of transnational projects and connective networks, registering the poet's investment in situating negritude and black internationalism as in conversation with other movements that exceed the geographical space of the black Atlantic. But it is worth noting that even these movements themselves are discursively constructed;

their participants/constituents need to be made legible to one another as well as to the rest of the world.

In the final pages of the poem, Césaire seems to retreat from his internationalist vision and to locate negritude's essence not in discrete histories of oppression but in a manifestation of *universal* humanity and an outgrowth of *universal* suffering. As the *Cahier* comes to a close, the enumeration of specific trans- and international solidarities begins to give way to a renewed focus on the ethical position of the poet-protagonist, who no longer seems to be in conversation with an antagonistic, absent colonizer-interlocutor, but rather with a higher power: in a "virile prayer" he calls for the universe to

> make me into the executor of these lofty works
> the time has come to gird one's loins like a brave man—
>
> But in doing so, my heart, preserve me from all hatred
> do not make me into that man of hatred for whom I feel only hatred
> (37–38)

Just as the speaker's wistful statements transitioned into their own miraculous fulfillment earlier in the text, so his prayer seems to bring about the desired transformation here: "Look, now I am only a man, no degradation, no spit perturbs him, / now I am only a man who accepts emptied of anger / (nothing left in his heart but immense love, which burns)" (39). The poet-protagonist can now distinguish between two kinds of humility—one cruelly demanded by the *béké*'s whip; the other a non-oppressive means of facing the future by respecting the past: "Presences, it is not on your back that I will make peace with the world" (41). Colonialism, imperialism, and racial exploitation have hardly disappeared from view, but in passages like this the emphasis is no longer on confronting those enemies through combative assertions of collective strength; the challenge the speaker now faces is an internal one.

The inward turn of the final pages of the poem is accompanied by an increased focus on needs, desires, and experiences that pertain to humanity as a whole rather than to specific groups or nations. Césaire's anaphoric stanzas celebrating "Those who invented neither powder or compass" refer less and less specifically with each repetition. His invocations of "my country," located so vividly in the Martinican morne in the opening pages of the poem, begin to feel more metaphorical than literal as well. And "entrenched as I am in this unique race," the speaker insists that "what I want / is for universal hunger / for universal thirst" (38). Moreover, the final (though not cumulative) definition of negritude offered by the poem is also its most capacious: "no longer a cephalic index, or plasma, or soma, but measured by the compass of suffering" (43). Biology is unequivocally displaced here in favor of the shared experience of historical trauma—but importantly historical trauma itself is delineated merely as undifferentiated "suffering." When, on the following page, the poet proclaims that "the work of man has only begun," the "man" in question bears no more specificity than the ubiquitous titular figure of the *Déclaration des droits de l'homme et du citoyen*—for, we are then informed, "no race has a monopoly on beauty, on intelligence, on strength / and there is room for everyone at the convocation of conquest" (44).

This shift from the situated internationalism Césaire has envisioned throughout the text to a final embrace of a more abstracted universal humanism at the end tends to be given a lot of weight in criticism as proof of Césaire's own humanist commitments[25]—or as evidence that the poet's ethical vision is transcendent enough to refute charges of essentialism.[26] Here, however, I wish to emphasize the significance of these gestures' appearance toward universal humanism only at the end of the poem—and as an outgrowth of the internationalism to which Césaire devotes so much imaginative attention beforehand. The Universal Declaration of Human Rights places its professions of universal humanity at the beginning of the document, asserting "the inherent dignity and . . . the equal and inalienable rights of all members of the human family" as "the foundation of freedom, justice and peace in the world" in its opening lines. Césaire's *Cahier* reverses that ordering; his final universalist claims thus read as claims that have been built and even earned over the course of the poem, constructed poetically rather than assumed as givens from the beginning. The negritude of the *Cahier* is not meant to be assimilated into a Eurocentric humanism; rather it asserts its right to define humanism from the outside, to draw on the immensely powerful fictions of universalism and humanism that are so constitutive of a First World global ethical imagination in the mid-twentieth century on its own terms.

POETRY OF THE THIRD WORLD REVOLUTION: SIDESTEPPING THE MANIFESTO

Césaire's poem critically reappropriates the internationalism of the Universal Declaration of Human Rights by overhauling its geographical scope, its imperialist claims to representative authority, and its obscuring of particularity. In this way it is a counterdeclaration, an alternative vision of global justice to that of imperial internationalism. And while the *Cahier* is not a "founding text" of the negritude movement in the same way that the Universal

Declaration could be said to found the contemporary human rights movement, certainly by the publication of the second and third editions of the poem Césaire (and his compatriots) probably thought of it in roughly those terms. We might, then, be tempted to describe the *Cahier* as a manifesto, which in the mid-twentieth century was the radical alternative to the juridico-political declaration as well as the liberal political traditions in which that form was ensconced. As Martin Puchner has shown, the modernist manifesto—in both its socialist and its avant-garde instantiations—was characterized first and foremost by its theatricality, its provocative seizure of contexts in which the declarative text and its author(s) enjoy no pre-existing claims to authority (25). This is precisely the kind of oppositional declarative work that the *Cahier* carries out. Well acquainted (and affiliated) with the socialist and avant-garde strains of the modernist manifesto tradition, Césaire certainly would have had that genre and its potential for declarative provocation in mind in the 1940s and 1950s, if not before.

And yet it is no accident that Césaire did not identify his poem as a manifesto—that, indeed, no one ever wrote a manifesto of negritude.[27] As a black, Antillean, and anticolonial student of Marxism and surrealism, Césaire had a complex relationship with each of these movements, whose centers of authority were unequivocally European and Eurocentric. Moreover, as Puchner observes, by the mid-twentieth century the manifesto had become as much a means of establishing and signifying new orthodoxies as it was a tool for discrediting older ones. André Breton's 1924 *Manifesto of Surrealism* is "a foundational scene from which surrealism emerges" (Puchner 185), a text that secures Breton's title as the sole legitimate author of surrealism's manifestos—and his authority over the movement writ large. And while the *Communist Manifesto* "defined for many subsequent writers what a manifesto should be" (11), it also—and because of this definitional and foundational task—discouraged subsequent writers from authoring new manifestos. It makes sense, then, that Césaire—for whom even "poetry" felt too restrictive a formal category when he was writing the first version of the *Cahier*—would have been uninterested in introducing negritude in programmatic terms.

The most clear-cut evidence of how careful Césaire was *not* to author a manifesto is provided by a text that flirts with, but deliberately does not quite inhabit, that genre. In 1942 Césaire published a poem in *Tropiques* whose text would later be incorporated into the revised 1947 edition of the *Cahier*. As it appeared in the Antillean journal, however, the poem was titled "En guise de manifeste littéraire" ["In the Guise of a Literary Manifesto"]—and dedicated to Breton. If Césaire assiduously avoided claiming the generic designation of "manifesto" in deference to Breton's exclusive control over surrealism's relationship with that form of writing, he nonetheless comes close to infringing on that monopoly by foregrounding the proximity of his poem to the manifesto form. "En guise de manifeste" gestures toward the very thing it proclaims itself not quite identical with; it raises the question of exactly what it takes to be a manifesto, what a good imitation thereof might look like, and most importantly what is accomplished by a text that purports to stand in for this other type of text while also refusing to be identified as such. Dedicated to Breton, this poem contains one of the longer work's most famous celebrations of negritudean-surrealist "folie," much of which gets incorporated into the 1947 edition of the *Cahier*:

Comptons:
la folie qui se souvient
la folie qui hurle
la folie qui voit,
la folie qui se déchaîne.

Assez de ce gout de cadavre fade!

Ni naufrageurs. Ni nettoyeurs de tranchée. Ni hyènes. Ni chacals. Et vous savez le reste:

Que 2 et 2 font 5
Que la forêt miaule
Que l'arbre tire les marrons du feu
Que le ciel se lisse la barbe
Et cetera, et cetera . . .
("En guise de manifeste" 7–8)

•

Let's count:
the madness that remembers
the madness that howls
the madness that sees
the madness that is unleashed

Enough of the taste of this insipid cadaver!

Neither shipwreckers. Nor trench cleaners. Nor hyenas. Nor jackals. And you know the rest:

> That 2 and 2 are 5
> that the forest miaows
> that the tree plucks the maroons from the fire
> that the sky strokes its beard
> etc., etc. . . . [28]

The refutation of Western rationality that takes place in these lines echoes—or perhaps more accurately does the work of—Breton's displacement of liberal humanism in his first *Manifesto of Surrealism*, where he declares that "the imagination is perhaps on the verge of reasserting itself, of reclaiming its rights" (10). And it echoes also Césaire's insistence, in his 1945 "Poetry and Knowledge," also published in *Tropiques*, that poetry's corrective to scientific knowledge lies in its accounting for a fuller, more holistic definition of humanity, one that sees the human as in partnership with the rest of the natural world rather than nature's oppressor. The poet, he asserts, is "someone who saves humanity, someone who restores it to universal harmony, someone who marries a human florescence to universal florescence" (Richardson and Fijałkowski 39). Within the text of the *Cahier*, the stakes of this revaluation of humanism in relation to history and politics become clear. "2 + 2 = 5" is not a game; the theatricality of surrealism's refutation of reason is not at odds with the very concrete problems of colonialism and racial exploitation that the poet-narrator must figure out how to successfully challenge. Not itself a manifesto, the *Cahier* nonetheless incorporates the poetic strategies of the surrealist manifesto tradition in identifying the aesthetic as a crucial weapon in the struggle against imperial authority.

Similarly, Césaire draws on key features of the urtext of the socialist manifesto tradition, the *Communist Manifesto*, in order to think negritudean solidarity as a transhistorical as well as a transnational/transregional phenomenon. Critics have paid much attention to the formal and stylistic relationship between Bretonian surrealism and Césaire's poetry; the aesthetic importance of communism, the other internationalism to which the manifesto form was central in the mid-twentieth century, has remained underexplored. It is worth noting that both the *Manifesto* and the *Cahier* were created amid a sense of generic flux, a search for a new textual form suited to a new historical and political moment (Puchner 19). More importantly, however, the *Communist Manifesto* supplies Césaire with the means of challenging the presentism of the juridico-political declaration by way of a radical alternative temporality of global ethics for a new world order. Césaire's poet-protagonist has representational obligations not only toward "those who cannot speak" in the present, but also toward past generations, who exert a ghostly presence in the text of the poem. The *Communist Manifesto*'s own staging of an ethical encounter with a ghost helps elucidate the stakes and inner workings of how Césaire imagines solidarity across time as well as space—how he imagines an ethics of declaring that opens itself up to black Atlantic history.

The *Manifesto* famously begins by defining communism as a specter—one of which, Jacques Derrida observes in *Specters of Marx,* the authors are both enamored and afraid. Specters, Derrida tells us, "have no more important role than that of throwing the time out of joint: the specter may appear to us at clearly identifiable points in time, but it appears as already existent: a specter is always a *revenant*. One cannot control its comings and goings because it *begins by coming back*" (11). Moreover, specters do not appear merely at the bidding of the conjurer; the paradox of conjuring as a speech act is that the *effects* of that speech act are always already beyond the speaker's control. In fact, the conjurer—also a witness and a kind of host—takes on an unexpected, and perhaps unwanted, ethical obligation to the specter. "The *Manifesto* calls, it calls for this presentation of the living reality: we must see to it that in the future this specter—and first of all an association of workers forced to remain secret until about 1848—becomes a *reality,* and a *living* reality. This real life must show itself and manifest itself, it must *present itself* beyond Europe, old or new Europe, in the universal dimension of an International" (101–2). Derrida issues a call to embrace this complex ethical obligation, to "learn to live by learning not how to make conversation with the ghost but how to talk with him, with her, how to let them speak or how to give them back speech, even if it is in oneself, in the other, in the other in oneself" (176). In Derrida's reading the ethical work of conjuring is central to the manifesto genre, in which the "future is not described, it is not foreseen in the constative mode; it is announced, promised, called for in a performative mode" (103). Communism is called forth performatively; but the paradox of performativity is that revolutionary time is unstable and ephemeral. "As soon as one identifies a revolution, it begins to imitate, it enters into a death agony" (115). The brilliance of Marx and Engels's text, but also the problem with which we, retrospectively, have to wrestle, is precisely this paradox.

The specters that haunt the *Cahier* do not make themselves manifest until midway through, but it is through them that Césaire holds negritudean internationalism accountable to not only a dispersed and disorganized present-day "throng" but also the past through which the African diaspora came to be. The spectral presences in Césaire's poem unhinge the speaker's search for an alternate mode of representational authority from the present; in throwing the time out of joint, conjuration establishes negritudean internationalism as crossing temporal as well as spatial boundaries. If remapping and listing are two of the principle means by which the *Cahier* establishes the transnational scope and implications of negritude, then conjuring is the means by which Césaire situates negritude as a trans*historical* phenomenon. Shortly before the poet-protagonist imagines himself as speaking for the dispossessed morne he witnesses in the present, he contemplates how he might use language on behalf of the spectral inhabitants of his native land.

> And you ghosts rise blue from alchemy from a forest of hunted beasts of twisted machines of a jujube tree of rotten flesh of a basket of oysters of eyes of a network of straps in the beautiful sisal of human skin I would have words vast enough to contain you. (*Notebook* 12)

Representational authority is identified, early along in the poem, as a means by which the speaker will affirm a loyalty to more than just the despairing present-day morne and its living inhabitants; his ethical obligation, this stanza makes clear, also extends backwards in time, to an ancestry whose presence is spectacularly active amid the vegetation of a "savage earth arisen from the storerooms of the sea" (13). The importance of this obligation becomes clear in the poem's first iteration of the word negritude, which "rose for the first time" ["se mit debout pour la première fois" (Césaire, *Cahier* 10)] in Haiti: a metropolitan colonial subject with a Western education, Césaire may have coined the *word* for negritude relatively recently, but his poet-protagonist can take no credit for inventing the phenomenon. Negritude makes its first appearance in the poem as a very old ghost, one that dates back to—or, as the reflexive verb "se mit" suggests, even predates—Haiti's revolution. The poet-protagonist's task is not to create negritude so much as to coax it into view, to instantiate another "rising" of this specter in the present.

Haunting, in Derrida's analysis, takes place on its own terms: "a specter is always a *revenant*. One cannot control its coming and goings because it *begins by coming back*" (11). Conjuring is a conscious, intentional speech-act under the control of Césaire's poet-protagonist; the ghosts that he conjures, however, are beyond his control. It is a risky task, one that threatens the speaker/author's authority even as it seems to cement it. The *Cahier* gives voice to negritude, but in doing so acknowledges the limitations of the voice that it gives. The poet-protagonist, the voice of the poem, will never satisfactorily speak for the political community he wishes to call forth. Césaire's poem embraces the impossibility of the task its speaker sets out to accomplish. These demands are dramatized in the final pages of the *Cahier* through Césaire's deployment of two closely linked motifs from classical epic: *katabasis* and *nekuia*. Gregson Davis describes the *Cahier*'s adaptation of *katabasis*—the epic hero's descent to the land of the dead—as the poet-protagonist's "descent into the psychological depths that brings him face to face with ghosts of his former self" (*Aimé Césaire* 43). Confrontation with the "confessions" he hears from the slave ships enables his own confession of identifying with the oppressor's disdain for the "comical and ugly" black man, and a revelation about the farcical nature of his own heroism. In other words, at the very moment that the poem employs a motif from epic that most explicitly figures the protagonist as the hero, it also draws his heroism into question. "It is against this painfully gained insight that we can best understand the positive affirmation of négritude we hear resounding through the later portions of the *Cahier*" (43). I read the *katabasis* episode as a means through which Césaire endows negritudean political solidarity with a vital transhistorical dimension. Ghosts first enter into the poem as objects of verbal desire; the poet-protagonist longs to "contain" them with his words. His confrontation with the slave ship that takes place midway through the poem thwarts that will to autonomous control, but also grants him admission to a negritudean fraternity that spans multiple centuries. Just as Virgil initiates Dante into a transgenerational community of great bards in the *Inferno*, so does the poet-protagonist's "descent" into the depths of an Atlantic past grant him solidarity with that past and its ghosts. The *katabasis* episode not only enables the poet-protagonist to confront and transcend his own complicity with European oppression and racism; it also establishes "his" negritude as multigenerational and transhistorical, a movement and an ethic that claims affinity with the dead as well as the living.

Katabasis distinguishes the *Cahier*'s relationship to history from that of the *Communist Manifesto*: while the *Manifesto* recounts the prehistory of the workers of the world, there is no urgent need in that text to establish transhistorical solidarity between the mid-nineteenth-century proletariat and laborers from earlier historical moments. In contrast, such a recognition is crucial in the *Cahier*. *Katabasis* allows Césaire to establish the spectral as a crucial ethical component of negritude: the ghosts of the slave ship are the ghosts to whom the poet-protagonist is responsible, and in turn they offer him a viable ancestry for a present-day transnational political community. He thus finds a way to bring together two strands of thought about modernity—"the catastrophic rupture of the middle passage" and "the dream of revolutionary transformation"—that Paul Gilroy argues are mutually exclusive for writers such as Douglass, Du Bois, and Wright (*Black Atlantic* 197). The *katabasis* episode recuperates the slave ship as a viable and indeed essential component of a contemporary black internationalist politics.[29]

The second epic motif of which Césaire makes use aligns much more closely with the *Communist Manifesto*'s strategies of integrating past and present. *Katabasis* is a narrative episode in which the hero plays the part of a visitor after undertaking a journey (even if, as in Dante's case, only a dream journey) to the land of the dead. *Nekuia*, in contrast, is an act of conjuring, a summoning forth and questioning of the dead in order to learn about the present—and the future. The conjurer is a host who issues an invitational speech-act and then plays a more passive role in welcoming a visitation by a specter. Césaire's poet-protagonist begins his descent to the Atlantic underworld with a speech act, an incantation:

> voum rooh oh
> voum rooh oh
> to charm the snakes to conjure the dead
> voum rooh oh
> to compel the rain to turn back the tidal waves
> voum rooh oh
> to keep the shade from moving
> voum rooh oh
> that my own skies may open
> (20)

A counterpoint to the words from the Catholic mass that appeared a few stanzas earlier, this incantation connotes both a specifically Caribbean oceanscape and more generally a set of distinctly non-Western modes of engaging with a spirit world, modes that allude to but also beyond African spirituality (e.g., the Indian snake charmer).[30] Conjuring signals the poet-protagonist's embrace of a set of original, syncretic strategies for forging transgenerational connection; the initiation of contact with ghosts takes place on his own terms. When the incantation (repeated twice more in subsequent stanzas) is finished, his role becomes notably more passive: at the completion of his "descent" to the slave ship, far from his earlier fantasy of finding words to contain the ghosts therein, he instead becomes first and foremost a listener:

> I hear coming up from the hold the enchained curses, the gasps of the dying, the noise of someone thrown into the sea . . . the baying of a woman in labor . . . the scrape of fingernails seeking throats . . . the flouts of the whip . . . the seething of vermin amid the weariness . . . (28)

These shades (or, rather, their voices) come up to meet the poet; while never himself entering the hold, the Atlantic's deepest circle of hell, he summons them forth from below. Césaire's speaker-hero is less a quester than an aural witness. In place of life stories, the poet-protagonist hears cries, gasps, splashes, whips. The slave ship releases new sounds and images into his consciousness that disrupt the narrative flow of the poem more than they contribute to it. If *katabasis* establishes the spectral as a crucial component of negritude, the means by which transhistorical as well as transnational solidarity becomes possible, then *nekuia* poses the question of what happens when one tries to invoke—which is to say, to declare—that solidarity in the present moment. Conjuring is unpredictable and overwhelming; the poet-protagonist relinquishes control over the project of negritude in welcoming these specters up from the hold, giving way to the ethical demand they place upon him.

Like Enlightenment-era revolutionary declarations, the *Communist Manifesto* derives its authority from a source beyond the text itself (the already-existent phenomenon of communism in place of nature or self-evident truths). But unlike these eighteenth-century texts, Marx and Engels's declaration identifies that authority as spectral—as an authority that haunts and in some sense challenges the authority of the text's declarative voice and the present in which it makes its intervention. Borrowing Derrida's language, we might say that Césaire's *Cahier* endows negritude with a similar hauntological structure; declaring negritude requires its conjuration. And conjuration introduces an ethical dimension to the work of declaring; Césaire cannot chart the revolutionary future he imagines for the colonized black Atlantic world without allowing for the fact that that future will be haunted by a past marked by slavery, colonialism, and revolutionary resistance to those institutions. To declare negritude into existence, the poet-protagonist must assume an audacious amount of authority, without which no act of declaration (or conjuration) can take place at all. Performative audacity enables the poet-protagonist to assume the inherent risks of the speech act. But the black Atlantic specters that the poet-protagonist (audaciously) conjures forth then assert their own authority over this rhetorical performance. They reveal this declarative text's affiliation with a much more capacious negritudean hauntology that dates back hundreds of years and spans both shores of the Atlantic. The poet-protagonist's embrace of negritude's transhistoricality humbles him, tempers his individual voice by acknowledging its debt to a multigenerational chain of voices of which it is a part. Conjuration offers Césaire a way out of the traps of presentism and unsituated universalism that threaten to derail the poet-protagonist at the outset of his quest.

PRESENTISM AND UNSITUATED UNIVERSALISM are precisely the traps into which the Universal Declaration of Human Rights falls. Without question, of course, much of the impetus behind the UN text stemmed from recent history, namely the horrors of the Holocaust and international law's failure to offer minority populations any protection in the wake of World War I. But the text itself quite purposely eschews reference to specific historical events; at a rhetorical level, its strategy for dealing with the past is exactly the opposite of the one that Césaire deploys in his poem. The utopian aspirations of speaking truth to power that many of the Universal Declaration's proponents and drafters shared were reined in by the practical realities of institutional constraints, Cold War politics, and the investments of many UN member states in the continued control of the colonial and "developing" world. The universalism of human rights discourse could not transcend the more narrowly internationalist contexts in which it was voiced. Even in its earliest days of institutional articulation, and well before its future complicities with a new world order were at all self-evident, human rights was endowed with an enormous amount of moral, pedagogical, and quasi-legal authority. The theory of universal authorship and applicability that underlies the Universal Declaration is constitutive of a twentieth-century imperial internationalism through which what Makau Mutua calls the "three-dimensional prism" of savages, victims, and saviors—the central metaphors of a Western human rights discourse—takes shape (10). And it is for this reason that Césaire's *Cahier*, with its challenging revaluation of the nature of the declaration, has much to tell us about the form through which the authority to declare human rights is asserted. Césairean negritude is not an "alternative" version of a declaration of human rights; it does not address the question of what the UN Declaration might have looked like had its drafters accounted for colonialism as a humanitarian disaster, or if there had been more representation from the colonized world within the Commission on Human Rights. Rather, Césaire confronts and reworks the declarative form in which human rights first gains its legibility and legitimation within First World international institutions. From within literary space, the *Cahier* interrogates the form of the juridico-political human rights declaration, and especially the pitfalls and opportunities that accompany its claims to authority. Césaire's poem, with its incorporation of the performative and spectral imperatives of the manifesto, provided a means of capaciously reimagining the nature and the parameters of legal and political belonging in the soon to be decolonized world.

CHAPTER 4

If You Could Make the Laws

Popular Authorship and the South African Freedom Charter

IF IN THE 1930s, when James's and Césaire's careers began, decolonization was virtually unthinkable to Europe's colonial powers, by 1960 the end of colonial rule was widely accepted as inevitable. The years in between have come to be thought of as the apex of anticolonial activity across South Asia, Africa, and the Caribbean. But of course many countries in the Global South do not fit neatly into this periodization of wartime anticolonial resistance followed by postwar decolonization: Haiti gained independence 150 years earlier; Martinique, Guadeloupe, and Réunion became departments of France rather than sovereign states; and much of southern Africa followed a notably different trajectory toward independence and liberation during this time period. And while South Africa had already "decolonized" in the narrowest sense of the term before the war, the country would continue to be ruled by a white minority until the 1990s. Accordingly, anticolonial resistance took on its own unique set of meanings and forms in this country in the late twentieth century. South Africa's "colonialism of a special type," and the apartheid regime that began taking shape in the wake of the National Party's electoral victory in 1948, called for a resistance movement designed to transform power relations within the country rather than to declare political independence from Europe. Contemporaneous with liberation movements taking place elsewhere on the continent, South Africa's own variety of anticolonialism in the 1950s would feature a different set of key terms from those of anticolonial movements elsewhere, foregrounding in unique ways the concepts of national belonging, enfranchisement, and both human and civil rights. Despite these political and discursive differences, it is important to recognize the extent to which the anti-apartheid movement was, nonetheless, an anticolonial struggle. It was revolutionary rather than reformist, intent not only on dismantling the institutional racism of the apartheid state but also on overturning the colonial power relations through which apartheid was made possible. In 1977 the African National Congress (ANC) would explain its response to Southern African "internal colonialism" in these terms—and cite the 1955 Freedom Charter, and its call for democratic majority rule, as an accurate and originary statement of the organization's vision.[1]

The end product of a nationwide grassroots campaign carried out by a coalition of anti-apartheid groups, the Freedom Charter puts forth an ambitious and liberatory vision of a South Africa yet to come, a multiracial national community rooted in democratic participation, social equality, and economic justice. In its own moment, the Charter—and the Congress of the People, the mass meeting at which the document was formally approved and endorsed in 1955—solidified the anti-apartheid movement as a mass resistance struggle dependent on solidarity across racial, ethnic, and ideological lines. The text's profession of racial inclusivity alienated some of the ANC's more committed Africanists, who would go on in 1958 to form the Pan Africanist Congress; and the Charter would have significantly less ideological purchase within the country during the 1960s and '70s, when the ANC was in exile and a much younger, student-based movement coalesced instead around Black Consciousness. But in the 1980s the Charter would be revived as a statement of the core values of the multiracial United Democratic Front, a means of establishing this umbrella organization's work to Mandela-era activism while also looking ahead to the anticipated end of apartheid rule. And indeed the 1994 Constitution echoed the Charter in language and tone, enshrining its call for civil and political rights into law.

The "Charterist" version of the history of the Freedom Charter foregrounds and celebrates this continuity between the text's moment of creation and the new South Africa of the late-twentieth and early-twenty-first centuries. Two decades later Raymond Suttner and Jeremy Cronin reissued their 1986 *Thirty Years of the Freedom Charter,* a collection of photographs, interviews, first-person accounts, and documents pertaining to the Congress of the People and the creation of the Charter. Originally published amid the censorship constraints of the late apartheid state, Suttner and Cronin's volume presents a remarkable account of the Charter's origins and legacies, one that provides invaluable source material for researchers of the anti-apartheid movement in the 1950s. The 2006 volume now also serves as a celebratory early-twenty-first-century revisiting of the Charter and its history—a testament to the triumph of the liberation struggle's emancipatory ideals in the new South Africa. In contrast, Naomi Klein's discussion of the Charter in *The Shock Doctrine* (2008) laments the betrayal of the radical political vision of the text—particularly its identification of land redistribution as a cornerstone of righting the wrongs of the past—in the early 1990s, as free-market ideology ruled the day in the ANC's negotiations with de Klerk. For Klein the Freedom Charter has become a reminder of the lost promise of the liberation movement, a document whose present-day memorialization as a tourist attraction in the Kliptown square that served as the site for the Congress provides bitingly ironic comment on the new South Africa's failure to address the economic violence that colonialism and apartheid inflicted on the country for centuries.

My goal in this chapter is to push past these two contemporary readings of the Freedom Charter—one celebratory/romantic, one sympathetic but ultimately tragic. I share with Suttner and Cronin as well as Klein a deep admiration for this text, but in order to honor it and suggest how and why it remains important today I want to avoid adjudicating its "success" or "failure" in South Africa's post-apartheid and postcolonial present. The betrayal of the Charter's vision in the new South Africa is not a failure of the anticolonial project at the heart of the country's liberation struggle; rather it is a vital reminder that that anticolonial project is not yet complete. Revolution's end goal, as the work of James and Césaire attests, cannot be reduced to the constitution of a new legal regime; the real work of revolution lies in the cultivation of a dynamic and radically democratic political community, one equipped to continually reconstitute the nation in the present. The Freedom Charter's greatest feat in 1955 was helping to constitute such a community of resistance. My reading of the text thus attends less to its content than to questions of how it was both formed and performed in its own historical moment. And I look not only at how the Charter challenged the authority of the South African state but also at how it critically engaged with a midcentury First World international legal imagination. The text draws inspiration from juridico-political forms that were enjoying a newfound prominence in international law in the mid-twentieth century—but does not appeal to international institutions for justice or assistance. In fact, its decidedly localized conception of human rights and political belonging contrasts sharply with the abstract universalism of contemporary international institutions' notions of the same. The Freedom Charter unsettles North Atlantic juridico-political discourse at the level of both form and content. It develops and performs innovative and subversive conceptions of authorship and representation that challenge law's discursive conventions.

And it engages, self-consciously and playfully, with the unique temporality of the declaration toward the purpose of putting forth a radical vision of political participation and societal transformation in the present and the future.

AFRICANS' CLAIMS

The Freedom Charter, and the grassroots campaign that led to its creation, could not have existed before the 1950s. Until that point the ANC saw itself as a traditional political party, with a hierarchical leadership structure, a membership composed mainly of urban black professionals, and no particular interest in mass mobilization or participation. This would begin to change with the formation of the Youth League in 1944, and gain momentum with the new political landscape that emerged in the wake of the 1948 election that brought the National Party to power and spurred the passage of the first apartheid legislation. New civil disobedience initiatives such as the 1952 Defiance Campaign, launched in response to these early new laws, increased ANC membership by four hundred percent (Gerhart 89). The Congress of the People Campaign and the Freedom Charter were products of this dramatic shift in focus for the ANC, evidence of the organization's new commitment to grassroots outreach as well as collaboration with other anti-apartheid constituencies. If the Freedom Charter's most provocative and lasting legacy lies in its insistence that "the people" themselves—*all* of them—should take part in the political life of the nation, then that legacy dates rather specifically to an approach to political organization that took hold after 1950.

The romance of radically democratic authorship that underpins the text of the Freedom Charter is one of its most remarkable features. But the implications of this romance only become clear in conjunction with another feature of the text, its critical engagement with international legal forms and institutions. And it is in relation to this feature that the Freedom Charter has an important textual precursor from the decade preceding the ANC's organizational transformation. In 1943, two years after Franklin Roosevelt and Winston Churchill pledged their countries' commitments to a peaceful and democratic postwar world order in the Atlantic Charter, the ANC formed a committee to study and develop a response to that document. The result was "Africans' Claims in South Africa," a two-part document that first reviewed the Atlantic Charter's contents point by point and then put forth a South Africa–specific "Bill of Rights," phrased as a series of demands for citizenship and social and economic welfare on behalf of the country's nonwhite population. Drafted by ANC leader Z. K. Matthews for presentation at a postwar peace conference, this text called on one hand for the fulfillment of the Atlantic Charter's promises—of the right to self-determination, the end of tyranny, and an open and nonexploitative trade policy, in particular—to Africans; and on the other hand for a set of international standards that would go further, and be far more explicit, than that text in securing the end of colonial and racial regimes. "Africans' Claims" was less a refutation of the contents of Roosevelt and Churchill's text than an annotated account of the points at which its gaps, silences, and evasions eroded its potential as a tool of envisioning a peaceful and democratic global future. The authors insisted, for instance, that the principles of territorial non-aggrandizement and the right to national self-determination needed to explicitly apply to Africa as well as to Europe. Moreover, the end of the war should mark the eradication not only of Nazism but of *all* kinds of oppressive political regimes: "Africans are in full agreement with the war aim of destroying Nazi tyranny, but they desire to see all forms of racial domination in all lands, including the Allied countries, completely destroyed" (Asmal, Chidester, and Lubisi 16). "Africans' Claims" calls on the international community to fulfill its vision for global justice on colonial soil. This call takes shape through the document's subtle drawing of parallels between Axis powers' aggrandizement in the midcentury and the aggression and oppression inherent in Europe's occupation of Africa.

But the ANC does not simply petition the Allied Powers for more extensive consideration of the needs and concerns of colonized peoples. It is not merely an African commentary on international law, an additional opinion for Western leaders to consider (or ignore) as they chart the future of a new world order for the late twentieth century. As ANC president Alfred Bitini Xuma explains in his introduction to the text, the real work of this document goes further than providing commentary and hoping for the best. "Africans' Claims" asserts much more authority over this "Atlantic" document, putting forth an "undisputed claim to full citizenship" in the postwar international community that is yet to come (7).

> As African leaders, we are not so foolish as to believe that because we made these declarations that our government will grant us our claims for the mere asking. We realise that for the African this is only a beginning of a long struggle entailing great sacrifices of time, means and even life itself. To the African people the declaration is a challenge to organise and unite themselves under the mass liberation movement, the African National Congress. (8–9)

"Africans' Claims" is ostensibly addressed to an international audience—the architects of the still-forming United Nations. But Xuma makes clear that petitioning the international community for support is only a starting point; (South) African readers bear the ultimate responsibility for instantiating the change that the text envisions. The "challenge" Xuma lays out in his introduction anticipates the impending sea change to the ANC's structure and mission, and calls upon black Africans themselves to rethink, and actively redefine, the nature of representation and authorship in a postwar world order. The exposition of the Atlantic Charter's facile universalism goes a step further, asserting the right of an African readership to reinterpret the document's geopolitical scope and intent:

> In considering the Charter as a whole, the Committee was confronted with the difficulty of interpreting certain terms and expressions which are somewhat loosely and vaguely used in the Atlantic Charter. Among the terms or words to which this stricture applies are "nations," "states," "peoples" and "men." *Whatever meanings the authors had in mind with regard to these terms, the Committee decided that* these terms, words or expressions are understood by us to include Africans and other Non-Europeans, because we are convinced that the groups to which we refer demand that they shall not be excluded from the rights and privileges which other groups hope to enjoy in the post-war world. (11; emphasis mine)

In their vagueness, the emancipatory claims of this North Atlantic document become exclusionary; it is the work of the text's non-European readers first to take note of the problems with its key terms and then to subject them to a more rigorously global redefinition. If the "Atlantic" of Roosevelt and Churchill's charter referred first and foremost to the oceanic setting in which it was written—on a ship, off the coast of Newfoundland, a secret and neutral wartime rendezvous point—then "Africans' Claims" broadens not only the conceptual scope of that document's content but also its imagining of the geography of authorship. An anticolonial transformation of Atlantic internationalism is more than a mere expansion of its geographical purview; such a transformation means interrogating the ways in which race and colonial power have long structured that oceanic space, both materially and imaginatively. This ANC text is an active intervention into the internationalism that underpins the North Atlantic world's declarative iterations of a postwar new world order. It begins as a reading of the Charter that seeks out its relevance to the domestic concerns of black South Africans—a query into how these new principles might apply locally. But that query quickly gives way to a broader consideration of what it would mean for Africans to see those principles through to their logical conclusion: what would happen if Africans enjoyed the right not only to choose and participate in their own government but also to author the statement of international principles in which such rights were iterated in the first place?

Unlike "Africans' Claims," the Freedom Charter was not (at least explicitly) a critical response to someone else's declaration of liberatory principles for a new world order. It was an autonomous declaration, addressed to a South African audience; more provocatively, it also claimed to have been authored by that audience. Yet the Freedom Charter shares with its 1940s predecessor a critical engagement with international institutions' ways of imagining juridico-political authorship and authority. Just as Haiti's founding texts aimed to authorize and enfranchise the nation's citizenry while also exposing the philosophical shortcomings of North Atlantic Enlightenment universalism and its manifestation in juridico-political texts, so the Freedom Charter interrogates postwar First World international and state-level legal norms. In the Charter's opening proclamation that "South Africa belongs to all who live in it, black and white," the magnitude of its affront to the South African state and its legal apparatus—including but not limited to apartheid policy—is clear. But the text also demands a revaluation of the form and content of the juridico-political documents meant to lay the groundwork for democracy, human rights, and self-determination in the mid-twentieth century, within and beyond South Africa. Moreover, this "collectively authored" declaration posits new means of imagining how such documents might be created and legitimized. To envision a truly postcolonial legal order is to confront the need for a new concept of legal authorship as well as legal authority. This is the confrontation that the Freedom Charter was meant to stage in 1955.

THE GENRE OF FREEDOM

The vision put forth by the Freedom Charter is a unique admixture of the national—an articulation of a South Africa yet to come—and the global, an invocation of international law that cites its authority while also critically commenting on the power structures through which that authority is made legible. These two levels of engagement, and the different modes of critique they provoke, are encapsulated in the document's title. The name of the document was never the subject of debate; Z. K. Matthews coined it when he first proposed the idea for the Congress of the People campaign in 1953 (173). The generic and political implications of that title, however, invite further comment. The text that Matthews originally had in mind was a preparatory draft in anticipation of the moment in which the time would come for a legal foundation for a new South African nation-state. His identification of this text as a

"Charter," then, suggests that he intended it to resemble a constitution; it was meant to be a document that would at least begin the work of articulating, if not actually founding, a new political order. This connection is explicit in the language of the ANC's resolution formalizing the beginning of the Congress of the People campaign, which referred to the text as "a Freedom Charter or constitution embodying a vision of a future South Africa, as we in Congress see it" (qtd. in Vadi 69). But a later memo by Matthews, circulated in early 1954 to leaders of the organizations that would come together to form the National Action Council, backs away significantly from this earlier formulation, even as the document's title remains unchanged:

> The main task of the Congress will be to draw up a "Freedom Charter" for all peoples and groups in South Africa. From such a Congress ought to come a Declaration which will inspire all the peoples of South Africa with fresh hope for the future, which will turn the minds of the people away from the sterile and negative struggles of the past and the present to a positive programme of freedom in our lifetime. Such a Charter properly conceived as a mirror of the future South African Society can galvanise the people of South Africa into action and make them go over into the offensive against the reactionary forces at work in this country, instead of being perpetually on the defensive, fighting rearguard actions all the time. (Matthews 176)

Matthews's language here aligns much more closely with how the Charter would be described in the wake of its ratification—as a source of inspiration and collective mobilization, a declaration rather than a constitution. The document's lack of constituting power would be of paramount importance when the state introduced the text as evidence during the Treason Trial a few years later, and would unsuccessfully argue that the text served as a blueprint for a communist state (South Africa, "Treason Trial Press Summaries"). Nelson Mandela was able to make the case, both at the trial and in print, that the Charter did no such thing; he and other ANC commentators pointed to the Charter's function as "more than a document" ("Does the Freedom Charter Mean Socialism?"), a text to be "transformed into a living instrument" poised to bring about revolutionary change, not provide the foundation of a new order (Mandela, "Freedom in Our Lifetime"). "Charter" in this sense serves as a more flexible and evocative generic alternative to "Constitution." It opens the text up to certain imaginative possibilities that the latter term would have foreclosed.

Yet "Charter" also suggests a generic connection between this text and some of the most well-known and rhetorically significant documents of mid-century international law. The word recalls the Atlantic Charter and its lofty, future-oriented vision for a peaceful global community. But as of 1954, the Charter of the United Nations would have been the more recent, prominent, and obvious referent for "charter" within the sphere of First World international politics. The South African text's challenge to state law also takes effect in part through its engagement at the level of form with First World internationalism, and more specifically with the moral force of the United Nations. The internationalist associations of "charter" as a genre offer up a way of thinking about political community that contrasts starkly with the romantic and nostalgic model of the nation in which, for example, Afrikaaner nationalism was grounded. First World international law provided an alternative political imaginary, a way of conceiving the possibility of diverse "national" populations naming common desires and beliefs that could constitute a just system of governance. Moreover, international law and its institutions could provide a powerful corrective moral authority to the South African state, which only a few years earlier had abstained from the UN vote that had ratified the Universal Declaration of Human Rights. Not long after W. E. B. Du Bois and other U.S. intellectuals had petitioned the UN as a way of shaming the United States for Jim Crow,[2] the Freedom Charter's title signals an affinity with an international organization whose norms threw the most egregious aspects of South Africa's apartheid government into sharp relief.

Formally and stylistically, however, the Freedom Charter has little in common with the UN Charter—a lengthy and detailed blueprint for the terms under which its member states would participate in a new postwar world order. The Freedom Charter, in contrast, is compact and lyrical. Its subheadings are decidedly untechnical; they focus readers' attention on the text's capacious vision for the future, and provide no specific information about terms of governance under which that future will materialize. The text declares independence from the existing South African state without quite constituting a new political order. The unity that the Freedom Charter professes and claims to have achieved among multiple constituencies is one that takes shape in opposition to an official system that has declared such unity impossible. The preamble proclaims the existence of this newly acknowledged, but long-awaited, collectivity.

> *We, the People of South Africa, declare for all our country and the world to know:*
>> that South Africa belongs to all who live in it, black and white, and that no government can justly claim authority unless it is based on the will of all the people;
>> that our people have been robbed of their birthright to land, liberty and peace by a form of government founded on injustice and inequality;

> that our country will never be prosperous or free until all our people live in brotherhood, enjoying equal rights and opportunities;
> that only a democratic state, based on the will of all the people, can secure to all their birthright without distinction of colour, race, sex or belief;
> And therefore, we, the people of South Africa, black and white together equals, countrymen and brothers adopt this Freedom Charter;
> And we pledge ourselves to strive together, sparing neither strength nor courage, until the democratic changes here set out have been won. ("Freedom Charter")

Opening with an all-important first-person plural, the preamble briefly narrates the people's dispossession at the hands of the state; puts forth the basic beliefs in racial equality and democracy that ground the contents of the Charter; and concludes by infusing the document, and its collective voice, with a strong sense of immediacy. The closing pledge "to strive together, sparing neither strength nor courage, until the democratic changes here set out have been won" gives the document some temporal specificity—the vision the Charter puts forth has yet to be realized—and simultaneously assigns the text's community of speakers and readers the task of closing the gap between the inadequate present and the projected future. The anaphoric structure of the opening declarative statements gives the preamble a chantlike quality, building to the drama of the pledge itself. The remainder of the Charter will adumbrate what it would take for an inclusive, democratic national community to come into being in the future; but these opening lines indicate that this community already exists, at least insofar as it has come together to instantiate this vision in textual form. Like the Haitian Declaration of Independence, this text ends with an oath of solidarity and determination: "let all people who love their people and their country now say, as we say here: THESE FREEDOMS WE WILL FIGHT FOR, SIDE BY SIDE, UNTIL WE HAVE WON OUR LIBERTY." The collective voice re-emerges in this final call for a voluntary, spontaneous expression of solidarity. Performance is inscribed into the text itself: the Charter serves as proof of the alternative, "real" South African nation, that it also envisions. In its sleek, declarative iteration of an alternative ethical basis for political community, the text bears some resemblance to the equally pithy and ideal-driven Atlantic Charter. Matthews, who chaired the committee tasked with drafting "Africans' Claims" ten years earlier, would have had that text in mind. There is a sense, then, in which the Freedom Charter serves as the declarative answer to the ANC's 1943 response to the Atlantic Charter—a follow-up and a fulfillment of that critical close reading of Churchill and Roosevelt's vision for a new world order. In its insistence on national particularity—the assurance of the rights of all peoples within a single nation-state rather than on the world stage—it reinforces the observations of the authors of "Africans' Claims." In its embrace of an ethos of populist authorship, it responds to Xuma's call for Africans themselves to undertake the challenge of realizing these international ideals locally.

No longer asking but telling, the Freedom Charter in its final form indicates a new imagined audience: not the present-day government, but rather the community about and by whom the text itself was written—the nation currently unrepresented by the state, which is also the nation-state yet to come. The text's declarative subheadings announce the document's major tenets in a prophetic vein: "The People Shall Govern!" "All National Groups Shall Have Equal Rights!" "The People Shall Share in the Country's Wealth!" "The Land Shall Be Shared Among Those Who Work It!" "All Shall Be Equal Before the Law!" "All Shall Enjoy Human Rights!" "There Shall Be Work and Security!" "The Doors of Learning and Culture Shall Be Opened!" "There Shall Be Houses, Security and Comfort!" "There Shall Be Peace and Friendship!" These statements appear as the simple, straightforward, and impassioned articulation of a set of popular demands; importantly, however, they are put forth not as demands but as promises for the future. This textual feature, Paul Rich explains, was the result of a change made to the draft of the Charter within the Executive Committee assigned the task of producing the text at the close of the Congress of the People (COP) campaign; between its first and second draft, the document underwent an important shift in tense—from the subjunctive "should" to the future "shall"—which also marked an important shift in tone, an eradication of the earlier version's "traces of the presupposition that by reasonable persuasion and argument its just demands could be conceded by the existing state" (270). In transforming grievances and requests into promises and prophecies, the Charter collapses the distance between the people as petitioners and the people as sovereign granters of petitions. Even though the text assiduously avoids making explicit claims to sovereignty, its rhetorical structure works aggressively to establish the basis for a radically altered political order for the South Africa of the future.

The aspirational and prophetic features of the Freedom Charter distinguish it from a charter intended to constitute, and the text's evocative opener—"We, the People of South Africa, declare for all our country and the world to know"—suggests that we might do better to describe it as a declaration of independence. Yet it matches up somewhat imperfectly with that genre as well. The Charter comes quite close to declaring independence in its assertion that "no government can justly claim authority unless it is based on the will of all the people"—a claim that is utterly incompatible with the apartheid state and which thus tacitly leaves no alternative to a complete structural overhaul of the existing political system. On the other hand, it stops short of positing a direct challenge to state sovereignty. Serving as rhetorical proof of the existence of an alternative political community to the one offered legitimacy by the current government, the Charter presents a new political order for South Africa as a future inevitability. Capitalizing on the ambiguity of its juridico-political authority, the text declares ideological independence from the South African state.

The Charter has a similarly ambivalent relationship to the genre of the rights declaration. The text proclaims that South Africa's (dreamt of, demanded, and anticipated) future lies in the country's guarantee of a long and detailed list of human rights—including many "second- and third-generation" rights (to health, shelter, economic security and peace, for instance). At the same time, it departs from the structural conventions of that genre in some crucial ways. Its means of establishing the source of the rights it enumerates is markedly different from that of the 1948 Universal Declaration. That text opens by announcing that "the recognition of the inherent dignity and the equal and inalienable rights of all members of the human family is the foundation of freedom, justice and peace in the world" (UN General Assembly, Preamble). In contrast, the Freedom Charter's preamble puts forth a regionally specific claim about ownership, authority, and membership in a political community: "*South Africa* belongs to all who live in it, black and white" ("Freedom Charter"; emphasis mine). This preamble's more universal principle, "that no government can justly claim authority unless it is based on the will of all the people," follows from this fact but does not ground it. Just as "Africans' Claims" presented an implicit challenge to the purported globalism of the international community envisioned by the authors of the Atlantic Charter, so the Freedom Charter insists on a realization of its principles in a specific time and place. The rights and freedoms inscribed in the Freedom Charter are nationally, geographically, and historically situated; the claimants of those rights and freedoms identify themselves in a collective first-person voice in the first clause of the document; and the basis of achieving these rights lies in collective action, not in reliance on pre-existing structures of natural and international law: "we pledge ourselves to strive together, sparing neither strength nor courage, until the democratic changes here set out have been won."

Further, by presenting those rights as prizes to be attained *in the future,* the document acknowledges the ease with which the state has been able to ignore them in the present. The Freedom Charter unravels the conventionally tautological structure of the rights declaration. As Joseph Slaughter explains, this genre depends on tautology as a productive and necessary strategy of articulating those "self-evident truths" of Enlightenment natural rights discourse:

> Tautology delimits the margins of a culturally situated logos, signaling the site where culture-bound knowledge confronts its own limits and turns back on itself to produce the most concise and chiastic formulation of communally constitutive common sense: Human rights are the rights of humans, inalienability is inalienable, imprescriptibility cannot be prescribed, a person is a person. (78)

But it seems to me that such tautologies only work if the declaration in which those rights are inscribed collapses the distance between present entitlement and future attainment. The 1789 *Déclaration des droits de l'homme et du citoyen* and the 1948 Universal Declaration of Human Rights accomplish this through their reliance on the present tense, their assertion that the rights they enumerate already exist. With the exception of the Preamble, however, the Freedom Charter is written entirely in the future tense. The emphatic and unrelenting "shall" at the beginning of each sentence reminds its reader at every turn of the distance between the present and the political community that is still to come. Human rights are presented in this text in decidedly pragmatic terms; they are rights that, as Hannah Arendt had observed just a few years previously, depended on "the right to have rights" for their meaningful implementation (*Origins of Totalitarianism* 296).

As was the case with Haiti's founding texts, the Freedom Charter's appropriation and reworking of multiple juridico-political genres, and especially genres associated with an emergent canon of international law, is a powerfully subversive move in and of itself. The Charter's generic heterogeneity allows it to put forth a wide range of liberatory claims and goals without locking it into one particular program, as doing so would have not only put the organizers of the Congress at further risk of prosecution for treason but also curtailed the radical possibilities of the text, its ability to speak in multiple ways to multiple audiences. Appearing nine years after the UN Charter and seven years after the ratification of the Universal Declaration of Human Rights, and at the outset of a global resurgence of the genre of the written state constitution,[3] the Freedom Charter draws on all of these forms, while not actually claiming to replace or replicate any of them. Engaging law and its genres *from outside* law and its genres, this text raises, and proposes a challenging answer to, the question of who can claim authority over forms of juridico-political expression in the mid-twentieth century.

The vision of this heteroglossic text is postcolonial in its prophesying of a new world order in which political authority has been fundamentally reorganized in non-imperial terms. Within this world order, nation serves a new kind of strategic purpose, a means of concretizing a cosmopolitan, multiethnic political community in which human rights are secured while also insisting that the origin and authority of those rights are local and historically specific, not universal and abstract. The Freedom Charter thus takes part of the broader transatlantic critique from below of international law that I began tracing in chapter 3. Even as it invokes the language of international law in order to expose the moral disjuncture with the South African state, the Charter does not look to international law or to the international community for a solution. It does not seek recourse from the UN, nor does it uncritically adopt that institution's forms of juridico-political expression wholesale. Instead it appropriates not one but several of international law's textual forms and creatively, liberally adopts those forms in order to articulate a new, nation-based vision for the political future. This difference in strategy signals a new attitude toward the authority of international institutions. Whereas "Africans' Claims" addressed international powers (such as they were) directly, the Freedom Charter addresses itself to a local audience and delineates a local plan for seeking political (and social and economic) justice for South Africa. This text borrows from texts of international law without granting its institutions much authority. The Universal Declaration put forth a universalist vision that was woefully incapable of recognizing its own limitations, its Eurocentrism and complicity with the rising powers of a new postwar geopolitical order. The Freedom Charter, in contrast, manages to capitalize on the ethical and juridical force of those texts while steering clear of their problematic claims and aspirations to universal applicability.

HOW TO DO THINGS WITH TEXTS: THE CONGRESS OF THE PEOPLE CAMPAIGN AND THE PROBLEM OF PERFORMATIVE TRANSCENDENCE

The formal elements of the text tell only part of the story of the Freedom Charter's disruption to a mid-twentieth-century transnational juridico-political imagination. The text was after all the end product of a fifteen-month grassroots national campaign, one intended to create a new kind of political community that would transcend regional, racial, socioeconomic, and linguistic divides by turning "the people of South Africa" into the authors of a blueprint for the nation's political future. At the behest of Matthews, in early 1954 the

ANC partnered with the Communist Party, the Indian Council, the Coloured People Organisation, and the Congress of Democrats to form a National Action Council that would plan a Congress of the People. The Council developed a three-stage plan or the campaign: publicity, networking, and recruitment; the collection of demands and delegate elections; and, finally, a mass meeting at which the Freedom Charter, containing the people's demands for a new South Africa, would be presented and ratified. The collection of demands would take place through a national canvass, carried out by "shock brigades" of trained volunteers (Suttner and Cronin 13) who would elicit and collect the peoples' demands in small group meetings around the country; special effort was made to canvass in areas with weak histories of ANC membership and support (14). As Suttner and Cronin explain in their collection of retrospective accounts of the campaign, the Congress of the People (COP) "was not so much a single event but a series of meetings held in huge rallies, small houses, flats, street and factory meetings, gatherings in kraals and on farms" (12–13). It was the most ambitious interorganizational anti-apartheid initiative of the decade, an attempt to draw new people into a conversation about nationhood, political identity, and human rights on an unprecedented scale. It was an effort to develop a form of popular engagement that would stand directly and dramatically in contrast to the political machine of the South African state—a practical instantiation of what would *become* a theory of South African anticolonial resistance.

The COP campaign strove to cultivate a new political community out of the most marginalized sectors of South Africa's population through conversation, face-to-face meetings, and the organization of existing social networks. As such, it was meant to do a very different kind of work from the polished, finalized text of the Freedom Charter that was intended as its end product. The campaign aimed to create through performance the community that the text of the Charter would express as a given. If the text of the Freedom Charter manifests what Paul Gilroy calls a politics of fulfillment—a counterdiscourse that takes shape within modernity and "play[s] occidental rationality at its own game" (*Small Acts* 134), making use of language and text in order to call upon "bourgeois civil society [to live] up to the promises of its own rhetoric" (135), then the COP campaign, in contrast, put forth what he identifies as a politics of transfiguration, a more utopian project that marks "the emergence of qualitatively new desires, social relations and modes of association within the racial community of interpretation and resistance *and* between that group and its erstwhile oppressors" (134). In Gilroy's formulation, a politics of transfiguration abandons the semiotic and the verbal in favor of the mimetic and the performative; it is a politics that "exists on a lower frequency where it is played, danced and acted, as well as sung about, because words, even words stretched by melisma and supplemented or mutated by the screams which still index the conspicuous power of the slave sublime, will never be enough to communicate its unsayable claims to truth" (134). A politics of transfiguration thus redefines the sphere of the political, insisting on its inseparability from other aspects of life. "Its basic desire is to conjure up and enact the new modes of friendship, happiness and solidarity that are consequent on the overcoming of the racial oppression on which modernity and the duality of rational Western progress as excessive barbarity relied" (134–35). In its emphasis on individual encounters and exchanges, culminating in a mass meeting at Kliptown at which the nation encounters itself for the first time, the COP strove toward a politics of transfiguration—a means of exceeding Western logos and its capacity for violent exclusion through a utopian series of acts of in-person encounters designed to destabilize the legitimacy of the state as representative of South Africa's political community.

Yet for all the faith the COP placed in performativity—the live enactment of a political community, both during the weeks and months of canvassing and organizing and through the Kliptown meeting—texts as material objects played an integral role in legitimizing the authority of that culminating performance. The end goal of the campaign, after all, was and was always intended to be the ratification of a Freedom Charter. And the grassroots campaign leading up to that event depended largely on the dissemination and collection of texts—texts which were more ephemeral and less polished or emblematic, to be sure, but also exhibiting an unquestioned faith in the ability of verbal representation to facilitate new forms of political representation. The people's demands for the future of the country were recorded in writing by organizers and then sent back to the National Action Committee (NAC) for synthetic inclusion in the final version of the Charter. Moreover, leaflets and pamphlets were key to the process of organizing volunteers, publicizing the campaign to communities, and creating a shared sense of purpose among organizers at all levels in the months leading up to the Congress. These textual materials mimicked the campaign's oral exchanges for which they also provided a script, enabling the extension of the NAC's outreach beyond the official face-to-face meetings, and blurring the line between Gilroy's two categories of politics within a culture of black countermodernity. What do we make of texts that aspire to transcend their textual status, and of live performances intended to constitute community both through the immediacy of the experience and through their efforts to ratify that moment of live constituting in textual form? We might understand these questions as symptomatic of a quintessential anticolonial dilemma: how to reconcile the strategically, deliberately utopian impulse of the project of liberation with the no less urgent need to render that project legible in order to constitute the postcolony? The process through which the Freedom Charter was publicized, conceived, and drafted throws into relief the extent to which it and the COP campaign brought such questions to the fore in mid-twentieth-century South Africa.

An early and important iteration of the COP's utopian project appears in a widely distributed leaflet, the *Call to the Congress of the People,* which set the stylistic pattern for the Freedom Charter itself, featuring a call-and-response structure that establishes the Charter as a profoundly communal project: "We call the people of South Africa black and white—Let us speak together of freedom!" ("Call"). This opening invocation of racial inclusivity is followed by a list enumerating the groups of people by vocation to whom it is addressed: "The farmers of the reserves and trust lands"; "The miners of coal, gold and diamonds"; "The workers of farms and forests"; "The workers of factories and shops"; "The teachers, students and the preachers"; and, finally, "The housewives and the mothers." The stress on political inclusion in very specific terms, the naming of groups of constituents at whom the canvass is directed, indicates the need to take nothing for granted when it comes to identifying membership in a political community. Like "Africans' Claims," the *Call* exhibits a wariness about assuming universal applicability and inclusivity. Each constituency is named and acknowledged in its particularity; at the same time, each constituency resides on the page alongside other constituencies. Only together do they become legible as a nation. This text enacts the first step of creating a political community among farmers, miners, teachers, housewives simply by naming these groups alongside each other on the page.

If the first part of the *Call* serves to begin the work of constituting a new political community by naming the members of that community, then its final instructions remind its readers that this process of constituting is dynamic, not static—and that, having been constituted within this community, through the act of reading, they must now continue the work of enfranchising others. The COP campaign's leaflets' value lay partly in their potential to circulate in unexpected ways, fall into new hands, and extend the reach of the *Call* beyond the purview of volunteers and their routes. The final lines of the *Call* draw attention to the text as a text, insisting that its readers interact with its material form in order to translate its message into action. "Do not throw this leaflet away! Pass it on to a friend. Discuss it with others. See that it is read by many people." The leaflet assigns its readers ultimate responsibility for perpetuating the conversation, becoming both teachers and disseminators in the process of answering the *Call.* The leaflet itself gets recycled, thrown back into the system where it can continue its work as it reaches new and wider audiences. Well in advance of the Kliptown meeting, these informal campaign materials self-consciously aim to blur the lines between oral and written political discourse.

Orality, ephemerality, and immediacy were both vital practical tactics and central ideological tenets of the COP campaign. If the law of the South African state was rigid, fixed, and impenetrable by most of the people subject to it, then the "law" envisioned by the campaign was fluid and dynamic, participatory in the most radical sense. Indeed, the process of collecting the people's demands—their direct contributions to the drafting of the Freedom Charter—took on a life of its own, embodying the radically democratic spirit of the campaign precisely through its *dis*organization. The structure of the canvass fell apart on the ground. People often wrote out their demands on their own paper, ignoring the forms provided them by the canvassers. And local organizers developed new methods of getting people together to draft demands, such as holding "gala festival" meetings in order to drum up energy within local communities (Rich 266–67). This confluence of careful organization, on one hand—the National Action Council's ambitious plan for a comprehensive canvass with universal participation—and, on the other, the chaotic and infinitely creative process by which the people themselves responded to the campaign plays no small part in how the story of the Congress of the People has been told retrospectively. Here is Ismael Vadi's account of this process in the only existing full-length history of the Freedom Charter:

> On the eve of the Congress it was reported that for months now the demands had been flooding into the COP headquarters, on sheets torn from school exercise books, on little dog-eared scraps of paper, on slips torn from COP leaflets ... The demands were spontaneous and were "characterised by a moving simplicity." Whatever political content that they had stemmed from the direct experiences of oppression and exploitation that people had in the country of their birth. (148)

This romantic take on the "flooding" of popular demands reveals its own set of narrative investments, and many of the Freedom Charter's critics have viewed such accounts of the Congress's unmediated incorporation of the words and desires of "the people" with far more skepticism.[4] Not all communities were canvassed; not all demands were recorded, collected, and returned to the national office. And, of course, organizational leadership remained firmly in control of the process of editing and selecting among the materials it did receive. Critics have noted that the final draft of the Charter bore a striking resemblance to the document these leaders had in mind well before they solicited popular input.[5]

The nation-yet-to-come declared and described by the Freedom Charter was a founding fiction. As such, one of its most unique features was its foregrounding of a narrative of a series of face-to-face encounters in which ordinary South Africans were asked to imagine themselves as lawmakers. These encounters were numerous enough that they could be imagined as the cumulative expression, as opposed to representation, of a "national" desire. Abstraction and representation were of course fundamental to the imaginative construction of South African nationhood, no less so for the anti-apartheid movement than for the state; but the Freedom Charter invited its readers to imagine that South Africans had found an alternative model—that they had literalized the creation of "We, the people" through the COP campaign. My aim here is not to bolster the COP campaign's own romantic claims about this text and its creation. But I do want to register and reflect on the extent to which this project—in all of its utopianism—did represent an attempt to radically rethink the possibilities of popular mobilization through the circulation and exchange of political desires in textual form. This process was not only about looking ahead to the ratification of an immutable final textual product; the imperatives of saving, recirculating, and (thereby) legitimizing the Executive Committee's draft were meant to establish an ongoing nationwide popular discursive provocation, which was intended to be just as important an outcome of the campaign as the Congress and Freedom Charter themselves. The COP campaign and the Freedom Charter take on the challenge of critically reappraising the idea of abstract representation as a necessary and beneficial component of a democratic political system.

The mystery and mystique surrounding the identity of those who actually drafted the Charter became part of the romance of collective authorship that was so central to the text's radically democratic claims. In the days leading up to the Kliptown meeting, after the national canvass had ended and most of the demands had arrived at the COP headquarters,[6] a small committee met to draft the long-anticipated Charter. No complete list of the members of this drafting committee exists, nor were records of their work kept at the time. Only tenuously allowed the right to organizational existence, the ANC and other groups involved in planning the Congress were, by the early 1950s, quickly becoming used to exercising caution when it came to keeping written records of their activities. But the identity of the drafters of the Freedom Charter—or, rather, the difficulty we have in identifying those drafters today—also plays right into the text's romance of collective authorship. Nelson Mandela and Albert Luthuli were legally banned in early 1955. While both of these

ANC leaders reviewed the Charter once it was in its final form, neither was able to attend or participate in the drafting meetings.[7] The Freedom Charter has few named drafters and no named signatories; the leaders of the anti-apartheid struggle in the 1950s are notably absent from, or at least exist in the shadows of, the origin stories surrounding this text. Even if figureheads of the ANC and its partnering organizations were responsible for mobilizing the national campaign and lending crucial support to the Congress of the People (which they would also be officially unable to attend), they could not take credit for "authoring" the text itself in the same way that, for example, the Committee of Five could for the U.S. Declaration of Independence, or that Eleanor Roosevelt and her core drafting committee could for the Universal Declaration of Human Rights.

There are few authorial heroes in the narrative of the Freedom Charter's creation other than the South African people, and this shift away from individual heroism has direct consequences for the nature of the claim this text makes to political authority. As discussed in chapter 1, Haiti's Declaration of Independence and 1805 Constitution undertake significant rhetorical labor in order to close the gap between speaker and spoken-for, between the exclusivity of the drafting process and the texts' claims to embody the will and desires of the Haitian people. But the literal authors of Haiti's founding documents are not—and are not meant to be—commensurate with the symbolic persona of the "We" posited in the texts. Named signatories at the end of each are in palpable tension with the presentation of their claims to speak the truth of a *popular* will, a tension that is reconciled, in the Constitution, by its establishment of a representative (though hardly democratic) governmental structure. No such tension plagues the South African Freedom Charter. Mass authorship—the voicing of demands from South Africans of all colors and classes—is meant to do the same kind of work that revolutionary war did for Haiti; it is meant to authorize the text as product *and* property of "the people," the entity it also brings into existence on paper. The absence of named signatories at the end of the document works to reinforce that authorization.

This shift in focus away from organizational leadership was replicated, once again partly out of necessity, during the mass meeting at Kliptown. The meeting was held over the course of two days in a large open square in Kliptown, a Soweto suburb just outside of Johannesburg. Nearly three thousand delegates, elected and financially sponsored by their local communities, traveled from across the country to attend; police harassment prevented many more from completing the journey. Beginning the morning of June 25, 1955, the meeting featured speeches, prayers, songs, and the reading out of prepared remarks by Luthuli and other absent leaders of the sponsoring organizations.

Each clause of the Charter was read aloud, and delegates were invited to come to the stage and offer remarks before it was formally adopted by means of a hand vote. Toward the end of the second day of the meeting—and importantly, only after the Charter had been read aloud and adopted in its entirety—the police, who had been observing the proceedings from the periphery, broke up the Congress, threatened all attendees with arrest, and confiscated all written materials related to the Charter and the COP campaign.

The thousands of people in attendance contributed to the COP's impressive visual display of national inclusivity. Yet the conspicuous absence of many key organizers and political leaders was also a constitutive feature of the proceedings. Albert Luthuli had been scheduled to give the opening address, but had been recently banned. Mandela, also banned at the time, could only sneak into the meeting in disguise and listen to the proceedings as a member of the crowd. Organizational leaders who did speak drew attention to the fact that many of the key organizers and leaders of the anti-apartheid movement were not there. Acting ANC president Robert Resha, for instance, argued that the Charter itself—its successful creation and ratification—rendered the state's deterrence of many leaders and delegates from coming to Kliptown essentially meaningless:

> Every Native section of the population is represented here. We have 2186 African delegates, 320 Indian delegates, 230 Coloured delegates, 112 European delegates, 721 women. Some were voiceless by the actions of the police, they were prevented from coming to the conference, their demands are here before us. Even though they are not here their voices will be heard. The Charter will have a greater support than any other document that has ever been drawn up. ("Transcript")

The speakers at Kliptown posited the collective voice formulated at—and through—the meeting itself as an inclusive surrogate for both the South African people at large and the individuals who were specifically prevented from attending. Just as the individual identities and personalities of organizational leaders did not play a central role in the Charter's composition (or at least in the narrative about its composition that developed after the fact), so the populist spirit of the COP was reinforced by the absence of organizational figureheads such as Luthuli and Mandela, who—like everyone else—had to rely on the Congress delegates to represent them and their interests at Kliptown.

The Kliptown meeting was a live staging of the experience of democratic participation that the COP campaign had been meant to facilitate across the country. One attendee put the estimated number of attendees at Kliptown at seven thousand, commenting: "This was certainly the most representative gathering there has ever been in South Africa. It was a real people's parliament, with one difference. It was not, of course, sovereign" (Suttner and Cronin 86–87). That lack of sovereignty was the reason a performance was necessary at all. The Kliptown meeting derived its political authority from its extralegality, and its extralegality demanded an enactment of that authority—a spectacle of democratic community formation. It was a performance in which all members of the audience took part (in some cases, as I explain below, incidentally and involuntarily) and one that proved that the real work of the COP campaign had already been accomplished. Kliptown was the tangible manifestation of a popular will that the campaign had both uncovered and helped to develop. The COP delegates' official task was to ratify the Charter by reading it aloud, discussing its contents, and putting each section of it to a vote. But the text of the document was already in its final form by the morning of June 25; neither the organizers nor the delegates anticipated that changes would be made to it at that point. Moreover, while the Congress was a spectacular occasion of democratic participation, the more fundamental democratic events had presumably already taken place during the canvass; "the people" had already spoken by voicing their demands at the grassroots level. The COP delegates, then, are better understood as *rereaders*, revoicers of previous speech-acts conducted by "the People of South Africa" whose desires the text was meant to encapsulate. The text of the Charter did not present the rights it posited for a future South Africa as inherent or inalienable, only in need of iteration and recognition in textual form. And yet by the time the document was read aloud at Kliptown, the rights and freedoms enumerated in that text *enjoyed the status of* inevitability because of the process through which they came to be articulated. At the COP meeting, the contents of the text were in need not of iteration but of *reiteration* in the form of public reading, discussion, and ratification. The Charter's performance in an open forum generated no new material, but sanctified the text, and provided live confirmation of the existence and passion of its nation of authors. "This ground on which we are standing here today is holy, friends," Resha declared to the Congress in his closing remarks ("Transcript"). The Kliptown meeting was a re-enactment, but it was a re-enactment with the weight of consecration.

Delegates and supporters of the anti-apartheid movement participated in the spectacle of representation at the COP, but they were not the only participants at the meeting, nor in the performance of authorization that was taking place at it. Though they only disrupted the proceedings toward the end of the second day, the police were also in attendance at Kliptown, observing it in its entirety from the periphery of the square. They broke up the proceedings only after the Charter had been fully ratified—a move the state believed would later allow the document to be subjected to a legal challenge (Suttner and Cronin 103). But standing on the edge of the proceedings for nearly two full days also put the police in the peculiar position of participating in the meeting—as witnesses. Indeed, the most extensive transcript of the proceedings of the COP that still exists was recorded by Detective Sargeant Van Zil Schoeman and submitted as evidence state in the Treason Trial a few years later. Two competing performances thus occurred simultaneously at Kliptown: that of the police, who were there to put on their own show, dressed in military garb and fully armed, and that of the delegates, ostensibly addressing one another but also, by necessity, speaking to the state authorities in attendance on the periphery. Chief Luthuli had—as a formality—invited the state to send its own delegates to the meeting; the police presence served as an ironic acceptance of that invitation. Accepting an award for his activism early on the first day of the meeting, Father Trevor Huddleston acknowledged the police in similar terms: "The Minister of Justice is very well represented here in the background and I hope they have a happy afternoon to see if they can spot some of their friends in this large gathering" ("Transcript"). Instead of creating a spectacle of intimidation, the police were incorporated into this other piece of theater, serving as witnesses to the Charter's ratification. In his autobiography, Mandela recounts the pedagogical value he found in engaging his prison guards in conversation during his long tenure on Robben Island (*Long Walk to Freedom* 418). The police's unwitting participation in the performance of the Freedom Charter's ratification in Kliptown similarly draws the state into this project of nation-making despite itself, demanding that it bear witness and proving the document's applicability to all South Africans, black and white.

THE CONGRESS OF the People offers up a wholesale refutation of the abstractions and obfuscations around which the First World international community constructed its key midcentury texts and institutions—its Kantian cosmopolitanism that erased the problem of power inequalities among the constituents of this new world order. Eschewing that model by imagining political community as constituted through live performance, the Congress and the Freedom Charter also foreground the South African nation as the political community to whom the tenets of the Charter are meant to apply. This text's embrace of the nation as the site of the postcolonial community yet to come counters an international system of colonialism and empire that aspires to global inclusivity but in fact works to uphold the systems of colonialism and empire that create unequal access to its promises of security, peace, and justice.

Yet what is most striking to me about the Freedom Charter is the way in which it enters into critical conversation with both international *and* national legal imaginaries. The colonialist South African state—including but not limited to the current apartheid government—had long defined the peoples living within its borders in terms of separate nations. Indeed, the whole idea of homelands was premised on the theory that Africans' tribal affiliations should and did overshadow any allegiance they might have to the state. The Freedom Charter, in contrast, insists that all of South Africa's peoples hold an equal stake in the idea of the nation. With all the irony of its complicities with both old and new forms of global empire, the UN serves in this sense as a model for the Congress of the People, in which regional delegates as well as a large number of organizations participated in a forum designed to emphasize unity within diversity, a common cause among peoples who had long been told to think of themselves and their concerns in isolation from one another.

This chapter and the previous one have focused on black Atlantic texts whose anticolonial vision emerges through their engagement with the discourses and institutions of mid-twentieth-century international law. Both Césaire's *Cahier* and the Freedom Charter take ethical inspiration from the global liberalism of the UN Charter and the universalist assumptions underpinning the Universal Declaration of Human Rights, while also subjecting those ideals to rigorous critique. These texts indicate the diversity of genres and platforms through which juridico-political authority is interrogated in the anticolonial black Atlantic world in the mid-twentieth century. Further, Césaire's and the Congress of the People's critical engagements with First World internationalism demonstrate that national liberation was only one component of a much larger anticolonial project. International and state legal institutions and norms develop in tandem in the late twentieth century—and anticolonial thinkers are aware of these interconnections. They take stock of how the norms governing the creation of new nation-states and the norms emanating from international institutions are part of one and the same juridico-political order—an order that has its uses as well as its problems. Anticolonial engagement with First World law is never merely a matter of acceptance or rejection; it is strategic and highly attuned to the ways in which the postcolonial community yet to come will have to negotiate national as well as international frames for imagining political belonging and community.

In my next chapter I turn to texts that, ostensibly at least, focus more narrowly on the possibilities of *national* political community on the eve of independence. But the forms in which they do so—especially the novel and the written state constitution—are unquestionably global forms by the late twentieth century, and the provocation they stage to a First World juridico-political imagination resonates, and is intended to resonate, transnationally. In my final chapter I return to a more explicit discussion of the links between two postcolonial essayists and universal human rights discourse in the final decades of the late twentieth century—a moment by which, supposedly, the dream of the postcolonial nation-state as the site of liberatory political community had become a thing of the past. But it is the continuity between these national and international spheres of anticolonial engagement with the idea of law that strike me as having much more to tell us about the capaciousness and ambition of the anticolonial project writ large.

CHAPTER 5

Novel Constitutions

The Genres of African Decolonization

> Forgetting, I would even go so far as to say historical error, is a crucial factor in the creation of a nation, which is why progress in historical studies often constitutes a danger for [the principle of] nationality. Indeed, historical enquiry brings to light deeds of violence which took place at the origin of all political formations, even of those whose consequences have been altogether beneficial. Unity is always effected by means of brutality.
>
> —Ernest Renan, "What Is a Nation?"

IN THE FALL of 1963 Jomo Kenyatta traveled to London to take part in the final stages of drafting Kenya's independence constitution, the legal text that would formalize the end of over seventy years of colonial rule and establish Kenya's national sovereignty. The figurehead of Kenya's liberation struggle and the newly elected prime minister, Kenyatta was one of a small number of Africans involved directly in planning the legal structure of the nation-state to come. In two public addresses in Nairobi, delivered just before and after his trip to England, he explained the significance of the constitution to an audience of Kenya's soon-to-be citizens. Both speeches tout the constitution as the culmination of a long process of negotiations among well-intentioned parties, and both reveal a fair amount of anxiety that ethnic and class-based fissures within the country itself will undermine the authority of the nation's future leadership. Before his departure for London, Kenyatta's words call for patience as the countdown to independence begins:

> I wish to take this opportunity to appeal to all the people of Kenya to keep calm and maintain the peace. The new era that Kenya will enter as an Independent nation—in the spirit of "harambee"—in December, is one which will call for dedication, hard work and unity. This is the challenge of the future. (Kenyatta 13)

Returning a month later, Kenyatta reported on the successful conclusion of the London talks, and confirmed December 12 as the official date for independence—also the date on which the final version of the Constitution would itself arrive in Kenya and be presented to him at the Uhuru ceremonies. Kenyatta's post-London account of the country's progress toward legal independence is accompanied again by an injunction for Kenyans to focus their energies on cultivating unity and solidarity. In language that echoes Ernest Renan's famous thesis about nationhood and memory, the prime minister ties legal independence to a project of willed collective amnesia: "I invite the Opposition leaders to forget the past and come together with us to form a united front to fight our real enemies—poverty, ignorance and disease," for "I see no shame in forgetting the past" if doing so will help bring about a unified postcolony in the future (14–15).

Of course, Kenyatta was counting on his audience to know exactly which "past" he was asking them to forget: a decade of popular uprisings against colonial rule; the colonial government's response in the form of a declaration of a state of emergency, during which 150,000 Gikuyu men were held in detention camps for six years (David Anderson 5); and a widespread, though never centrally organized, guerrilla struggle (dubbed the "Mau Mau Rebellion" by the British) in which—contrary to depictions in Western media—most of the violence occurred among Africans.[1] Fissures between loyalists and freedom fighters, as well as among Kenya's numerous ethnic and cultural groups, remained palpable well after the end of colonial rule was in sight. But the former freedom fighters in particular had cause to be skeptical of Kenyatta's call for reconciliation and forgetting in the moment of the formation of the new sovereign state: they knew they were being asked to let go not only of violence and discord, but also of some of their most basic demands for the undoing of colonialism's brutal dispossessions of land and resources. Kenyatta and other members of the former colonized elites would benefit from the economic legacies of colonialism after independence; the majority of Kenya's future citizens would not.

The kind of authority that Kenyatta claims in these two speeches clearly positions him in relation to this same past he wants badly for the new nation to put out of its mind. Kenyatta presents himself first and foremost as an emissary, charged with conveying the concerns and desires of the Kenyan people to the Constitutional Conference, but he also insists on his role as constitutional author: he is a member of the elite cadre of drafters who will participate in the creation of the country's founding legal text. These speeches, moreover, are intended to frame, translate, and summarize the essence of the new law to a lay audience. Detailed, technical, drily worded and laboriously long (at over a hundred and fifty pages), the Independence Constitution was never intended to circulate widely. To those who did read the text, its meaning derived from its technical precision regarding the legal organization and administration of the country; its meaning for those who did not read it depended on its symbolic value within a broader discourse of postcolonial nationhood—a discourse of which Kenyatta's public addresses played an important part. Kenyatta's claims to these two very distinct kinds of authorship contribute, in these speeches, to his ability to identify the kinds of memories that will constitute the new nation. But more to the point, his constitutive authority empowers him to designate the kinds of memories that must be left out as Kenya looks ahead to its postcolonial future. The recent and traumatic anticolonial past is here cut off from the current project of state-building, a project that will take place far away and out of sync with the Nairobi in which Kenyatta speaks. The Constitutional Conference, in fact, is meant to stand in for and indeed even replace revolutionary action, leaving the responsibility for the final steps of decolonization in the hands of a chosen few rather than with the people themselves. Kenyatta's speeches are constitutive performances, speech acts through which the political community of the new nation-state is imagined and declared—and through which the speaker/constituter places definitive limits on the project of national liberation.

Thus even as these public performances seem to fetishize the written state constitution and bolster the notion of postcolonial law as a hermetic and elite, they reveal that the process of constituting this newly independent African nation-state was in fact porous and discursively complex. While state officials staked their claim to constitutive authority via the imaginative potency of law, the new nation in fact came into being as both a lived reality and an idealized concept through a range of rhetorical forms. This chapter argues that decolonization is a process characterized by multiple, sometimes incommensurate or even antagonistic, attempts to constitute the postcolony through language. Taking Kenya as my central example, but drawing as well on key texts associated with the decolonization of another settler colony, Algeria, I explore the staging of dramatic postcolonial African constitutive moments across a wide variety of genres. Extralegal constitutive forms such as fiction point to, and recuperate, subjectivities and visions of postcolonial community that the state leaves out or even works to obliterate.[2] Yet I also seek to challenge the way in which postcolonial criticism and theory generally tends to position law and legal texts in relation to the literature of decolonization. In the years surrounding African independence, legal texts were themselves—among other things—sites of innovation and experimentation. African decolonization is largely responsible for the explosion of the written constitution into a global genre in the 1960s and '70s; and Africa's independence constitutions are characterized by a fascinating range of formal experiments that represent efforts to transform the genre into one well suited to the specificity of the continent's postcolonial condition. These constitutions are often read as failures, when in fact this first generation of postcolonial legal texts innovatively redefines the generic contours of the state constitution. The genres I discuss here, legal and extralegal, serve as vital correctives to a postcolonial juridico-political structure that proved neither long-lasting nor able to account for or transform the economic and political legacies of decades of colonial rule. Yet these genres are not completely disillusioned with the romance of legal independence, or with the possibilities of constituting a new political order that more fully embodies the radical aims of the liberation struggle. Rather, they develop and enact alternative concepts of what it means to constitute postcolonial political community.

What all of decolonization's forms have in common is a preoccupation with performative context. While not all of these forms are equally successful, and while each has different audiences and aims, they all conceive of constituting first and foremost as an event, a speech act tied closely to the process of revolutionary political change. The texts I examine in this chapter work to instantiate national political community amid the tumult of revolution, whose endpoint is difficult to determine and in some sense feared—for should it arrive too soon, or on the wrong terms, it will introduce a new political order that threatens to foreclose national liberation's radical anticolonial potential. The antidote to this threat, as evidenced across multiple genres of African decolonization, lies in conceiving of the act of constituting as profoundly performative. That investment in performance is central to my critical approach to Kenya and Algeria's state constitutions, Mau Mau loyalty oaths, Frantz Fanon's *Wretched of the Earth,* and Ngũgĩ wa Thiong'o's *A Grain of Wheat.* Far from naive, though often romantic, in their assessment of decolonization and its aftermath, these texts insist that the constitution of postcolonial political community is a multifarious process that neither abandons the idea of law nor reifies it. Created in a moment in which "the state" and "the people" were still often imagined as commensurate, these texts of African decolonization are not simply relics of a bygone anticolonial past but rather vital components of a long genealogy of critical anticolonial thought whose implications extend well into the postcolonial present.

AFRICAN DECOLONIZATION AND CONSTITUTIONAL NOVELTY

In the twenty-first century, the legal texts that formalized national independence in Africa are often viewed as emblems of postcolonial failure. Postcolonial constitutions signal the shortcomings of political independence, the ascent of the neocolonial state, and the onset of an era in African history of "constitutions without constitutionalism" (Okoth-Ogendo). Moreover, very few of Africa's "independence constitutions"—that is, the very first constitutions that transferred sovereignty from colonial powers to Africans—lasted long in their original form. Whatever changes these texts enacted in the legal structure of the former colonies, their short-lived legal currency undercut their ability to have lasting effects in postcolonial African society.

It is easy, therefore, to lose sight of the extent to which independence constitutions really did mark a meaningful departure from Western and colonial law by reworking some of the most basic conventions governing what a constitution is and what it should do. African constitution-making in the 1960s was one trajectory in a broader historical narrative of the proliferation of the written state constitution in the decades following World War II. Once considered exclusively the province of North Atlantic nation-states, and more recently devalued by interwar failures such as the Versailles Treaty and the Weimar Constitution, in the late twentieth century the written constitution fast became the genre that bestowed legal and political legitimacy on the sovereign states of the globe's newly decolonized regions (Ackerman). But the reasons for this revived investment in the constitution *as a text* during decolonization are not self-evident. Postcolonial constitutions, Julian Go observes, are "remarkable in the sense that constitutions are not logically necessary. That is, there is no immediately necessary connection between having an independent state and writing a single-document constitution. A constitution does not *have* to exist in written form, neither does it have to be issued in a single document" (72). What, then, prompted the popularity of the written constitution among newly sovereign nation-states in Africa, South Asia, and the Caribbean?

In some ways, the stakes of textuality for late-twentieth-century decolonization were similar to the stakes faced by Haiti in the early 1800s. In both cases, the written constitution presented an opportunity to critically and creatively engage with First World law. Like post-revolutionary Haiti, newly decolonized African countries borrowed from but also challenged the conventions of Western legal genres as well as the imaginative scope of law and its relationship to the nation-state with which those genres were associated. The thirty-six African state constitutions that held legal currency in 1964 are diverse in terms of length, structure, ideological orientation, and ways of narrating—or choosing not to narrate—a national history or cultural identity within the space of the text.[3] Several African (and Asian) nations experimented with socialist constitutional models, conceiving of the text as a space for the articulation of the ideological origins and basis for the postcolonial future.⁴ Even the Westminster model that many of the former British colonies adopted—the model which would garner quick criticism domestically for its Eurocentrism—was, of course, not actually a "model" from Britain at all (since Britain has no written constitution) and in fact signaled an important shift from the structures of colonial rule: in their call for parliamentarism, these constitutions abandoned the model of centralized, executive power that had grounded the colonial state.

A comparative overview of Kenya and Algeria's 1963 constitutions illustrates the range of styles, formal features, and philosophical underpinnings at work in Africa's independence constitutions. Kenya's is by far the longest African constitution in existence as of 1963: it occupies 168 pages in the 1965 edition of Amos Peaslee's *Constitutions of Nations*. Not one of those 168 pages is devoted to a preamble. Two opening chapters—which span thirty articles and twenty-five pages—lay out the basis of citizenship (including generous and flexible citizenship provisions for European and Indian residents) and basic rights; because these chapters are concerned with the question of what it means to be Kenyan rather than with the structural procedural features of the new government (the preoccupation of the remaining 143 pages), they comprise the portions of the document that most explicitly speak to national identity. But the constitution's front-ending of citizenship and rights is also the *only* way in which it defines Kenya as a people (the phrase "the people" never appears in the text), and this definition takes place in nonnarrative form. The document's avoidance of a narrative voice and emphasis on technical detail are features that owe much to the kinds of internal tensions signaled in Kenyatta's speeches, and specifically to the split between the Luo- and Gikuyu-dominated Kenya African National Union—until 1963, the only Kenyan political party—and the Kenya African Democratic Union, which claimed to advocate for the rights and interests of the region's smaller ethnic groups. Yash Ghai and Patrick McAuslan identify the 1963 Constitution's excess of detail as a symptom of confusion and nervousness, among the drafters, over how to deal with the controversial issues of minority protection, regional versus central control, and land distribution; length, they assert, correlates in this text to the tenuous and fraught nature of the negotiations over a constitution whose deadline, by 1963, was no longer flexible (197, 210). The document presented to Kenyatta by the Duke of Edinburgh at the 12 December Uhuru ceremonies, a document which Kenyatta held up to the crowd to applause, was, by all accounts, a legal mess—and would be superseded by a new constitution within twelve months.

Algeria's first constitution, by contrast, is one of Africa's shortest constitutions as of 1964, and epitomizes the postcolonial constitution's experimentation with a distinctly socialist version of the genre. In a sweeping historical narrative put forth in the first paragraphs of a dramatic and lengthy preamble, the text locates the origins of Algeria's new legal order in the violence of a resistance movement born at the same moment as the inception of colonial rule:

> The Algerian people have waged an unceasing armed, moral and political struggle against the invader and all his forms of oppression, for more than a century following the aggression of 1830 against the Algerian State and the occupation of the country by French colonial forces.
>
> On November 1, 1954, the National Liberation Front called for the mobilization of all the energies of the nation, since the battle for the independence had reached its final phase of realization.
>
> The war of extermination waged by French imperialism was intensified and more than a million martyrs paid with their lives for the love of their country and liberty.
>
> In March 1962 the Algerian people emerged victorious from the seven and a half year's struggle waged by the National Liberation Front.
>
> Upon recovering its sovereignty, after a hundred and thirty two years of colonial domination and a feudal regime, Algeria has given itself new national political institutions. (Peaslee 6)

The preamble identifies the constitution as the culmination of Algeria's revolutionary struggle in these opening lines, but then goes on to issue a call for the continuation of that struggle: "the Algerian people will continue its march toward a democratic and popular revolution" through the program of social economic and development that the text charges the National Liberation Front to carry forth in the new country (6). Algeria's postcolonial future is presented here as an organic and necessary extension of its colonial past, as well as of its national past which the Constitution identifies as *preceding* colonialism— France's 1830 occupation is characterized as an act of war against an already-existent sovereign Algeria. Written and ratified in Algeria, and without the participation of France, this constitution lays claim to indigenous nationalism in both its drafting process and its content, which contrast starkly with the literal and figurative importation of the Kenyan text.

Stylistically, then, Kenya and Algeria's 1963 texts demarcate opposite ends of the spectrum of African independence constitutions, from the meticulously technical to the ideological and poetic. At the same time, both texts were also products of a hermetic and carefully managed drafting process. The generic origins of the written constitution were understood, by the creators of the independence constitutions, to be Western. Whereas the colonial state strove, earlier in the century, to "locate" (which usually meant "create") indigenous sources of legitimacy for the legal structures of indirect rule, by the 1960s all participants in the drafting of independence constitutions took for granted that there were no local precedents for the legal text that would confer political sovereignty on new African nation-states.[5] Indeed, colonial constitutions had been in place in most of Africa for well over a decade, implemented as a means of establishing at least a nominal measure of representative government in the face of intensified anticolonial struggles as well as international support for nations' rights to self-determination in the wake of World War II. While members of Africa's political elites like Kenyatta participated in the drafting and ratification of the legal instruments of independence, those instruments ultimately had to be approved by colonial officials who, of course, had yet to formally cede power to African leaders. Moreover, there was no meaningful participation in the process by the African people at large, who were assumed to be both uninterested in and unable to understand constitution-making.[6] Newly independent countries adopted many of the trappings of parliamentarianism, representative democracy, and civil and human rights; but these changes had little impact on the lived experience of most of the nations' new citizens, and in fact served largely to perpetuate the structural features of indirect rule that colonialism had set in place. Decolonization-era African constitutions were mired in multiple paradoxes. They were at once overloaded with significance and devoid of value. They were intended to implement democratic structures of rule in the new nation-states, but were created with very little input or participation from the majority of the citizenry of Africa's new nation-states.

For legal historians and political theorists, however, the most significant shortcoming of Africa's independence constitutions is their ephemerality. Both Kenya and Algeria's first postcolonial constitutions were discarded and replaced with new, dramatically different constitutions within a short period of time (one year for Kenya, three for Algeria); in this respect, both texts are typical of the history of constitutionalism across Africa as well as other postcolonies around the globe in the wake of decolonization.[7] Regime changes account for some of the rapid constitutional turnover that took place in the 1960s and '70s, but scholars' more pervasive explanation has pointed to new governments' discomfort with a post-independence legal code that was designed and drafted so extensively by the former colonial powers. Africa did not take long after independence to start looking for constitutional forms better suited to the continent. This version of the story grants postcolonial lawmakers at least some integrity, acknowledging—importantly, I believe— African constitution-making as part of the broader process of negotiating new realities in the wake of decolonization. A more skeptical assessment of independence constitutions argue that these documents did little more than "provide a fig leaf of popular legitimation for illegally acquired power, or . . . symbols of the political authenticity of particular régimes" (Le Vine 188). In this reading, the short shelf lives of so many independence constitutions is a testament to the devaluation of the rule of law in the postcolony, a symptom of a broader trend toward the failure of the African state in the late twentieth century. This version of the story situates African constitutionalism within a broader narrative of Afro-pessimism (Mamdani 287), echoing the narrative framing of Haiti's post-revolutionary history—from the early 1800s to the present—that I discuss in chapter 1. And for the same reasons that I find that sort of framing of Haiti's constitutional history unsatisfying, I want to trouble such interpretations of African constitutional history in favor of examining what the significance of Africa's earliest constitutions *was* rather than focusing on what it was not. Ephemerality, in other words, does not have to be interpreted only as failure.

In an early account of Africa's colonial and postcolonial constitutional history, Yash Ghai proposes some ways out of an overdetermined evaluation of the "failure" of the textual turbulence of postcolonial law. He notes, for example, that even if state leaders did claim to overturn their countries' independence constitutions in order to replace colonial forms and structures with indigenous ones, the next generation of African constitutions does not suggest that they succeeded in doing so. African political leaders cited a return to traditional African law as the reason for constitutional revision and reform, but the content of the constitutions themselves did not match the rhetoric. The real changes, Ghai asserts, took place beyond the texts themselves, as charismatic individual leaders amassed more power within the political system; the authority to rewrite and replace the constitution in this sense came to matter more than the contents of the text (417). Further, Ghai urges his readers to re-examine their expectations for the temporal longevity of constitutions. Citing the autocratic and arbitrary nature of colonial law, he notes that "if we apply a rather orthodox definition of the constitutional order . . . one will have to conclude that there was no constitutional order under the colonial regime" either (406), and indeed the final years of the colonial era—a flurry of constitutional revisions and amendments—had at least as tempestuous a legal history as the post-independence era. We need, he insists, to get rid of "the notion of permanence of a particular constitutional document" (405), a notion that ultimately prevents us from understanding the important work that the short-lived independence constitutions *did* accomplish: the work of achieving independence (432).

To evaluate independence constitutions not according to their longevity or durability but rather according to their intervention at a particular moment in time is to recognize that constitutions are performative texts, with concerns and audiences that do not easily translate into the postcolonial future. From this perspectives, what might the first postcolonial Kenyan and Algerian constitutions reveal about their moment of articulation—and, more broadly, about the meaning of constitution-making during decolonization? Though their strategies for doing so are drastically different, both texts are invested in defining a national past, the role it will play in the new nation-state, and what it means to claim postcolonial authority over that past. Algeria, on one hand, foregrounds a national history in its preamble, but in so doing also circumscribes the scope and meaning of that history in ways that serve the interests of the postcolony's centralized leadership: Algerian independence and the National Liberation Front are inseparable by the end of the preamble. Kenya's constitution, which eschews not only any explicit historical narrative but also the past tense, erases the pre-independence past completely, and in so doing carries out the kind of forgetting-through-silencing that Kenyatta calls for in his public addresses. Further, both of these texts—though in quite disparate ways—register historical trauma. Both are born of violent struggles. Both try and work through those events, Kenya by painstakingly charting a course for a nation-state that will protect minorities and distribute power regionally, Algeria by rehearsing the revolutionary struggle in the preamble and assigning it a continuing role in the nation's present. In both cases, the constitutions' "nervous conditions" are evident in the lengths the texts go to in order to avoid and iron out aspects of the colonial past that challenge the present with troubling ambiguity.

Africa's independence constitutions engage directly and creatively with the problems of translating the anticolonial past into a viable and liberatory postcolonial future. They do so, in part, by offering up alternatives to the First World's generic conventions for the written state constitution. We of course need to be mindful of the ways in which these texts set in place authoritarian and short-lived political orders whose terms were most favorable to the countries' former colonial rulers. But we shortchange these texts, and impoverish our own sense of complexity and creativity of the moment of legal decolonization, if we do not also recognize them as active participants in the project of instantiating postcolonial through formal innovation in the mid-twentieth century.

THE CONSTITUTIONAL COUNTERDISCOURSE OF MAU MAU

What the bulky, bureaucratic text of Kenya's 1963 Constitution leaves out—the historical trauma that it cannot name but to which it nonetheless responds, if only through its silences—is the "Mau Mau" liberation struggle of the 1950s, an armed uprising against the colonial government and its supporters conducted by a loosely organized group of fighters, dubbed terrorists by colonial officials and the press, who fled to and operated out of the forests. The colonial government's response to Mau Mau was sweeping and violent: in 1952 a state of emergency was declared, and a number of national liberation leaders including Kenyatta—most of whom had nothing to do with the armed insurgency—were arrested. The 1956 trial and execution of Dedan Kimathi, a Mau Mau leader, effectively brought the resistance movement to an end, though the Emergency was not officially over until 1959. Around two hundred white settlers and British police died during the rebellion; between 12,000 and 20,000 Africans were killed, most at the hands of other Africans (D. Anderson 4).

Mau Mau haunts constitutionalism in postcolonial Kenya in two ways. First, it serves as the event that cannot be named or assimilated into the official narrative of nationhood; it is the liberation project that exists in excess of the formation of a new state. But it also serves as a discursive alternative to that narrative. Colonial and European depictions of Mau Mau figured the movement as a surge of barbaric and irrational violence, a primal force that existed only in excess of institutions of law and order. In fact, however—and despite the movement's lack of centralized organization or leadership—by the early 1950s Mau Mau had a quasi-legal structure of its own, one that developed in response to the colonial state's ever-growing privileging of the written constitution. Mau Mau oath-taking served as a powerful alternative to, and challenge to the legitimacy of, the forms of constituting that were taking shape within the colonial legal system. This challenge continued, albeit in new contexts, after Kenya's independence: while Kenyatta's government would perpetuate British colonialism's fetishization of the written constitution in the 1960s, the Mau Mau oath enjoyed an important afterlife in popular memory and written memoirs in postcolonial Kenya—an afterlife that celebrated nonstatist bases for loyalty, solidarity, and collective action.

Drawing in part from Gikuyu rite-of-passage traditions as well from decades-old practices within Kenya's anticolonial movement,[8] the Mau Mau oath was symbolically significant to colonialists, loyalists, and freedom fighters alike as a speech act of resistive solidarity. Supporters of the freedom struggle first took a loyalty oath, *muma wa chuba,* which bound them to others in the movement in general (but rhetorically powerful) terms; the second oath, *batuni,* bound its takers to active military service, and specifically to be willing to kill for the cause.[9] The oaths were, of course, oral forms; their exact language varied, and they were only recorded and circulated as written texts a decade after the Mau Mau struggle had come to an end. Mwangi Kariuki and Waruhiu Itote's transcriptions, from their 1963 and 1967 memoirs, reflect the variation among written versions of the *batuni* oath:

Mwangi Kariuki, *Mau Mau Detainee*:

1.
I speak the truth and vow before our God
And by this *Batuni* oath of our movement
Which is called the movement of fighting
That if I am called on to kill for our soil
If I am called on to shed my blood for it
I shall obey and I shall never surrender
And if I fail to go
    May this oath kill me,
    May this he-goat kill me,
    May this seven kill me,
    May this meat kill me.

2.
I speak the truth and vow before our God
And before our people of Africa
That I shall never betray our country
That I shall never betray anybody of this movement to the enemy
I shall go forth without fear and I shall never surrender

Waruhiu Itote, *"Mau Mau" General*:

I swear in truth before God and this Council that I will obey the laws of the Council and will be a steadfast soldier who will obey the Council's and the commander's orders. If I disobey or fail to fulfil any commission, let this meat turn against me and let my legs be fractured.

I swear that if I become a commander I will judge all cases fairly, without fear or favour to any person, whether friend or relative. (Again, he bit and swallowed the meat.)

I swear that I will never forget our people, our women and children, or those killed in the forest or in Government camps. If ever I refuse to help them when I am able to do so, or if I forget them, let this meat turn against me;

> And if I fail to do this
> May this oath kill me, etc.
> (Kariuki 29)

> I swear to give my life as a sacrifice for the nation in the fight for Independence, without demanding any reward except our freedom. If I speak falsely, let this oath kill me... (Itote 276)

Kariuki and Itote's transcriptions differ significantly in both form and content, but both illustrate the extent to which the *batuni* oath was meant to bind its taker to protect the secrecy and sanctity of the freedom movement—and both stress the agency of the oath itself to enact repercussions for any failure on the part of that oath-taker to fulfill his or her obligations. During the height of Mau Mau activity, oathing ceremonies inducted men and women into the movement often en masse, but always in person, and always in a context that made the community to which the oath-taker would be bound an immediate and visible reality. The sense of the oath as a speech act embedded in a kind of *legal* order was a consequence both of the words spoken and of a more general awareness of the Kikuyu community as laying claim to a more legitimate sovereignty than that of the colonial government, which had, by the early 1950s, outlawed Kikuyu political organizations as well as oathing ceremonies (D. Anderson 44, 53). The oathing ceremony, then, was paradoxically public and performative in one sense and covert and illicit in another; oaths existed beyond the purview of the colonial state, but the act of oath-taking was also a powerful means of forging political community within that extralegal space.

There is little mystery as to how the oaths served, in Frederick Cooper's words, as a counterpoint to Europe's "relentless belief in modernity" that underlay colonial ideology (320). The oaths were, of course, no less "modern" than the colonial institutions whose authority they sought to challenge, but the kind of modernity they proposed was one that presented itself as consistent with traditional Kikuyu practices *and* as accessible to the population at large, as a political community with which Africans with no educational, political, or economic privilege could directly engage.[10] In these ways, the oaths contrasted starkly with another new trend in the 1950s: the colonial government's drafting and ratification of a flurry of colonial constitutions, which were intended to facilitate a transition to representational government and eventually self-rule in Kenya. While to European settlers (and, to some extent, Asians and elite Africans who stood to benefit from the reforms) colonial constitutionalism signaled a major policy shift, it had little meaning for the majority of the colonized population. And to the extent that these changes in the legal system *were* felt or experienced by non-elite Africans, they were part of a reformist agenda that would only solidify the legal justification for colonialism's dispossession of the country's land and resources. The Mau Mau memoirs quite explicitly juxtapose colonial constitutionalism and its shortcomings with the political potency of the oaths, and even identify constitutional reform as a catalyst for action in the liberation struggle. For Waruhiu Itote, the causal connection between colonial constitutionalism and the Mau Mau oath is unambiguous. He reports taking his first loyalty oath just after—and largely in response to—reading the Electors' Union's 1949 "Kenya Plan," which put forth a scheme for minority rule quite similar to South Africa's apartheid system (39–41). In an appendix to his memoir, he asserts the legitimacy of the oath by comparing it to testimonial practices within Western systems of law:

> The word "oath" in connection with the "Mau Mau" Movement has somehow been associated in the minds of many people with "savagery," "atavism," and the most imaginative stories about human beings gone "mad." Yet the same people will have only the most solemn thoughts when they hear the word "oath" in connection with legal testimony, where it stands for "honesty," or in connection with allegiance to a country, where it stands for "devotion" or "commitment." For those of us in the Movement, oaths had the same solemn and peculiar "binding" quality as they have had for other groups and organizations throughout history. We used them for many purposes, and we had many different oaths for these purposes.[11]

Itote's comments point to the stakes of political legitimation that were attached to the liberation struggle's use of oathing. But they also, more interestingly and provocatively, suggest the way in which Mau Mau had developed its own code of legal legitimacy—had developed a means, in other words, of constituting a people, through individual pledges of national loyalty,[12] at exactly the same moment in which the newly (and only very tentatively) "representative" government of the colony was generating one intermediary constitution after another. During the final years of Kenya's anticolonial struggle, the Mau Mau oath provided an alternative mode of constituting political community in the almost-but-not-quite nation-state, one with considerably more popular legitimacy than legal texts.

To the chagrin of Kenyatta's government, the Mau Mau oaths continued to play a prominent role in cultural memory well after independence through their evocation in a popular new textual genre, the Mau Mau memoir. In these texts, the oaths serve as a means of repudiating the postcolonial state's efforts to focus popular attention on the independence constitution and to present political independence as a meaningful break with the colonial past. The Kenyatta government, Marshall Clough notes, "shaped a new discourse about Kenya's colonial history that centered on constitutional anticolonialism, downplayed the role of Mau Mau, condemned violence, and called for reconciliation of all Kenyans in the spirit of 'forgive and forget'" (26). For a moderate/conservative government trying to establish itself as modeled on a Western (and colonial) conception of the rule of law, the Mau Mau oath was one of the most uncomfortable features of the story of the forest fighters' role in achieving independence; it represented an embarrassing alternative basis of political solidarity that was absolutely incompatible with the state's legal authority.[13] In recalling anticolonial unity as the basis for postcolonial unity, the oaths directly challenge not only an earlier moment in Kenya's history of legal constitutionalism, but also the post-independence Kenyatta government and a postcolonial constitution that makes no pretense of embodying the voice of "the people." The antagonism between constitutionalism and the oath from the final years of colonial rule re-emerges in the postcolony, but this time refracted through competing narratives of what it means to constitute the nation. If after independence the national bourgeoisie fetishizes the constitution and figures the rule of law as the basis for national unity, then the memoirs' accounts of the Mau Mau oaths put forth a counternarrative of national solidarity, one that revolves around a politics of economic and social justice, but also around a politics of constitutional performativity. The Mau Mau oath recalls a moment in which the people themselves were invited to help shape Kenya's political future through individual declarative acts of solidarity that took place in real time and in person—and that could hardly contrast more starkly with the insulated and bureaucratic process of constituting the independent Kenyan state in the early 1960s.

The discursive landscape of decolonization is populated by competing claims to constitutive authority. The provocation of the Mau Mau oaths, both before and after independence, lies in their exposition that the work of constituting can be—and is being—carried out beyond the pale of the state's official iterations. The oaths both enact and theorize a more radical and performative mode of postcolonial political community formation. Amid the backdrop of a different African national liberation struggle, and in a markedly different genre, Frantz Fanon's *Wretched of the Earth* undertakes this same project.

FRANTZ FANON AND THE POSTCOLONIAL SPEECH-ACT

Three decades after the original publication of *The Wretched of the Earth*, Robert Young described Fanon's text as "both a revolutionary manifesto of decolonization and the founding analysis of the effects of colonialism upon colonized peoples and their cultures" (119–20). The declarative and critical functions of this work are tightly linked: Fanon's is an analysis that founds, one that brings to light the essence of anticolonial struggle and decolonization in a form that, in the twentieth century, connotes absolute novelty. Young's brief reading of *Wretched* attends more or less exclusively to the final pages of the text, in which Fanon rallies his readers to action: "We must shake off the great mantle of night which has enveloped us, and reach for the light" (235); "For Europe, for ourselves and for humanity, comrades, we must make a new start, develop a new way of thinking, and endeavor to create a new man" (239).

Young does not elaborate on how "manifesto" might in fact describe the rest of Fanon's text, despite the fact that *Wretched* spans over two hundred pages that feature a more analytical and critically detached narrative voice. Recalling Césaire's and James's somewhat fraught relationship between black internationalism and the genre of the modern manifesto, I want to interrogate what it might mean, and why it might be useful, to read Fanon's text in its entirety as a revolutionary manifesto.[14] In Austinian terms, *Wretched*'s constative function—its description of the colonial world and analysis of the process of decolonization—is accompanied by a performative function, a rhetorical intervention into the landscape of anticolonial struggle that joins forces with (though, for Fanon, certainly does not stand in place of) that struggle. Extrapolating from Benita Parry's observation that Fanon (like Césaire before him) exhibits "an unwillingness to abstract resistance from its moment of performance" (43), I read Fanon's text as itself a performance of anticolonial resistance. The stylistic energy of Fanon's prose, a certain attitude of presentation that gives urgency and immediacy to the argument, speaks to this author's refusal to separate out a call to action from the activity of critique.[15] In the place of juridico-political articulations of nationhood, Fanon imagines the conditions of rhetorical performance under which the populism of the anticolonial struggle might translate and transition into a radical postcolonial democratic community. But *Wretched* is also itself a rhetorical performance, one that straddles the descriptive "are" and the aspirational "ought to be" from which the revolutionary declaration derives its rhetorical power.

Decolonization, in Fanon's account, is a highly creative process. The opening chapter of *Wretched* posits creativity as an intrinsic part of mass resistance to colonial rule—"gripped in a kind of creative frenzy the nation plunges into action of a hugely disproportionate nature" (52)—and in a fiery coda (the part of the text that most explicitly reads like a manifesto), Fanon also cites creativity as the most valuable resource in the project of the reinvention of humanity after the anticolonial struggle has come to an end: "if we want humanity to take one step forward, if we want to take it to another level than the one where Europe has placed it, then we must innovate, we must be pioneers" (239). But creativity for creativity's sake is not necessarily beneficial or liberatory. In his 1959 *A Dying Colonialism* Fanon explored the way in which Algerians appropriated and transformed symbols such as the veil and communicative tools such as the radio, which had been controlled by the colonizer, for revolutionary purposes. "This illiterate people that is writing the finest and the most stirring pages of the struggle for freedom cannot draw back nor be silent" (31), and the tools that enable this "writing" are precisely those that once served to retain colonial control over the adjudication of Algerian women's morality and over the news media. In *Wretched* Fanon again cites the malleability of the "technical instrument" of anticolonial activity (*A Dying Colonialism* 76), but this time does so in order to explain how such instruments can also be reappropriated, in damaging ways, by a counterrevolutionary national bourgeoisie on the eve of independence. Lambasting second-generation negritudean fetishizations of African cultural particularism, and calling instead for a "combat literature" that will cultivate collective political engagement, Fanon cautions the engaged black poet to remember that "nothing can replace the rational and irreversible commitment on the side of the people in arms" (*Wretched* 162). No form or cultural tradition is inherently liberatory. Decolonization's creative force depends on its performative contexts.

Fanon's critique of anticolonial creativity is most frequently discussed in relation to "On National Culture," the fourth chapter of *Wretched* and originally a speech given at the 1959 Second Congress of Black Writers and Artists in Rome. But reproduced in the 1961 text, this argument appears only in the wake of three chapters that focus on the manipulability of forms of creative expression as they are deployed in *political* contexts. As independence draws near, the national bourgeoisie can sabotage political creativity by falling back on stale and hierarchical forms of communication. The leader who once gave voice to anticolonial ideals is now likely to "unmask his inner purpose: to be CEO of the company of profiteers composed of a national bourgeoisie intent only on getting the most out of the situation" (112). What Fanon fears in the wake of anticolonial revolution is an official language that masks an abandonment of that revolution's aims, a mismatch of words and deeds: "The nationalist political parties never insist on the need for confrontation precisely because their aim is not the radical overthrow of the system . . . They are violent in their words and reformist in their attitudes" (21–22). Political leaders' rhetorical authority enables this duplicity. In their hands, political speech becomes a dangerous tool that deploys a narrative of the nation's heroic past to divert attention away from present-day concerns:

The leader with his militant past as a loyal patriot constitutes a screen between the people and the grasping bourgeoisie ... He helps to curb the growing awareness of the people. He lends his support to this caste and hides its maneuvers from the people, thus becoming its most vital tool for mystifying and numbing the senses of the masses. Every time he addresses the people he recalls his life, which was often heroic, the battles waged and the victories won in the people's name, thus conveying to the masses they should continue to place their trust in him. (113)

During the struggle for liberation the leader roused the people and promised them a radical, heroic march forward. Today he repeatedly endeavors to lull them to sleep and three or four times a year asks them to remember the colonial period and to take stock of the immense distance they have covered. (114)

Political speeches reinforce an official, top-down symbolics of discursive authority. They flatten out the dynamic experience of the public meeting, turning it into an occasion for further infantilization of the people rather than an opportunity to foster collective growth and reconfigure power among the future postcolony's citizenry. This rhetorical form, in the hands of an exclusionary and centralized national party, thus simultaneously reflects and perpetuates a politics that true decolonization should be working to overturn.

In his descriptions of the wayward neocolonial political leader, Fanon repeatedly casts this figure—at his most dangerous and deplorable—as a rhetorician, a manipulator of heroic tales whose language works primarily to reinforce his own identity as a national hero. Out of joint with the nation-time of the postcolony, the leader imagines himself as a speaker-hero, assuming the same kind of representational authority that he claimed (with more legitimacy) before decolonization—and failing or refusing to recognize that in the postcolony, that figure is woefully out of place. Here is the voice of (political *and* aesthetic) representative authority from Césaire's *Cahier d'un retour au pays natal,* but stripped of all of his ambivalence and self-consciousness—and translated into a different historical moment. The figure of the speaker-hero signals a refusal, on the part of the postcolony's political leadership, to step out of the way and facilitate the ultimate coup of decolonization—its overturning of existing structures of representation and authority. The task of the decolonized nation is to obliterate this figure from its imaginative scope as well as from its political sphere. True decolonization eliminates the need for the very form of leadership that made it possible to begin with:

> When they have used violence to achieve national liberation, the masses allow nobody to come forward as "liberator." They prove themselves to be jealous of their achievements and take care not to place their future, their destiny, and the fate of their homeland into the hands of a living god. (51–52)

In Hegelian fashion, the anticolonial hero should fade away once the fight he led has been won. His resuscitation in this new historical moment constitutes an act of regression: "We must not cultivate the spirit of the exceptional or look for the hero, another form of leader. We must elevate the people, expand their minds, equip them, differentiate them, and humanize them" (137).

Rejecting the speaker-hero is part and parcel of a rethinking of the basic premise of representation upon which that figure depended. At the level of political organizations, this entails "rid[ding] ourselves of the very Western, very bourgeois, and hence very disparaging, idea that the masses are incapable of governing themselves" (130). Such a transformation means eschewing technocratic language which, under the guise of fulfilling the technical requirements of a democratic state, serves to mystify and alienate the very people whose interests it claims to uphold:

> Resorting to technical language means you are determined to treat the masses as uninitiated. Such language is a poor front for the lecturer's intent to deceive the people and leave them on the sidelines. Language's endeavor to confuse is a mask behind which looms an even greater undertaking to dispossess. The intention is to strip the people of their possessions as well as their sovereignty. You can explain anything to the people provided you really want them to understand. (130–31)

Reworking a political community's representational structure is thus first and foremost a pedagogical project: the postcolony needs a program of political education that clears space for constituents to cultivate a new mode of *collective* heroism. Fanon explains this process as one that explicitly calls for an overhaul of the genre of political speech.

> It is commonly thought with criminal flippancy that to politicize the masses means from time to time haranguing them with a major political speech. It is thought that for a leader or head of state to speak on major current issues in a pedantic tone of voice is sufficient as obligation to politicize the masses. But political education means opening up the mind, awakening the mind, and introducing it to the world. It is as Césaire said: "To invent the souls of men." To politicize the masses is not and cannot be to make a political

speech. It means driving home to the masses that everything depends on them, that if we stagnate the fault is theirs, and that if we progress, they too are responsible, that there is no demiurge, no illustrious man taking responsibility for everything, but that the demiurge is the people and the magic lies in their hands and their hands alone. In order to achieve such things, in order to actually embody them, we must, as we have already mentioned, decentralize to the utmost. The flow of ideas from the upper echelons to the rank and file and vice versa must be an unwavering principle, not for merely formal reasons but quite simply because adherence to this principle is the guarantee of salvation. (138)

Fanon excoriates political leaders' inflexible and unimaginative assumption that the dynamic and complex work of transforming national consciousness can be accomplished by delivering prepared remarks to a crowd. So much of Fanon's argument about postcolonial leadership comes down to the question of what kind of speech enables—and serves as proof of—the existence of a true postcolony. The postcolonial speech-act is a vital, constitutive component of this process, an utterance that is also an event in its instantiation of the political community that also authors it. "The living expression of the nation is the collective consciousness in motion of the entire people . . . If the national government wants to be national it must govern by the people and for the people, for the disinherited and by the disinherited" (144). After decolonization, "the people" becomes the true speaker-hero of the nation. This vision of democratization through decentralization not only prompts Fanon to cite Césaire, but also aligns with the conception of aesthetic and political representation that Césaire put forth in his *Cahier*. The Césairean echoes continue in Fanon's presentation of this new representational order in idealist terms: the means by which the people seize their rightful authority is described as a kind of magic. Moreover, the pronouns in these passages remind Fanon's readers that this transformation remains theoretical: a "You" is still responsible, here, for taking on the role of educator, and "*we* must . . . decentralize to the utmost." Fanon calls for the dissolution of an exclusionary "we," a political elite whose subject position is inherently separate from that of the masses; but his use of the pronoun itself is proof that no such dissolution has happened yet. The magic of a truly popular embodiment of progress is yet to come.

Fanon's indictment of the anti-/postcolonial political elite is emphatic and sustained. In contrast, *Wretched* provides relatively few concrete discussions of what the new, collective heroism of the truly decolonized political community will look like or how it will form. As I will explain below, this vagueness serves an important strategic purpose in the text. But Fanon's vision of decolonized community formation does crystallize around one specific scene: the open, democratically run public meeting is the context in which he imagines that a new postcolonial participatory political order can be realized.

> The masses must be able to meet, discuss, put forward suggestions and receive instructions. Citizens must have the opportunity to speak, to express themselves and innovate. The meeting of the local cell or the committee meeting is a liturgical act. It is a privileged opportunity for the individual to listen and speak. At every meeting the brain multiplies the association of ideas and the eye discovers a wider human panorama. (136)

The kind of speech that emerges through Fanon's conception of the local, public meeting is eminently creative and communal. Through such an event, the work of language creation should be entirely commensurate with the work of community-building and nation-building, and sustain itself through a distinctive, powerful tension between ritual and innovation. In the opening pages of the text Fanon identifies traditional public forums in precolonial Africa as spaces of public exchange and, importantly, self-criticism—spaces that are blissfully free of the egoism of the colonized intellectual, which undercuts communal will.[16] The public meeting that Fanon envisions in post-independence contexts is one in which these long-standing forms of public exchange are translated and incorporated into a postcolonial public event that gives way to what Pierre Bourdieu terms the "social magic" of constituting a collective political identity.[17] Fanon not only reconceives democratic participation and the work of language in this vision of the public meeting; he also reconceives authorship, which is no longer about individuals but rather about a particular time, place, and spirit of creation. Public speech entails a performative, "liturgical" use of language, a language that is freed from the national bourgeoisie's discursive betrayals precisely because it takes place as part of an "act." While Fanon lays out a vision of what the innovative discourse of the local public meeting should look like, the vagueness of this prescription is equally telling; "We" might need the discursive foundation for national consciousness, but "the masses" are charged with the act of founding itself.

"One often speaks of the masses as one speaks of the people," Trinh T. Minh-ha observes. "One invokes them and pretends to write on their behalf . . . Yet to oppose the masses to the elite is already to imply that those forming the masses are regarded as an aggregate of average persons condemned by their lack of personality or by their dim individualities to stay with the herd, to be docile and anonymous" (113). The masses of Fanon's text are hardly depicted as docile, and it is worth noting that Fanon's second chapter opens by troubling classical Marxism's own "aggregation" of largely rural and indigenous colonized populations into theoretical terms better suited for a Western, urban proletariat. Fanon's championing of popular resistance came at a time when, after relying heavily on mass agitation from Algeria's rural population, the National Liberation Front was beginning to revert to a more insular and centralized model of party leadership; *Wretched* voiced a protest against that shift. Nonetheless, Fanon's presentation of the masses in abstract terms is both directly connected to the more utopian aspects of the text and analytically unsatisfying. This is particularly the case in relation to the text's gender politics: Fanon's colonized subject is unequivocally male. And while, as many critics have noted, Fanon recognizes that men and women experience colonialism differently, he never thinks through the implications of those differences in his theorization of anticolonial resistance and the formation of postcolonial community.[18] Fanon's own class and gender identity shape the way in which he portrays "the wretched," and marks the limitations of that portrayal.

But the points at which the limits of Fanon's own representational authority present themselves in this text also elucidate why it is productive to think of *Wretched*, in its entirety, as a manifesto. Whereas the abstract and even hyperbolic resonances of "the people" make for a weak analytical term, to the manifesto (as well as to the revolutionary declaration more generally) these features are a rhetorical asset. In "Colonial War and Mental Disorders," Fanon presents a series of "case studies" of Algerian and French patients whom he himself treated, and whose psychic ailments epitomize the effects of colonial and anticolonial violence that the previous four chapters have theorized. Fanon's narrative voice in this chapter is that of the emotionally detached physician and scientific observer; this detachment throws into relief the horror of the experiences of the patients themselves, who are victims or perpetrators of rape, torture, and murder in the context of anticolonial war. But in one or two extraordinary moments, they are also responsible for disrupting the doctor-narrator's detachment from these case studies by drawing him into dialogue and asking him unanswerable questions. "What would you do if it happened to you?" a National Liberation Front militant, suffering from impotence after the rape and torture of his wife, asks his doctor (189). When Fanon asks an Algerian teenager why he killed a European boy, he is asked by way of response "if I had ever seen a European in prison" (200)—and then, "In your opinion, what do you think we should have done?" (201). These interrogative moments pierce through the omniscience and stability of Fanon's narrative perspective by drawing attention to his subject position and that of his interlocutors/patients, whose involvement in the war of independence is far more immediate than Fanon's will ever be. The epilogue that follows chapter 5 recuperates a more prominent and self-assured authorial voice, the voice of the activist; but these starkly anomalous and unsettling trauma narratives haunt and even undercut the bold, vindicationist message of those closing pages. The paradox of Fanon's own position, as a colonized intellectual who seeks both to represent the plight of a colonized people and to insist on the eradication of the need for that people to be represented, becomes a component of his own authorial voice. Fanon's final call to revolutionary action—which also became his last published words—is not oblivious to the high stakes of speaking for a population with whom he cannot always identify.

Another crucial symptom of *Wretched*'s own involvement in the kind of language of decolonization that it theorizes is Fanon's enigmatic present tense, which shifts—often imperceptibly—between descriptive and subjunctive modes, between, to borrow once again from Derrida's reading of the U.S. Declaration of Independence, the "are" and the "ought to be." This ambiguity is encapsulated in the text's early assertion of the absolute novelty of the moment of decolonization.

> Decolonization never goes unnoticed, for it focuses on and fundamentally alters being, and transforms the spectator crushed to a nonessential state into a privileged actor, captured in a virtually grandiose fashion by the spotlight of History. It infuses a new rhythm, specific to a new generation of men, with a new language and a new humanity. Decolonization is truly the creation of new men. But such a creation cannot be attributed to a supernatural power: The "thing" colonized becomes a man through the very process of liberation.[19]

So much hinges, in this passage (as well as, indeed, in the first four chapters of this text), on whether the decolonization to which Fanon refers is one that he sees actually occurring in the world around him—or whether instead this is a decolonization that as of yet Fanon can only imagine, a decolonization, as Césaire might put it, that is "made to the measure of the world."[20] This ambiguity reflects the fact that Fanon was witnessing the advent of political independence in some African countries while at the same time imagining it as a future reality in others; his enigmatic present tense reflects the tension between the descriptive and the theoretical, the real and the being-made-real, that characterized the moment of revolutionary activity in which he was writing. *The Wretched of the Earth* is neither strictly a theory of anticolonial struggle emerging out of the precedent set by past struggles, nor a projection of what the struggle will look like when it eventually comes to pass; rather, it is self-consciously situated in the midst of the revolutionary moment itself. In accordance with Martin Puchner's most basic definition of the manifesto, Fanon's text "not only records revolutionary history but wants to make this history as well" (Puchner 22). In the moment of true decolonization, *being* must change; *humanity* must fundamentally be altered; *language* must be created anew. Words are part of the process of bringing into existence this "new rhythm, specific to a new generation of men," even as they also emerge out of that newness. The temporality of Fanon's prose enacts the radical disruption of his proposed definition of decolonization, and his own words thus prove inseparable from the work of the struggle itself.

The paradox of representational authority with which *Wretched* contends is thus also a paradox of revolutionary temporality. Like Africa itself in the late 1960s, this text is caught between what Fanon posits as two crucially distinct moments, the moment of the anticolonial struggle and the moment of independence. The narrative voice of *Wretched* is similarly trapped between these two temporalities, but it also exists in another double bind: decolonization's radical reworking of representational authority draws into question the role that Fanon himself, as a colonized intellectual, plays in narrating (and/or prophesying) the decolonized nation. Coming to terms with the performativity of the text involves recognizing the ambiguity of Fanon's own narrative authority. Fanon's greatest feat, Robert Bernasconi asserts, lies in his recognition of the value of conceiving of the postcolonial future as beyond the analytical grasp of the theorist of decolonization.

> Fanon was at his most explicit and most precise when he translated the claim "the violence is a positive [new] humanism" into the claim that the new humanism is to be "prefigured in the objectives and methods of the struggle" (*Dt* 294/*WE* 246). This does not mean that there is nothing beyond violence, still less that violence is the goal. Violence helps to mobilize the masses and introduces ideas of national destiny and of collective history, but Fanon also speaks, for example, of a second phase that is the building up of the nation to which these ideas, born of the struggle, contribute (126–7/93). To say that the new humanism is prefigured in the struggle allows for a restoration of the unforeseeable to its place within historical becoming and promises a refiguring of the relation between theory and practice. One could still set objectives, organize priorities, and develop strategies locally, but one would no longer try to envisage the end of the dialectic. To do so would threaten the novelty of the new humanism and its claim to have put the old humanism behind it. Not that novelty of itself was the crucial issue for Fanon. What Fanon's account of the two logics suggested was that a new humanity could arise only

through the creative praxis of the colonized. Theirs was a violence that would not only destroy the old order, but produce a new one. Theoreticians should avoid trying to disarm it ahead of time by presuming that they always know where it will lead. ("Casting the Slough" 120–21)

Fanon's hazy descriptions of true decolonization, and its advent of a "new humanism," owe something, to be sure, to his awareness of the extent to which his vision was already being undermined in newly independent African nation-states such as Ghana and the Congo; one might argue that the idealism of *Wretched* is meant to project an imagined alternative to the realities of decolonization of which Fanon was already cognizant, and the ominous future trends to which those realities were already giving way, as early as 1960. But I am intrigued by Bernasconi's suggestion of another way to read futurity in *Wretched*—as an aspect of the text that gets intentionally left open-ended, whose possibilities are not foreclosed by the theorist's efforts to control them through narrative projection. Fanon's resistance to concretizing his vision of the postcolonial future signals a recognition of the limitations of his own authorial voice in constituting that future.

Wretched both thematizes and discursively stages the problem of speaker-heroism in contexts of decolonization. This is a problem that remains unsolved by the end of the text. The lesson of *Wretched*—one which, as we will see below, Ngũgĩ wa Thiong'o takes to heart—is that narratives of anticolonial struggle and theories of decolonization are themselves part of the web of rhetorical performance through which the postcolony gets constituted. To theorize and/or narrate decolonization is also to put on a rhetorical performance within the historical moment of decolonization itself. This is a performance through which new possibilities for representational authority emerge.

NOVEL RECONSTITUTION IN *A GRAIN OF WHEAT*

Like *The Wretched of the Earth*, *A Grain of Wheat* reflects the complex temporality of the moment of decolonization: political independence, very recently achieved when Ngũgĩ published this novel, had not yet lost its luster as an ideal, but by 1967 decolonization was also a lived reality in Kenya, one whose early aftereffects could be analyzed as well as celebrated. Neil Lazarus positions *A Grain of Wheat* as a "transitional work" in Ngũgĩ's career, "poised on the border between an intellectualist field of vision" that characterizes his earlier fiction and the "more soberly materialist, long-historical socialist internationalism" to which his writing would give voice beginning in the late 1970s with *Petals of Blood* (*Resistance* 21–22). But because Ngũgĩ's intellectual and political development map so closely onto Kenya's shift from decolonization to neocolonialism, his 1967 novel is transitional in a broader historical sense as well. In an intriguing reversal of the trajectory that David Scott delineates for C. L. R. James, Ngũgĩ becomes less invested in European modernist tropes of realist tragedy, and more committed to the political mobilization of his audience, the further he, and Kenya, get from political independence. In *A Grain of Wheat,* Ngũgĩ begins to experiment with some of the formal and ideological provocations for which his mid-career fiction of the 1970s and '80s becomes known. Among the most important of these is the way Ngũgĩ begins to conceive of the novel both as a space in which to theorize the constitution of postcolonial political community as performative, and as a form through which such a performance can be enacted. The novel is structured around a series of public meetings and speeches that provide occasions for the inhabitants of a small Gikuyu village to reflect on their much-anticipated postcolonial future. I read these performances as scenes of constituting, as well, for the author, as scenes of theorizing performativity as crucial to the instantiation of a truly postcolonial community as Fanon had envisioned it just a few years earlier. Also like Fanon, Ngũgĩ seeks to create a work that will not only critically reflect on but also actively participate in the work of constituting the postcolony.

Set in the fictional village of Thabai, *A Grain of Wheat* opens in the days leading up to Uhuru (independence), and traces the crises of conscience that haunt several residents of the village back through the events of the preceding decade, including the most intense period of the "Mau Mau" guerrilla war, the colonial government's declaration of an Emergency, and the detention and displacement of hundreds of thousands of Kenyans during a violent final decade of colonial rule. Ngũgĩ's protagonist is Mugo, an orphan and a loner in the otherwise close-knit village community; he wrestles with the secret (revealed to readers halfway through the novel) that he was responsible for turning over Kihika, Thabai's most beloved freedom fighter, to the British in the early days of the Emergency. The novel culminates with Mugo's public confession of his betrayal at Thabai's Uhuru ceremonies. Mugo is one amid a cast of characters through whom Ngũgĩ explores the forms of culpability and complicity created in the turbulent final years of colonial rule in Kenya. The subplot centers around Gikonyo, a would-be businessman who returns home from the detention camps only to discover that his wife Mumbi has had a child with Karanja, Gikonyo's one-time romantic rival who joined the Home Guard, the native colonial police force—and eagerly wielded this power over Thabai during the Emergency.

A Grain of Wheat is structured around three public meetings, each one featuring rhetorical performances designed to create and sustain, at the local level, a sense of national community among attendees. The first of these takes place before the Emergency, and in the early days of Thabai residents' awareness of the liberation struggle; most importantly it serves as the occasion for Kihika's entrance into public life as a charismatic leader—Thabai's own speaker-hero. When Jomo Kenyatta fails to show up for a scheduled public address in Thabai in the early 1950s, Kihika takes the stage in his place. Readers access this important moment in Thabai's recent history through Mugo's memory of the event.

> Kihika unrolled the history of the tribe, the coming of the whiteman and the birth of the Party. Mugo glanced at Gikonyo and Mumbi. Their eyes were fixed on Kihika; their lives seemed dependent on his falling words . . .
> People laughed. Kihika did not join them. He was a small man with a strong voice. Speaking slowly with emphasis on the important words, he once or twice pointed at earth and heaven as if calling them to witness that what he spoke was the truth. He talked of the great sacrifice.
> "A day comes when brother shall give up brother, a mother her son, when you and I have heard the call of a nation in turmoil."
> Mugo felt a constriction in his throat. He could not clap for words that did not touch him. What right had such a boy, probably younger than Mugo, to talk like that? What arrogance? Kihika had spoken of blood as easily as if he was talking of drawing water in a river, Mugo reflected, a revulsion starting in his stomach at the sight and smell of blood. I hate him, he heard himself say and frightened, he looked at Mumbi, wondering what she was thinking. (*A Grain of Wheat* 15)

Kihika's speech mesmerizes; his ability to engage the crowd comes from voice and presence, body and words all at once. Summoning the power of a preacher and a prophet, he adopts an affect which distances him from his audience (they laugh; he doesn't), and his voice quickly transcends the space of his body, connecting him not merely to the people in front of him but also to a cosmology—heaven and earth, in Mugo's retrospection, are witness to this spectacle. Mugo, however, remains painfully alienated from this transformative audience experience and instead registers the speech first and foremost muscularly: his throat constricts; his stomach turns; and through these physiological responses he becomes keenly aware of his distance from others in the crowd.

The embodied nature of Mugo's reaction to Kihika's speech both recalls and complicates a key component of Fanon's theory of the origins of popular revolt within a colonized population. Spontaneity, Fanon argues, is a powerful force in propelling the rural masses to consciousness and action—but it is also unpredictable, unsustainable, and likely to result in directionless, unproductive violence if no structure exists to channel and organize popular energies. The colonial subject's spontaneity is linked to his capacity for violence, which surfaces in his physiological response to the discursive dissemination of Western culture.[21] This physiological response most specifically ties together aural perception—what the colonized subject hears—and muscular activity—what the colonized subject's body does in response to what is heard: "Now it so happens that when the colonized hear a speech on Western culture they draw their machetes or at least check to see they are close at hand." The colonized subject's capacity for physical violence has been recognized, brought to the surface, and even conditioned to respond to the stimulus of cultural imperialism. "In the period of decolonization, the colonized masses thumb their noses at these very values, shower them with insults and vomit them up" (8). The origins of spontaneity, for Fanon, lie in the colonized subject's reaction to public speech, in which that subject detects hypocrisy and betrayal.

Yet Kihika is no hypocrite; he is more earnest than his audience, and Mugo is wrong to interpret his passion as arrogance. Further, Kihika's words do not propel Mugo toward violent, active rejection. If anything they have the opposite effect. And it is in Mugo's physical reaction to the speech, not his conscious thoughts, that the novel sets us up to detect the shortcomings of Kihika's performance at a structural level in this scene. The contraction of Mugo's throat muscles prevents him from speaking up, speaking with, responding to, or sharing in the imagined community which Kihika's words are meant to help instantiate. Kihika's voice shuts down other voices; in taking the stage, he takes the stage away from others. This rhetorical performance does nothing to reconfigure the relationship between speaker and audience—which means that self-identified outsiders like Mugo remain outsiders at its close, and enthralled listeners like Mumbi and Gikonyo remain happy to be led through the liberation struggle by this powerful rhetorician, but have no vision for how to lead themselves once he is gone.

Criticism of *A Grain of Wheat* has tended to shortchange the complexity of Mugo's internal struggle in this scene, and in the novel as a whole: Mugo tends to be read either as mad[22] or as a somewhat awkwardly constructed character whose horror and paralysis in the face of revolution signals Ngũgĩ's continued dependency on the conventions of Western modernism.[23] Ngũgĩ's use of this character to critically engage with a Fanonian concept of spontaneity troubles such interpretations. Mugo's thoracic difficulties direct our attention toward problems of anticipating and controlling audience response, and reveal the extent to which the speaker-hero model embodied by Kihika is limited in its ability to recognize, account for, and adjust for fissures within the crowd he addresses. Mugo's discomfort registers more than just his own alienation, and foreshadows more than just the personal betrayal that that alienation will lead to later in the novel. Incorporating a refracted version of Fanonian spontaneity onto the scene of this pre-Emergency public meeting, Ngũgĩ registers the fact that there are dangerous conditions attached to the kind of unity that Kihika envisions for Kenya—and that he assumes of his audience. At best, Kihika's speaker-heroism will be ineffective: it will not bring about the "flow of ideas" between Thabai's (burgeoning) political leadership and the community as a whole. At worst, it will betray the development of that community by oppressively erasing points of view that challenge the sovereign power of the speech-giver.

The problematic strain of speaker-heroism that Ngũgĩ identifies in Kihika's speech has close ties to Kenyatta's own reputation as a formidable public speaker. A "small man with a strong voice," Thabai's Mau Mau martyr ascends to heroism not on a battlefield (we have no indication that he was a particularly gifted fighter) but on a stage. Kihika's speech, delivered in the early 1950s, echoes Kariuki's account of what it was like to hear—and witness—a young Kenyatta speak in public around that same time: "The effect of his voice and personality was immediate and magnetic so that even the smallest children became still and quiet as Kenyatta talked to us of his doings in England and of the future of our country. He was mixing Kikuyu and Swahili words in a wonderful way and the doubters found that he knew more old Kikuyu phrases than they had ever heard" (Kariuki 11). Kenyatta's charisma and cosmopolitanism not only impress Kariuki but commit him permanently to the cause: "fundamentally changed by his statesmanlike words and his burning personality," he "vowed there and then that I would struggle with him for justice and freedom for our country" (12). Kariuki recalls the version of Kenyatta that Ngũgĩ would later, in his prison diary, identify as "the Kenyatta of 'the burning spear,' of whom the Kenyan masses then rightly sang as their coming saviour" (*Detained* 87). Kihika is modeled after Kenyatta, whose absence in the novel points to Ngũgĩ's disillusionment with the much less fiery leader who by the 1960s "was talking in an entirely different language" (87–88).

Even in his pre-Emergency innocence, Kihika's shortcomings point to how the model of speaker-heroism sets up problems of unification and democratic participation that will emerge later on in the narrative. If Kihika is a gifted speaker, he is less gifted as a listener. When he passionately presents India as a paradigm of anticolonial action to his sister and friends, extolling instances of personal martyrdom, his audience is once again cowed by his words, but also confused about the content of his story. Mumbi has trouble with Kihika's suggestion that nation should replace kinship ties and "could not visualize anything heroic in men and women being run over by trains" (*A Grain of Wheat* 77). Gikonyo, who is "touched more by the voice of Kihika and the glint in his eyes than by the argument which he did not follow anyway," asks a pivotal question—"How do we unite the people?" (78). Kihika never answers this question, and thus never reflects on, for example, what kinds of social fissures, such as gender and class, might serve as obstacles to the national unity he has in mind.[24] The dissonance between the intention of Kihika's words and their reception by his audience is thrown into sharper relief shortly thereafter when he completely misreads an exchange with Wambuku, his lover, who desperately wants to get him to switch topics from politics to their future together. His retort to her—"'It is not politics, Wambuku,' he said, 'it is life'" (85)—is no less telling than his body language: he "spoke [to her] with his hands as to a large audience in front of him" (85). Kihika cannot change registers: while other characters will modulate the tone and tenor of their voices depending on context, Kihika seems to put on the same performance every time he speaks. Kihika's motives are pure, but his rhetorical style resembles that of Fanon's party leader who speechifies without educating and retains a monopoly on representational authority.

Because Kihika dies in the mid-1950s, his political vision and leadership skills are not directly put to the test by the Emergency and by the even more politically fraught period of Kenya's post-Emergency transition toward independence. As Eileen Julien observes, "there is no sense of a struggle on Kihika's part" in signing on as a freedom fighter (141); shielded from violence until the day of his death, and protected by that death from the experience of detention, he has the luxury of maintaining an ideological purity that becomes impossible for the novel's other central characters, all of whom face Uhuru with guilt and doubt about their roles in the struggle and with anxieties about their futures in the new nation. And in this Kihika's and Kenyatta's fates crucially part ways: Kihika dies a hero's death just as the future prime minister disappears from the scene—and comes back a different kind of leader. Yet the novel hints that had Kihika survived the Emergency, he might have undergone a similar transformation. Ngũgĩ's anticolonial hero exhibits what Ato Quayson identifies as a "will to transcendence": "the desire to transcend social and political contradictions and to provide discursive material contexts through which the dangerous energies of such contradictions can be channeled in particular directions rather than in others." The will to transcendence is "an essentially totalitarian impulse" that gains legitimacy through its recourse to a local, purportedly organic cultural heroism (49–50). While Quayson briefly notes that in some historical instances—the anti-apartheid struggle, for example—this effacement of contradictions is "necessary work," he sees it as a phenomenon with primarily negative consequences for the "peculiar phenomenology" of leadership in the contemporary African state.[25]

If Kihika's pre-Emergency speech suggests that anticolonial speaker-heroism was a limited mode of political engagement even well before decolonization, then in the subsequent two scenes of rhetorical performance Ngũgĩ goes on to explore alternatives to that model as his fictional village recovers from a decade of brutal colonial oppression and prepares for independence. In contextualizing Thabai's first post-Emergency public meeting, Ngũgĩ draws attention first not to individual speakers, but rather to the communal needs, desires, and energies that shape the meaning and structure of this village event: "Many people from Thabai attended the meeting because, as you'll remember, we had only just been allowed to hold political meetings; other people came, hoping to be diverted with escape stories and other heroic deeds" (57). The meeting is structured around two distinct genres of public performance. Villagers (all male) who were arrested and sent to detention camps during the Emergency take the stage to share their memories of the experience. These first-person testimonials convey the particularity of individual memories; they inscribe the recent past into the present while giving honor to the community members recognized as having made heavy sacrifices during the Emergency. But between speakers the audience itself breaks into song, incorporating individual testimonials into collectively voiced narratives of anticolonial heroism that date back to the onset of colonial rule in Kenya. The songs also look forward to the future, folding detainees' stories into a prophetic narrative of the nation still to come. Individual stories, and individual voices, do not stand alone at the post-Emergency meeting; no single speaker stuns the crowd into silence. Rather, everyone in attendance participates in the creation of a heterogeneous and multitextured national narrative; participation itself is the constitutive performance that matters.

In their assessment of the first three decades of Ngũgĩ's literary career, Alamin Mazrui and Lupenga Mphande cite 1970 as the point at which he "begins to explore orality as a creative process rather than as a received tradition" through his "creative deployment of song and ritual" (167) which "give his narrative style a combative thrust that goes beyond the traditional use of orality for mere authentication" (171–72). But Ngũgĩ's use of song in *A Grain of Wheat* suggests that he had already begun this exploration as of the late 1960s. Song proved a crucial form of collective resistance for the (largely female) population of Thabai that lived out the Emergency performing forced labor under the oppressive and often violent watch of the Home Guard. Mumbi recalls song's transformative power among a group forced to spend the morning digging the Great Barrier Ditch, meant to isolate villages from one another and thus short-circuit fighters' flow of supplies and communications (Lutz 187): "A woman or a man from one end of the trench would start [singing] and all of us joined in, creating words out of nothing" (*A Grain of Wheat* 126). Song provides another model of popular spontaneity in the novel, emerging out of and rebuffing the Emergency's efforts to impose an expressive void on a colonized population. In the context of the post-Emergency public meeting, song thus also serves as a citational trace of a form of resistant cultural expression that did not wait for the closing of the detention camps, or for independence, to constitute community. Song in post-Emergency Thabai is in fact a revival of an earlier performance that did its real work, and had its real effect, during the freedom struggle's darkest hours—and this performance, a form of resistant anticolonial action, took place not in the forests or the detention camps, but on the supposed home front, which of course was no more immune to Emergency violence than the camps or the forests. In *A Grain of Wheat,* song is an anticolonial, not a precolonial, "tradition," one whose strategic function is similar to that of the Mau Mau oaths. And it is a crucial medium through which a plurality of voices and memories are incorporated into the post-Emergency meeting—suggesting heterogeneous and inclusive possibilities for how the village might go about constituting the decolonized nation to come.

For all of the attention Ngũgĩ pays at the beginning of this scene to audience participation, his narration of the meeting centers around a dramatic solo performance that significantly disrupts the communal dynamic of the events and points again to the very real limits of Thabai's protonational unity. When Mugo takes the stage at the meeting, he tells a story that contrasts with those of other detainees in both form and content. While other speakers "talked of suffering under the whiteman and illustrated this with episodes which revealed their deep love of Kenya" (57), Mugo's words rawly and myopically center around the lived experience of detention.

> "They took us to the roads and to the quarries even those who had never done anything. They called us criminals. But not because we had stolen anything or killed anyone. We had only asked for the thing that belonged to us from the time of Agu and Agu. Day and night, they made us dig. We were stricken ill, we often slept with empty stomachs, and our clothes were just rags and tatters so that the rain and the wind and the sun knew our nakedness. In those days we did not stay alive because we thought our cause strong. It was not even because we loved the country. If that had been all, who would not have perished?

"We only thought of home.

"We longed for the day when we would see our women laugh, or even see our children fight and cry. When we thought that one day we would return home to see the faces and hear the voices of our mothers and our wives and our children we became strong. Yes. We became strong even in days when the cause for which blood was spilt seemed—seemed—"

At first Mugo enjoyed the distance he had established between himself and the voice. But soon the voice disgusted him. He wanted to shout: that is not it at all; I did not want to come back; I did not long to join my mother, or wife or child because I did not have any. Tell me, then, whom could I have loved? He stopped in the middle of a sentence and walked down the platform towards his hut. (58)

Other detainees attribute their survival and endurance in the camps to love of country; Mugo explicitly rejects this explanation and replaces country instead with a more generalized longing for home. Mugo's disruption of the public meeting is not just tonal; his words pose a challenge to the kind of truth that the detainee testimonial is expected to tell. The authority of the personal testimonial depends on its authentic conveyance of the speaker's own lived experience. The truth of Mugo's story is collective, not individual—hence his use of the plural rather than the singular pronoun—but it is also not his own. As he speaks, Mugo comes to realize how the possibilities of representation are complicated and ironized by knowledge gaps, complicities, and ambiguous allegiances within the community, and how these complications are embedded into the structure of the post-Emergency public meeting. *A Grain of Wheat* asks: How honest and inclusive will that unity be? How well will this new national consciousness account not only for specific categories of difference, but more basically for the principle of difference itself?

The pronoun problem—which is also a problem of representational authority—that emerges in Mugo's speech in 1959 intensifies in the novel's climactic scene of public rhetorical performance, Thabai's Uhuru celebration. Distraught after having told Mumbi the truth about his part in Kihika's death, Mugo has sent word that he will not speak at the ceremony after all; General R., a former forest fighter who self-identified much earlier along as a doer, not a speaker ("'I can't use my tongue,' he used to say with a streak of pride, 'but I can use my hands'" [135]), decides to take the stage in Mugo's place. General R.'s speech, and the one that Mugo finally does make at the last minute, introduces yet another performative genre into the new nation's heterogeneous discursive field: that of the confession. General R. intends to do honor to Kihika's memory by recounting his heroic acts for the crowd. Once onstage, however, he finds himself overwhelmed by unexpected memories of his own actions, chief among them his assassination of a minister, Reverend Jackson, who had long vilified the liberation struggle from the pulpit. Jackson's memory takes on attributes of a ghostly presence for General R., and dramatically transforms his mode of address: "Words came out, and it seemed he was pleading innocence, giving evidence in a crowded court" (191). General R. shifts focus from the past, and its attendant ghosts, to the future: "We get Uhuru today. Tomorrow we shall ask: where is the land? Where is the food? Where are the schools? Let therefore these things be done now, for we do not want another war . . . no more blood in my . . . in these our hands" (192). General R.'s prophecy poses the novel's most explicit articulation of the questions of Kenya's former freedom fighters that Kenyatta's government was in the process of failing to answer by 1967; these words are as close as Ngũgĩ comes, in this text, to directly criticizing his president.[26] General R. at first rehearses the Mau Mau rebel's party line in his speech, but then his words give way to a more awkward fluctuation between the first-person singular and plural. Rev. Jackson's ghost pushes General R.'s speech in the direction of public confession—a push that the speaker, stumbling between "we" and "I," tries to resist. General R.'s use of "we" serves as a deflection device, a means of averting confrontation with the memory of his own acts of violence during the Emergency. But his use of the plural pronoun also poses the question for readers of what it might mean to think about that "we," the entity being reborn as a national persona on this day of independence, as having blood on its hands, as needing to incorporate the memory of a violent recent past into that more celebratory identity charted out for it through the symbolics of the flag, the foot race, and song.

When Mugo finally takes the stage, he proves able to do what General R. cannot (and what he himself could not do earlier): speak consistently in the first person, identify precisely his own role in the country's recent history, and, of course, reveal the secret of his own culpability to the community at large.

> "You asked for Judas," he started. "You asked for the man who led Kihika to this tree, here. That man stands before you, now. Kihika came to me by night. He put his life into my hands, and I sold it to the whiteman. And this thing has eaten into my life all these years."
>
> Throughout he spoke in a clear voice, pausing at the end of every sentence. When he came to the end, however, his voice broke and fell into a whisper. "Now, you know." (193)

This short declaration marks the only *public* speech in the novel that is delivered unequivocally in the first person, and that functions as a proper confession.²⁷ It is also the final public speech-act of the novel: Thabai's Uhuru celebration closes on an empty stage. Mugo has already confessed his betrayal of Kihika to Mumbi, but the higher narrative stakes of this climactic public confession match up with the novel's privileging of the communal over the interpersonal.²⁸ In both cases, however, the content and form of Mugo's confession is roughly the same: he speaks in short, declarative sentences, and he provides no explanation of his motives nor outward expression of remorse. Perhaps in keeping with his taciturn nature, but also, in this final scene, in keeping with General R.'s own perception of the public meeting as a kind of courtroom, Mugo gives away nothing, in his moment of public purgation, except for the bare facts of the case. In fact, it takes an omniscient narrator to flesh out that picture more fully for readers. Mugo's whispered tones do convey a crucial intimacy, mimicking a more private conversation between confidants within the space of a large public event; and while Mugo later gets led away presumably to his death, the crowd seems more awed by the bravery of the confession itself than horrified by its content. When a village elder approaches Mugo about speaking at the Uhuru celebrations early along in the novel, he puts forth the text's most crucial rhetorical principle: "You need not talk the whole day. I have seen many people ruin good speeches because they would talk till their mouths were drained of all saliva. A word to touch the hearts—that is all" (23). Mugo's confession, in its sorrowful brevity, finally achieves that effect—but also dissolves, once and for all, Thabai's faith in speaker-heroism. Confession constitutes community by placing the burden of action back onto a public audience, which now also must adopt new responsibilities as jurist, confidant, and confessor.

 The rise of the confession in Western modernity, Peter Brooks has argued, coincides with the point at which it becomes not only possible but imperative for the subject to ruminate on his or her interiority. Mugo's confession calls for a non-Western adjustment of Brooks's formulation in order to reflect the fact that interiority means differently in mid-twentieth-century Kenya. A Conradian obsession with the inscrutability of the self meets up, in this novel, with a social context in which individual and collective identity call for a new mode of adjudicating guilt. Mugo's confessional speech-act, indeed, may be most significant in terms of how it collapses the public and private spheres into one another. The confession is also perhaps the rhetorical form best suited to Mugo the anti-speaker-hero: Mugo needs to profess guilt, not rally his listeners to arms, and it is through this more humble genre of speech that he will ultimately become part of the community at long last. The truth of confessions, Brooks explains, "is often not straightforward but deviated from its apparent referent: a truth of performance and dialogue, a truth created by the bond of confessant and the confessional situation" (63). The consequence of Mugo's speech act is the creation of just such a bond. In Ngũgĩ's novel, confession is a performance that enables a productive collapse of the "I" and the "we," a means of foregrounding the inability of the representation-laden "we" to fully and meaningfully account for the "I" that signifies the singularity of the individual psyche and experience that the voice of the new nation will struggle, unsuccessfully, to fully capture in its official texts.[29]

In this climactic scene, the terms of public speech that Kihika and his community once accepted as a given have been disrupted and transformed. The most effective and important "solo performances" at Thabai's Uhuru celebrations are those that expose the speaker's own culpability and alienation, not those that fuel the crowd into a patriotic fervor. Audience members are no longer just audience members; their participation pulls the speakers onstage into a model of collective rather than individual heroism. The replacement of inspirational address with confession posits at least one model of the genre of speech act that is best suited to the new moment of decolonization and its complicities and uncertainties that cast the old anticolonial "will to transcendence" in a new and far less appealing light. But the question remains as to how these transformations at the level of plot inform the disruption of the novel as a whole to other discursive modes in which the African nation gets constituted in the 1960s. Constitutions and constitutionalism, upon which so many hopes were pinned during decolonization, quickly turned into what H. W. O. Okoth-Ogendo has called a situation of "constitutions without constitutionalism," a continued preoccupation with defining state power textually but without a corresponding effort to make the constitution match the realities of African political orders (or vice versa) beyond the text. In contrast to a lengthy, highly technical, and technocratic constitution, *A Grain of Wheat* asserts the importance of other, extralegal kinds of constitutive speech-acts. Forms of verbal expression that disrupt legal discourse have the potential to reinvigorate radical democracy as a popular habit.

Like Fanon's *Wretched of the Earth*, *A Grain of Wheat* not only thematizes and theorizes extralegal constitutive performances in post-independence Kenya; the novel itself is also meant to stage such a performance. Mugo struggles—and ultimately fails—to channel, in his own voice, a "we" that constitutes a truly collective "we," one that simultaneously describes and creates a national voice that accounts for the complicities and culpabilities of the country's colonial past as well as the heroism of that past. Ngũgĩ's narrative is meant to create precisely that kind of "we"—a collective political identity that mainly eludes his characters but might come to fruition instead through his readers. Ngũgĩ conceives of readers of the novel of decolonization as active participants in the historical processes that the fictional narrative recounts. Perhaps the most innovative and important aspect of how this author builds on a Fanonian model of revolutionary discourse lies in this effort to "reconstitute" his readers, and their orientation toward the nation-in-the-making, over the course of the novel.

At a key moment in the narrative, Ngũgĩ juxtaposes the decidedly local frame of action for the story—Thabai—with the postcolonial metropolitan stage on which the official, metropolitan narrative of Kenyan nationhood is composed. The opening paragraphs of the final chapter dramatize the tensions between different kinds of performances through which Kenya celebrated its independence.

> Kenya regained her Uhuru from the British on 12 December 1963. A minute before midnight, lights were put out at the Nairobi stadium so that people from all over the country and the world who had gathered there for the midnight ceremony were swallowed by the darkness. In the dark, the Union Jack was quickly lowered. When next the lights came on the new Kenya flag was flying and fluttering, and waving, in the air. The Police band played the new National Anthem and the crowd cheered continuously when they saw the flag was black, and red and green. The cheering sounded like one intense cracking of many trees, falling on the thick mud in the stadium.
>
> In our village and despite the drizzling rain, men and women and children, it seemed, had emptied themselves into the streets where they sang and danced in the mud. Because it was dark, they put oil-lamps at the doorsteps to light the streets. As usual, on such occasions, some young men walked in gangs, carrying torches, lurked and whispered in dark corners and the fringes, really looking for love-mates among the crowd. Mothers warned their daughters to take care not to be raped in the dark. The girls danced in the middle, thrusting out their buttocks provokingly, knowing that the men in corners watched them. Everybody waited for something to happen. This "waiting" and the uncertainty that went with it—like a woman torn between fear and joy during birth-motions—was a taut cord beneath the screams and the shouts and the laughter. People moved from street to street singing. They praised Jomo and Kaggia and Oginga. They recalled Waiyaki, who even before 1900 had challenged the white people who had come to Dagoreti in the wake of Lugard. They remembered heroes from our village, too. They created words to describe the deeds of Kihika in the forests, deeds matched only by those of Mugo in the trench and detention camps. They mixed Christmas hymns with songs and dances only performed during initiation rites when boys and girls are circumcised into responsibility as men and women. (177)

At the outset of this climactic public meeting, the village's improvisational and syncretic approach to marking and giving meaning to independence completely dissolves between speaker and audience—and contrasts starkly with the formal and orderly independence ceremony that takes place in Nairobi. The official staging and narrative of national independence are not quite rejected here—the narrator presents the Nairobi version of Uhuru as tangentially connected to what happens locally, an event of which Thabai's residents are in some sense aware—but that official performance does get crucially supplemented by the story of the village's creative and spontaneous approach to marking independence and assigning it meaning. It is in the gaps between events on the official schedule that real celebration takes place in Thabai—the tension of waiting gives way to communal song; a disappointing lack of energy among the crowd is broken by a sudden decision to orchestrate a footrace. Further, there is a strong suggestion here that this creative appropriation of celebrating Uhurus is connected to a longer history of metropolitan neglect: just as Kenyatta never showed up at that early pre-Emergency meeting at which Kihika first spoke, in December of 1963 regional representatives to the new government send their regrets to the village, having opted to appear at the Nairobi ceremonies rather than the local ones (190). Thabai's festivities are thus not only more creative and multilayered than the Nairobi flag raising; they are also facilitated and necessitated by the village's existence beyond the purview of the metropole. Nairobi and the state marginalize Thabai; official discourses that define nationhood through the symbolics of the flag, the constitution, and the president (whom the 1963 Constitution endows with remarkably little power) marginalize other discourses, made manifest through fiction, that threaten to challenge and complicate these official narratives.

Nairobi and Thabai's concurrent Uhuru celebrations epitomize the kind of shared temporality, the Andersonian "meanwhile," that constitutes the nation as imagined community. But the possessive pronoun at the beginning of the second paragraph troubles that common ground: in identifying Thabai as "our village," the narrator reveals his affiliation with the village rather than the capital. The opening of this chapter does not simply juxtapose Nairobi and Thabai, urban and rural, metropolitan and local, real and fictional; it also makes an assertion about the kind of narrative voice best suited to tell the story of decolonization. The first-person voice that wins out here is the last in a series of instances in which Ngũgĩ's narrator breaks away from his omniscient distanced stance and inserts himself into the action unfolding in Thabai. Such intrusions assign concrete and historicized roles for narrator and reader alike. More provocatively, these intrusions indicate that narrator, readers, and character share a common historical experience: "Many people from Thabai attended the meeting because, *as you'll remember,* we had only just been allowed to hold political meetings" (57; emphasis mine); and "Learned men will, no doubt, dig into the troubled times which we in Kenya underwent, and maybe sum up the lesson of history in a phrase" (115). Here, readers are not outside observers of historical processes; they are positioned as knowing and owning that history as a consequence of having lived it. Further, the distinction between readers' identity and "learned men" ironizes the fact that in order to access *A Grain of Wheat,* Ngũgĩ's readers must themselves be "learned" in written English. Ngũgĩ famously develops another solution to this problem a decade later when he begins writing and publishing his creative work in Gikuyu; even in this English-language novel, however, he achieves similar effects by asking readers to rethink the text itself as orature—to think of themselves as insider participants in a live performance rather than as consumers of a story of events that happened to other people in other places at other times.

Ngũgĩ takes this one step further when his narrator addresses readers not only as Kenyans, but indeed as Thabai locals who saw Mugo walking in the rain a few days before the ceremony: "Most of us from Thabai first saw him at the New Rung'ei Market the day the heavy rain fell. You remember the Wednesday, just before Independence? Wind blew and the rain hit the ground at an angle" (155). Ngũgĩ's narrator here does not simply assign readers a common nationality, one that requires non-Kenyans to imaginatively identify as national citizens. He also requires all readers, even Kenyan ones, to suspend themselves into a self-consciously fictional identity and, thus, to abandon the readerly distance enabled by the static, written form of the novel in favor of a performative, oral context for the unraveling of the story. Far from a technical weakness on Ngũgĩ's part (Williams 74), or an indication that this narrator is a "neutral" adjudicator of decolonization (Gikandi, *Ngũgĩ wa Thiong'o* 124), Ngũgĩ places greater ethical demands on his readers at such moments by implicating them in the process of constituting community with which his characters also struggle.

Moments of direct narratorial address in *A Grain of Wheat* posit an "insider" identity for Ngũgĩ's readers, an identity whose fictionality has some important consequences for how we understand the author's conception of the novel's disruption to a discourse of national constituting. In earlier chapters I discussed the importance of performative immediacy—as a practice but also as a discursive mode that gets re-presented in writing—to black Atlantic conceptualizations of liberatory anti- and postcolonial speech. In *A Grain of Wheat,* Ngũgĩ similarly juxtaposes live public rhetorical performance and its creative, popular energies with writing, which is associated with a hypocritical colonial education system and with Thabai's colonial administrators' perverse obsession with classification. *A Grain of Wheat* is typically identified by critics as Ngũgĩ's last novel to model itself primarily on European modernist incarnations of the genre. As such, it evidences the author's debt to writers such as Conrad and Lawrence, remains fixated on issues of individual agency, identity, and alienation, and lacks the formal innovativeness and commitment to a robust Marxian critique of neocolonialism that *Petals of Blood* and *Devil on the Cross* will showcase a decade later.[30] But through these moments of direct address to and identificatory involvement of his readers, Ngũgĩ also infuses this earlier novel with the ethical demands of orature. In this sense *A Grain of Wheat* prefigures the radical reworking of form that appears more explicitly in his later work—and this prefiguration is closely connected to this earlier novel's historical proximity to the constitutive moment of Kenyan decolonization.

In *A Grain of Wheat* Ngũgĩ seeks to combat the foreclosure of anticolonial aspirations for social and economic justice that state discourses of nationhood were enacting in early postcolonial Kenya. The novel's relationship with official narratives of decolonization is in this sense antagonistic and subversive. But the novel shares with early postcolonial law a certain contextual conservatism: written in European languages by Africans educated under the colonial system and immersed in Western literary traditions, African postcolonial fiction was (and to some extent continues to be) accessible only to a small fraction of the population of the new nation. Ngũgĩ's thematization of the problems of individual versus collective authorship, class fissures, and the violence of colonial education are, of course, problems with which he himself was struggling at this time. Unlike the 1963 Constitution, *A Grain of Wheat* dramatizes these conflicts and invites its readers to reflect on the importance of performative context for the successful emergence of postcolonial community.

After *A Grain of Wheat* Ngũgĩ did not publish another novel for ten years. His shift in focus to drama in the interim has much to do with its potential to provide a less mediated grassroots aesthetic-political experience. The Kamĩrĩĩthũ Community Education and Cultural Centre in Limuru, the village-based theater collective through which he (in conjunction with Ngũgĩ wa Mirii) staged *Ngaahika Ndeenda* (*I Will Marry When I Want*) in 1977, epitomized Ngũgĩ's vision for a radically democratic authentic art form: Kamĩrĩĩthũ "provided the first meaningful challenge to imperialist cultural domination in Kenya by changing the whole terms of the struggle—in location, audience, language, values, and even style of production, i.e. the communal participation" (*Writers in Politics* 47).

A Grain of Wheat nonetheless poses, and tries to answer, the question of what such a challenge might look like. What would it take for Kenya to constitute itself in the manner envisioned by and through the anticolonial struggle? I have argued that Ngũgĩ's novel is intended as a radical reflection upon, but also as a contribution to, the transformation of a colonized people into a postcolonial nation. In this, it aligns with other, contemporaneous forms of constituting that had currency in Africa during decolonization: the written state constitution, the Mau Mau oath, the anticolonial theoretical tract. These forms are products of the unique and tumultuous revolutionary temporality of decolonization: all stage their discursive interventions in response to the needs of that moment. And all, though particularly the extralegal forms, insist that constitution-making is meaningless unless it is closely tied to a community that creates and sustains it. True constituting is an inventive, participatory, and heterogeneous process. It is also incredibly fragile and rare, and dependent upon both political good faith and an ineffable creativity in a particular moment in time.

THREE DECADES AFTER *The Wretched of the Earth* appeared in print, Achille Mbembe built on Fanon's insights about the compromised nature of decolonization in the hands of a national bourgeoisie. His "Provisional Notes on the Postcolony" presents a more challenging, and (even) more pessimistic, diagnosis of the conditions under which resistance to the postcolonial African state is possible. Just as Fanon argued that it was crucial to recognize the psychic damage inflicted on *both* the colonizer and the colonized by colonialism, so Mbembe asserts that both the state and the people suffer under the power economy of postcolonialism:

> The postcolonial relationship is not primarily a relationship of resistance or of collaboration but can best be characterised as illicit cohabitation, a relationship made fraught by the very fact of the *commandement* and its "subjects" having to share the same living space . . . it has resulted in the mutual zombification of both the dominant and those whom they apparently dominate. (4)

This mutual zombification is made manifest in moments of public spectacle: "The dramatisation of the postcolonial *commandement* takes place especially during those ceremonies which make up the state's liturgical calendar" (17), scenes in which, under Cameroon's Ahidjo regime, "'Massive, spontaneous and enthusiastic' participation was expected of the masses" (18). Such performances, Mbembe contends, "have become the privileged language through which power speaks, acts, coerces" (21). Their success depends, however, on the willing participation of the people, who no longer confront or resist power but instead engage more intimately with the obscene and often ridiculous means by which the state attempts to position itself "simultaneously as indistinguishable from society and as the upholder of the law and the keeper of the truth" (5). The impulse toward escapist diversion that the Thabai villagers exhibit after the Emergency in Ngũgĩ's novel has transformed, in Mbembe's postcolony, into a tool of state control. And the public performances through which both Fanon and Ngũgĩ once imagined the realization of the anticolonial struggle's liberatory ideals are transformed into scenes of the most aggressive and spectacular co-option of those ideals. To Mbembe's litany of examples from Cameroon we might add the instance of Kenyatta's 1969 appropriation of the central discursive symbol of Mau Mau—which just a few years earlier he had perceived as a threat to state power—in a state-sponsored mass oathing campaign designed to (coercively) promote loyalty (Clough 52).

In the postcolony of Mbembe's 1992 account (reiterated and more substantially developed in his 2003 *On the Postcolony*), the liberatory potential of performance no longer has undergone some major changes since the early days of decolonization. Mbembe locates the devaluation of sovereign power in the postcolony in the same place as its expression: "instead of keeping silent in the face of obvious official lies and the effrontery of elites, this body breaks into laughter. And by laughing it drains officialdom of meaning and sometimes obliges it to function empty and powerless" (25). And "the real inversion takes place when, in their desire for a certain majesty, the masses join in the madness and clothe themselves in cheap imitations of power so as to reproduce its epistemology; and when, too, power in its own violent quest for grandeur makes vulgarity and wrongdoing its main mode of existence" (29). Just as Fanon provided little detail about what liberatory performance would look like and do, so Mbembe remains vague about the outcome and implications of this inversion. But he insists on the need for a new vantage point from which to interrogate "how the practices of those who command and of those who are assumed to obey are so entangled as to render them powerless" (29), and he calls for revaluation of the relationship between performance and resistance in the postcolony beyond the terms set out by the radical thinkers of the era of decolonization. Mbembe's assessment of the aesthetics of postcolonial power and powerlessness at the turn of the twenty-first century indicates that Fanonian and (at least early) Ngũgĩan theories of rhetorical performance are no longer sufficient. But his account also suggests the importance of the *legacies* of these theories for thinking through the challenge that radical discursive interventions pose to postcolonial juridico-political discourse after the chaotic moment of decolonization has given way to a disappointing postcolonial present and its grotesquely figured version of political community. It is to these legacies, and their presence in the postcolonial essay in the 1980s and '90s, that I turn in my final chapter.

CHAPTER 6

The Right to Opacity

Ngũgĩ, Glissant, and Radical Multilingualism

AT WHAT POINT, and with what consequences, do writers whose careers began before or during decolonization become known as "postcolonial" writers? My aim in posing this question is not to limit the term "postcolonial" to a reductively linear historical trajectory that privileges the very colonial era that postcolonial theory has always aimed to decenter.[1] Rather, I am curious about how and why this term has been applied to writers whose early work was produced and circulated against the backdrop of mid-twentieth-century national liberation struggles and their immediate aftermath. Why has "anticolonial" gained far less traction than "postcolonial" as a descriptive term for this type of African and Caribbean author—and what is lost or obscured by that choice of nomenclature? As I argued in the previous chapter, if Ngũgĩ wa Thiong'o's *A Grain of Wheat* is a postcolonial novel, it inhabits that identity most fully in its efforts to critically situate anticolonialism within the new postcolony—by probing what it would mean for revolutionary change to continue well after the advent of political independence, which on its own could not create the new postcolonial community aspired to by the national liberation struggle.

Shifting focus from the 1960s to the final decades of the twentieth century, this chapter reads comparatively between Ngũgĩ and the Martinican poet, novelist, and essayist Édouard Glissant. Both writers' careers began during rather than after "decolonization" (which meant very different things in late-twentieth-century Kenya and Martinique), and well before "postcolonialism" had any purchase as a theoretical category. In the 1980s, only Ngũgĩ was explicitly associated with postcolonial theory, a newly emergent field of critical inquiry which was (and to a large extent continues to be) an overwhelmingly anglophone enterprise. But by the end of that same decade, translations of two of Glissant's volumes of essays—*Caribbean Discourse* and *Poetics of Relation*—had begun to circulate widely in the Anglo-American academy, and by the 1990s the Martinican writer was fully ensconced in Caribbean postcolonial studies. Nonetheless, the long-standing and quite formidable disciplinary divide between francophone and anglophone literature means that as of Glissant's death in 2011 these two writers had never been in contact, nor had they ever referenced one another in their work. Ngũgĩ began writing fiction in Gikuyu rather than English in the 1970s, and subsequently became one of postcolonial theory's most vocal proponents of resisting the cultural hegemony of English by writing and publishing in non-Western languages. In contrast, by the early 1990s Glissant—who wrote in French throughout his career—had staked out significant distance between his own critical investments and those of Martinique's *Créoliste* writers, and what he saw as their overly celebratory, and borderline essentialist, claims about the subversive potential of the Creole language. Few attempts have been made, to date, to bring these two figures together for comparative study.[2]

This lack of contact between the two writers during Glissant's lifetime—and the relative dearth of critical work that reads between them—is unfortunate given the myriad areas of overlap in their intellectual and creative interests. Both Ngũgĩ and Glissant are innovators of the postcolonial literary-critical essay form. Both set out to interrogate the depths of the impact of colonialism on culture. Both are prominent theorists of language in postcolonial contexts, heavily influenced by an earlier generation of black internationalist anticolonial thinkers such as Césaire and Fanon. Moreover, their critical essays pose similar questions and problems. Ngũgĩ and Glissant approach postcolonialism with a deep historical consciousness, and a preoccupation with the question of what kinds of political, economic, imaginative conditions might bring about a politically radical new world order, the kind at least partially envisioned, if not instantiated, by midcentury anticolonial thinkers and activists. They embrace poststructural insights about language and power, an anti-/postcolonial analysis of the politics of language in the wake of colonial occupation, and a vision of the postcolonial future that sees linguistic liberation as central to other kinds of liberation. Most importantly, both champion what I am calling radical multilingualism, a politics of linguistic diversity for the postcolonial world that is also an aesthetics. Ngũgĩ's and Glissant's radical multilingualism gets worked out in their playful but also pugnacious and defiant critical essays—texts that are part of the long genealogy of declarative interventions I have traced throughout this book. Below I argue that these authors lay out the stakes of linguistic diversity in the postcolonial world by appropriating the rhetorical strategies of an increasingly prominent and powerful late-twentieth-century discourse of universal human rights.

I situate Ngũgĩ's and Glissant's critical writing within two distinct but interconnected historical frames, the first of which is the rise to prominence of universal human rights as a discursive tool of Third World activism. At forty years' distance from the moment of the drafting and ratification of the Universal Declaration of Human Rights, the geopolitical landscape of human rights discourse had changed dramatically by the 1980s. Whereas colonized peoples were largely left out of the institutions and founding texts of the postwar new world order in the 1940s, by the late twentieth century Third World concerns had become central to the missions of the UN, the Bretton Woods Institutions, and a burgeoning population of international nongovernmental organizations. Moreover, Third World emancipatory projects, for which national liberation and the creation of strong independent states had once been a focal point, were now more likely to be pitted *against* state governments—and had begun to make use of the rhetoric and institutions of universal human rights as a means of bringing international pressure to bear on oppressive postcolonial states. Beginning in the 1960s and '70s, human rights discourse proved a potent tool for postcolonial struggles for social, political, economic, and environmental justice in the Third World (Rajagopal). At the same time, the very pervasiveness of human rights as a lens through which to read and solve Third World problems has raised questions about both its limitations and its potential complicities in the context of late-twentieth- and early-twenty-first-century empire. Easily appropriable by Western policymakers as well as activists from below, human rights discourse has the potential to depoliticize, deprioritize, or drown out other kinds of social justice projects.[3]

If human rights discourse is one contemporary transnational project at constant risk of complicity with the oppressive structures it seems to be charged with resisting, postcolonial theory—of which Ngũgĩ's and Glissant's work became constitutive in the 1980s and 1990s—is another. As Neil Lazarus and others have argued, this newly ascendant field has threatened to crowd out other, potentially more radical, ways of thinking and talking about the decolonized world in the academy.[4] Postcolonial theory presupposes a historical *and* ideological break between midcentury anticolonialism and the political, cultural, and philosophical conditions of the 1980s and '90s. Through their potency and ubiquity, both postcolonial theory and human rights discourse risk occluding alternative frameworks for thinking and talking about the non-Western world; and both are premised on the belief that anticolonial struggles and their attendant discourses are part of an earlier historical moment, one with limited relevance to the postcolonial landscape of the late twentieth century and beyond.

Invested in a different vocabulary and an ostensibly separate set of historical and political concerns, postcolonial studies only began expressly interrogating human rights discourse in the twenty-first century. While arguably there are few seminal texts of postcolonial theory for which human rights is not implicitly central—the *sati* case at the heart of Spivak's "Can the Subaltern Speak?" is a prime example, illuminating the conflict between "cultural" and "women's" rights and, for Spivak, exposing the problem of choosing between these alternatives at all—human rights was not a key term for the field during its first two decades of existence. Yet it was during this period that Glissant's and Ngũgĩ's critical essays made a human rights imaginary vital to their articulation of radical multilingualism, and to their framing of the relationship between postcolonial poetics and politics. Inhabiting while also critically interrogating the rhetorical work of the rights declaration, their work explores the possibilities and the limitations of the concept of human rights for a postcolonialism that retains the revolutionary imagination of midcentury anticolonialism.

GLISSANT'S ANTI-/POSTCOLONIAL POETICS: DECLARING THE UNDECLARABLE

In an early essay of *Caribbean Discourse,* Édouard Glissant reproduces the full text of one of Martinique's most important historical documents: Louis Thomas Husson's 1848 proclamation to the island's field slaves, in which this colonial functionary announces the passage of emancipation law in France and the imminent—though not instantaneous—abolition of slavery in the French Antillean sugar colonies. Husson gave his speech on March 31, shortly after France's National Assembly had issued its initial abolition decree, but before this decree was scheduled to actually take effect in Martinique. Assuring the field slaves that freedom was imminent, he urged them to wait patiently and peacefully until the legal apparatus of abolition had been fully instituted. Husson was not entirely successful on either count, as evidenced by the slave revolts that took place across the island just a few weeks later. Yet for Glissant, the more significant effects of this text, "the thinly veiled declaration of our alienation" (27), took shape over a longer swath of time. They continue to be felt in the late twentieth century on an island which twice, once in 1848 and again in 1946, forfeited a more radical, Haiti-esque form of liberation in favor of continued submission to French rule. The paternalistic circumscription of the terms of Martinique's nineteenth-century liberation are palpable in the opening words of Husson's speech:

> My Friends,
> You have all heard the good news that has just come from France. It is true: it is General Rostoland and myself who brought it. We took the steamer in order to get here very quickly.
> Freedom will come! Good luck, my children, you deserve it . . .
> But the republic needs time to gather the funds for the purchase [of the slaves' freedom from the planters] and to pass the law of abolition. So, nothing has changed, for the present. You remain slaves until the law is official. Then Governor Rostoland will send me to tell you: "Freedom has come, long live the republic!" (*Caribbean Discourse* 31)

But before he quotes Husson, Glissant offers up his own liberal and ironic gloss of his words, illuminating the consequences of this speech for Martinique's cultural, economic, and political dispossession over the next century and a half.

> *Glad Tidings!* This will be the principle of our political and collective existence. Herein lies the first formulation of the Other Land.
> The steamer. To get there more quickly. The transatlantic liner, the *Latécoère*, the Boeing: the infinite manifestations of the umbilical cord. (27–28)

If Husson's proclamation is an all too familiar component of Martinican history, then Glissant's reading thereof—or rather, his *pre*reading—is meant to defamiliarize it for his readers. Inverting the relationship between the original text and his own satirical commentary by presenting the latter first, he challenges the speech's status as historical artifact, stressing instead its discursive continuity with Martinique's present-day relationship with France. The 1848 text makes manifest the way in which the historical moment of abolition is responsible for undermining Martinique's liberation from colonial exploitation while purporting to do the opposite. In order to carve out a new emancipatory project for Martinique, one that meets the demands of the not-quite-postcolonial present, Glissant insists on the need to approach this historical document with new eyes.

Glissant's engagement with Husson's text at the outset of *Caribbean Discourse* speaks to just how deeply engrained this speech is in his own historical imagination.[5] And as he notes, he is not the first twentieth-century Martinican writer for whom this is true: several decades earlier Aimé Césaire rendered this famous document infamous by exposing its racist paternalism in *Victor Schoelcher et l'abolition de l'esclavage*. Glissant's aim is not to reiterate Césaire's assessment of the document's "repulsive, hypocritical, sanctimonious, and basically proslavery posture" (*Caribbean Discourse* 30), but rather to suggest that such a scathing critique is no longer sufficient:

> I feel we have never considered this text in its entirety, never clarified its implications or its consequences. It is certainly not a text that *created* the historical events that followed; it is nothing but their prefiguration expressed in a public form. But it is certain that therein lies the expression, for once in written form, of a political will whose strategic orientation will be increasingly difficult to evaluate. (27)

The very familiarity of Husson and his words masks the true implications of the speech—which is also a historical event in and of itself—for Martinique's post-emancipation future. The colonial institutions and discourses surrounding the proclamation bear much of the blame for Martinique's cultural and economic alienation, but so do Martinicans, who, in Glissant's assessment, have become far less adept at maintaining a vital critical distance from France over time: "We know that the slaves of 1848 did not fall for these pretty words, and that the proclamation at the end of March did not forestall the revolts in May, which led to the promulgation of the decree of abolition *before* it arrived properly signed" (30). Husson's original audience, in other words, was not seduced by this performance of legal authority. But that resistant collective consciousness has dissipated since 1848: "We have all listened to M. Husson, and little by little stopped sneering" (30). Glissant's project, then, is to reintroduce the sneer to the interpretive contexts of the discourse of abolition.

A century and a half after emancipation, and decades after departmentalization, the Husson proclamation has much to tell Glissant and his readers about the role of law in late-twentieth-century Martinique. Carried across the vast space of the Atlantic by self-consciously benevolent agents who control its contents as well as the time frame and method of its execution, emancipation law is an import: it comes from France, and arrives and takes effect in the Caribbean on France's schedule. Glissant's rephrasing of Husson's words shifts the emphasis away from the bureaucratic hurdles that slow the legal emancipation process, and onto the problem of oceanic space. The Atlantic interrupts the legal space–time continuum between metropole and colonial outpost. This interruption, of course, was exactly what made it possible for the *Déclaration des droits de l'homme et du citoyen* and Atlantic slavery to coexist in the first half of the nineteenth century. And it creates the buffer that Husson needs in order to present himself, the governor of Martinique, and the colonial administration writ large as essential mediators between two different legal spaces and temporalities. The interruption of oceanic space becomes a powerful rhetorical tool for Husson as well as a crucial component of how the Antilles' relationship to French law is defined in the speech. The Atlantic is an ocean that only Husson can cross; and it must be crossed in order to enable the law to make its arrival. By the time law arrives in Martinique, it has transformed from a primarily conceptual entity to a primarily *material* entity. Further, Glissant explains, this transatlantic economy of law has remained intact over time, even if abolition (following enslavement) is no longer the commodity making the journey: "The good news still comes from elsewhere. Today it deals with the publication of the figures for *official aid*" (35). Freedom and economic self-sufficiency transform from rights to gifts as they travel across the ocean.

Husson's text largely disappears from *Caribbean Discourse* after this early essay. But 1848 remains an important historical touchstone throughout the volume, and Glissant does reference the proclamation once more, in a concluding assertion of the dream of Martinican independence. Husson's speech is the legal-literary textual artifact that mocks that dream. Whereas in Haiti the abolition of slavery went hand in hand with national independence at the outset of the nineteenth century, in Martinique emancipation was a legal achievement that bound the island all the more tightly to France, and undermined the possibility of more expansive and subversive forms of liberation for years to come. Husson's proclamation serves as an insidious, farcical substitute for the types of founding documents that Martinique never had, a declaration of independence and a sovereign state constitution. Moreover, the text serves as a reminder of the absence of revolution in Martinican history. Glissant hints at this absence as he reflects on recent efforts to commemorate the May 1848 slave revolts with a national holiday. "The 'liberation' of 1848, paradoxically, has nothing to do with the community," he observes, for it was at that time that "the latter lost any sense of organization or future; any ability to conceive of themselves as a group." The nationalism to which Martinicans aspire remains a dream deferred, and one in which, at least as of 1981, Glissant remains heavily invested: "The 'national holiday' for Martinique is yet to come; that will be the day when the reality of the nation will have been established" (252).

Glissant's (pre)reading of Husson's proclamation in *Caribbean Discourse* prompts two interconnected questions for me. The first is a question that has become a focal point for several recent critical appraisals of this writer: what importance should we assign to what we might loosely define as a set of anticolonial concerns—national independence, political liberation, and, more generally, the category of the political—in *Caribbean Discourse* as well as in Glissant's later volumes of essays?[6] The second question, though closely related to the above, has conspicuously not yet been explored by critics. What do we make of Glissant's preoccupation with *law* at the beginning and end of *Caribbean Discourse*? In this early volume of essays Glissant is much more explicitly and unequivocally invested in questions of Martinican national identity than in his later work; and even so, this text expresses plenty of dissatisfaction with what for him is an unproductive dialectic of nationalist/nativist celebrations of "authentic" Martinican culture. For Glissant, the way out of this dialectic is through a focus on poetics rather than politics—an exploration of new imaginative possibilities for Martinican identity and cultural expression, not the formulation of a political response to France's economic and political dispossession of its overseas departments.

Glissant's opening engagement with Husson's speech is more important to the fabric of *Caribbean Discourse,* and indeed to the "poetics of relation" with which he becomes increasingly preoccupied throughout the 1980s, than it seems. The legal authority of Husson's speech goes hand in hand with an authority it claims over language. It is the bilingual dissemination of this text that reveals the intimate and insidious link between colonialism's legal discourse and a politics of language that has long served as a distraction from Martinique's more fundamental disenfranchisement under French rule.

> To put the final touch to the quality of "historical document" in M. Husson's text, the poster was displayed in a *bilingual* form. In French on the left and in Creole on the right. Yes. A bilingual proclamation. How not to be amazed? Something "fundamental," like the treaty dividing the Carolingian empire. And if one can imagine that the Creole text was read aloud to the inhabitants of Martinique, who were no more literate in that language than in French, then imagine as well some civil servant commissioned to do the Creole "translation," cursing this extra, absolutely absurd task, and setting to work on this crazy black pidgin that will later fill us with wonder. (37)

An ostensibly liberal gesture toward inclusivity and diversity, the translation of Husson's proclamation into Creole obscures the fact that the contents of that proclamation undermine the development of a subversive, anticolonial Martinican national identity—one that, in the late twentieth century, the Creole language has come to represent. Husson's French converts from a singular oral performance to a reproducible textual form; it is this textualized version of French for which an equally diminutive, "equivalent" textualized version of Creole is found for the poster.

As Glissant explains at length in the remainder of *Caribbean Discourse*, Creole's status as a "native" language, and its historical role as a tool of resistance to colonial oppression, are riddled with ambivalence. Creole has certainly served a powerful role as a language of protest in Martinican history, but on its own—particularly in its increasingly standardized orthographic form, developed and disseminated by policymakers and writers—it is ill equipped to address monolingualism, which for Glissant is the much more serious problem that Martinique faces in its quest to give voice to itself as a national community. Creole "has not been able so far to reflect on itself"; in remaining just as locked into a rigid, rule-based concept of language, and specifically in remaining unreflective about the nature and possibilities of expression, the language "falls short of its potential" (166). Through Husson's speech Glissant exposes monolingualism masquerading as bilingualism, an instance in which the colonial authorities seem to exhibit respect for linguistic diversity while at the same time reaffirming the system of legal and linguistic authority in which Sameness rules the day.

This masquerade has significant consequences for Martinican nationalism and language politics in the twentieth century. To merely celebrate Creole as a subversive national language is to perpetuate the fiction that a Martinican national identity has actually had the chance to come into existence; "To claim that Creole has always been our national language is to even further obscure . . . the disturbing self-doubt that is the source of our insecurity but that also establishes our presence" (167). If Creole were to truly become a national language, free of that self-doubt, "the ambiguity of the relationship of French to Creole would disappear and . . . each Martinican would have access to the sociocultural means of using French without a sense of alienation, of speaking Creole without feeling confined by its limitations" (167). Creole's greatest success has been its usefulness as a tool of protest, a means of challenging the hegemony of French and asserting the existence of a national identity at least as a potentiality. But the more profound change has yet to come, for it is a change that entails not merely giving primacy to a non-European language but also reconfiguring the expressive universe in which both languages exist.

> We will perhaps be the ones to teach others a new poetics and, leaving behind the poetics of not-knowing (counterpoetics), will initiate others into a new chapter in the history of mankind. Indeed, we may be the ones (except in the eventuality of some monolithic language that suddenly descends and

covers over all our countries) who will fuse, one with the other, these new forms of expression through our combined poetics, and far removed from abstract universality, with the fertile yet difficult relationship with our willed, collective need for obscurity. (169–70)

The problem with championing Martinican Creole is that doing so accepts wholesale the idea of language as a fixed and above all a transparent, translatable system. As such, it cannot meet "our willed, collective need for obscurity." Monolingualism, for Glissant, is not just about language. It is a false universal, a claim to mastery that forecloses the possibility of future engagements with otherness. There is nothing inherently universal, and nothing inherently liberatory, about any language. But the fixity that Glissant associates in the bilingual presentation of Husson's 1848 proclamation with both textuality and translatability is inherently oppressive. The poster's attempt to render the law accessible to all in fact achieves the opposite, affirming the formal and imaginative fixity of both language and law—a fixity that Glissant will devote much of his intellectual energy, in *Caribbean Discourse* and beyond, to dispelling.

Husson's is not the only declarative text that fares badly in *Caribbean Discourse*. In the early pages of *Caribbean Discourse* Glissant establishes some distance between his project and that of his negritudean predecessors by critiquing those writers' formal choices. He does not spend much time in this text engaging Césaire's work—having done so at more length in his earlier *L'Intention poétique*—but a hefty footnote early along in this collection does summarize his sense of the historical distance between their projects.

> M. Aimé Césaire comes to this conclusion (in the euphoria, admittedly, of 1948) in his introduction to the (Selected Works) *Oeuvres choisies* of Victor Schoelcher: "He brought political freedom to blacks in the French Caribbean ... created a startling contradiction that cannot but explode the old order of things: *that which makes the modern colonized man at the same time a full citizen and a complete proletarian.* From this time on, on the edge of the Caribbean sea as well, the motor of History is about to roar into life."
> It is difficult today to identify with these declarations.
> Because we know that here political freedom has been only a constant lure. That the Martinican is neither a full citizen (he is not from the city) nor a complete proletarian (but a "dispersed" proletarian). That History is that which has been opposed unrelentingly to the converging histories of the Caribbean, and that since the "liberation" of 1848 what has indeed increased is the snoring of the sleep of assimilation, interrupted by tragic explosions of popular impulses, never enough to resolve the dilemma. (50)

Glissant's long-standing political differences with Césaire are made clear here: as the co-founder of the Front Antillo-Guyanais de l'Autonomie in 1959, he was arguably far *more* "anticolonial" than the mayor of Fort-de-France who brokered Martinique's transition from colony to department in the mid-twentieth century. At some years' remove from his anti-departmental activism, Glissant here makes the case for why anticolonialism in the (late-twentieth-century) present needs to encompass much more than just the goal of political liberation.

But it is noteworthy that in order to do so, he points not to the content of Césaire's comments on Schoelcher so much as to the form in which those comments are made. Glissant's unease lies with Césaire's declarations rather than with Césaire himself. We are removed, he explains, not only from the unbridled optimism of Césaire's "euphoric" historical moment, but also from the impact of the rhetorical form that such optimism took in 1948. Declarations eschew ambiguity, and a certain amount of ambiguity is constitutive of the later twentieth century, in which, Glissant explains, drawing clear distinctions between categories such as "citizen" and "proletarian" is no longer possible. He reiterates this point about Césaire in an interview many years later: "The political declarations in *Notebook of a Return to the Native Land* have always seemed slightly rhetorical to me. And that's all we retain because it's easy, it's clear, it reassures, everyone, it lends courage and all of that. But the rest—and what is most important— we don't even see" (Dash and Troupe 50). His evaluation of declarations in *Poetics of Relation* echoes this sentiment; "grounded in the old Manichaeanism of liberation," declarations "are of no use [in the present], because they only contribute to reinforcing a stereotypical language with no hold in reality. These are all liabilities whose dialectics must first be either realized or bypassed" (152). Anticolonial declarative rhetorics ultimately fall prey to the very rigidities and oppressions that they were meant to oppose: "The West," he writes,

> is where [the] movement [of the people] becomes fixed and nations declare themselves in preparation for their repercussions in the world. This fixing, this declaration, this expansion, all require that the idea of the root gradually take on the intolerant sense that Deleuze and Guattari, no doubt, meant to challenge... Most of the nations that gained freedom from colonization have tended to form around an idea of power—the totalitarian drive of a single, unique root—rather than around a fundamental relationship with the Other. Culture's self-conception was dualistic, pitting citizen against barbarian. (*Poetics* 14)

These forms of expression have proved equally inadequate to the post-decolonization Third World:

In poor countries any appeal for self-sufficiency grounded solely in economics and good sense is doomed to failure. Good sense is of no consequence in the tangle of world Relation. Sensibilities have become so profoundly contaminated, in most cases, and the habit of material comfort is so well established, even in the midst of the greatest poverty, that political dictates or proclamations are inadequate remedies. (149)

Declarations are the formal means of expression for imaginatively impoverished political goals—for projects that rely on essentialist or empirical thinking at the expense of a fluid and more capacious notion of cultural exchange and creativity that is central to Glissant's work. The "totalitarian" fixity that he abhors materializes in self-assured, affirming declarative texts that depend on an intolerant dualism. Critiquing the declaration, in both *Caribbean Discourse* and *Poetics of Relation,* is a means for Glissant to distance himself from an older anticolonial politics that has outlived its usefulness. And, in keeping with the assessment of the evolution of his writing espoused by critics such as Peter Hallward and Chris Bongie, it also seems to imply a retreat, in his later work, from political questions and concerns.

I wish to offer an alternative perspective on the development of Glissant's thought between the publication of these two texts. Despite this repeated insistence on the imaginative paucity of declarative forms, on a deeper level, Glissant's preoccupation with the disruptive potential of the declaration is one of the most important points of continuity between his work and that of the negritudean writers he most admired, Césaire and Fanon. Glissant is ultimately less critical of negritude and the oppositional anticolonialism of its Martinican figureheads than the passages quoted above suggest. Moreover, he is deeply invested—albeit not uncritically—in the same *anticolonial* question Césaire and Fanon confronted: that of how to develop a novel rhetorical form through which to express the political novelty of the anticipated and desired postcolonial future. Glissant's treatment of Fanon in *Caribbean Discourse,* as well as the myriad Fanonian echoes that run through this text, make this common investment manifest.[7] Like Fanon, he writes in French while also serving as a scathing critic of the French language's claims to purity and universal humanism. Moreover, the problem he aims to address in *Caribbean Discourse*—that of how to cultivate a national consciousness that retains a vigilant critical edge, and that resists the lure of merely fetishizing the local— is quintessentially Fanonian. "What is missing from the notion of Caribbeanness is the transition from the shared experience to conscious expression; the need to transcend the intellectual pretensions dominated by the learned elite and to be grounded in collective affirmation, supported by the activism of the people" (*Caribbean Discourse* 222). But for the word "Caribbeanness," this statement might well have come straight from the pages of one of the middle chapters of *Les Damnés de la terre*. In "On National Culture" Fanon warns against the colonial intellectual's capacity for exoticism, distinguishes national culture from folklore, laments the sapping of "creativity" and "ebullience" from native cultural expression under colonial rule, and insists that political liberation and the emergence of new cultural and aesthetic forms are inextricably linked (*Wretched* 177). Practically quoting his predecessor, Glissant "define[s] national literature as the urge for each group to assert itself: that is, the need not to disappear from the world scene and on the contrary to share in its diversification" (*Caribbean Discourse* 99). Even if suspicious of declarations themselves, Glissant takes the *desire* to declare—a desire manifested in literature—very seriously. If, as he contends, the history of modernity is shaped by the West's attempt to impose an oppressive Sameness on the world, the non-West responds by exploding that Sameness through self-assertion, which for Glissant is a fundamentally literary activity: "I define national literature as the urge for each group to assert itself; that is, the need not to disappear from the world scene and on the contrary to share in its diversification" (99). National literature is situated and responsive; self-assertion requires more than either mere reversion to folklore or an appropriation of European aesthetic forms. "We say that a national literature emerges when a community whose collective existence is called into question tries to put together the reasons for its existence" (104). A new global humanism is at stake in this work of declaring a collective identity; "If [the peoples of the world] do not assert themselves, they deprive the world of a part of itself" (99). Far less invested in cultural expression as part of a dialectic than Fanon, Glissant nonetheless shares his predecessor's opinion that the work of challenging the oppressively totalizing authority of the West ultimately saves the West from itself.

Throughout *Caribbean Discourse* Glissant acknowledges his debt to Césaire and Fanon—and, specifically, to the way in which these negritudean forefathers united words and action in powerful new ways. Both did the work of "acting one's ideas," and of "tak[ing] full responsibility for a complete break" from colonialism (25). For Fanon that break was political; for Césaire, poetic. Both kinds of break are crucial, and both must happen through language: "The word must be mastered. But such a mastery will be insignificant unless it is an integral part of a resolute collective act—a political act" (163). Even as Glissant figures negritude as troublingly dependent on declarative forms and their associated restrictive identity politics, he ultimately reaffirms these earlier writers' commitment to the creation of new, emancipatory identities through rhetorical performance: "To declare one's own identity is to write the world into existence" (169).

Glissant thus rejects what he sees as the declaration's tendency toward fixity and totalization while at the same time affirming and embracing the desire and need to declare. In both *Caribbean Discourse* and *Poetics of Relation* he recognizes this desire and need as integral to the increasingly unproductive dialectic of colonial control and resistance that continues to play out in the late twentieth century. Indeed this impulse—articulated in declarative form—frames these two texts. Here is the dramatic rights claim that appears in the opening pages of *Caribbean Discourse*:

> We demand the right to obscurity [*Nous réclamons le droit à l'opacité*].[8] Through which our anxiety to have an existence becomes part of the universal drama of cultural transformation: the creativity of marginalized peoples who today confront the ideal of transparent universality, imposed by the West, with secretive and multiple manifestations of Diversity. Such a process is spectacular everywhere in the world where murders, shameless acts of genocide, tactics of terror, try to crush the precious resistance of various peoples. It is imperceptible when we are dealing with communities condemned to such a painless oblivion.
>
> The discourse of such communities (those shadowy threads of meaning where their silence is voiced) must be studied if we wish to gain a profound insight into the drama of creolization taking place on a global scale. Even if we consider this silence and this emptiness as meaningless in the face of the terrible and definitive muteness of those peoples physically undermined and overwhelmed by famine and disease, terror and devastation—which well-heeled countries accommodate so easily. (2)

Introduced here for the first time, *opacité* will remain a central aesthetic principle in Glissant's work for years to come. And yet here at the beginning of *Caribbean Discourse* the stakes of this concept are tied to a whole host of material realities such as genocide, famine, terror—realities which in the late twentieth century are associated both with the Third World writ large and with other, very different kinds of rights claims—the claims of human rights. Glissant here links Martinique to a number of postcolonial/global crises from which his own island has been mainly sheltered due in part to its ongoing political and economic ties to France. Moreover, he establishes a relationship between the major claims of the volume—about language, literature, culture, and aesthetics—and a "terrible and definitive muteness" that crosses national and regional boundaries. It is here that *Caribbean Discourse* reveals itself as an ethical project, a volume in which Glissant's lyricality complements criticism in order to insist that social, political, and economic problems are also fundamentally problems of the imagination:

> Yes. The anxious serenity of our existence, through so many obscure channels linked to the trembling world. In our detached stillness, something somewhere breaks free from someone's suffering or hurt and comes to rest in us. The salt of death on exhausted men, wandering across a desert that is certainly not freedom. The devastation of entire peoples. Those who are sold. Children blinded by their incomprehensible agony. Victims of torture who see death lingering in the distance. The smell of oil on dusty skins. The growing layers of mud. We are at the outer edge and remain silent. (2–3)

The collective demand and accompanying confident "we" with which *Caribbean Discourse* opens might be read as a symptom of this early work's investment in Martinican nationalism, and in a more affirmative kind of political project that fades away later in Glissant's career. But the broader vision of this declaration, its rapid unfolding into a call for the recognition of creolization as a global phenomenon poised to combat the existential *and* material violences of empire, belies such a reading. So does Glissant's energized reiteration of this declaration toward the end of *Poetics of Relation*: "We clamor for the right to opacity for everyone" (194) ["*Nous réclamons pour tous le droit à l'opacité*" (*Poétique* 209)]. "Everyone," as I discuss in more detail in relation to Ngũgĩ below, is a pronoun loaded with global connotations in the age of the Universal Declaration of Human Rights; it is a pronoun that signals a dream of global justice, of an indiscriminate principle through which national boundaries and even the particularities of international communities give way to a utopian vision of equality based in a very specifically twentieth-century sense of the global. In one of the final essays of this later collection, Glissant reasserts *Caribbean Discourse*'s opening demand, tweaking it slightly to stress its universal applicability—and thereby phrasing it more explicitly as a kind of human rights claim. A decade of widespread interest in theories of difference, he explains, may account for the fact that this demand seems to make more sense to readers now than it did when he first articulated it (189). But difference and opacity are importantly not identical:

> Agree not merely to the right to difference but, carrying this further, agree also to the right to opacity that is not enclosure within an impenetrable autarchy but subsistence within an irreducible singularity. Opacities can

coexist and converge, weaving fabrics. To understand these truly one must focus on the texture of the weave and not on the nature of its components. For the time being, perhaps, give up this old obsession with discovering what lies at the bottom of natures. There would be something great and noble about initiating such a movement, referring not to Humanity but to the exultant divergence of humanities. Thought of self and thought of other here become obsolete in their duality. Every Other is a citizen and no longer a barbarian. What is here is open, as much as this there. I would be incapable of projecting from one to the other. This-here is the weave, and it weaves no boundaries. The right to opacity would not establish autism; it would be the real foundation of Relation, in freedoms. (190)

Opacity is meant to mark an end to essentialism, the self/Other binary, and the categories of sameness and difference that have enabled (and been created by) the same structures responsible for slavery, colonialism, and empire. The language Glissant uses to explain their replacement is a language of internationalism—but not an internationalism that is composed of a collection of entities defined by boundaries, citizenship, and essences. Rooted in opacity rather than difference, this internationalism does not easily accommodate the nation. But neither does it give way to a totalizing universalism; note the pluralization of "humanities," "freedoms," and even "opacities."

The importance of the concept of *opacité* to both *Caribbean Discourse* and *Poetics of Relation* is hard to miss. What is less obvious is why in both texts opacity is presented as a *right*. Why draw upon a juridico-political language of rights claims in order to give weight and resonance to this concept? The stakes of rights discourse in francophone postcolonial contexts are somewhat unique—a point Glissant comes to by way of a discussion in *Poetics of Relation* about the historical role of French in Martinique. French has long served as "the a priori bearer of values that could help remedy the anarchistic tendencies of the various cultures that are, completely or partially, a product of its expression" (112). The French-language international community has traditionally reflected that view of French as both humanistic and humanitarian, "inseparable from the pursuit of the dignity of mankind, insofar as man is conceived as an irreducible entity." French has direct ties not only with humanism's literary and cultural appendages but also with humanism's translation into the political sphere—it is an agent not only of universal humanism but of universal human rights. "In the present conceptual debate the French language, the language of the Rights of Man, would provide useful protection against excesses set in motion by the presuppositions of any proclamation of the Rights of Peoples. *La francophonie* would provide that transcendency by giving the correct version of humanism" (113). Glissant here invokes what in the 1980s and '90s was a major source of tension for human rights activists and policymakers: how to negotiate the set of individual civil and political rights whose discursive and philosophical origins could be fairly straightforwardly traced back to Enlightenment thinkers and texts from the Age of Revolution, and a more recent way of thinking about collective rights that owed much to a critique of the Eurocentrism of universal human rights in theory and practice.[9] Glissant situates the Rights of Peoples in opposition to the Rights of Man in this formulation because the former are essentially *postcolonial* rights; they represent an alternative vision of the possible scope of contemporary human rights discourse that has gained some discursive and even institutional legitimacy by the '80s—for example, in the form of the 1981/1986 African Charter on Human and People's Rights and the 1989 International Labour Organization Convention Concerning Indigenous and Tribal Peoples in Independent Countries. Group rights are ultimately no less problematic for Glissant than their Enlightenment-era counterparts; "poor nations, by their very eruption, had made it possible for new ideas to be born: ideas of otherness, of difference, of minority rights of peoples. These ideas, however, seemed only to dust the surface of the swirling magma" (136).

To assert *opacité* as a right is to first embrace a juridico-political discourse closely associated with both France and the French language, and to then explode that discourse by challenging its association with a monolingual politics of identity, a politics by which *opacité* cannot be contained. But it is the *declaration* of opacity that constitutes the central "event" that ties *Caribbean Discourse* and *Poetics of Relation* together. And that event evokes not just Western rights discourse but also a contemporary Caribbean appropriation of the declaration from which Glissant was busy distancing himself in the '80s and '90s. The declarative text that Glissant did *not* write during this time was *Éloge de la Créolité*, Jean Bernabé, Raphaël Confiant, and Patrick Chamoiseau's lyrical manifesto of a Creole poetics defined by its celebration of the racial, cultural, and linguistic hybridity in which Caribbean identity is grounded. The authors cite Glissant as a chief source of inspiration, and much of the language in which they articulate Creoleness is thoroughly Glissantian: Creoleness is "an open specificity," "an annihilation of false universality, of monolingualism, of purity" (Bernabé et al. 90). Creoleness is characterized by a Glissantian resistance to linguistic fixity; it "is not monolingual. Nor is its multilingualism divided into isolated compartments ... Living at once the poetics of all languages is not just enriching each of them, but also, and above all, breaking the customary order of these languages, reversing their established meanings" (107–8). Yet the major difference between Glissantian and *Créoliste* approaches to identity is announced in the *Éloge*'s opening sentence: "Neither Europeans, nor Africans, nor Asians, we proclaim ourselves Creoles" (75). Though the "we" is defined in the negative, and though the *Éloge* will go on to assert the global implications of the concept, Creoleness presumes the existence of a fixed identity—a self available for triumphalist and affirmative proclamation. "We declare ourselves Creoles. We declare that Creoleness is the cement of our culture and that it ought to rule the foundations of our Caribbeanness" (87). Contrast these formulations with Glissant's introduction to the concept of creolization in *Poetics of Relation,* also one of the few moments in this text in which he obliquely references his *Créoliste* contemporaries:

> We propose neither humanity's Being nor its models. We are not prompted solely by the defining of our identities but by their relation to everything possible as well—the mutual mutations generated by this interplay of relations. Creolizations bring into Relation but not to universalize; the principles of creoleness regress toward negritudes, ideas of Frenchness, of Latinness, all generalizing concepts—more or less innocently. (*Poetics* 89)

The critical antagonism between Glissant and the *Créolistes* is a gentle one—presented here as more of a concern or a preference than a theoretical fault line.[10] As Chris Bongie has observed, the two critiques are part of one and the same "Creole Continuum" (*Islands and Exiles* 42). The difference between them—the element in Glissant's radical multilingualism that prevents it from "regressing" in the way he ascribes to Creoleness—is at least as much a formal as it is a conceptual difference. Like negritude before it, Creoleness has surrendered a crucial ambiguity in the service of declaring itself; unlike negritude, Creoleness makes this trade-off at a historical moment in which that ambiguity is needed more than ever.

Though the authors themselves do not label their text as such, the *Éloge* is widely regarded as a manifesto.[11] "*Praise*'s cosigners," Mylène Priam argues, "creatively adapted the main function of literary and artistic manifestos"—she has in mind particularly the manifestos of Italian futurists—"which is to allow art to continue exerting its influence on the social body by viewing reality through the prism of aesthetic, literary, or poetic vision" (24). The structure and rhetorical features of the text conform to the conventions of the genre, but even more importantly, its authors are intent on bringing the program they described to life through their craft; in their creative work, they go on to enact the Creoleness that they describe, celebrate, and demand on the page. The essentialist elements of the *Éloge,* we might infer from Priam's reading, are perhaps not lacking in strategy; for if this text is a manifesto, then it is a *performative* presentation of selfhood, one "tied to the present time and to the Caribbean space, while perceiving this space in a multi-relational perspective and considering its future in an open way" (31).

This practical, strategic imperative at the heart of the *Éloge* marks the most significant point of divergence between this text and Glissant's own work—not because Glissant, himself a novelist as well as a critic, was not also preoccupied with the question of how to "exert influence on the social body" through art, but rather because he did not articulate a specific program for such exertion. Just as, forty years earlier, Césaire skirted the genre of the manifesto and its attendant ideological orthodoxies, so Glissant distances himself from a form that distills Creoleness to a fixed identity. The manifesto, whose etymological origins connect it to the work of bringing things to light, cannot accommodate the concept that Glissant comes closest to presenting declaratively in his own work. The right to opacity, "not enclosure within an impenetrable autarchy but subsistence within an irreducible singularity" (*Poetics* 190), supersedes the discourse of difference, rooted in identity politics, which Glissant claims has been "exhausted" by the end of the 1980s (189).

The declarative moments embedded within *Caribbean Discourse* and *Poetics of Relation* do not aim to make manifest a new identity. What they do instead is assert a rights claim. Glissant's engagement with a discourse of rights is a provocative rhetorical flourish, but here I have aimed to show that it signals more than that. Opacity breaks new ground within the terrain of poetics that Glissant explores in these volumes. But what if it also had the potential to break new ground within a juridico-political discourse of rights? If first-generation rights are civil and political, second-generation social and economic, and third-generation collective—rights, in other words, that protect and affirm difference—then perhaps we might think of *opacité* as a "fourth-generation right," a harbinger of a rights discourse (and movement) that is yet to come. Moreover, *opacité* would call into question the nature of (human) rights itself. Is the logical end of human rights discourse, of a global striving for a new humanism, one that necessarily privileges poetics—not as an escape from politics, but as the strategy that has the potential to give politics what it has been missing? *Caribbean Discourse* begins with a satirical deconstruction of legal discourse. It ends with a meditation on the same problem of the relationship between expression and action that confronted the writers of negritude many years earlier: "Let us not stop with this commonplace: that a poetics cannot guarantee us a concrete means of action. But a poetics, perhaps, does allow us to understand better our action in the world" (199). Less intent on escaping or transcending the political than on redefining it, Glissant draws on a discourse of human rights—and its long history of muddling the lines between the political and the ethical—in order to put forth a vision of how a poetics of opacity might be able to help reconfigure that discourse.

NGŨGĨ'S WORLD OF LANGUAGES: PERFORMING GIKUYU FOR THE NORTH AMERICAN ACADEMY

In January 1989, a decade into his forced exile from Kenya, Ngũgĩ wa Thiong'o arrived at Yale University as a visiting professor. While he spent his first weeks there doing his best to "completely shut New Haven out of [his] consciousness" (*Moving the Centre* 156), he enjoyed teaching, liked the library, and discovered a graduate student population with a great deal of interest in African languages and literatures. His time in New Haven also afforded him the opportunity to publish, for the first time, a Gikuyu-language essay in a North American scholarly journal.

> When I had dinner with one of the editors of the prestigious *Yale Journal of Criticism* I tried to get out of her request that I contribute an article by telling her that I only wrote in Gikuyu. She looked me in the eye and said: write in Gikuyu. We shall publish it. (156–57)

Accordingly, Ngũgĩ submitted an article for publication in the Fall 1990 issue of the journal entitled "Kĩĩngeretha Rũthiomi Rwa Thĩ Yoothe?" / "English: A Language for the World?" The text appeared first in Gikuyu and was followed by an English translation (prepared by himself and Wangũi wa Goro). Ngũgĩ's claim to the editor was not entirely accurate: he had indeed written and published all of his *literary* works from 1978 onward in Gikuyu, but had also, during that same period, published several volumes of essays of political and cultural criticism in English. Nonetheless, the publication of this essay in his native tongue was the first time he had staged the project of "decolonizing the mind"—so central to his work since the late 1960s—in critical prose.

By 1990 Ngũgĩ was a prominent and provocative voice in Anglo-American postcolonial studies.[12] Novels such as *The River Between* (1964) and *A Grain of Wheat* had become a staple of postcolonial literature syllabi, and by the mid-1990s excerpts from his 1986 *Decolonising the Mind: The Politics of Language in African Literature* appeared in multiple anthologies of postcolonial theory. However, in the preceding decade his life and career had also been dramatically shaped by the international human rights movement. He was a former prisoner of conscience, having been arrested and held in prison without charge for a year in the late '70s in the wake of the Limuru production of his

Ngaahika Ndeenda (*I Will Marry When I Want*), which put forth a scathingly critical appraisal of Daniel Moi's neocolonial state. Banned by Moi from university employment in Kenya, and released from prison due to pressure from Amnesty International, Ngũgĩ moved to England in the 1980s, where his work with the Committee for the Release of Political Prisoners in Kenya gave him a robust profile as a human rights activist as well as a novelist and critic. Yet in his published work Ngũgĩ rarely discusses human rights as such. He does not analyze his experience in terms of a world of human rights violators and victims but instead in terms of the destructive effects of neocolonialism and global capitalism on Africa and the rest of the Third World. Even his prison memoir, *Detained,* spends relatively little time dwelling on the author's status as a political prisoner per se, instead contextualizing his experience in relation to Kenya's long struggle for national liberation and figuring the Moi state as a new incarnation of the oppressive colonial regime that preceded it. Third World liberation, not universal human rights, remain at the heart of Ngũgĩ's politics in the late twentieth century.

Thus when Ngũgĩ does make use of human rights rhetoric in his work, his reasons for doing so are worthy of some interrogation. "Kĩĩngeretha" is not one of Ngũgĩ's more well-known critical essays, nor does it break much new ground in terms of content; its argument about the tyranny of English in a postcolonial world and the need to cultivate literary and cultural expression in African languages would have been familiar to his readers as of 1990. As discussed in chapter 5, he had been working with the rudiments of this argument in his fiction as early as the 1960s. Neither is Ngũgĩ's investment in thinking transnationally and comparatively a new development at this moment in time. A black internationalist from his first exposure to George Lamming at university, Ngũgĩ has always situated his analysis of Kenya's struggle for a national culture as part of a global struggle against colonialism and imperialism; his first volume of collected essays, *Homecoming,* begins with a focus on language and culture as tools of anti-imperial resistance within Kenya and then broadens its scope, first to Africa and then to the Caribbean. One distinguishing feature of "Kĩĩngeretha" is its use of metaphors that evoke another kind of internationalism, one to which, before the 1990s, Ngũgĩ had paid little heed: that of twentieth-century global institutions and the crises of human rights that helped lead to their creation. It is to Ngũgĩ's choice of metaphors that I devote much of my attention below.

At first glance, Ngũgĩ's argument in "Kĩĩngeretha" seems the perfect target of a Glissantian critique of an essentializing language politics which is also part of what that francophone author would identify as an "exhausted" politics of difference at the end of the twentieth century. Much like Thomas Husson,

Ngũgĩ assigns a political value to the multilingual presentation of a single text; the simple fact of his essay's appearance in a language other than English is assumed to have some emancipatory effects. But the second distinctive feature of this essay complicates such a critique. The bilingualism of the *Yale Journal of Criticism* (*YJC*) essay stages a declarative performance, one that puts much heavier demands on its readers to critically reflect on the ethical and political stakes of linguistic alterity. Below I explore the connections between the somewhat distinct formal features of this 1990 essay—its affinity with the modernist manifesto in its visual as well as rhetorical provocations—and Ngũgĩ's evocation of a contemporary discourse of human rights and international relations in order to problematize the purportedly banal ubiquity of "global English" in the late-twentieth-century postcolonial world. It is this disjuncture between Ngũgĩ's decidedly *anti*colonial brand of postcolonialism and a contemporary discourse of human rights that makes the appearance of this 1990 essay in Gikuyu so intriguing. The purported universalisms of both human rights discourse and celebratory accounts of global English come under fire in this declarative text, whose proposal of a new "language for the world" ultimately gives way to an argument about radical multilingualism and its promise of a more convincing and ambitious postcolonial vision of global justice.

A prefatory paragraph to "Kĩĩngeretha" explains its origins as "a talk under the title 'The Imperialism of Language' in a seminar organized by the BBC on the theme 'English: a Language for the World' that took place on October 27, 1988" ("English" 283). The essay that appears in the *YJC* is a reiteration not only of some of Ngũgĩ's general claims about the relationship between imperialism and the English language, but also of a specific public lecture on that topic. At least as important as the content of the BBC talk was its multilingual delivery; Ngũgĩ explains to his *YJC* readers that the lecture "was first introduced in both Gikuyu and Kiswahili," and subsequently translated into English for the audience. This prefatory narrative alerts *YJC* readers to questions about the audience for whom the substance of his talk was intended. With one important amendment, a question mark at the end of the phrase, the title of the English version of Ngũgĩ's essay is not his own; it was the title given by the BBC to a seminar in which Ngũgĩ's was one of the only literary voices, as well as the only voice from the postcolonial world: "speakers included H. R. H. the Duke of Edinburgh who opened the seminar, the novelist Anthony Burgess, Timothy Edgar M. P., then the Undersecretary of State in the Foreign and Commonwealth Office, Sir Anthony Parsons, former British Ambassador to the United Nations, and Robert Horton, then Managing Director of BP." Ngũgĩ's interlocutors are, like him, stakeholders in a conversation about globalization—but the philosophical and geopolitical stakes that the other seminar participants hold in this conversation differ quite dramatically from those of this writer-activist. The voice of Ngũgĩ's talk, the voice that haunts the *YJC* essay, offers up a postcolonial disruption to a conversation that is both about and the product of a late-twentieth-century neoliberal version of globalization.

Readers familiar with Ngũgĩ's work will know from the start that the answer to the question he poses in his title—is English, or should it be, a "language for the world," a common global language shared by all peoples and regions?—is a resounding *no*. In the talk turned essay, he situates English as imperialism's discursive weapon—the Bible that accompanied the sword as Europe occupied Africa in the nineteenth century (284). The connection between language and violence is central to his own memories of learning English in a colonial school as a child: "In some cases, our mouths were stuffed with pieces of paper picked from the wastepaper basket, which were then passed from one mouth to that of the latest offender" (285–86). Had these tactics succeeded in eradicating native languages completely, the result would have been, to borrow Orlando Patterson's famous expression, social death:

> An oppressor language inevitably carries racist and negative images of the conquered nation, particularly in its literature, and English is no exception... some works bearing these offensive images, like those of Elspeth Huxley, Karen Blixen, Rider Haggard, Robert Truark, Nicholas Monserratt, to name just a few, found their way into the school English curriculum. Imagine it: if the African languages had all died, African people would have had to define themselves in a language that had such a negative conception of Africa as its legacy. (287–88)

Versions of this account of the violence of colonial education and its consequences appear in many of Ngũgĩ's previously published essays, as well as his early fiction and drama. In "Kĩĩngeretha," however, he spends much more time situating languages themselves as the inflictors and victims of colonial and subsequently neocolonial violence. English is figured, in the above passage, not as the language *of* the oppressor but as the oppressor language. Upon the arrival of the Bible and the sword, the languages of Africa and other colonized regions of the globe were "thrown into the rubbish heap and left there to perish" (284–85). English takes on ghoulish qualities, "grow[ing] on the graveyard of other peoples' languages" and "swallow[ing] up" native tongues "in regions where they are putting up a last ditch struggle to prevent their languages from being killed and buried forever" (288).

There is, of course, nothing terribly original about describing languages as dead or dying, and indeed the member of the Welsh Language Society that Ngũgĩ quotes in the essay describes Welsh—another victim of empire—as "under threat of death" (288). But over the course of the essay Ngũgĩ's personification of languages sharpens around metaphors of death and burial. Graveyard imagery forces us to imagine these languages as embodied, as endowed with the same physical and therefore the same *symbolic* properties as human bodies. African and other Third World languages are threatened not only with death but with unconsecrated burial; they are transformed into waste. The kind of "death" threatened by the genocidal campaign of English, French, Portuguese, and other European imperial languages exposes imperialism's biopolitical stakes.

Yet if African languages have been rendered disposable by empire, they have also served as vital tools of anti-imperial resistance: "The rural and urban masses, who had refused to surrender completely in the political and economic spheres, also continued to breathe life into our languages and thus helped to keep alive the histories and cultures they carried" (288). And in the present, languages can continue fighting back by helping to create a new and different landscape of international relations: "All our languages should join in the demand for a new international economic, political, and cultural order" (291). Ngũgĩ insists that languages themselves—not the speakers of those languages—should "be encouraged to talk to one another through the medium of interpretation and translation" (291). With the emergence of a common global language, "the different languages of the world could further communicate with one another" (292). At once victims of a rapacious imperial order and activists fighting for their right to exist, the languages of the world are part of an international community all their own—stakeholders in search of a means of coordination and cooperation across differences of region, culture, and history.

This vision of linguistic activism and diversity challenges some of the assumptions behind the title of the BBC conference, which Ngũgĩ has literally already called into question by re-punctuating its title. What needs and desires underlie the search for a language of the world? What is behind the perceived need for linguistic unity, for a lingua franca to stave off the anarchy of Babel? Ngũgĩ does not confront these questions head-on; but, extending the international relations metaphor still further, he does explain why he finds English to be a poor candidate for the job. A language for the world only has potential when the "world" in question plays host to an international community predicated on social, economic, political, and racial equality—a world in which languages from all regions and cultures enjoy equal status, as do the regions and cultures whence they come. The absence of any African languages among the official languages of the United Nations thus directly correlates to Africa's relative powerlessness within that international institution, and within the international community more broadly (290). At the same time, multilingualism can play a part in working to *achieve* the kind of international community that is also its precondition:

> Where there is real economic, political, and cultural equality among nations and there is *democracy*, there will be no reason for any nation, nationality, or people to fear the emergence of a common language, be it Kiswahili, Chinese, Maori, Spanish, or English, as the language of the world. A language for the world? A world of languages! The two concepts are not mutually exclusive provided there is independence, equality, democracy, and peace among nations. (292)

"A language for the world" is a formula that, at least under present conditions of linguistic and political-economic inequality, threatens to best serve the goals of global capitalism; "a world of languages," conversely, anticipates a cosmopolitan future that rejects the hierarchies of the colonial past. Ngũgĩ here embraces a version of multilingualism that rejects the hierarchical, centralized model of cultural and political power implicit in the concept of global English. Yet he retreats from such a vision when, in the final paragraphs, he makes a case for Kiswahili as "an excellent candidate for [a] world language" in the interim, as it "already has the advantage of never having grown in the graveyard of other languages" (293). The essay ends in ambiguity. Which should come first, the new era in human relations in which linguistic diversity wins out over the search for a lingua franca, or the supplanting of English with that of a purportedly innocent and transnational African language? Ngũgĩ never fully commits to the espousal of a somewhat modest but concrete alternative to global English—its replacement with Kiswahili—and a more ambitious but less well-defined questioning of the hegemonic structures of globalization under which a "language of the world" becomes desirable in the first place.

"Kĩĩngeretha" is not Ngũgĩ's first or best articulation of this argument for a radical postcolonial multilingualism that topples the ever-expanding hegemony of global English. What makes the essay unique is less its substance than its form: here Ngũgĩ draws on a utopian version of internationalism and a rhetoric of universal human rights in order to present this argument about critical humanism to a predominantly Western audience. The essay's origins in the commercial cosmopolitanism of the BBC conference, as well as in Ngũgĩ's status as a postcolonial intellectual in exile in the North American academy, intersect with a set of metaphors about languages as rights-bearing members of a global community all their own. Ngũgĩ opens the essay by describing language in universal terms, as a birthright—and, indeed, a *human* right.

> Everyone in the world has a language, either the language of his or her parents or one adopted at birth or at a later stage in life. So when we consider English as a possible language for the world, we are all drawing from the languages and cultures in which we are rooted. (283)

One way of glossing the twentieth-century project of developing a concept, and a declaration, of universal human rights is as a problem of developing a kind of political-ethical Esperanto—a language of justice that enjoys legitimacy worldwide because of its inherent legibility to all peoples everywhere. But for Ngũgĩ, these universal precepts then quickly give way to other issues that have less to do with language in its natural state and more to do with languages in an inherently social world: "The topic also brings up the question of choosing one language from among many languages. What we are therefore discussing is the relationship between English and the various languages of the world. In short, we are really talking about the meeting of languages" (283). European Enlightenment-era philosophical tracts on the state of nature ponder language as a sign of humans' inherent sociability; Ngũgĩ's interest, in contrast, lies with the intrasocial work of languages in the plural—with what happens when multiple languages come into contact, and more specifically with the power dynamics inherent in such encounters. And it is within this framework that the connection between language and human rights at the heart of Ngũgĩ's essay comes into view. How could the "meeting of languages" that preoccupies Ngũgĩ, and his fellow participants at the BBC seminar, be about anything other than the creation of the means of communication for an inclusive, just, and powerful international community? The protagonist of the Universal Declaration of Human Rights, "Everyone," Ngũgĩ's choice for an opening pronoun, evokes a contemporary universalization of an Enlightenment concept of rights. In the Universal Declaration, the articles that begin with "Everyone" stipulate specific rights—to habeas corpus, a nationality, property ownership, social security, education, and so forth—to which an infinitely inclusive but also positively defined set of living bodies can lay claim by virtue of their humanity. Ngũgĩ does not explicitly identify language as a human right, but his use of this pronoun, so central to the foundational text of late-twentieth-century human rights discourse, brings this context to mind. "Everyone" calls forth not abstract "man" but a concrete, identifiable group of humans that can be brought into a juridico-political order without exclusion.

While certainly the essay aims to expose the injustice of colonialism and imperialism's alienation of the *speakers* of African languages from their native tongues, and while that injustice might well be described as a human rights violation, Ngũgĩ is actually arguing a somewhat different point. His identification of languages rather than humans as rights-bearing entities instead foregrounds the aesthetic consequences of linguistic imperialism. Recalling André Breton's declaration of the rights of the imagination in his 1924 *Manifesto of Surrealism*, Ngũgĩ's twisting of a human rights rhetoric borrows from the conventions of the modernist manifesto, complicating conventional assumptions about the use and meaning of juridico-political language in order to insist on the urgency of expressive diversity. Unlike Breton, however, Ngũgĩ also points to crucial parallels between the rights of languages and other kinds of rights (of nations, peoples, individuals), in a way that maintains the autonomy of language from the realm of the political just far enough for languages to directly experience a variety of violence and injustice all their own:

> The quality of the encounter between languages both in the past and in the world today, and hence the dominance of one aspect over the other at a given time, has been determined by the presence or absence of independence and equality between the nations involved. (284)

In this phrasing, the violence that languages inflict upon each other is always tied to a violence enacted on human bodies, on peoples and nations. It also exists semi-autonomously; languages, as much as people, are presented in this essay as original participants in the drama of the colonial encounter. In the fall of 1990, *YJC* readers might well have been familiar with at least two contemporaneous scholarly accounts of this same drama in the Western literary tradition: Peter Hulme's *Colonial Encounters* (1986) and Stephen Greenblatt's *Learning to Curse* (1990). Colonial encounter was proving a pivotal point of intersection between literary and scholarly postcolonialisms at the moment in which Ngũgĩ opened this essay with a staging of linguistic confrontation as overshadowed by the power dynamics of colonialism. Ngũgĩ's intervention into this conversation is to reroute his readers' attention from the human actors involved in the moment of colonial encounter to their means of communication—not simply in order to point out, as Greenblatt did in the same year, that "the primal crime in the New World was committed in the interest of language" (17), but rather to situate language in two roles, as *both* perpetrator and victim in this colonial crime scene.

Consequently, at the outset of a talk-turned-essay pitched at a couple of different types of international communities—scholarly and political-economic—languages themselves are described as constituting their own international community. The languages of the world effectively have their own politics, and their own democratic imperative, and thus are subject to the same betrayals of democracy as are peoples, nations, and human bodies. The problem of the claim of English as "a language for the world" stems from a long-standing disconnect between the empirical reality of languages on the ground—who speaks them, what they mean, the cultures and nations they support—and an uneven global distribution of power, of which the spread of global English serves as just one manifestation. This world community of languages has long been dispossessed of its ideal equilibrium, in which "languages meet" democratically. Ngũgĩ thus establishes the impossibility of talking about a politics of language and culture in isolation from a discussion of how sovereign nation-states interact under conditions of colonialism and neocolonialism.

Long-standing injustices in international relations do not merely provide Ngũgĩ with a convenient metaphor for the inner workings and external pressures of the literary and cultural sphere. When languages extend beyond the boundaries of their populations of native speakers, they effectively take part in a semi-autonomous global civil society—one that is subject to the same failures and inadequacies of a global civil society of nations. The historical development of language and culture cannot be discussed without reference to the geopolitics to which this process has been linked over the past several hundred years. Neither can its solution.

> We must avoid the destruction that English has wrought on other languages and cultures in its march to the position it now occupies in the world. The death of many languages should never be the condition for the life of a few. On the contrary, the lives of many languages should add life to whichever language emerges as the transnational or universal language of communication between people. We, the present generation, must distance ourselves from the false and bloody logic of development theory handed to us by imperialism: the claim that the cleanliness of one person must depend on pouring dirt onto others; that the health of a few must depend on their passing their leprosy onto others; that the wealth of a few people or a few nations must be rooted in the poverty of the masses of people and nations. ("English" 291)

Here again, Ngũgĩ assigns value to languages as living beings in order to illuminate the ethical stakes of countering the destructive and totalizing spread of global English. The choice in this passage is clear: we either render ourselves complicit in more of the same, the destructiveness of the "march" of English to world prominence and dominance, or we forge a new path for the future of language that achieves universality *through* particularity.

Ngũgĩ's presentation of languages as rights-bearing participants in a global community stunted by empire draws a connection between the straightforward problem of language rights as human rights—all peoples should be able to communicate freely in their own languages—and the ethical and aesthetic problem of cultural diversity, of multilingualism as a means of ensuring a robustly democratic ethos. But—again, in the fashion of the modernist manifesto—he also performs the multilingualism that he theorizes. The BBC lecture, he explains in his preface, "was first introduced in both Gikuyu and Kiswahili, with Wangũi wa Goro interpreting . . . After this initial presentation I presented an English translation, all the while explaining the procedure as I went along" (283). Supplied with an "interpreter" and willing to translate into English, Ngũgĩ nevertheless staged an unfamiliar linguistic encounter for his audience in the BBC seminar, enacting his rejection of English as a worthy lingua franca and presenting his talk in a language that none of the other participants would have spoken or understood—as well as in Kiswahili, the African language that Ngũgĩ posits in his concluding remarks as transnational and thus more palatable as a candidate for a "language for the world" in his conclusion.

At the seminar, Ngũgĩ's audience had no choice but to take in this multilingual performance in its entirety. His *YJC* readers, by contrast, do have the choice of skipping over, or only briefly glancing at, the eleven pages of Gikuyu that precede the English translation.[13] The bilingual presentation of the essay was a gesture of respect to the principle of multilingualism, an invitation to readers to consider what it would be like to be able to read Ngũgĩ's words in the original—and, more broadly, what it would be like for a journal of literary criticism to be able to anticipate readers' fluency in not only Gikuyu but in African and other non-Western languages. The major intervention of "English: A Language for the World?" into the discourse of the *Yale Journal of Criticism*, and more broadly of North Atlantic academic cosmopolitanism, had to do with what the essay looked like on the page—how it performed a disruption in the material presentation of the journal, and what the stakes of that disruption were and might be. Like the modernist manifesto, Ngũgĩ's text not only wants to be read, but also wants to transform its readers' notions of how to read. The appearance of those eleven pages in Gikuyu opens up a new kind of imaginative space in North Atlantic scholarly discourse. We do not need to read those pages; we only need to see them (and read them in translation) to have the experience of ethical engagement that Gikuyu's linguistic alterity invites. What would a radically multilingual community of literary critics look like? In what ways would the norms of authorship, authority, and First World privilege be disrupted by such a transformation?

"Kĩĩngeretha" stages a linguistic disruption on the pages of the *YJC*. But the entrance of Gikuyu into First World scholarly discourse is more broadly suggestive of the possible implications of Third-Worldism into the North Atlantic academy. By 1990 Ngũgĩ was a postcolonial intellectual whose exile had come with the dubious gift of transnational mobility and a heightened international reputation. The journal essay makes no direct comment on the Western academic community of which he had been a part for the past ten years. But just as he used his status as an outsider to unsettle the BBC conference participants' assumptions about language, culture, and colonialism through the multilingual delivery of his talk, so in the essay we can detect a distance from and skepticism toward his largely First World audience. The links between colonialism and the birth of the English department, accounted for most notably in Gauri Viswanathan's 1988 *Masks of Conquest*, would not have been opaque to Ngũgĩ, who had narrated his own version of this history many times over in print by this point.[14] Nor would Gayatri Spivak's concept of the native informant, an early iteration of which also appeared in 1988 in "Can the Subaltern Speak?" Below the surface of this essay about global English are questions about the complicities of Ngũgĩ's readers—and of Ngũgĩ himself—with a rather comfortably institutionalized First World postcolonialism which Arif Dirlik charges with "obfuscat[ing] . . . its own relationship to what is but a condition of its emergence: a Global Capitalism which, however fragmented in appearance, serves nevertheless as the structuring principle of global relations" (*Postcolonial Aura* 54). One prong of Ngũgĩ's answer to this problem of complicity consists of his persistent reiteration of a narrative of colonial oppression and anticolonial resistance during a decade in which postcolonial criticism largely shifted its focus from the material history of the postcolonies to discourse analysis. In "Kĩĩngeretha," his playful and critical engagement with the rhetoric of human rights serves as another means of confronting the troubling elisions among global neoliberalism, First World humanitarian approaches to reading the Third World, and First World postcolonialism.

I HAVE FOCUSED much of my attention in this book on instances in which African and Caribbean writers' engagements with juridico-political forms were closely and quite explicitly tied to the project of imagining an inclusive, democratic postcolonial nation-state, a political community capable of living up to the aspirations of the national liberation struggles of the midcentury.

This chapter, in contrast, has attended to a later set of texts for which postcolonial nationhood is less of an explicit concern. Written in the 1980s and '90s, at over twenty years' distance from the decolonization of Kenya and at nearly fifty years' distance from the departmentalization of Martinique, Ngũgĩ's and Glissant's essays reflect political realities that the earlier national liberation struggles—which were formative for both of these writers—were not able to anticipate. Their shift in focus to questions of global aesthetics not only suggests that the nation is no longer the focal point for their critical interests; it also signals the historical distance between these writers' late-twentieth-century contexts and the anticolonial politics of earlier decades.

We might readily counter such claims by citing any of the myriad instances in these authors' published works that indicate an ongoing investment in an "older" oppositional politics and an attention to postcolonial national identity, if not exactly nationalism or national liberation per se. Across the genres of fiction, autobiography, and criticism, Ngũgĩ continues to situate the present-day plight of Kenya, Africa, and the Global South in terms of the colonial past—and persistently recounts what for him was at least a fleetingly successful Fanonian program of popular resistance to colonialism. And even if scholars argue over the degree to which Glissant's critical prose remains politically engaged past the 1990s, Glissant himself certainly was, as an outspoken critic of Sarkozy's cultural politics, for example, and of France's perpetuation of its overseas departments' economic dependency on the metropole in the twenty-first century.[15] Proof abounds that neither of these writers ceased to vociferously engage with the material realities that speak to the legacies of colonialism, and its power imbalances, in Africa, the Caribbean, and other postcolonial regions in the twenty-first century.

But my argument in this final chapter has been that a certain kind of anticolonialism also persists in—and is crucial to—work in which these writers seem to be preoccupied with other issues. Ngũgĩ's and Glissant's critical prose of the 1980s and '90s engages global contexts, appropriates and manipulates the rhetoric of human rights, and foregrounds problems of language, culture, and identity—the central concerns of postcolonial theory during those years. But it is my sense that these shifts do not signify a turn toward a bland and apolitical cosmopolitanism. Rather, these authors have reconfigured the rhetorical tools of anticolonialism for the postcolonial present. Their essays engage the "internationalism" of universal human rights discourse in order to suggest, as Bruce Robbins would do around the same time, that "internationalism is not a utopian idealism, an infinitely deferred ideal of ultimate justice for all. It is not a synonym for the one universal rationality. There are many versions, and they are all imperfect" (7). The differences between the concept of political community that appears in Ngũgĩ's and Glissant's late work and that of Césairean negritude or Jamesian Pan-Africanism are stark. But like those midcentury writers, Ngũgĩ and Glissant work to construct an alternative international imagination, one that counters the logic of a form of globalization organized around empire with a radical multilingualism grounded in a definitively anticolonial politics and aesthetics.

In reading comparatively between these two writers, I am asking that we re-evaluate our sense of the role of anticolonialism in the postcolonial present. In doing so I do not mean to overstate my case—to suggest, for example, that Ngũgĩ's and Glissant's investments (or those of other postcolonial writers at the turn of the century) have not changed over time. The essays I have looked at in this chapter make, at best, small and subtle gestures toward the anticolonial. They do not put forth bold new political agendas or even name a new political collectivity. Indeed, as I discussed in relation to Glissant, these texts are intent on *avoiding* that kind of project, pushing instead at a conjectural and conjunctural way of imagining political belonging in the postcolonial world.

But that avoidance can also be read as part of the work of carving out imaginative and rhetorical space for a new version of anticolonialism, one better suited to the demands of the present. Declarations, Glissant cautions, do not work the way they used to. And yet Glissant is also an author who holds on tightly to a belief in the disruptive potential of the declarative gesture, of the revaluation of official juridico-political discourse through the performance of imaginative alternatives, of the countering of a stagnant and oppressive political discourse with a new poetics. This book closes with an acknowledgment rather than a resolution of that paradox. Radical anticolonial rhetorical performances have not disappeared in the transatlantic postcolonial world. They are there if we know where and how to look for them.

Coda

> Authority stealing pass armed robbery
> We Africans we must do something about this nonsense
> We say we must do something about this nonsense
> I repeat, we Africans we must do something about this nonsense
> Because now authority stealing pass armed robbery
> Authority man him go dey steal
> Public contribute plenty money . . .
>
> —Fela Kuti, "Authority Stealing"

MIDWAY THROUGH CHRIS ABANI'S 2004 *GraceLand,* sixteen-year-old Elvis Oke wanders into a public square in Lagos. It is 1983, nearly two decades after Nigeria's independence from Britain, and a little more than a decade after the end of the Biafran War. Unemployed, living in a slum, and deeply skeptical of a government whose overdependence on oil revenues has had disastrous consequences for the country's economy and civil society, Elvis comes to Tinubu Square in search of his mentor, the King of Beggars, who is just about to begin an impromptu public performance.

> The King of the Beggars got up onstage and began plucking reluctant chords from a battered out-of-tune guitar. The crowd grew silent as he performed a series of tone poems. He was talking about the beauty of the indigenous culture that had been abandoned for Western ways. It was essentialist, maybe even prejudiced, because the culture he spoke of was that of the Igbo, only one of nearly three hundred indigenous people in this populous country. He spoke of the ancient systems of governance that were like a loose democracy, leaning more to a socialist system, a governance based on age-grades that gathered to discuss the way forward in any crisis. This system produced a tight-knit community, where the good of the group was placed before individual stake. He spoke of the evils of capitalism that the United States

of America practiced—a brand of capitalism, he said, that promoted the individual interest over the communal. It was a land of vice and depravity, infested with a perverse morality based on commercial value rather than a humanistic one. The King called for everyone to return to the traditional values and ways of being. (154–55)

The King's age and generational affiliations are readily apparent in this speech: he is somewhere between forty and fifty years old, or roughly the same age as first-generation postcolonial writers such as Chinua Achebe and Ngũgĩ, and his own adolescence coincided with Nigeria's independence. Identifying Igbo traditions as the basis for a cultural resistance to the corruptions of Western capitalism, his argument resorts to the kind of ethnic-identity politics that helped facilitate Nigeria's civil war a decade earlier. Elvis is quick to identify the anachronism and chauvinism in the speech:

The King's rather preachy sermon sounded a lot like the ideas of Obafemi Awolowo, an independence advocate from the early days of the nation. Elvis's main problem with the King's theories was that they didn't account for the inherent complications he knew were native to this culture, or the American. As naive as Elvis was, he knew there was no way of going back to the "good old days," and wondered why the King didn't speak about how to cope with these new and confusing times. (154–55)

Elvis's reflections are in line with what the first half of the novel already amply demonstrated about the impossibility of a return to a precolonial Nigeria, or even to the early days of independence. Elvis's mother has died, his father moved to the city and became an abusive drunk after a failed run for public office in his village, and Igbo culture has more often than not served as an excuse for members of Elvis's community to overlook serious internal problems—including sexual violence and murder—rather than as the basis for a harmonious and robust polis. And whatever the validity of the King's critique of capitalism and its effects on the country, his words cannot account for the attraction that American culture holds for Elvis and other Nigerians of his generation, from John Wayne films to James Baldwin novels. Elvis marks his own generational distance from the content of this speech in his rejection of the idea of cultural purity, not only in the West but within Africa; the "good old days" are inaccessible to him not because they are gone, but because they never existed in the first place.

The King's speech is anachronistic in yet another sense: its mode of delivery seems to suspend his listeners' ability to remain critical of its content.

"Elvis was mesmerized by the richness of the King's voice. It was seductive, eliciting the listener's trust, and he soon forgot his concerns and began to believe the King was right" (155). While onstage, the King inhabits the role of the anticolonial speaker-hero as theorized by James and depicted via the character of Kihika in Ngũgĩ's *A Grain of Wheat*. His performance, while effective, harks back to an earlier time in which appeals to national solidarity on cultural grounds and Marxist critiques of "American" capitalism were—or at least seemed—appropriate and adequate strategies of anti-imperial resistance. The content *and* the form of the King's speech thus contrast starkly with that of the speaker who takes the stage after him and unflinchingly addresses the "new and confusing times" that Elvis has in mind.

> When the King finished, a nervous-looking young man in round glasses got up onstage and began to recite a speech. Though he tried to shout over the noise of the now animated crowd, Elvis could only make out snatches.
> "... A country often becomes what its inhabitants dream for it. Much the same way that a novel shapes the writer, the people's perspective shapes the nation, so the country becomes the thing people want to see. Every time we complain that we don't want to be ruled by military dictatorship; but every time there is a coup, we come out in the streets to sing and dance and celebrate the replacement of one despot with another one. How long can we continue to pretend we are not responsible for this? How long..." (155)

Just as Ngũgĩ juxtaposes Kihika's polished, seductive, and romantic public performances to Mugo's awkward, guilt-ridden public confessions in *A Grain of Wheat*, so Abani here draws his readers' attention to the stylistic differences between the older, suaver King and the earnest but unpolished younger speaker. The content of this second speech is theoretical, analytical, and future-oriented. This speaker omits any reference to tradition, culture, or even Nigeria or Africa, homing in instead on the struggle taking place between the country's citizenry and its own government. Likening the nation to a writer, he insists that the people themselves, the "we" he invokes, are and have long been in charge of authoring their own national destiny. But instead of a glorious ideal, this authority has led to a national nightmare; the people themselves are responsible for conjuring forth the totalitarian regimes of which they have since become the victims. While the King's speech pandered to his audience members' cultural pride, the unnamed speaker issues a scolding, a fraught call to collective accountability.

The Tinubu Square speeches thus seem to present Elvis—and Abani's readers—with two competing diagnoses for what ails Nigeria in the late twentieth century: Westernization on one hand, internal corrosion on the other. But as the scene continues and the King joins Elvis in the crowd, the relationship between the two performances becomes more complex.

> Elvis lost the thread again as the King materialized beside him.
> "Good evening," Elvis said.
> "Sshh, listen. Dis speaker is good."
> "But I can't hear him . . ."
> "Sshh!"
> Elvis strained to hear the young man over the crowd. In the distance somewhere, someone was playing a radio loudly, and he could hear Fela Kuti blowing a saxophone riff. It was an amazing thing to hear, a saxophone player in full flight. He had to really struggle to focus on the young man's words.
> ". . . Malcolm X once said America is a prison. So is this country and we are both the jailer and the inmates, imprisoning ourselves by allowing this infernal, illegal and monstrous regime of military buffoons to continue. They continue to play us like fools, buying off our allegiance with money, or with force when they cannot pay the price. I am calling for a rebellion . . ."
> "Let us move away," the King said. "He is getting carried away, and de army go soon come." (156)

The King's generosity toward the second speaker is much more in keeping with what we know about this character from the first half of the novel; while onstage he may have adopted an authoritative oratorical persona, in reality he is poor, homeless, and disfigured, having been nearly killed by a rapacious Nigerian army officer during the Biafran War. He is also Elvis's mentor, and so his insistence that Elvis listen carefully to the next speaker suggests that he anticipates and even welcomes Elvis's skeptical appraisal of the limitations of his own performance. The reductive essentialism of the King's words onstage are in fact somewhat out of step with this character's role as one of the few people in Elvis's life who has regularly offered him the opportunity to engage in critical reflection about his world, its history, and the ethical demands placed on him amid the violence and desperation of Lagos in the 1980s. The negritudean clichés of the King's speech create a backdrop against which the second speaker's scathing indictment of the nation in ruins is thrown into relief. Further, the messages of these two speeches may have more in common than they seem to: both call attention to the forces of alienation and disaffection at work in postcolonial Lagos, as well as to the capitalism that is, in fact, global rather than American, and that has been a destructive part of the fabric of Nigerian life in the years since independence. To the extent that this softspoken, awkward second performer has an audience at all, it is because the King drew the crowd.

The two speeches present Elvis (and readers) with two very different but, perhaps, ultimately symbiotic rhetorical approaches to protest—and they are joined by a third approach in the form of Fela Kuti's music, which blares from the radio and competes directly for the attention of the second speaker's audience. Elvis registers the music as a distraction from the performance underway in the Square, a familiar but unwanted noise that interferes with his ability to pay attention to the real show. But as is the case elsewhere in the novel, Abani's insertion of an iconic black musician into this scene is far from innocuous or random. Elvis recognizes the artist by his saxophone solo, but if he had also listened to the lyrics of the song blaring from the radio he would likely have noticed much continuity with the second speech: Fela was a well-established protest singer extraordinaire who had been enraging state authorities with his music for years by the early 1980s. While Elvis perceives the speech and the music as in cacophonous competition, the content of their messages overlaps significantly, de-exceptionalizing the lone (and incredibly vulnerable) speaker on the stage and suggesting that the frustrations to which he gives voice are widespread, permeating the aural landscape of Lagos through multiple mediums. The accidental confluence of these two performances in fact adds to the threat they pose: here is protest spontaneously erupting on the streets without coordination, without a centralized orchestrator of a message that is too deeply and broadly understood by the inhabitants of Lagos to require organization. The King's politically conservative and anachronistic speech is, it turns out, the only performance in this collection of performances that can safely avoid creating an opportunity for the state to put its own power on display in the form of police violence. And the King seems to know it.

If the generically disparate modes of anticolonial protest at work in this scene are in fact part of a single multidimensional performance rather than incommensurate visions of justice and nationhood, then Elvis's interpretation of events requires some amendment, for he has missed the more nuanced ways in which older and newer rhetorical strategies can interact with each other in an age of empire. *GraceLand* criticism has tended to focus on the novel's pessimistic or ambivalent view of present-day Nigeria.[1] But the scene in Tinubu Square complicates such interpretations for me. As the contrast between the two speeches breaks down, so does our sense of what the novel is saying about the relationship between the anticolonial past and the postcolonial present— or, rather, the multiple postcolonial presents, as we read this 1983 moment in Nigerian history through the lens of our own twenty-first-century knowledge of the two decades of dictatorships that lie ahead for the country after Elvis's story comes to a close. Public performances of nationhood, including *both* their radical potential and their potential shortcomings, remain central to a postcolonial imagination inflected by a multigeneric history of anticolonial critique. In contrast to an approach that either celebrates anticolonialism or registers it only as anachronism, *GraceLand* presents us with the possibility of ethical intergenerational exchange, a dialogic and performative way of thinking about how anticolonialism confronts the postcolonial present with its lost pasts.

The performances to which Elvis bears witness in Tinubu Square have a long history, one that this book has traced back to the eighteenth-century Caribbean. It is a history of the romance of rhetorical performance, the public declaration of the courageous speaker-hero who aims to both name and inaugurate a new political community. But the well-kept secret of that romance is that there are few instances in which such performances do not also contain a powerful self-critique. The speaker-hero of Césaire's *Cahier* counterbalances his audacious affirmation of the negritudean self with an anxious acknowledgment of the impossibility—and the ethical complications—of the representational task he has set himself. And in their critical prose, Fanon, Ngũgĩ, and Glissant seek to harness the revolutionary energy and drama of the manifesto with the control and critical capabilities of the essay form. In black Atlantic anticolonial writing, even texts that seem at first glance to offer up only reductive essentialist claims often demand, and deserve, a reading that explores how they invite their readers to move beyond their ostensible reductiveness. And even texts that seem to distance themselves from the crass work of performatively embracing affirmative identities and politics often interact with such performances in complex and subtle ways.

In *Literature, Law, and Rhetorical Performance in the Anticolonial Atlantic* I have sought to stage a series of encounters among a generically and even ideologically diverse set of rhetorical performances with the idea that none of them were ever really meant to stand alone. Rhetorical success depends on context, and no context is more vital to these declarative texts than their audiences' exposure to *multiple* forms of articulating real and imagined postcolonial community. The anticolonial project takes shape across numerous genres, registers, and disciplines: literary as well as legal texts; public meetings as well as novels; oaths performed surreptitiously in the forests as well as constitutions handed over to new authorities in official ceremonies in the new nation's capital. My aim has been to suggest how increased attention to this diversity might open up the field of postcolonial studies to new modes of inquiry—by indicating new ways of connecting underexplored genres and archives with more canonical materials, to be sure, but also by challenging us to reconsider the relevance and resonance of the rhetorical strategies of anticolonial writing for the not-quite-postcolonial present. At its core, anticolonialism is a project of imagining postcoloniality. That project remains active and urgent in the twenty-first century.

NOTES

INTRODUCTION

1. "'Are and ought to be'; the 'and' articulates and conjoins here the two discursive modalities, the to be and the ought to be, the constation and the prescription, the fact and the right. *And* is God: at once creator of nature and judge, supreme judge of what is (the state of the world) and of what relates to what ought to be (the rectitude of our intentions). The instance of judgment, at the level of the supreme judge, is the last instance for saying the fact *and* the law. One can understand this Declaration as a vibrant act of faith, as a hypocrisy indispensable to a politico-military-economic, etc. coup of force, or, more simply, more economically, as the analytic and consequential deployment of a tautology; for this Declaration to have a meaning *and* an effect, there must be a last instance" ("Declarations of Independence" 11–12).

2. See Ania Loomba's critique of Michael Hardt and Antonio Negri's *Empire* in the conclusion of her *Colonialism/Postcolonialism* (216).

3. See, in particular, Arjun Appadurai, *Modernity at Large*; Michael Hardt and Antonio Negri, *Empire*; as well as the commentary of some of the participants in the MLA Roundtable entitled "The End of Postcolonial Theory?" (Yaeger). These accounts are countered by a number of others—Simon During, Simon Gikandi, and other participants in the MLA Roundtable, to name a few—that insist on the continued relevance of the historical and ethical imperatives of postcolonialism in the twenty-first century.

4. I borrow the word "transversal" from Ian Baucom, who in turn is drawing on Édouard Glissant's description of the kind of "cross-cultural relationship" that is constituted through the evocation of slaves thrown overboard—a "network" of "submarine roots" that grounds a comparative critical practice not through "the universal transcendence of the sublime" but instead through an oceanic history of slavery and colonialism (quoted in Baucom par. 6). Baucom connects this reading practice with the stakes of postcolonial studies' balancing the capaciousness of an oceanic geohistorical framework against the uncritical embrace of global hybridity thus: "one of the most valuable and most particular lessons that 'postcolonialism's' texts have communicated to us is, in Glissant's terms, precisely the lesson of the 'transversal.' The coral-become bodies of those slaves drowned in the Middle Passage do link the waters washing the coast of Martinique with an eighteenth- and nineteenth-century history of the Caribbean, with the past and present legacies of the triangular trade, with the Victorian and Edwardian underdevelopment of Africa, Rastafarian and Pan-Africanist narratives of return, the poetry of Aimé Césaire, Afrocentric curricula, and the commodification of Kente cloth . . . To refuse to read these linkages is not to eschew indiscriminate acts of totalization, it is to refuse to read" (par. 9).

5. As Charles Piot observes, the omission of present-day Africa from black Atlantic studies "not only silences a major entity in the black Atlantic world but also leaves unchallenged the notion that Africa is somehow different—that it remains a site of origin and purity, uncontaminated by those histories of the modern that have lent black Atlantic cultures their

distinctive character—and thus risks reinscribing a conception of culture that Gilroy, Hall, and many of the new diaspora scholars otherwise spend much of their work critiquing. This ellipsis also suggests, of course, that Africa has played little role in the development of black Atlantic cultural production, other than as provider of raw materials—bodies and cultural templates/origins—that were then processed or elaborated upon by the improvisational cultures of the Americas" (156).

6. See, for example, Chrisman and Nixon.

7. See Yogita Goyal's introduction to the Fall 2014 special issue of *Research in African Literatures*, devoted to a consideration of Africa and the black Atlantic in the twenty-first century, for a thorough and insightful discussion of the implications of incorporating the new African diaspora(s) into a black Atlantic critical framework.

8. See also Koskenniemi and Mazower.

9. See also Orford; Douzinas; Mutua; Rajagopal; and Berman.

10. See Escobar; Hardt and Negri; and Cheah.

11. Other key works in this subfield include Schaffer and Smith; Cheah; Goldberg; Goldberg and Moore; and Anker. Not all of these critics explicitly identify their work with postcolonial studies; we might much more readily identify Schaffer and Smith's book within a World Literature critical framework, for instance. However, overwhelmingly, the literary texts that these studies choose as their objects of analysis come from postcolonial canons.

12. See Crenshaw et al., and especially Harris; Patricia Williams; Guinier and Torres; and Holloway.

CHAPTER 1

1. See Nesbitt, *Universal Emancipation*.

2. See, for example, Trouillot; Fick; Geggus; Buck-Morss; Nesbitt; Garraway; and Jenson.

3. For overviews of the formal antecedents of each of these genres, see Lucas; Lyon (especially chapter 1); Wasserstrom, Hunt, and Young; and McIlwain.

4. See Fliegelman; Armitage; Slauter; Ozouf; and Friedland.

5. Critiques of Arendt's political/social distinction appear in Hardt and Negri; Wellmer; and Bernasconi, "The Double Face of the Political and the Social."

6. It should be noted that while Arendt judged the American Revolution as originating in a more solid, "political" foundation, *On Revolution* also enumerates the ways in which she thought the United States itself fell short of its own revolutionary ideal within decades of its founding.

7. As Philippe Girard has recently observed, the distinction between Toussaint's "antislavery" and Dessalines's "anticolonial" programs may be less stark than scholarship has tended to assume; Dessalines's commitment to national independence was not unequivocal until quite shortly before he issued the Declaration of Independence, for example. See Girard.

8. For a more thorough analysis of Dessalines's "Africanness," see Jenson.

9. Deborah Jenson makes a compelling case for recognizing Dessalines rather than Boisrond-Tonnerre as "the crucial conceptual voice" of this and other official proclamations written during the same year (88).

10. Curiously, this passage precedes a series of paragraphs that contain the Declaration's most notable compromises: Dessalines assures the North Atlantic community that Haiti has no plans to instigate revolt or let its own dismantling of colonialism and plantation slavery spread beyond the geographical boundaries of Haiti.

11. See Madiou 3 and Rainsford 262–63.

12. See Jenson 139–40. Other accounts of the sensationalized reception of the 1804 massacres elsewhere in the north Atlantic world appear in Geggus *Impact* and Fischer.

13. See Harris.
14. In this sense Dessalines's constitution has more in common with Napoleon's 1799 Constitution of the Year VIII.
15. "En conséquence, l'Assemblée Nationale reconnaît et déclare, en présence et sous les auspices de l'Etre suprême, les droits suivants de l'Homme et du Citoyen" ("Déclaration des droits de l'homme"). ["Thus, the National Assembly recognizes and declares, in the presence and under the auspices of the Supreme Being, the following rights of man and citizen."]
16. Enemy status in this instance specifically did not apply to Britain or Spain, as the Declaration of Independence had already made clear.
17. See Bernasconi, "Double Face"; Negri; Wellmer; Hardt and Negri; and Frank, who helpfully elucidates Arendt's misreading of "the people" in U.S. revolutionary contexts as well as offering analysis of the limitations of her treatment of France.

CHAPTER 2

1. See Christian Høgsbjerg's account of James's transformation from liberalism in the 1930s.
2. See Robinson; Idahosa; San Juan; Henry; and Miller.
3. See Edmondson and Pinto.
4. Another prime example: "The leaders of a revolution are usually those who have been able to profit by the cultural advantages of the system they are attacking, and the San Domingo revolution was no exception to this rule" (19). Cedric Robinson's chapter on James in *Black Marxism* does a particularly nice job of situating James as far more self-aware and focused on the potential of the black masses as revolutionary actors than were many of his peers (Padmore, Nkrumah, Kenyatta, Williams), while still circumscribed by his own class affiliations.
5. Deborah Jenson usefully cautions against an overly skeptical assessment of Toussaint's claims to authorship, however: "The singularity of his voice calls into question strict associations of authorship with the individual print genesis of texts, since he is arguably very much the author of his dictated writings" (67).
6. James's experiences with Eric Williams's Trinidad and Nkrumah's Ghana overlap both chronologically and thematically; James briefly references this overlap toward the beginning of the introduction to this volume, but does not, for example, note that he was ousted from Williams's good graces right around the same time that Nkrumah shocked him by dismissing his Chief Justice. Nowhere in the introduction does he fully explain the extent to which his experience with both countries in the early 1960s was one of disillusionment and profound disappointment. Apart from *The Life of Captain Cipriani* and *The Case for West Indian Self-Government*, both written and published in the 1930s, James never writes a full-length history of Trinidad's independence movement (nor does he ever label that movement a "revolution," to the best of my knowledge); but in his 1960 *Modern Politics* he does comment critically on the island's postcolonial government in much the same way that he comments on Ghana in the speeches published in part 2 of *Nkrumah*.
7. See Scott 2014.

CHAPTER 3

1. Beginning in the 1950s, UN delegates from the Third World as well as participants in the Bandung Conference would begin more aggressively framing self-determination as the most basic and pressing human right to which Third World peoples were entitled; as Moyn points out, however, this move was less an embrace of a human rights agenda than an additional

means of demonstrating its limited applicability to the anticolonial struggle. For a very different assessment of the relationship between the early years of contemporary human rights discourse and anticolonial movements, see Roland Burke, who asserts that "anticolonialism was in part conceived of as a struggle for human rights, the two concepts proceeding together in the campaign for freedom and independence" (14).

2. See Mazower.

3. See especially Walker; Rabbitt; Rosello; Melas; Garraway, "'What Is Mine'"; Nesbitt, "The Incandescent I, Destroyer of Worlds"; and Davis, "Negritude-as-Performance."

4. I have chosen to confine my discussion in this chapter to Césaire and his own particular brand of negritude in order to do justice to the complexity of his work—and as a result have not considered the way in which the work of Léopold Sédar Senghor might also be responding to a First World juridico-political imagination. Much of Senghor's poetry relies heavily on an essentialist African racial identity in far less nuanced terms than that of Césaire—though recent scholarship, by Gary Wilder and others, has demonstrated that he was far more canny about race as a social and political construct than is often assumed. See Wilder, *Freedom Time*, as well as the work of many contributors to the 2002 special issue of *Research in African Literatures* on Senghor.

5. Key critical interrogations of "human rights" include Arendt's *Origins of Totalitarianism*; Lyotard; Agamben; and essays by Rancière, Hamacher, Maslan, Brown, and Spivak in the 2004 special issue of *South Atlantic Quarterly*, edited by Balfour and Cadava.

6. In contrast to its eighteenth-century generic predecessors, which *preceded* revolution and the establishment of new legal orders, the Universal Declaration came into being *after* a war and *after* the law of the UN Charter, the constituting text of the postwar period. Already, in a sense, a repetition of key tenets of the Charter, a *reaffirmation* of faith rather than an original commitment, the Universal Declaration does not stand on its own. Morsink observes that much of the first paragraph of the preamble to the Universal Declaration is purposely an exact reproduction of the opening language of the UN Charter (315).

7. Brian Simpson notes that Eleanor Roosevelt did make an (unsuccessful) attempt to persuade the State Department to reconsider its position on implementation; on the Commission, however, she never wavered in upholding that official position as it stood (429).

8. Cassin's draft declaration is reproduced in full in Glendon 275–80.

9. See Morsink, chapters 5 and 6, for a detailed account of the CHR's debates over economic and social rights.

10. "One of the discursive gambles of contemporary human rights law is its articulation of a fictional international human rights personality that it aspires to bring to life; in other words, contemporary human rights law projects an artificial international legal personality from the human being as a goal to be achieved through the recognition and enjoyment of the rights and duties that the law ascribes it" (Slaughter 60–61).

11. See, in particular, Glendon; Ishay; Hunt; and Donnelly. For more critical recent assessments of the text and its claims to authority, see Douzinas; Moyn; and Normand and Zaidi.

12. See Du Bois as well as Carol Anderson, *Eyes Off the Prize*.

13. Such conflicts continue to be read primarily as symptoms of how Cold War politics infected the work of the Commission. See, in particular, Glendon.

14. Haiti, Liberia, and Ethiopia, although members of the UN, had no delegates on the Commission.

15. For extensive treatment of this subject, see Morsink; Moyn; and Burke. See Klose for a detailed account of the extensive efforts Britain and France took to defend their suppression of political and civil rights in their colonial territories during the wars of decolonization.

16. See also Anghie; Mutua; and Orford.

17. "With the official acceptance of the right to self-determination, the process of decolonization itself became a human right, and lent moral legitimacy of human rights to anticolonial struggles in Asia and Africa" (Burke 37).

18. These two narratives are ultimately quite compatible. Throughout its (contemporary) history, human rights discourse has served as both a powerful means of critiquing empire and as a means of enabling empire to reform and thereby strengthen itself. Such is Hardt and Negri's argument in *Empire*. See also Rajagopal.

19. See especially Arnold, *Modernism and Negritude*; and Hountondji. Césaire himself articulated this same distinction: "Vous trouvez qu'il y a une sorte de hiatus entre ma pensée théorique et mon action pratique? Mais c'est vrai parce que ma pensée théorique s'inscrit dans l'absolu et mon action pratique dans un contexte bien déterminé. Je n'ai pas dit qu'il y a une pensée ésotérique et une pensée publique, mais enfin, il y a une doctrine et une action" (qtd. in Armet 92).

20. See especially Glissant, *Caribbean Discourse*.

21. See also Dalleo's discussion of Caribbean anticolonial writers' critical engagement with the U.S. presence in the region, as well as with North American capitalism more generally.

22. "For Césaire in 1946, as for generations of economically marginalized Martinicans since 1848, [dissidence] meant appealing to the norms of the French Republic in order to bypass the particularist, antidemocratic dimensions of French colonial policy." Nesbitt, "Departmentalization and the Logic of Decolonization" (38).

23. See Arnold, "Césaire's *Notebook* as Palimpsest" and "Beyond Postcolonial Césaire."

24. Eshleman and Smith were also the first English translators to remove the possessive pronoun from the title; "*My* Native Land" became, more accurately, "*The* Native Land" in their 1983 translation.

25. "It is important that Césaire's version of negritude never rested on a determinate notion of black identity, but rather always consisted in an expansive and open-ended celebration of the black man's mobility and contact with the other. Césaire's negritude is already infused with the humanist values upheld at the end of the poem, and anticipates the ethical concerns that dominate the celebration of universal humanity. Even when he appears to champion the specificity of black identity, Césaire dissolves that specificity and describes negritude as an opening out and a gesture of contact with otherness" (Hiddleston 90).

26. See especially C. Miller, *The French Atlantic Triangle*.

27. It is important, for instance, that while the 1932 single-issue journal *Légitime défense*— an important, Caribbean-authored precursor to the negritude movement—opens with a declaration, *Tropiques* does not.

28. My translation borrows from Eshleman and Smith's translation of the *Cahier*, though not all lines from this poem appear in the *Cahier*.

29. Christopher Miller's *The French Atlantic Triangle* offers an elegant and more extensive exploration of the significance of negritude's refusal to comply with the francophone world's long-standing erasure of the memory of the slave trade.

30. My reading of the content of this stanza draws heavily on Irele's gloss (84).

CHAPTER 4

1. "The conference endorses the position of the African National Congress which declares that the people of South Africa, like those of Namibia and Zimbabwe, are colonised people. The conference further endorses the position of the United Nations declaring the Pretoria regime illegitimate. In doing so, it notes with satisfaction that the African National Congress, the vanguard movement spearheading the broad alliance of the indigenous people and the other oppressed black people, including white democrats, recognises the fact that the white population in South Africa has severed ties with their respective metropoles, that they recognise South Africa as their homeland. It is for that reason that the conference fully endorses and hails the ANC position, reflected in the Freedom Charter, which declares that South Africa belongs to

all who live in it, black and white, and that no government can justly claim authority unless it is based on the will of the majority of the people" ("Statement of the Lisbon Conference March 1977").

2. See Du Bois; as well as Von Eschen and C. Anderson.
3. See Ackerman.
4. See, in particular, Dennis Davis.
5. See Lodge 72; D. Davis 4; and Rich 268–69.
6. Many of them got there at the last minute (Vadi 148).
7. Matthews was not banned but was out of town when the Charter was drafted.

CHAPTER 5

1. "More European civilians would die in road traffic accidents between 1952 and 1960 than were killed by Mau Mau. These figures should be contrasted with the 1819 African civilians assassinated by Mau Mau, and another 916 African civilians wounded over the same period. These later figures do not include the many hundreds of Africans who 'disappeared,' and whose bodies were never found" (D. Anderson 84).

2. I build here not only on Benedict Anderson's pivotal insight about the importance of nationhood as an imaginative construct, but also on the work of scholars such as Cathy Davidson, Priscilla Wald, Doris Sommer, and Katie Trumpener, who have demonstrated the ways in which literary forms do the work of constituting the modern nation, often in ways that exceed and correct the limitations and exclusions inherent in the written state constitution's definition of nationhood.

3. See Peaslee.
4. See Go and Arjomand.
5. Arguments in favor of, or explaining ex post facto, the replacement of independence constitutions often cited a need for more constitutional autochthony—though as Ghai notes, autochthony proved most powerful as a rhetorical claim and rarely translated into substantive changes in the legal texts themselves (416).
6. See Le Vine.
7. "By the end of the twentieth century," Go reports, "at least 59 out of 91 independence constitutions had been significantly amended or displaced by the promulgation of new ones" (78). Zanzibar's independence constitution lasted exactly one month (De Winton 189). In West Africa alone, by Victor Le Vine's count, there were "no less than 50 post-independence constitutions and constitutional documents for all of West Africa up to 1989" (189). Only Senegal and the Ivory Coast, Le Vine observes, "have survived with their independence constitutions more or less intact" (202).
8. See Clough, *Mau Mau Memoirs* 311–20.
9. For Mau Mau memoirists' descriptions of the *muma wa chuba* and *batuni* oaths and transcriptions of their contents, see Kariuki 25–31; Barnett and Njama 130–33; and Itote 273–84.
10. See Kershaw for a critical assessment of the Mau Mau oaths' relationship to Kikuyu oathing practices from the nineteenth and early twentieth centuries.
11. Itote 273. Kariuki makes a similar move in his memoir when he recalls reflecting on the *muma wa chuba* oath with his comrades in detention: "Like most oaths of this type all over the world it was secret. We often discussed in the detention camps the oaths of Freemasons which were also taken secretly at night, and wondered why people thought ours were so much worse" (18).
12. The qualification here is that particularly in the later years of the struggle many people took oaths—or more accurately *were oathed*—in mass ceremonies presided over by Mau Mau leadership. One could draw many parallels between the way in which the Mau Mau oath got

"taken to scale" and the mass female excisions conducted in the 1920s, beautifully explored in Lynn Thomas's *Politics of the Womb*. I do not wish to idealize the Mau Mau oath here: even Kariuki and Itote report that their own initiations into the movement involved a degree of coercion (both were brought to the ceremony by friends who hadn't told them where they were going; see Kariuki 25; Itote 40). Popular *narratives* of the oath, however, foreground individual will in ways that matter, for my purposes, at least as much as do the actual conditions under which people actually participated in the oathing ceremonies.

13. The state's awareness of the continued potency of the oath becomes clear in its cynical and short-lived effort to reappropriate the form in a 1969 mass oathing campaign designed to promote national loyalty as a palliative to ethnic divisions. See Clough 52–54. The memoirs are not the only texts in which the oaths and their significance are framed in ways that differ sharply from the official narrative; see Tirop Simatei for an analysis of several Kenyan novels that offer alternative narratives of the history of Mau Mau in the 1960s and beyond.

14. In formulating these questions, I am inspired by Shalini Puri's reading of late-twentieth-century hybridity theory as manifesto—"an interpretive choice," she explains, that "turns [theory] outward to history, locating it inescapably in a specific situation, dated event, or conjecture and resisting claims to transhistorical abstraction or authority" (99). At a distance of four decades from African decolonization and the publication of *Wretched*, we are perhaps less likely to forget to historicize Fanon than postcolonial theorists from the 1990s and onward. But Puri's point nonetheless helps clarify that the "manifesto-ness" of Fanon's text may have less to do with its presentation of a concrete program of action, and more to do with the relationship between theory and historical time—between the activity of imagining and narrating decolonization, and the temporal dynamics of anticolonial revolution that shape the form and content of Fanon's work.

15. This urgency and immediacy were reflected in Fanon's writing process. Alice Cherki notes that Fanon had long been in the habit of dictating his prose to his wife or another trusted (always female) scribe, but that *Wretched*'s ties to orality are even more pronounced: "This is a much less *written* book than his previous ones: the ideas are laid out, dispersed, and then repeated like the stanzas of a poem. Fanon did not have time to revise or edit. The style is unquestionably his, persuasive rather than illustrative, and the rhythm that characterizes all his writings is more rapid, choppy. As in *Black Skin, White Masks,* his writing is a bodily feat; in this case, the feat is literally and figuratively more precipitous than ever" (Cherki 27).

16. "Self-criticism has been much talked about recently, but few realize that it was first of all an African institution. Whether it be in the *djemaas* of North Africa or the palavers of West Africa, tradition has it that disputes which break out in a village are worked out in public. By this I mean collective self-criticism with a touch of humor because everyone is relaxed, because in the end we all want the same thing" (12).

17. "But do we really know what it means to consecrate, and particularly to consecrate a difference? How is what I would call the 'magical' consecration of a difference achieved, and what are its technical effects? Does the fact of socially instituting, through an act of *constitution*, a pre-existing difference—like the one separating the sexes—have only symbolic effects, in the sense that we give to this term when we speak of the symbolic gift, in other words, no effects at all? . . . To institute . . . is to consecrate, that is, to sanction and sanctify a particular state of things, an established order, in exactly the same way that a *constitution* does in the legal and political sense of the term" (Bourdieu 119).

18. See McClintock, "Fanon and Gender Agency"; Sharpley-Whiting; and Chow, *Ethics after Idealism*.

19. *Wretched* 2. The original French reads: "La décolonisation ne passé jamais inaperçue car elle porte sur l'être, elle modifie fondamentalement l'être, elle transforme des spectateurs écrasés d'inessentialité en acteurs privilégiés, saisis de façon quasi grandiose par le faisceau de l'Histoire. Elle introduit dans l'être un rythme propre, apporté par les nouveaux hommes,

un nouveau langage, une nouvelle humanité. La décolonisation est véritablement création d'hommes nouveaux. Mais cettre création ne reçoit sa légitimité d'aucune puissance surnaturelle: la «chose» colonisée devient homme dans le processus même par lequel elle se libère" (*Damnés* 30).

20. "At the very time when it most often mouths the word, the West has never been further from being able to live a true humanism—a humanism made to the measure of the world" (*Discourse* 73).

21. My use of the masculine pronoun is intentional, in part because I want my language to align with Fanon's own, and in part because, as indicated above, Fanon's colonized subject is gendered, with profound consequences for the author's conception of community. See Chow, "The Politics of Admittance." Other discussions of Fanon's gendered language that I have found particularly useful include McClintock and Sharpley-Whiting, as well as Bergner; Dubey; and Fuss.

22. See Cook and Okenimkpe 71 and Kessler 83.

23. The most vehement articulation of this argument is found in Vaughan. See also Ogude.

24. While I want to make the case that Ngũgĩ *registers* Kihika's obliviousness to these identity categories, it's also important to note that *A Grain of Wheat* contains no such critical reflection on the problem of ethnicity.

25. Quayson xxxviii. Quayson first introduces this term as a means of describing the ideological didacticism of Ngũgĩ's *Petals of Blood*. I would quibble with Quayson's assessment of that later novel (which, I believe, is not devoid of moments that invite readers to dwell in the ambiguities of the political philosophy underlying the narrative), but the fact that Ngũgĩ's speaker-hero from this earlier text exhibits that same tendency brings up some fascinating possibilities for how to think about the connections *between* these two texts.

26. Kenyatta's title changed from prime minister to president when Kenya became a republic in 1964.

27. Certainly the confessional narratives that Mumbi, Gikonyo, and Mugo deliver to one another serve a similar function, but since they take place in private they lack the capacity for communal transformation that Mugo's pivotal speech has the potential to bring about.

28. Harry Sewlall notes that this emphasis on the community is one of Ngũgĩ's most important adjustments to Conrad's *Under Western Eyes*, which privileges Razumov's relationship with Haldin's sister and mother over his relationship to the Russian revolutionaries' cause (63).

29. In making this claim I do not wish to uncritically privilege a concept of individual selfhood which, as much African literary and philosophical criticism has argued, is an inheritance from a Western Enlightenment tradition, and at odds with a long history of indigenous definitions of selfhood in more collective terms. Quite the opposite; my point about the role of song, spontaneous improvisation, and audience participation at these key moments in Ngũgĩ's novel is that they are the mechanisms through which Ngũgĩ is imagining forms of postcolonial expression that will shed this inheritance and prove thoroughly African. However, to the extent that *A Grain of Wheat* is a novel steeped in a European modernist (Conradian) tradition of depicting the alienated protagonist whose individual circumstances trouble the social tapestry writ large, *and* to the extent that postcolonial Kenyan civil society is articulated overwhelmingly in what Mahmood Mamdani cites as the "modernist" forms of the European nation-state, a similarly oriented framework of the relationship between the self and the collective is apposite. Ngũgĩ, and his novel, accepts a vision of Kenya's future that revolves around its identity as a modern nation-state, one that will have to at least draw upon a Western notion of the relationship between individual and group identity as one starting point.

30. See Cook and Okenimkpe; Lazarus, "(Re)turn to the People"; Ogude; Patrick Williams; and Gikandi, *Ngũgĩ wa Thiong'o*.

CHAPTER 6

1. This is McClintock's apprehension about the term's (mis)use, as articulated in "The Angel of Progress." For an especially compelling recent reconfiguration of the term "post-colonialism" in relation to anticolonial movements that registers the pitfalls of overstating the divide between the anticolonial past and the postcolonial present, see Dalleo.

2. To the best of my knowledge, the only published comparative analysis of Ngũgĩ's and Glissant's work is Duncan McEachern Yoon's brief but suggestive "Translation and the Global South."

3. See Rajagopal as well as Moyn and Kennedy.

4. In *The Postcolonial Unconscious* Lazarus offers up a recent and particularly compelling account of postcolonial theory's role as "a rationalisation of, and pragmatic adjustment to, the demise of the ideologies that had flourished during the 'Bandung' years" (9). See also Ahmad; Dirlik, *The Postcolonial Aura*; Gandhi; San Juan; and Parry.

5. While some of the essays in *Caribbean Discourse* appeared elsewhere in print before the publication of the original (French) version of this collection, to the best of my knowledge, this one—entitled "In the Beginning" in English, "L'Amorce" in French—did not.

6. See in particular Bongie, *Islands and Exiles*; Britton; Hallward; and Nesbitt, *Voicing Memory*.

7. For a useful analysis of Fanon's influence on Glissant's work, see Mardorossian.

8. Dash translates *opacité* as "obscurity," whereas in *Poetics of Relation* Wing translates it as "opacity," which has since become the overwhelming term of choice for anglophone critics.

9. See, for example, Benhabib.

10. Glissant does articulate his differences with the *Créolistes* more forcefully elsewhere; see Bongie's brief discussion of the argument between these theorists in his *Islands and Exiles* 64–65.

11. See Puri as well as Priam.

12. See, for example, Williams and Chrisman as well as Ashcroft, Griffiths, and Tiffin.

13. No Kiswahili version of the essay appears in the journal. When the essay is reprinted in *Moving the Centre* three years later, the Gikuyu version disappears as well—though Ngũgĩ discusses its composition in the introduction to the volume.

14. For Ngũgĩ's account of the relationship between imperialism and the discipline of English, see "On the Abolition of the English Department" in *Homecoming*; "Literature in Schools" in *Writers in Politics*; the first several essays in *Moving the Centre*; and *Decolonising the Mind*.

15. See Forsdick.

CODA

1. See Omelsky and Dawson.

WORKS CITED

Abani, Chris. *GraceLand*. New York: Farrar, 2004.
Ackerman, Bruce. "The Rise of World Constitutionalism." *Virginia Law Review* 83.4 (1997): 771–97.
Adéèkó, Adélékè. "Power Shift: America in the New Nigerian Imagination." *Global South* 2.2 (2008): 10–30.
Agamben, Giorgio. *Homo Sacer: Sovereign Power and Bare Life*. Stanford: Stanford UP, 1998.
Ahmad, Aijaz. *In Theory: Classes, Nations, Literatures*. London; New York: Verso, 1992.
Anderson, Benedict R. *Imagined Communities: Reflections on the Origin and Spread of Nationalism*. London: Verso, 1983.
Anderson, Carol. *Eyes off the Prize: The United Nations and the African American Struggle for Human Rights, 1944–1955*. Cambridge; New York: Cambridge UP, 2003.
Anderson, David. *Histories of the Hanged: The Dirty War in Kenya and the End of Empire*. New York: Norton, 2005.
Anghie, Antony. *Imperialism, Sovereignty, and the Making of International Law*. Cambridge; New York: Cambridge UP, 2005.
Anker, Elizabeth S. *Fictions of Dignity: Embodying Human Rights in World Literature*. Ithaca: Cornell UP, 2013.
Appadurai, Arjun. *Modernity at Large: Cultural Dimensions of Globalization*. Minneapolis: U of Minnesota P, 1996.
Arendt, Hannah. *On Revolution*. New York: Viking, 1965.
———. *The Origins of Totalitarianism*. New York: Harcourt, 1966.
Arjomand, Samir. "Constitutions and the Struggle for Political Order." *Archives Européennes de sociologie / Archives of European Sociology* 33 (1992): 39–82.
Armet, Auguste. "Aimé Césaire, homme politique." *Etude littéraire* 6.1 (1973): 81–96.
Armitage, David. *The Declaration of Independence: A Global History*. Cambridge: Harvard UP, 2007.
Arnold, A. James. "Beyond Postcolonial Césaire: Reading *Cahier D'un Retour Au Pays Natal* Historically." *Forum for Modern Language Studies* 44.3 (2008): 258–75.
———. "Césaire's *Notebook* as Palimpsest: The Text Before, During, and After World War II." *Research in African Literatures* 35.3 (2004): 133–40.
———. *Modernism and Negritude: The Poetry and Poetics of Aimé Césaire*. Cambridge: Harvard UP, 1981.
Ashcroft, Bill, Gareth Griffiths, and Helen Tiffin, eds. *The Post-Colonial Studies Reader*. London; New York: Routledge, 2006.
Asmal, Kader, David Chidester, and Cass Lubisi. *Legacy of Freedom: The ANC's Human Rights Tradition: Africans' Claims in South Africa, the Freedom Charter, the Women's Charter, and Other Human Rights Landmarks of the African National Congress*. Johannesburg: Ball, 2005.
Austin, J. L. *How to Do Things with Words*. Cambridge: Harvard UP, 1962.

Bailyn, Bernard. *The Ideological Origins of the American Revolution*. Cambridge: Harvard UP, 1967.

Balfour, Ian, and Edouardo Cadava, eds. *And Justice for All? The Claims of Human Rights*. Spec. issue of *South Atlantic Quarterly* 103.2–3 (2004).

Barnett, Don, and Karari Njama. *Mau Mau from Within*. New York: Monthly Review, 1966.

Baucom, Ian. "Charting the 'Black Atlantic.'" *Postmodern Culture* 8.1 (1997): n. pag. Web. 2 June 2015.

Benhabib, Seyla. *The Rights of Others: Aliens, Residents and Citizens*. Cambridge; New York: Cambridge UP, 2004.

Bergner, Gwen. "Who Is That Masked Woman? Or, the Role of Gender in Fanon's *Black Skin, White Masks*." *PMLA* 110.1 (Jan. 1995): 75–88.

Berman, Nathaniel. "Modernism, Nationalism, and the Rhetoric of Reconstruction." *Yale Journal of Law and the Humanities* 4.2 (1992): 351–80.

Berman, Nathaniel, Euan MacDonald, and Emmanuelle Jouannet. *Passion and Ambivalence: Colonialism, Nationalism, and International Law*. Leiden: Brill, 2011.

Bernabé, Jean, Patrick Chamoiseau, and Raphaël Confiant. *Éloge de la Créolité / In Praise of Creoleness*. Trans. Mohamed Bouya Taleb-Khyar. Paris: Gallimard, 1993.

Bernasconi, Robert. "Casting the Slough: Fanon's New Humanism for a New Humanity." *Fanon: A Critical Reader*. Ed. Lewis R. Gordon, T. Denean Sharpley-Whiting, and Renée T. White. Cambridge, MA: Blackwell, 1996. 113–21.

———. "The Double Face of the Political and the Social: Hannah Arendt and America's Racial Divisions." *Research in Phenomenology* 26 (1996): 3–24.

Bogues, Anthony. Afterword to C. L. R. James's "Lectures on *The Black Jacobins*." *Small Axe* 8 (2000): 113–17.

———. *Caliban's Freedom: The Early Political Thought of C. L. R. James*. London; Chicago: Pluto, 1997.

Bongie, Chris. *Friends and Enemies: The Scribal Politics of Post/colonial Literature*. Liverpool: Liverpool UP, 2008.

———. *Islands and Exiles: The Creole Identities of Post/colonial Literature*. Stanford: Stanford UP, 1998.

Bourdieu, Pierre. *Language and Symbolic Power*. Cambridge: Harvard UP, 1991.

Breton, André. *Manifestoes of Surrealism*. 1924. Trans. Richard Seaver and Helen R. Lane. Ann Arbor: U of Michigan P, 1969.

Britton, Celia. *Edouard Glissant and Postcolonial Theory: Strategies of Language and Resistance*. Charlottesville: UP of Virginia, 1999.

Brooks, Peter. *Troubling Confessions: Speaking Guilt in Law & Literature*. Chicago: U of Chicago P, 2000.

Buck-Morss, Susan. *Hegel, Haiti, and Universal History*. Pittsburgh: U of Pittsburgh P, 2009.

Burke, Roland. *Decolonization and the Evolution of International Human Rights*. Philadelphia: U of Pennsylvania P, 2010.

"Call to the Congress of the People." *African National Congress*. Web. 31 May 2015. <http://www.anc.org.za/show.php?id=2602>.

Cantalupo, Charles, ed. *The World of Ngũgĩ wa Thiong'o*. 1st ed. Trenton, N.J.: Africa World Press, Inc, 1995.

Carby, Hazel. *Race Men*. Cambridge: Harvard UP, 1998.

Césaire, Aimé. *Aimé Césaire, the Collected Poetry*. Trans. Clayton Eshleman and Annette Smith. Berkeley: U of California P, 1983.

———. *Cahier d'un retour au pays natal*. Ed. Abiola Irele. Ibadan: New Horn, 1994.

———. *Discourse sur le colonialisme*. Paris: Présence Africaine, 1955.

———. *Discourse on Colonialism*. Trans. Joan Kelley. New York: Monthly Review, 2000.
———. "En guise de manifeste." *Tropiques* 5 (1942): 7–8.
———. *Lettre à Maurice Thorez*. Paris: Présence Africaine, 1956.
———. *Lyric and Dramatic Poetry, 1946–82*. Trans. Clayton Eshleman and Annette Smith. Charlottesville: UP of Virginia, 1990.
———. *Notebook of a Return to the Native Land*. Trans. Clayton Eshleman and Annette Smith. Middletown, CT: Wesleyan UP, 2001.
———. *Victor Schoelcher et l'abolition de l'esclavage: suivi de trois discours*. Lectoure: Editions le Capucin, 2004.
Cheah, Pheng. *Inhuman Conditions on Cosmopolitanism and Human Rights*. Cambridge: Harvard UP, 2006.
Cherki, Alice. *Frantz Fanon: A Portrait*. Trans. Nadia Benabid. Ithaca: Cornell UP, 2006.
Chow, Rey. *Ethics after Idealism: Theory, Culture, Ethnicity, Reading*. Bloomington: Indiana UP, 1998.
———. "The Politics of Admittance: Female Sexual Agency, Miscegenation, and the Formation of Community in Frantz Fanon." *Frantz Fanon: Critical Perspectives*. Ed. Anthony Alessandri. New York: Routledge, 1999. 34–56.
Chrisman, Laura. *Postcolonial Contraventions: Cultural Readings of Race, Imperialism, and Transnationalism*. Manchester; New York: Manchester UP, 2003.
Clough, Marshall S. *Mau Mau Memoirs: History, Memory, and Politics*. Boulder, CO: Rienner, 1998.
Cook, David, and Michael Okenimkpe. *Ngũgĩ wa Thiong'o: An Exploration of His Writings*. Oxford: Currey; Portsmouth, NH: Heinemann, 1997.
Cooper, Frederick. "Mau Mau and the Discourses of Decolonization." *Journal of African History* 29.2 (1988): 313–20.
Crenshaw, Kimberlé et al., eds. *Critical Race Theory: The Key Writings That Formed the Movement*. New York: New Press; dist. Norton, 1995.
Dalleo, Raphael. *Caribbean Literature and the Public Sphere: From the Plantation to the Postcolonial*. Charlottesville: U of Virginia P, 2011.
Dash, J. Michael, and Quincy Troupe. "Interview with Edouard Glissant: March 22, 2006." *Black Renaissance / Renaissance Noire* 6-7.3-1: 50–56.
Davidson, Cathy N. *Revolution and the Word: The Rise of the Novel in America*. Expanded ed. New York: Oxford UP, 2004.
Davis, Dennis. "The Freedom Charter: A Challenge and Bequest." *The Freedom Charter and Beyond: Founding Principles for a Democratic South African Legal Order*. Ed. Nico Steytler. Cape Town: Wyvern, 1991. 1–19.
Davis, Gregson. *Aimé Césaire*. Cambridge; New York: Cambridge UP, 1997.
———. "Negritude-as-Performance: The Interplay of Efficacious and Inefficacious Speech Acts in *Cahier d'un retour au pays natal*." *Research in African Literatures* 41.1 (2010): 142–54.
Dawson, Ashley. "Surplus City: Structural Adjustment, Self-Fashioning, and Urban Insurrection in Chris Abani's *Graceland*." *Interventions* 11.1 (2009): 16–34.
Dayan, Joan. *Haiti, History, and the Gods*. Berkeley: U of California P, 1995.
de Gennaro, Mara. "Fighting 'Humanism' on Its Own Terms." *differences* 14.1 (2003): 53–73.
De Winton, M. G. "Decolonisation and the Westminster Model." *Africa in the Colonial Period III. The Transfer of Power: The Colonial Administrators in the Age of Decolonization*. Ed. A. H. M. Kirk-Greene. Oxford: U of Oxford Inter-Faculty Committee for African Studies, 1979. 183–92.
Déclaration des droits de l'homme et du citoyen de 1789. *Conseil constitutionnel*. Web. 24 Oct. 2013. <http://www.conseil-constitutionnel.fr/conseil-constitutionnel/francais/la-constitution/la

-constitution-du-4-octobre-1958/declaration-des-droits-de-l-homme-et-du-citoyen-de-1789.5076.html>.

Derrida, Jacques. "Declarations of Independence." *New Political Science* 15 (1986): 7–15.

———. "Force of Law: The 'Mystical Foundation of Authority.'" *Acts of Religion*. Trans. Gil Anidjar. New York: Routledge, 2001. 228–98.

———. *Specters of Marx: The State of the Debt, the Work of Mourning, and the New International*. Trans. Peggy Kamuf. New York: Routledge, 1994.

Dessalines, Jean-Jacques. "Liberté ou la mort. Proclamation. Jean-Jacques Dessalines, Gouverneur Général, aux habitans d'Haiti." *Haiti and the Atlantic World*. Ed. Julia Gaffield. Web. 2 June 2015. <http://haitidoi.com/2013/08/02/i-have-avenged-america/>.

Dirlik, Arif. *The Postcolonial Aura: Third World Criticism in the Age of Global Capitalism*. Boulder, CO: Westview, 1997.

———. "Rethinking Colonialism: Globalization, Postcolonialism, and the Nation." *Interventions* 4.3 (2011): 428–48.

"Does the Freedom Charter Mean Socialism?" *New Age* 17 Nov. 1957. Web. 28 Aug. 2013. <http://anc.org.za/show.php?id=2604>.

Donnelly, Jack. *International Human Rights*. Boulder, CO: Westview, 2007.

Douzinas, Costas. *The End of Human Rights: Critical Legal Thought at the Turn of the Century*. Oxford; Portland, OR: Hart, 2000.

———. *Human Rights and Empire: The Political Philosophy of Cosmopolitanism*. London; New York: Routledge, 2007.

Du Bois, W. E. B. *Color and Democracy: Colonies and Race*. Chesapeake, NY: ECA, 1990.

Dubey, Madhu. "The 'True Lie' of the Nation: Fanon and Feminism." *differences* 10.2 (1998): 1–29.

Dubois, Laurent. *Avengers of the New World: The Story of the Haitian Revolution*. Cambridge: Harvard UP, 2004.

Dubois, Laurent, and John D. Garrigus, eds. *Slave Revolution in the Caribbean, 1789-1804: A Brief History with Documents*. Basingstoke: Palgrave, 2006.

"Duke Graduate Student Discovers Haiti's Original Declaration of Independence in British Archives." Duke U Office of News and Communications, 1 Apr. 2010. Web. 24 Oct. 2013. <http://today.duke.edu/showcase/haitideclaration/newsarchive.html>.

During, Simon. "Postcolonialism and Globalization: Towards a Historicization of Their Inter-Relation." *Cultural Studies* 14.3-4 (2000): 385–404.

Edmondson, Belinda. *Making Men: Gender, Literary Authority, and Women's Writing in Caribbean Narrative*. Durham: Duke UP, 1999.

Edwards, Brent Hayes. *The Practice of Diaspora: Literature, Translation, and the Rise of Black Internationalism*. Cambridge: Harvard UP, 2003.

Escobar, Arturo. *Encountering Development: The Making and Unmaking of the Third World*. Princeton: Princeton UP, 1995.

Esterhammer, Angela. *The Romantic Performative: Language and Action in British and German Romanticism*. Stanford: Stanford UP, 2000.

Fanon, Frantz. *Les damnés de la terre*. Paris: Maspero, 1961.

———. *A Dying Colonialism*. Trans. Haakon Chevalier. New York: Grove, 1967.

———. *The Wretched of the Earth*. Trans. Richard Philcox. New York: Grove, 2004.

Farred, Grant. *What's My Name? Black Vernacular Intellectuals*. Minneapolis: U of Minnesota P, 2003.

Fick, Carolyn E. *The Making of Haiti: The Saint Domingue Revolution from Below*. Knoxville: U of Tennessee P, 1990.

Fischer, Sibylle. *Modernity Disavowed: Haiti and the Cultures of Slavery in the Age of Revolution*. Durham: Duke UP, 2004.

Fliegelman, Jay. *Declaring Independence: Jefferson, Natural Language & the Culture of Performance*. Stanford: Stanford UP, 1993.
Forsdick, Charles. "Late Glissant: History, 'World Literature,' and the Persistence of the Political." *Small Axe* 14.3 (2010): 121–34.
Frank, Jason A. *Constituent Moments: Enacting the People in Postrevolutionary America*. Durham: Duke UP, 2010.
"The Freedom Charter." *African National Congress*. 26 June 1955. Web. 31 May 2015. <http://www.anc.org.za/show.php?id=72>.
Friedland, Paul. *Political Actors: Representative Bodies and Theatricality in the Age of the French Revolution*. Ithaca: Cornell UP, 2002.
Fuss, Diana. "Interior Colonies: Frantz Fanon and the Politics of Identification." *Diacritics* 24.2–3 (1994): 19–42.
Gandhi, Leela. *Postcolonial Theory: A Critical Introduction*. New York: Columbia UP, 1998.
Garraway, Doris L. "'What Is Mine': Césairean Negritude between the Particular and the Universal." *Research in African Literatures* 41.1 (2010): 71–86.
———, ed. *Tree of Liberty: Cultural Legacies of the Haitian Revolution in the Atlantic World*. Charlottesville: U of Virginia P, 2008.
Geggus, David Patrick. *Haitian Revolutionary Studies*. Bloomington: Indiana UP, 2002.
———, ed. *The Impact of the Haitian Revolution in the Atlantic World*. Columbia: U of South Carolina P, 2001.
Gerhart, Gail M. *Black Power in South Africa: The Evolution of an Ideology*. Berkeley: U of California P, 1978.
Ghai, Yash P. "Constitutions and the Political Order in East Africa." *International and Comparative Law Quarterly* 21.3 (July 1972): 403–34.
Ghai, Yash P., and Patrick McAuslan. *Public Law and Political Change in Kenya: A Study of the Legal Framework of Government from Colonial Times to the Present*. Nairobi; New York: Oxford UP, 1970.
Gibson, Nigel C., ed. *Rethinking Fanon: The Continuing Dialogue*. Amherst, NY: Humanity, 1999.
Gikandi, Simon. "Globalization and the Claims of Postcoloniality." *South Atlantic Quarterly* 100.3 (2001): 627–58.
———. *Ngugi wa Thiong'o*. Cambridge; New York: Cambridge UP, 2000.
Gilroy, Paul. *The Black Atlantic: Modernity and Double Consciousness*. Cambridge: Harvard UP, 1993.
———. *Small Acts: Thoughts on the Politics of Black Cultures*. London: Serpent's Tail, 1993.
Girard, Philippe. "Jean-Jacques Dessalines and the Atlantic System: A Reappraisal." *William and Mary Quarterly* 69.3 (July 2012): 549–82.
Glendon, Mary Ann. *A World Made New: Eleanor Roosevelt and the Universal Declaration of Human Rights*. New York: Random, 2001.
Glissant, Édouard. *Caribbean Discourse: Selected Essays*. Trans. J. Michael Dash. Charlottesville: UP of Virginia, 1989.
———. *Le Discours Antillais*. Paris: Seuil, 1981.
———. *L'Intention poétique*. Paris: Seuil, 1969.
———. *Poetics of Relation*. Trans. Betsy Wing. Ann Arbor: U of Michigan P, 1997.
———. *Poétique de la relation*. Paris: Gallimard, 1990.
Go, Julian. "A Globalizing Constitutionalism? Views from the Postcolony, 1945–2000." *International Sociology* 18.1 (2003): 71–95.
Goldberg, Elizabeth Swanson. *Beyond Terror: Gender, Narrative, Human Rights*. New Brunswick: Rutgers UP, 2007.
Goldberg, Elizabeth Swanson, and Alexandra Schultheis Moore. *Theoretical Perspectives on Human Rights and Literature*. New York: Routledge, 2012.

Goyal, Yogita. "Africa and the Black Atlantic." *Research in African Literatures* 45.3 (2014): v–xxv.

Greenblatt, Stephen. *Learning to Curse: Essays in Early Modern Culture.* New York: Routledge, 1990.

Guinier, Lani, and Gerald Torres. *The Miner's Canary: Enlisting Race, Resisting Power, Transforming Democracy.* Cambridge: Harvard UP, 2002.

Haitian Declaration of Independence. 1804. National Archives, Kew, UK. Web. 24 Oct. 2013.

Hale, Thomas A., and Kora Véron. "Is There Unity in the Writings of Aimé Césaire?" *Research in African Literatures* 41.1 (2010): 46–70.

Hall, Stuart, and Bill Schwarz. "Breaking Bread with History: C. L. R. James and *The Black Jacobins.*" *History Workshop Journal* 46 (1998): 17–31.

Hallward, Peter. *Absolutely Postcolonial: Writing between the Singular and the Specific.* Manchester: Manchester UP, 2001.

Hardt, Michael, and Antonio Negri. *Empire.* Cambridge: Harvard UP, 2000.

Harris, Cheryl. "Whiteness as Property." *Harvard Law Review* 106.8 (1993): 1707–91.

Henry, Paget. *Caliban's Reason: Introducing Afro-Caribbean Philosophy.* New York: Routledge, 2000.

Hiddleston, Jane. "Aimé Césaire and Postcolonial Humanism." *Modern Language Review* 105.1 (2010): 87–102.

Høgsbjerg, Christian. *C. L. R. James in Imperial Britain.* Durham: Duke UP, 2014.

Holloway, Karla F. C. *Private Bodies, Public Texts: Race, Gender, and a Cultural Bioethics.* Durham: Duke UP, 2011.

Hountondji, Paulin J. "La 'Fin du monde': Césaire et l'invention de la liberté." *Black Renaissance / Renaissance Noire* 3.1 (2000): 166–80.

Hulme, Peter. *Colonial Encounters: Europe and the Native Caribbean, 1492–1797.* London; New York: Methuen, 1986.

Humphrey, John P. *Human Rights & the United Nations: A Great Adventure.* Dobbs Ferry, NY: Transnational, 1984.

Hunt, Lynn. *Inventing Human Rights: A History.* New York: Norton, 2007.

Idahosa, Paul. "James and Fanon and the Problem of the Intelligentsia in Popular Organizations." *C. L. R. James: His Intellectual Legacies.* Ed. Selwyn R. Cudjoe and William E. Cain. Amherst: U of Massachusetts P, 1995. 388–404.

Ishay, Micheline. *The History of Human Rights: From Ancient Times to the Globalization Era.* Berkeley: U of California P, 2004.

Itote, Waruhiu. *"Mau Mau" General.* Nairobi: East African Institute P, 1967.

James, C. L. R. *At the Rendezvous of Victory: Selected Writings.* London: Allison, 1984.

——. *The Black Jacobins: Toussaint L'Ouverture and the San Domingo Revolution.* 1963. 2d ed., New York: Vintage, 1989.

——. *A History of Negro Revolt.* New York: Haskell, 1969.

——. *A History of Pan-African Revolt.* Washington, DC: Drum and Spear, 1969.

——. "Lectures on *The Black Jacobins.*" *Small Axe* 8 (2000): 65–112.

——. *The Life of Captain Cipriani: An Account of British Government in the West Indies, with the Pamphlet "The Case for West Indian Self Government."* Durham: Duke UP, 2014.

——. *Modern Politics: A Series of Lectures on the Subject Given at the Trinidad Public Library in Its Adult Education Program.* Detroit: bewick/ed, 1973.

——. *Nkrumah and the Ghana Revolution.* Westport, CT: Hill, 1977.

Janvier, Louis Joseph. *Les Constitutions d'Haïti (1801–1885).* Paris: Marpon, 1886.

Jay, Paul. *Global Matters: The Transnational Turn in Literary Studies.* Ithaca: Cornell UP, 2010.

Jefferson, Thomas. "Notes of Proceedings in the Continental Congress" (7 June–1 Aug. 1776). *The Papers of Thomas Jefferson.* Vol. 1. Ed. Julian P. Boyd. Princeton: Princeton UP, 1950.

Jenson, Deborah. *Beyond the Slave Narrative: Politics, Sex, and Manuscripts in the Haitian Revolution.* Liverpool: Liverpool UP, 2011.
Johnson, Chris W. "Sex and the Subversive Alien: The Moral Life of C. L. R. James." *International Journal of Francophone Studies* 14.1-2 (2011): 185-203.
Joseph, Miranda. *Against the Romance of Community.* Minneapolis: U of Minnesota P, 2002.
Julien, Eileen. "Heroism in *A Grain of Wheat.*" *African Literature Today* 13 (1983): 136-45.
Kamugisha, Aaron. "The Hearts of Men? Gender in the Late C. L. R. James." *Small Axe* 34 (2011): 76-94.
Kariuki, Josiah Mwangi. *Mau Mau Detainee; the Account by a Kenya African of His Experiences in Detention Camps, 1953-1960.* London: Oxford UP, 1963.
Kennedy, David. "The International Human Rights Movement: Part of the Problem?" *Harvard Human Rights Journal* 99 (2002): 101-25.
Kenyatta, Jomo. *Harambee! The Prime Minister of Kenya's Speeches, 1963-1964, from the Attainment of Internal Self-Government to the Threshold of the Kenya Republic.* Nairobi; New York: Oxford UP, 1964.
Kershaw, Greet. *Mau Mau from Below.* Eastern African Studies. Oxford: Currey; Athens: Ohio UP, 1997.
Kessler, Kathy. "Rewriting History in Fiction: Elements of Postmodernism in Ngugi Wa Thiong'o's Later Novels." *ARIEL* 25.2 (1994): 75-90.
King, Richard H. "Hannah Arendt and the Concept of Revolution in the 1960s." *New Formations* 71 (2006): 30-45.
———. "The Odd Couple: C. L. R. James, Hannah Arendt, and the Return of Politics in the Cold War." *Beyond Boundaries: C. L. R. James and Postnational Studies.* Ed. Christopher Gair. Ann Arbor: Pluto Press, 2006. 108-27.
Klein, Naomi. *The Shock Doctrine: The Rise of Disaster Capitalism.* New York: Holt, 2007.
Klose, Fabian. *Human Rights in the Shadow of Colonial Violence: The Wars of Independence in Kenya and Algeria.* Trans. Dona Geyer. Philadelphia: U of Pennsylvania P, 2013.
Koskenniemi, Martti. *The Gentle Civilizer of Nations: The Rise and Fall of International Law, 1870-1960.* Cambridge; New York: Cambridge UP, 2002.
Kuti, Fela. "Authority Stealing." *VIP & Authority Stealing.* New York: Knitting Factory, 2010.
Lauren, Paul Gordon. *The Evolution of International Human Rights: Visions Seen.* Pennsylvania Studies in Human Rights. Philadelphia: U of Pennsylvania P, 1998.
Lazarus, Neil. *The Postcolonial Unconscious.* Cambridge; New York: Cambridge UP, 2011.
———. *Resistance in Postcolonial African Fiction.* New Haven: Yale UP, 1990.
———. "(Re)turn to the People: Ngũgĩ wa Thiong'o and the Crisis of Postcolonial African Intellectualism." Cantalupo 11-26.
Léopold Sédar Senghor. Spec. issue of *Research in African Literatures* 33.4 (Winter 2002).
Le Vine, Victor T. "The Fall and Rise of Constitutionalism in West Africa." *Journal of Modern African Studies* 35.2 (1997): 181-206.
Lodge, Tom. *Black Politics in South Africa since 1945.* London; New York: Longman, 1983.
Loomba, Ania. *Colonialism/Postcolonialism.* 2nd ed. New York: Routledge, 2005.
Lucas, Stephen E. "The Rhetorical Ancestry of the Declaration of Independence." *Rhetoric and Public Affairs* 1.2 (1998): 143-84.
Lutz, John. "Ngugi's Dialectical Vision: Individualism and Revolutionary Consciousness in *A Grain of Wheat.*" *Ufahamu* 29.2-3 (2003): 171-98.
Lyon, Janet. *Manifestoes: Provocations of the Modern.* Ithaca: Cornell UP, 1999.
Lyotard, François. "The Other's Rights." *On Human Rights: The Oxford Amnesty Lectures 1993.* Ed. Stephen Shute and Susan Hurley. New York: Basic, 1993. 135-48.
Madiou, Thomas. *Histoire d'Haïti.* Port-au-Prince, Haiti: Deschamps, 1987.

Malouf, Michael. *Transatlantic Solidarities: Irish Nationalism and Caribbean Politics*. Charlottesville: U of Virginia P, 2009.
Mamdani, Mahmood. *Citizen and Subject: Contemporary Africa and the Legacy of Late Colonialism*. Princeton: Princeton UP, 1996.
Mandela, Nelson. "Freedom in Our Lifetime." *Liberation* 30 June 1956. Web. 13 Aug. 2013. <http://www.anc.org.za/show.php?id=2603>.
———. *Long Walk to Freedom: The Autobiography of Nelson Mandela*. Boston: Little, Brown, 1994.
Mardorossian, Carine. "From Fanon to Glissant: A Martinican Genealogy." *Small Axe* 30 (2009): 12–24.
Matthews, Z. K., and Monica Wilson. *Freedom for My People: The Autobiography of Z. K. Matthews, Southern Africa 1901 to 1968*. London: Collings, 1981.
Mazower, Mark. *No Enchanted Palace: The End of Empire and the Ideological Origins of the United Nations*. Princeton: Princeton UP, 2009.
Mazrui, Alamin, and Lupenga Mphande, "Orality and the Literature of Combat: Ngũgĩ and the Legacy of Fanon." Cantalupo 159–84.
Mbembe, Achille. "Provisional Notes on the Postcolony." *Africa* 62.1 (1992): 3–37.
McClintock, Anne. "The Angel of Progress: Pitfalls of the Term 'Postcolonialism.'" *Social Text* 31–32 (1992): 84–98.
———. "Fanon and Gender Agency." *Rethinking Fanon: The Continuing Dialogue*. Ed. Nigel C. Gibson. Amherst, NY: Humanity, 1999. 283–93.
McIlwain, Charles Howard. *Constitutionalism, Ancient and Modern*. Ithaca: Cornell UP, 1940.
Melas, Natalie. "Untimeliness, or Négritude and the Poetics of Contramodernity." *South Atlantic Quarterly* 108.3 (2009): 563–80.
Miller, Christopher L. *The French Atlantic Triangle: Literature and Culture of the Slave Trade*. Durham: Duke UP, 2008.
Miller, Paul B. "Enlightened Hesitations: Black Masses and Tragic Heroes in C. L. R. James's 'The Black Jacobins.'" *MLN* 116.5 (2001): 1069–90.
Morsink, Johannes. *The Universal Declaration of Human Rights: Origins, Drafting, and Intent*. Philadelphia: U of Pennsylvania P, 1999.
Moyn, Samuel. *The Last Utopia: Human Rights in History*. Cambridge: Harvard UP, 2010.
Mutua, Makau. *Human Rights: A Political and Cultural Critique*. Philadelphia: U of Pennsylvania P, 2002.
Negri, Antonio. *Insurgencies: Constituent Power and the Modern State*. Trans. Maurizia Boscagli. Minneapolis: U of Minnesota P, 1999.
Nesbitt, Nick. "Departmentalization and the Logic of Decolonization." *L'Esprit Créateur* 47.1 (2007): 32–43.
———. "The Incandescent I, Destroyer of Worlds." *Research in African Literatures* 41.1 (2010): 121–41.
———. *Universal Emancipation: The Haitian Revolution and the Radical Enlightenment*. Charlottesville: U of Virginia P, 2008.
———. *Voicing Memory: History and Subjectivity in French Caribbean Literature*. Charlottesville: U of Virginia P, 2003.
Ngũgĩ wa Thiong'o. *Decolonising the Mind: The Politics of Language in African Literature*. London; Portsmouth, NH: Heinemann, 1986.
———. *Detained: A Writer's Prison Diary*. London; Exeter, NH: Heinemann, 1981.
———. "English: A Language for the World?" *Yale Journal of Criticism* 4.1 (1990): 269–94.
———. *A Grain of Wheat*. London: Heinemann, 1967.
———. *Homecoming: Essays on African and Caribbean Literature, Culture and Politics*. London: Heinemann, 1972.

———. *Moving the Centre: The Struggle for Cultural Freedoms*. London; Portsmouth, NH: Heinemann, 1993.

———. *Writers in Politics: Essays*. Studies in African Literature. London: Heinemann, 1981.

Nixon, Rob. *Homelands, Harlem, and Hollywood: South African Culture and the World Beyond*. New York: Routledge, 1994.

Normand, Roger, and Sarah Zaidi. *Human Rights at the UN: The Political History of Universal Justice*. Bloomington: Indiana UP, 2008.

Ogude, James. *Ngugi's Novels and African History: Narrating the Nation*. London; Sterling, VA: Pluto, 1999.

Okoth-Ogendo, H. W. O. "Constitutions without Constitutionalism: Reflections on an African Political Paradox." *Constitutionalism and Democracy: Transitions in the Contemporary World*. Ed. Douglas Greenberg, Stanley N. Katz, Melanie Beth Oliviero, and Steven C. Wheatley. New York: Oxford UP, 1993. 65–82.

Omelsky, Matthew. "Chris Abani and the Politics of Ambivalence." *Research in African Literatures* 42.4 (2011): 84–96.

Orford, Anne. *Reading Humanitarian Intervention: Human Rights and the Use of Force in International Law*. Cambridge; New York: Cambridge UP, 2003.

Orgel, Stephen. "Prospero's Wife." *Representations* 8 (1984): 1–13.

Ozouf, Mona. *Festivals and the French Revolution*. Cambridge: Harvard UP, 1988.

Parry, Benita. *Postcolonial Studies: A Materialist Critique*. London; New York: Routledge, 2004.

Patterson, Orlando. *Slavery and Social Death: A Comparative Study*. Cambridge: Harvard UP, 1982.

Peaslee, Amos J. *Constitutions of Nations*. Prep. Dorothy Peaslee Xydis. Rev. 3rd ed. The Hague: Nijhoff, 1965.

Pinto, Samantha. *Difficult Diasporas: The Transnational Feminist Aesthetic of the Black Atlantic*. New York: New York UP, 2013.

Piot, Charles. "Atlantic Aporias: Africa and Gilroy's Black Atlantic." *South Atlantic Quarterly* 100.1 (2001): 155–70.

Priam, Mylène. "Beyond 'The Drama of Consciousness' and Against the 'Drama of the Manifesto': Poetic License and the Creolist Discourse." *Research in African Literatures* 44.1 (2013): 19–35.

Puchner, Martin. *Poetry of the Revolution: Marx, Manifestos, and the Avant-Gardes*. Princeton: Princeton UP, 2006.

Puri, Shalini. *The Caribbean Postcolonial: Social Equality, Post-Nationalism, and Cultural Hybridity*. New York: Palgrave, 2004.

Quayson, Ato. *Calibrations: Reading for the Social*. Minneapolis: U of Minnesota P, 2003.

Rabbitt, Kara M. "Prose Poem, Anti-poème, Political Force: The Critical Function of Genre in Aimé Césaire's *Cahier d'un retour au pays natal*." *Romance Notes* 39.1 (1998): 35–46.

Rainsford, Marcus. *An Historical Account of the Black Empire of Hayti*. Ed. Paul Youngquist and Grégory Pierrot. Durham; London: Duke UP, 2013.

Rajagopal, Balakrishnan. *International Law from Below: Development, Social Movements, and Third World Resistance*. Cambridge; New York: Cambridge UP, 2003.

Renan, Ernest. "What Is a Nation?" Trans. Martin Thom. *Nation and Narration*. Ed. Homi Bhabha. London; New York: Routledge, 1990. 8–22.

Rich, Paul. "Reviewing the Origins of the Freedom Charter." *Peace, Politics and Violence in the New South Africa*. Ed. Norman Etherington. London; New York: Zell, 1992. 254–83.

Richardson, Michael, and Krzysztof Fijałkowski, eds. *Refusal of the Shadow: Surrealism and the Caribbean*. London; New York: Verso, 1996.

Robbins, Bruce. *Feeling Global: Internationalism in Distress*. New York: New York UP, 1999.

Robinson, Cedric J. *Black Marxism: The Making of the Black Radical Tradition*. London; Totowa, NJ: Zed, 1983.

Roosevelt, Eleanor. *What I Hope to Leave Behind: The Essential Essays of Eleanor Roosevelt*. Brooklyn, NY: Carlson, 1995.
Rosello, Mireille. "The 'Césaire Effect,' or How to Cultivate One's Nation." *Research in African Literatures* 32.4 (2001): 77–91.
San Juan, E. *Beyond Postcolonial Theory*. New York: St. Martin's, 1998.
Schaffer, Kay, and Sidonie Smith. *Human Rights and Narrated Lives: The Ethics of Recognition*. New York: Palgrave, 2004.
Scott, David. *Conscripts of Modernity: The Tragedy of Colonial Enlightenment*. Durham: Duke UP, 2004.
———. *Omens of Adversity: Tragedy, Time, Memory, Justice*. Durham: Duke UP, 2014.
Sewlall, Harry. "Writing from the Periphery: The Case of Ngugi and Conrad." *English in Africa* 30.1 (2003): 55–69.
Sharpley-Whiting, T. Denean. "Fanon's Feminist Consciousness and Algerian Women's Liberation: Colonialism, Nationalism, and Fundamentalism." *Rethinking Fanon: The Continuing Dialogue*. Ed. Nigel C. Gibson. Amherst, NY: Humanity, 1999. 329–53.
Simatei, Tirop. "Colonial Violence, Postcolonial Violations: Violence, Landscape, and Memory in Kenyan Fiction." *Research in African Literatures* 36.2 (2005): 85–94.
Simpson, A. W. Brian. *Human Rights and the End of Empire: Britain and the Genesis of the European Convention*. Oxford; New York: Oxford UP, 2001.
Slaughter, Joseph R. *Human Rights, Inc.: The World Novel, Narrative Form, and International Law*. New York: Fordham UP, 2007.
Slauter, Eric Thomas. *The State as a Work of Art: The Cultural Origins of the Constitution*. Chicago: U of Chicago P, 2009.
Soboul, Albert, Jean-René Suratteau, and François Gendron, eds. *Dictionnaire historique de la révolution française*. Paris: PUF, 1989.
Sommer, Doris. *Foundational Fictions: The National Romances of Latin America*. Berkeley: U of California P, 1991.
South Africa. Treason Trial Press Summaries, 1956–61, nos. 1–58. *1956 Treason Trial*. AD1812.I1. U of the Witwatersrand Historical Papers Research Archive. Web. 30 May 2015. <http://www.historicalpapers.wits.ac.za/?inventory/U/collections&c=AD1812/R/>.
Spivak, Gayatri Chakravorty. "Can the Subaltern Speak?" *Colonial Discourse and Post-Colonial Theory: A Reader*. Ed. Patrick Williams and Laura Chrisman. New York: Columbia UP, 1994. 66–111.
Springfield, Consuelo Lopez. "Through the People's Eyes: C. L. R. James's Rhetoric of History." *Caribbean Quarterly* 36.1-2 (1990): 85–97.
"Statement of the Lisbon Conference March 1977." *African National Congress*. 24 Mar. 1987. Web. 28 Aug. 2013. <http://www.anc.org.za/show.php?id=4518>.
Stephens, Michelle Ann. *Black Empire: The Masculine Global Imaginary of Caribbean Intellectuals in the United States, 1914–1962*. Durham: Duke UP, 2005.
Suttner, Raymond, and Jeremy Cronin. *50 Years of the Freedom Charter*. Pretoria: Unisa, 2006.
Thomas, Lynn M. *Politics of the Womb: Women, Reproduction, and the State in Kenya*. Berkeley: U of California P, 2003.
"Transcript of Shorthand Notes Taken by Dt. Sgt. Van Zil Schoeman at the Congress of the People: Kliptown, Johannesburg, 25th and 26th June, 1955." *1956 Treason Trial*. AD1812, Item No. B4.75. U of the Witwatersrand Historical Papers Research Archive. Web. 30 May 2015. <http://www.historicalpapers.wits.ac.za/?inventory_enhanced/U/Collections&c=132531/R/AD1812-B4-75>.
Trinh, T. Minh-ha. *Woman, Native, Other: Writing Postcoloniality and Feminism*. Bloomington: Indiana UP, 1989.

Trouillot, Michel-Rolph. *Silencing the Past: Power and the Production of History.* Boston: Beacon, 1995.
Trumpener, Katie. *Bardic Nationalism: The Romantic Novel and the British Empire.* Princeton: Princeton UP, 1997.
Unesco. *Human Rights: Comments and Interpretations.* New York: Columbia UP, 1949.
UN General Assembly. Universal Declaration of Human Rights. 10 Dec. 1948, 217 A (III).
Vadi, Ismail. *The Congress of the People and the Freedom Charter Campaign.* New Delhi: Sterling, 1995.
Vaughan, Michael. "African Fiction and Popular Struggle: The Case of *A Grain of Wheat.*" *English in Africa* 8.2 (1981): 23–52.
Viswanathan, Gauri. *Masks of Conquest: Literary Study and British Rule in India.* New York: Columbia UP, 1989.
Von Eschen, Penny M. *Race Against Empire: Black Americans and Anticolonialism, 1937–1957.* Ithaca: Cornell UP, 1997.
Wald, Priscilla. *Constituting Americans: Cultural Anxiety and Narrative Form.* Durham: Duke UP, 1995.
Walker, Keith Louis. "In Quest of the Lost Song of Self: Aimé Césaire and the Problem of Language." *Callaloo* 17 (1983): 120–33.
Warner, Michael. *The Letters of the Republic: Publication and the Public Sphere in Eighteenth-Century America.* Cambridge: Harvard UP, 1990.
Wasserstrom, Jeffrey N., Lynn Hunt, and Marilyn Blatt Young, eds. *Human Rights and Revolutions.* Lanham, MD: Rowman, 2000.
Watt, Ian. *The Rise of the Novel: Studies in Defoe, Richardson, and Fielding.* Berkeley: U of California P, 1957.
Wellmer, Albrecht. "Arendt on Revolution." *The Cambridge Companion to Hannah Arendt.* Ed. Dana Villa. 220–41.
Wilder, Gary. *Freedom Time: Negritude, Decolonization, and the Future of the World.* Durham: Duke UP, 2015.
———. *The French Imperial Nation-State: Negritude & Colonial Humanism between the Two World Wars.* Chicago: U of Chicago P, 2005.
Williams, Patricia J. *The Alchemy of Race and Rights.* Cambridge: Harvard UP, 1991.
Williams, Patrick. *Ngugi wa Thiong'o.* Manchester: Manchester UP; New York: St. Martin's, 1999.
Williams, Patrick, and Laura Chrisman, eds. *Colonial Discourse and Post-Colonial Theory: A Reader.* New York: Columbia UP, 1994.
Winkiel, Laura A. *Modernism, Race, and Manifestos.* Cambridge; New York: Cambridge UP, 2008.
Yaeger, Patricia. "Editor's Column: The End of Postcolonial Theory? A Roundtable with Sunil Agnani, Fernando Coronil, Gaurav Desai, Mamadou Diouf, Simon Gikandi, Susie Tharu, and Jennifer Wenzel." *PMLA* 122.3 (2007): 633–51.
Yoon, Duncan McEachern. "Translation and the Global South: Comparing Ngugi's *Globalectics* to Glissant's *Poetics.*" *Journal of Contemporary Thought* (Summer 2013): n. pag. Web.
Young, Robert. *White Mythologies: Writing History and the West.* London; New York: Routledge, 1990.

INDEX

Abani, Chris, 220, 221, 222, 223, 224, 225
abstraction, 25, 29, 46, 99, 123, 139, 143, 161, 167, 197, 213, 233
Achebe, Chinua, 221
African Americans, 88, 100
African Charter on Human and People's Rights, 204
African diaspora, 8, 9, 58, 105, 115
African National Congress (ANC): 122, 124, 135, 140, 231–32n1
African National Congress Youth League, 124
African socialism, 73, 74
Africans' Claims in South Africa, 124–25, 126–27, 130–31, 132
Afro-pessimism: 154. *See also* pessimism
Age of Revolution, 17, 18, 19, 78, 204
Algeria: anticolonialism, 9, 148, 151, 162, 167; constitution (1963), 149, 151–152, 153, 155; National Liberation Front, 152, 155, 167
American Law Institute, 86
American Revolution, 18, 228n6
Amnesty International, 208
Anderson, Benedict, 69, 183, 232n2
Anghie, Antony, 10
anticolonial theoretical tract, 186
anticolonialism: 2, 6, 54, 63, 160, 191, 218–19; in Africa, 8–9, 14; betrayals and failures of, 4, 5, 6, 14; black Atlantic, 9, 16, 23, 46, 51, 52, 76, 105, 225; as critical frame, 6, 9, 12, 15, 17, 67, 93, 126, 136, 144–45, 188, 209, 217, 219, 225–26; critiques of, 63, 198, 199; definitions of, 92, 93; as distinct from federation/departmentalization, 22, 23, 53, 91, 92, 195, 198, 228; as distinct from national liberation, 53, 79, 80, 92, 93, 122, 144, 198; heroism, 27, 39, 69, 75, 164, 175, 176, 222; human rights, 77–78, 190; and internationalism, 10, 12, 78; as periodizing term, 4, 5, 6, 30, 66, 76, 148, 155, 169, 191, 199, 224–25; as political movement, 15, 23, 66, 71–73, 77–8, 78–79, 121–22, 149, 153, 161, 181, 190, 218, 229–30, 230; resistance, 50, 121, 135, 167; revolution, 4, 14–15, 17, 21–22, 30, 47–48, 50, 63, 170, 187, 230; rhetorical performance, 2–3, 48, 52, 66, 96, 198, 224
antiwhite sentiment, 22, 25, 33, 39
Arendt, Hannah, 3, 34, 42, 46, 49, 133
Armitage, David, 25
Arnold, A. James, 93
assimilation, 92, 111
Atlantic (as concept), 1, 3, 7, 8, 9, 12, 13, 16, 17, 21, 22, 24, 25, 33, 46, 56, 57, 58, 93, 105, 108 109, 117, 118, 119, 126, 193, 194
Atlantic Charter, 7, 14, 93, 124–25, 126, 129, 130, 132
Austin, J. L.: *How to Do Things with Words*, 3, 19
authority: 4, 19–20, 21, 112, 120, 133, 162, 163, 178, 193, 195, 217; critiques of, 90, 94, 106; First World, 6, 10, 48–49, 78, 90, 103, 114; legal, 13, 42, 82, 84–85, 120, 127, 160, 193, 195; postcolonial, 3, 14, 17, 18, 47, 51–52, 54, 56–59, 65; representative, 96, 98–99, 108, 111, 115–16, 163, 167, 169–70, 175; textual assertions of, 72, 79, 80, 81–83, 88, 89, 102, 104, 107, 119, 123, 125, 136, 147; universal, 79, 81, 88, 89, 94, 106
authorship: 1, 2, 6, 22, 36, 37, 86, 94, 162, 217, 222; collective efforts, 56, 81, 85, 88, 96, 124, 127, 130, 131, 135, 136, 138, 139, 140, 176, 183, 185; conceptions, 81, 88, 126; legal authority, 14, 17, 127, 148; non-individual, 86, 166; reimaginings of, 13, 14, 18, 23, 123–24, 126–27, 166; and revolution, 49, 56–57, 229n5; universalism, 14, 89, 120
avant-garde aesthetics, 77, 111

Baldwin, James, 221
Bandung Conference, 104, 229–30n1

249

Berger, John, 94
Berman, Nathaniel, 81
Bernabé, Jean, 204
Bernasconi, Robert, 169, 170
Biafran War, 220, 223
Bible, 210
bills of rights (general), 83
black Atlantic: 1, 3, 9, 16, 17, 18, 28, 33, 40, 42, 47, 64, 82, 96, 105, 108, 123, 126, 127, 150, 216, 217, 227–28n5; history, 45, 115; negritude movement, 80, 109, 119; slave revolts, 13, 17, 49, 58, 65, 67, 71; studies, 7, 8, 9, 16, 117, 227–28n5
Black Consciousness, 122
black internationalism, 8, 9, 46, 51, 53, 62, 66, 76, 105, 109, 115, 117, 161, 189, 208
black nationhood: romance, 22–23
black personhood, 24
Black Power, 103
black transnationalism, 8–9, 46, 51, 53, 62, 66, 76, 105, 109, 116, 161, 189
blackness, 3, 15, 22, 36, 39–40, 41–42, 77, 108
Blixen, Karen, 210
Boisrond-Tonnerre, Louis, 24–25, 228n9
Bongie, Chris, 27, 199, 205
Bostock, Anna, 94
Bourdieu, Pierre, 166, 233n17
Breton, André, 93, 113, 114, 214
Bretton Woods Institutions, 93, 190
Brooks, Peter, 180
Burgess, Anthony, 209
Burke, Edmund, 54

cahier (as genre), 94, 95, 96
Cahier d'un retour au pays natal (Césaire): 14, 62–64, 72, 75, 76–80, 95, 81, 101–2, 104, 109, 119, 163–65, 168, 198, 225; as antimanifesto, 112, 113, 114; birthing imagery, 102, 103; conjuring and incantation, 118, 119; critique of imperialism, 90, 110, 199; critique of universality, 90, 99, 111; internationalism, 104, 109–10; negritude movement, 80, 94, 99–100, 104–5, 107, 109–11, 115–16, 119–20, 219, 230n4, 231n25; as speech act of anticolonial resistance, 96–97, 98, 104
Cameroon, 186, 187
Carby, Hazel, 51
Caribbean Discourse (Glissant): 191–93, 194–95, 199, 201, 203–4, 218, 235n5; Creole language, 195, 196–97, 204, 206; declarative form, 200, 201, 202, 206

Cassin, René, 85, 86
Castro, Fidel, 61
Césaire, Aimé: 2, 13–14, 23, 41, 46, 66, 103, 105, 114, 121, 161, 189, 193, 197, 198; anticolonialism, 92, 93; *Discours sur le colonialisme*, 10, 91; French National Assembly, 91–92, 231n22; *Lettre à Maurice Thorez*, 105, 106. See also *Cahier d'un retour au pays natal* (Césaire)
Césaire: 227n4
Chamoiseau, Patrick, 204
charismatic leadership, 4, 154, 172
charterism, 122
charters (as genre), 128, 129
Christophe, Henri, 34, 44, 53, 57, 58
Churchill, Winston, 124, 125, 126, 130
circulation of texts, 36, 65, 66, 68, 69, 136, 137, 138, 139
citizenship: 3, 13, 24, 28, 31, 35–38, 40–41, 68, 124–25, 151, 197, 198, 203. See also political belonging
civil rights, 87, 122, 153
class, 42, 50, 51, 99, 146, 167, 175, 185, 229n4
Cold War politics, 10–11, 77, 83, 84, 93, 120, 230n13
colonialism: 2, 4, 7, 21, 22, 68, 80, 82, 83, 89, 92, 103, 105–6, 114, 120, 125, 143, 149, 151, 156, 159, 161, 167, 186, 193, 195, 203, 208, 210, 214–15; in Africa, 2, 9, 14, 73, 105, 121–23, 143, 147, 152–53, 162; in Caribbean, 2, 28, 40, 43, 45, 49–50, 52, 105, 119, 200, 217n4; discourse, 2, 65, 70, 99, 103, 104; impacts of, 162, 167, 186, 189, 214–15, 217, 218; and law, 154, 155; racial exploitation, 7, 33, 82, 88, 110, 114, 203; of a "special type," 14, 121, 122, 231–32n1; struggle against, 208, 218, 228n10
Coloured People Organisation (South Africa), 135
Committee for the Release of Political Prisoners in Kenya, 208
communism: 66, 105, 114, 115, 119, 128. See also France: Communist Party; *Communist Manifesto*; Engels, Friedrich; Marx, Karl; Marxism
Communist Manifesto (Marx and Engels), 55, 112, 114–15, 117, 119
community: imagined, 18, 173, 183, 232n2; international, 2, 7, 10, 17–18, 24, 42–43, 47, 85, 211–12, 213–14, 215; postcolonial, 4, 13, 15, 17, 73, 122–23, 143–44, 148–49, 160, 167, 171, 185, 188; romance of, 22, 23, 138

comparative methodology, 2, 8, 11, 15, 55, 59, 61, 76, 104, 108, 109, 188, 189
confession, 178, 179, 180, 234n27
Confiant, Raphaël, 204
Congo, 170
Congress of Democrats (South Africa), 135
Congress of the People (COP), 122, 131, 133, 134–43, 144
Conrad, Joseph, 185
constitution-making (general), 19, 37, 42, 44, 150, 154–55, 186
constitutions: 4, 13, 34, 35, 38, 44, 86, 181, 233n17; African independence constitutions, 4, 12, 148–55, 159–60, 232; colonial versions, 34, 53, 153, 156, 158–59; "constitutions without constitutionalism," 150, 181; making of, 4, 19–20, 34–37, 42–44, 68, 146–48, 150–51, 153–55; postcolonial versions, 33, 35, 150–51, 153; written state as genre, 13, 17–18, 35–36, 42, 44, 128, 133, 144, 148–50, 152–53, 155–56, 186
convention (as genre), 84
Cooper, Frederick, 158
Corbet, Edward, 31
cosmopolitanism, 2, 11, 105, 109, 134, 143, 174, 212, 216, 218
covenant (as genre), 84
creativity, 52, 64, 69, 155, 161–62, 186, 199–200, 201
Creole: Haitian, 46, 47; Martinican and Guadeloupean, 189, 195, 196
Créoliste writers, 189, 204, 205, 206, 235n10
Creolization, 201, 202, 205
critical legal studies, 10
Critical Race Theory, 11, 12, 35, 40, 41, 228n12
Cronin, Jeremy, 122, 123, 135
Cuba, 61
cultural imperialism, 173
cultural rights, 85, 90, 132

Dalleo, Raphael, 79, 92–93
Damas, Leon, 104
Dante, 117
Davis, Gregson, 100, 116–17
Dayan, Joan, 36, 46
Déclaration des droits de l'homme et du cityoen, 3, 16, 18, 24, 28, 39, 54, 96, 111, 133, 194, 229n15
declarations of independence (as genre), 13, 18, 24, 28, 131, 132
declarations of international law, 84, 85, 123, 124, 127

declarations of rights (as genre), 18, 19, 24, 81, 83, 132, 133, 191
decolonization: 1, 4, 5, 12–14, 52, 60, 64, 76, 79, 146, 160–62, 165, 188, 233–34n19; in Africa, 9, 48, 50, 52, 53, 67, 73, 121, 148–50, 153–55, 160, 170–71, 185–86, 218, 233n14; aftereffects, 30, 73, 75–76, 92–93, 165, 198–99; in Caribbean, 4, 48, 50, 60, 150; European reaction, 121; rhetorical and performative contexts, 149, 162, 163, 168–69, 173, 176, 181, 182–84, 187; political and representational authority, 46, 163, 169
Deleuze, Gilles, 198
democracy, 17, 21, 22, 38, 127, 130, 153, 181, 212, 215, 220
departmentalization, 79, 91, 92, 93, 193, 198, 218, 231n22
Depestre, René, 90–91
Derrida, Jacques: 4, 19, 42, 119, 168; "Declarations of Independence," 20, 21; *Specters of Marx*, 115, 116
Dessalines, Jean-Jacques, 2, 24, 26, 27–28, 57–58, 228n9; anticolonialism, 22–23, 25, 38, 53, 228n7; Constitution of 1805 (Haiti), 33–34, 35–38, 41, 43–45, 229n14; Declaration of Independence (Haiti), 13, 29, 31, 31–32, 46, 54, 228n10
detour, 97
development, 11, 87, 90, 215
diaspora, 9, 105, 107, 109, 115, 228n7
Diderot, Denis, 59
difference (vs. opacity), 202, 208
Dirlik, Arif, 217
Douglass, Fredrick, 117
Du Bois, W. E. B., 88, 117, 129
Dubois, Laurent, 17

Edgar, Timothy, 209
Edmondson, Belinda, 51
Edwards, Brent Hayes, 8, 9
Eliot, T. S., 62
elites/elitism, 51, 58, 67, 147, 148, 153, 160, 165, 199, 229n4
Éloge de la Créolité (Bernabé, et al), 204, 205–6
emancipation law (French Antilles), 191, 192, 193, 194
empire: 6, 7, 10, 15, 202, 203, 210, 211, 216, 224, 231n18; as concept, 6; European, 1, 53, 88, 92; globalization, 15, 143, 144, 219; human rights/humanitarianism, 89, 90, 190; international law, 10; race, 12, 48

Engels, Friedrich: 55, 66. See also *Communist Manifesto* (Marx and Engels)
English, 184, 189, 207, 208, 209, 210, 211, 212, 213, 215, 216
Enlightenment, 16, 54, 56, 58, 80, 86, 119, 127, 133, 204, 213
ephemerality, 45, 47, 101, 115, 138, 153, 154, 155
equality, 16, 20, 21, 24, 34, 36, 38, 39
Eshleman, Clayton, 94
essay (postcolonial), 189, 190, 225
essentialism: 42, 111, 189, 199, 203, 205, 208, 223. *See also* strategic essentialism
Esterhammer, Angela, 59
ethics: anticolonialism, 14, 46, 78, 88, 90, 93, 94, 114, 119; as concept, 202, 215, 216, 223, 225; representational, 94, 96–99, 102–4, 110–11, 114–17, 119, 168, 178, 185, 225
Ethiopia, 49, 52
ethnicity, 122, 134, 146, 147, 151, 233n13, 234n24
Eurocentrism, 80, 111, 112, 123, 134, 151, 204
everyone (as concept), 202, 213
expressive lawmaking, 41
extralegality, 35, 81, 84, 85, 133, 142, 148, 158, 181, 186

failure: 5, 6, 14, 30, 45, 92, 93, 123, 149, 150, 154. *See also* success
family, 39, 40, 41, 42
Fanon, Frantz: 9, 17, 30, 162, 189, 218, 225, 233n14–15. *See also Wretched of the Earth* (Fanon)
Farred, Grant, 49, 71, 73
Fick, Carolyn, 46
First World: 10, 217; internationalism, 15, 116, 123, 129, 144; juridico-political imagination, 3, 6, 7, 12–13, 23, 79, 123, 144–45, 230n4; law and imperial rule, 2, 3, 78, 80, 150; political texts, 1, 48, 76, 79, 80, 127, 155; universalism, 14, 123
Fischer, Sibylle, 17, 34, 40, 41, 45
form, 3, 13, 14, 36, 80, 90, 91, 114, 120, 123, 162, 199, 200, 212
France: 54, 93, 95, 121; *cahiers de doleances*, 95, 96, 99; colonialism, 22, 89, 152, 201, 203; Communist Party, 93, 105; constitution of 1791, 4, 20, 38, 44; French Revolution, 16, 20, 34, 45; Frenchness, 26, 27, 91; National Assembly, 24, 54, 191
Fraser, Nancy, 109
Freedom Charter (South Africa): 9, 14, 122, 124, 129–30, 136, 143; critics, 138, 139; drafting, 131, 133, 137, 138–39, 140; international law, 133, 134, 144; as North Atlantic juridico-political challenge, 123–24, 130–31; racial equality, 130, 137, 144, 231–32n1; as South African regime challenge, 123, 127, 128, 130–32, 139
Friedland, Paul, 95
Front Antillo-Guyanais de l'Autonomie, 198
futurity, 170, 205

Gaffield, Julia, 31
Garraway, Doris, 25
Garvey, Marcus, 62, 109
gender, 8, 41–42, 50–52, 167, 175–76, 234n21
Gennaro, Mara de, 108
genocide, 83, 201
Ghai, Yash, 151, 154, 232n5
Ghana, 67–68, 69, 70–72, 75, 170
Gikuyu (language), 184, 207, 209, 216, 217, 235n13
Gilroy, Paul, 7, 8, 9, 16, 117, 135–36, 227–28n5
Girard, Philippe, 228n7
Glissant, Edouard: 2, 15, 76, 97, 188–89, 219, 227n4; critiques of Césaire, 197, 198, 199, 200; negritude, 199, 200, 205; *opacité*, 201, 202–3, 204, 206, 207, 235n8; *Poetics of Relation*, 189, 198, 199, 201, 202, 203, 204, 205; postcolonial theory, 189, 190, 199, 218; radical multilingualism, 15, 189–90, 191, 205, 209, 219. *See also Caribbean Discourse* (Glissant)
global capitalism, 208, 212, 217, 221, 222, 223
Global North, 5, 8, 10, 13, 17, 105
Global South, 4, 6–7, 10, 89, 90, 133, 218
globalization, 5–6, 11, 15, 209–10, 212, 219
Go, Julian, 150
Grain of Wheat (Ngũgĩ), 14, 149, 170–73, 177–85, 184, 188, 222, 234n24, 234n29; criticisms of, 172, 174, 176; readers as active participants, 181, 182; speaker heroism, 174, 176, 234n25; testimonials as narrative device, 176, 178
Great Britain. *See* United Kingdom (UK)
Greenblatt, Stephen, 214
Grenada, 76
Guadeloupe, 91, 121
Guattari, Félix, 198
Guberina, Petar, 104

Haggard, Rider, 210
Haiti: 40, 43, 72, 93, 116, 121, 150, 154; anticolonialism, 23, 46–47, 79; Constitution (1805), 3, 4, 12, 13, 17, 22, 33–47, 140; 184

INDEX · 253

Declaration of Independence (1804), 1, 13, 17, 22, 23–33, 34, 35, 37, 54, 130, 140; end of slavery, 13, 53, 194; Haitian Revolution, 13, 16–17, 21–22, 45, 47, 49, 57–58, 61, 62, 65–66, 229n4
Hall, Stuart, 65, 227–28n5
Hallward, Peter, 199
Harambee, 146
Hardt, Michael, 92
hauntology: 119. *See also* spectrality
heroism: 117, 140; anticolonial, 27, 69, 176; collective, 164, 165, 181; devotional, 98, 99; revolutionary, 50, 51, 52, 58, 85; rhetorical, 71, 73, 75. *See also* speaker-heroism
history: from below, 51, 58; of the present, 49, 61, 64, 65, 67, 70, 71, 72; revolutionary, 49, 55–56, 58, 62, 64–67, 70–74, 76; writing of, 49, 51, 58, 61, 64, 65, 66, 70, 71
Høgsbjerg, Christian, 52, 53
Holocaust, 120
Horton, Robert, 209
Huddleston, Trevor, 143
Hulme, Peter, 214
human rights: 4, 10–11, 14, 81–84, 87–89, 94, 112, 132–35, 153, 191, 208; activism, 204; and anticolonialism, 77–78, 80, 90; discourses of, 6–7, 17, 78, 87, 89–90, 120, 145, 190–91, 206, 208–209, 214, 217–18, 229–30n1, 231n18; as internationalism, 78, 82, 88; law, 11, 105, 242n10; movements, 79, 89, 90, 190, 204; as mechanisms of empire, 89, 101; universalism, 15, 16, 77, 79–80, 94, 123, 190, 202, 204, 212–13. *See also* Universal Declaration of Human Rights
humanism, 54, 63–64, 76, 80, 110–11, 114, 161–62, 168–70, 199–200, 203–4, 206, 212, 234n20
humanitarian law, 10
humanitarianism, 6, 89, 120, 203, 217
Humphrey, John, 83, 86
Husson, Louis Thomas, 191, 192, 193, 194, 195–96, 197, 208
Huxley, Elspeth, 210

immediacy, 32–33, 58, 68, 130, 136, 138, 161, 184, 233n15
imperialism: 6, 7, 10, 92, 105, 109–110, 152, 173, 208; internationalism, 78, 82, 88, 111, 120, 123, 124, 129, 134, 143, 144, 208, 212; and language, 207, 208, 209–17, 209–11, 214, 215
incarnation, 59, 61

India, 89, 174
Indian Council (South Africa), 135
indigeneity, 27, 39, 152, 154, 220, 234n29
instability, 4, 45
Institute of the Black World, 64
intellectuals/intellectualism, 8, 23, 48–49, 55, 69, 71, 73, 76, 99, 103, 166, 168–70, 200, 212, 213. *See also* organic intellectual; postcolonial intellectual; vernacular intellectual
Inter-American Juridical Committee, 86
International Labour Organization Convention Concerning Indigenous and Tribal Peoples in Independent Countries, 204
international law: 1, 5, 10, 14, 80–81, 84, 88, 120, 132–33, 143, 144; changes in, 46, 81; postcolonialism, 11–12, 77, 78, 120, 123; reappraisals of, 80, 125, 126–29, 134; revisionist histories of, 10, 11
internationalism: 81, 94, 144, 203; Atlantic, 126; black, 105; imperialism, 88, 120
internationalism(s), 7, 15, 77–79, 94, 104–6, 108–11, 114–15, 120, 126, 203, 208, 218
Irele, Abiola, 102, 109
Itote, Waruhiu, 157, 159

James. C. L. R.: 2, 9, 13, 16, 23, 46, 51–53, 121, 171; anticolonialism, 52, 53, 67, 79; *At the Rendezvous of Victory*, 66, 75; *Beyond a Boundary*, 71; black internationalism, 161, 229n4; *Black Jacobins*, 49, 50, 51, 52, 53–54, 56, 57, 58, 59–62, 64–66, 72, 75, 229n6; *A History of Negro Revolt*, 50, 53, 57, 58, 66, 72–73; *A History of the Pan-African Revolt*, 66, 72, 73, 74, 75; *Nkrumah and the Ghana Revolution*, 50, 66, 67–71, 72–73, 74, 75; Pan-Africanism, 219; revolutionary heroism, 51, 52, 57, 58, 75; use of romance, 50, 51, 52, 59, 62, 66, 71
Jefferson, Thomas, 18, 55, 86
Jenson, Deborah, 17, 27, 29, 228n9, 229n5
Jim Crow, 88, 129
Johnson-Forest Tendency, 60
Joseph, Miranda, 22
Julien, Eileen, 175

Kadalie, Clements, 57
Kariuki, Miwangi, 157, 232n11, 232–33n12
katabasis, 116, 117, 118, 119
Kennedy, David, 10
Kenya: 9, 52, 151, 170, 189, 149; anticolonialism, 147, 156, 157, 158, 159, 160, 179, 187,

208, 218; colonial state of emergency, 147, 156, 171, 172, 175, 176, 177, 179, 187; Constitutional Conference, 147, 148; cultural memory, 148, 159–60; Electors' Union's "Kenya Plan," 159; independence constitution, 146, 147–48, 151, 153, 155, 156, 185; Kenyan African Democratic Union, 151; Kenyan National African Union, 151; Mau Mau liberation struggle, 147, 155, 157, 160, 171, 179, 232n1
Kenyatta, Jomo, 146, 147, 148, 151, 153, 156, 159–60, 234n25
Kimathi, Dedan, 156
King, Richard, 49
Kiswahili, 209, 212, 216, 235n13
Klein, Naomi, 123
Kuti, Fela, 223, 224

L'Ouverture, Toussaint: 13, 22, 34, 64, 66, 228n7, 229n5; critiques of, 45, 50, 51, 53, 55–59, 61, 72, 76; Haitian Constitution (1805), 34, 37; relationship with France, 54–55, 68
Lamine Guèye Act (1946), 91
Lamming, George, 9, 208
language (general), 15, 36, 46–47, 184–85, 189, 195, 197, 200, 203–4, 208–11, 213–18
laughter, 182, 187
Lauren, Paul Gordon, 87
law: 1, 35; and force, 4, 20, 21, 35, 42; legality and legal legitimacy, 45, 158, 159; and literature, 11, 80, 81, 148; paradoxes of, 2, 47; United States, 3, 12. *See also* colonialism: and law; international law
Lawrence, D. H., 185
Lazarus, Neil, 5, 6, 170, 190, 235n4
League of Nations, 48, 88
legal positivism, 83
Lenin, Vladimir, 48, 74
Levellers, 68
linguistic diversity, 189, 190, 196, 211, 216
literacy: 36, 46–47, 57–58, 68–69, 74, 162, 195. *See also* prodigal literacy
literary (concept), 79
logos, 133, 136
Loomba, Ania, 5
Louis XVI, 95
Luthuli, Albert, 139, 140, 141, 143
Lyon, Janet, 68

Malouf, Michael, 109
Mandela, Nelson, 128, 139, 141, 143

manifesto: 54, 120, 160, 161167, 168, 206, 225, 233n14; modernist/surrealist, 78, 94, 112–14, 205, 209, 214, 216; socialist, 94, 112, 114, 115. *See also Cahier d'un retour au pays natal* (Césaire): as antimanifesto; *Communist Manifesto* (Marx and Engels); *Wretched of the Earth*: as manifesto
Martinique: 97, 121, 194, 198, 201–2, 218, 227n4; departmentalization, 79, 92, 93, 193, 194, 198; national identity, 195, 196, 197, 199, 202; slavery emancipation, 189, 193, 197
Marx, Karl: 48, 55, 66. *See also Communist Manifesto* (Marx and Engels)
Marxism, 50, 106, 112, 222
masses: 4, 51, 56, 57, 58, 65, 70, 163, 164, 165, 166, 167, 169, 172, 174, 186, 187. *See also* people
Matthews, Z. K., 122, 127, 130, 134
Mau Mau loyalty oaths, 14, 149, 156–58, 159, 160, 177, 186, 187, 232n11, 232–33n12, 233n13
Mau Mau memoirs, 156, 157, 158, 159, 160, 232n11
Mau Mau movement, 147, 156, 157, 158, 159, 171, 172, 178, 232n1, 232–33n12
Mayflower Compact, 35
Mazower, Mark, 82, 88
Mazrui, Alamin, 176
Mbembe, Achille, 186, 187
McAuslan, Patrick, 151
McKay, Claude, 109
meetings (public), 140, 141, 166, 171, 172, 176, 177, 178, 179, 180, 183, 184, 187
Melas, Natalie, 97
Melville, Herman, 51
Michelet, Jules, 65
Middle Passage, 103, 107, 117, 227n4
Miller, Paul, 57
Minh-ha, Trinh T., 166
mode of emplotment, 49, 50, 51
modernism: legal/political, 81, 234n29; literary, 78, 112, 171, 185, 234n29
modernity: 24; counterculture, 7, 16; revolutionary, 2, 3, 47
Moi, Daniel, 9, 208
monolingualism, 196, 197, 204
Monserratt, Nicholas, 210
Morsink, Johannes, 84, 85, 88, 230n6
Moyn, Samuel, 10, 77–78, 82, 229–30n1
Mphande, Lupenga, 176

Mussolini, Benito, 49, 52
Mutua, Makau, 120

Napoleon, 22, 33, 40, 53
nation-state (as concept), 5, 6, 11, 12, 17, 18, 105, 144, 234n29
National Action Council (South Africa), 135, 136, 138
National Association for the Advancement of Colored People (NAACP), 88
national bourgeoisie, 160, 162, 163, 186
national consciousness/identity: 24, 31, 40, 62, 178, 195; in Haiti, 17, 26, 41–42, 54, 62; in Kenya, 151, 218; in Martinique, 195, 196; transformation of, 165, 166, 199
national liberation, 5, 12, 49, 53, 78–79, 92, 121, 144, 148–49, 160, 188, 190, 208, 217–18
national literature, 200
National Negro Congress, 88
national self-determination, 78, 80, 90, 93, 125, 127, 153, 229–30n1
nationalism, 5, 25, 79, 105, 109, 129, 152, 194, 196, 202, 218
nationhood, 17, 19, 22–23, 34, 37, 39, 135, 139, 147, 156, 161, 183, 185, 218, 224
natural law and rights, 24, 33, 38, 39, 41, 132, 133, 213
Nazism, 125
Negri, Antonio, 92
negritude movement: 62, 63, 66, 77, 106, 111. *See also* black Atlantic: negritude; *Cahier d'un retour au pays natal* (Césaire): negritude movement; Glissant, Edouard: negritude
nekuia, 116, 118, 119
neocolonialism, 4, 73, 92, 150, 163, 171, 185, 208, 210, 215
neoliberalism, 5, 11, 210, 217
Nesbitt, Nick, 92
Ngũgĩ wa Thiong'o: 2, 9, 15, 76, 170, 202, 207–8, 219, 221, 225, 235n13; "Kĩĩngeretha Rũ thiomi Rwa Thĩ Yoothe?" / "English: A Language for the World," 207, 208, 209–14, 216–17, 218; *Petals of Blood,* 171, 185, 234n25; postcolonial theory, 188–89, 190, 207; radical multilingualism, 15, 216–17, 189, 191, 209, 212, 219. See also *Grain of Wheat* (Ngũgĩ)
Nigeria, 221, 222, 223, 224
Nkrumah, Kwame, 60, 67–68, 69–70, 71, 72, 229n6
novel (as genre), 144, 148, 171, 181, 184, 185
Nyerere, Julius, 13, 73, 74, 75, 76

oaths/oath-taking: 4, 24, 28, 29, 30, 31, 32, 33, 37, 130, 149, 156, 159. *See also* Mau Mau loyalty oaths
obscurity: 197, 201. *See also* Glissant, Edouard: *opacité*
Okoth-Ogendo, H. W. O., 181
On Revolution (Arendt), 18–20, 21, 45, 228n6
opacity. *See* Glissant, Edouard: *opacité*
oral/live performance, 28–29, 31, 33, 35, 36, 43–44, 68, 70, 135–36, 140, 141–43, 158, 176, 182, 184, 209
orality, 3, 33, 136, 138, 157, 176, 184, 233n15
orators/oratory, 50, 54, 57, 70
orature, 184, 185
organic intellectual, 55
Orgel, Stephen, 103

Padmore, George, 53
Pan Africanist Congress, 122
Pan-Africanism, 49, 50, 53, 63, 65, 73, 219, 227n4
Parry, Benita, 5, 161
Parsons, Anthony, 209
particularity, 104–5, 106, 108, 111, 131, 137, 162, 216
Patterson, Orlando, 210
Peaslee, Amos, 151
people (the): 13, 31, 33, 35, 36, 37, 38, 42, 49, 58, 67, 69, 70, 73, 74, 124, 129, 132, 134, 135, 138, 139, 140, 142, 149, 151, 159, 160, 162, 163, 164, 165, 166, 167, 175, 186, 200
performance/performativity: 4, 13, 15. *See also* anticolonialism: rhetorical performance; decolonization: rhetorical and performative contexts; oral/live performance; *Wretched of the Earth* (Fanon): performance of anticolonial resistance
pessimism: 46, 73, 186, 224. *See also* Afro-pessimism
Pétion, Alexandre, 22, 44, 53
Philip (Duke of Edinburgh), 209
Piot, Charles, 227–28n5
poetics, 191, 195, 196, 197, 204, 206, 207, 219
poetry, 91, 112
political action techniques, 4, 135, 137, 139, 166, 178, 180
political ambivalence, 50, 51, 52, 163, 168
political belonging, 6, 12, 13, 14, 18, 76, 79, 81
political community: 6, 45, 49, 51, 69, 76, 78, 116, 117, 129, 137, 145, 164, 217, 219, 234n21; authorship/authority, 18, 19, 79; performance, 13, 31, 136, 143, 158, 159, 165, 171, 225;

postcolonial, 3–4, 23–24, 70, 78, 123, 130, 132–33, 134–36, 149, 160, 187; race, 8, 34, 42; rhetoric, 20, 50, 132, 148, 158, 159, 165, 225
political legibility, 1, 3, 12, 40, 41, 47, 54, 58, 105, 110, 127, 137
political representation: 6, 51, 81, 158; in Aimé Césaire's work, 78, 90, 94, 95, 96, 108, 114, 115, 116, 165, 225; in C. L. R. James's work, 59, 61; in Frantz Fanon's work, 163, 164, 165, 167, 169, 225; in Haiti, 13, 17, 36–37, 47; in Ngũgĩ wa Thiong'o's work, 175, 178, 181, 225; in South Africa, 136, 139, 142; United Nations, 89, 120, 123, 126
politics of fulfillment, 135, 136
politics of transfiguration, 135, 136
populism, 9, 14, 68, 73, 131, 141, 161
post-colonial bildungsroman, 11
post-independence period, 5, 6, 7, 45, 72, 153–55, 160, 181
postcolonial (periodizing term), 188
postcolonial human rights studies, 11
postcolonial intellectuals, 63, 73, 212, 217
postcolonial legal studies, 10
postcolonial literature, 11, 12, 185, 188, 207, 214, 228n11
postcolonial present, 2, 6, 52, 64, 66, 218, 219, 224
postcolonial rights, 204, 206
postcolonial states, 4
postcolonial studies, 5, 6, 11, 46, 148, 189, 191, 207, 214, 217, 227n4, 228n11
postcolonial theory, 5, 15, 45, 52, 188–89, 190–91, 207, 217, 218, 227n4, 235n4
postcoloniality as imagined future, 2, 17, 67, 73–76, 79–80, 93, 127, 131, 134, 143–44, 147–48, 152, 155, 161, 165–66, 169–71, 189, 199, 209, 226
poststructuralism, 189
Priam, Mylène, 205
print culture, 35, 36, 69
problem-space, 78, 80, 81
prodigal literacy, 57, 58, 73–74
public sphere, 50, 180
Puchner, Martin, 112, 169

Quayson, Ato, 175, 234n25

race: 8, 11, 12, 22, 34, 36, 40, 41, 47, 106, 122; colonial racism, 17, 77; exploitation, 9, 34, 109, 114; paternalism: 192, 193; violence, 21, 33. See also African Americans; blackness; scientific racism

radical multilingualism. See Glissant, Edouard: radical multilingualism; Ngũgĩ wa Thiong'o: radical multilingualism
reading publics, 29, 48, 69
reappearance, 61, 62, 64
reconciliation, 147
relation, 193, 190, 203, 205
Renan, Ernest, 147
representation: abstract, 78, 96, 99, 167; aesthetic, 94, 165; subalternity, 37, 51, 57, 59, 60, 64, 65, 70, 99, 166
representative democracy, 153, 158
republication, 50, 64, 65, 66, 70, 72, 112
Resha, Robert, 141, 142
resistance: 2, 8. See also anticolonialism: resistance; Cahier d'un retour au pays natal (Césaire): as speech act of anticolonial resistance; Wretched of the Earth (Fanon): performance of anticolonial resistance
Réunion, 121
revolution: anticolonial/black, 14–15, 17, 21, 30, 48–50, 59, 63–64, 66–67, 73, 75, 162; as concept, 3, 4, 15–16, 18–21, 24, 35, 49, 51–52, 58, 79, 96, 102, 115, 123, 140, 149, 162, 194, 228; from below, 51, 74. See also American Revolution; France: French Revolution; Haiti: Haitian Revolution
revolutionary discourse, 51, 55
Rights of Man, 17, 21, 24, 25, 44, 54, 203, 204
rights/rights discourse, 35, 81, 133, 142, 151, 191, 201, 203, 204, 206, 216
Robbins, Bruce, 104, 106, 218
Robespierre, Maximilien, 59
Robinson, Cedric, 9, 229n4
romance: 49, 62–63, 66, 70, 71, 75, 76, 103, 123, 124, 138–39, 149, 222, 225; anticolonial/black, 2, 3, 13, 14, 22, 23, 50, 51, 52; romanticism, 59, 60; romanticization, 22, 45, 51, 85, 91, 104
Roosevelt, Eleanor, 83, 140, 230n7
Roosevelt, Franklin Delano, 82, 124, 125, 126, 130
Rousseau, Jean-Jacques, 39

Saint-Lot, Émile, 85
Saracen Indians, 10
Sarkozy, Nicholas, 218
Saudi Arabia, 88
Schoelcher, Victor, 193, 198
Schoeman, Van Zil, 143
scientific racism, 10

Scott, David, 2, 49, 50, 60, 78, 81, 171
Second Congress of Black Writers and Artists, 162
self-determination (as a right), 78, 89, 90, 125, 127, 153, 229–30n1
Senghor, Léopold Sédar, 104, 230n4
Slaughter, Joseph, 11, 12, 87, 132, 230n10
slavery: 16, 17, 19, 21–22, 25, 34, 35, 40, 45, 47, 53, 54, 56, 99, 191, 194, 203, 227n4; abolition of, 23, 36, 53, 191, 192, 193, 194, 197; Atlantic slave trade, 7, 8, 9, 105, 108, 231n29; in Haiti, 36, 44, 47; slave ships, 107, 117, 118, 119; in U.S., 36, 40. *See also* Middle Passage
Smith, Annette, 94
Smuts, Jan, 88
Snyder, Émile, 94
social and economic rights, 87, 132, 206
social death, 210
socialism, 74, 152
solidarity, 8, 22, 37, 41, 51, 59, 61, 78, 94, 104, 106, 107–10, 114–15, 117, 119, 122, 130, 136, 147, 156–57, 160, 222
song, 176, 177, 182, 183, 223, 224
South Africa: 57, 122, 124, 128, 129, 140, 135; anticolonialism, 121–22, 144, 231–32n1; anti-apartheid movement, 122, 124, 135, 139, 140, 176; apartheid, 88, 121, 123, 127, 132, 144, 159, 159; civil disobedience, 124–25; Congress of the People Campaign, 2, 124, 127, 128; Kliptown meeting, 135, 138, 139, 140–43; National Party, 121, 124; Treason Trial, 128, 143. *See also* Freedom Charter
Soviet Union, 84, 88
speaker-heroism: 170, 225; in Aimé Césaire's work, 118–119, 163, 164, 165, 225; in C. L. R. James's work, 50, 51–52, 67, 71, 75. *See also Grain of Wheat* (Ngũgĩ): speaker-heroism
spectrality, 115, 116, 117, 118, 119, 120, 179
speech acts/speech acts theory, 3–4, 19–21, 30–33, 50, 58, 64, 79, 96–99, 115–16, 118–19, 148–49, 157–58, 160–61, 165, 180–81
speeches (public/political): 3, 35; in Aimé Césaire's work, 63, 64, 78; in C. L. R. James's work, 50, 57, 58, 69–70, 71; in Chris Abani's work, 220, 221, 222, 223, 224; in Edouard Glissant's work, 191, 192, 193, 194; in Frantz Fanon's work, 162, 163, 164–65; Haitian Declaration of Independence, 28, 29, 30, 32–33;

Haitian Constitution, 47; Kenyan freedom struggle, 146, 147, 147, 151; in Ngũgĩ wa Thiong'o's work, 172, 173, 174, 176, 177, 178, 179, 180, 181, 234n27; South African freedom struggle, 140, 141
Spivak, Gayntri Chokravortv, 191, 217
spontaneity, 42, 59, 74, 130, 172, 173, 174, 177, 183, 186, 224
Springfield, Consuelo, 50
Stephens, Michelle, 51, 105
strategic essentialism, 41, 42, 45, 63, 108
success: 5, 6, 14, 47, 92, 123. *See also* failure
surrealism, 93, 105, 112, 113, 114
Suttner, Raymond, 122, 123, 135

Taino-Arawaks, 27, 39
Tanzania, 13, 73, 75
temporality: 5, 17, 18, 23, 25, 36, 46, 47, 56, 73, 74, 75, 87, 135, 136, 137, 138, 139, 140, 150, 157, 181, 184, 195, 197, 216; constitutional, 42, 44, 152; declarations, 19, 20, 21, 24, 31, 32, 33, 54, 124, 132, 133, 161, 227n1; nationhood, 183, 193, 194; revolutionary, 19, 20, 21, 30, 34, 35, 42, 62, 79, 114, 115, 168, 169, 186; textual representation, 59, 131, 142, 168
theatricality, 112, 114
Third World, 50, 90, 92, 190, 198, 201, 217, 229–30n1
Tocqueville, Alexis de, 96
tragedy, 20, 49, 50, 123, 171
transatlanticism, 15, 18, 56, 134, 192, 194, 219
Transcontinental Railroad, 109
transhistoricism, 61, 62, 114, 116, 117, 118, 119
translation, 8, 195, 197, 207, 211, 216
transnationalism, 8, 9, 51, 78, 79, 104, 106, 109, 114, 116, 119, 134, 145, 211, 215, 216, 217
transversal reading practice, 7, 227n4
Trinidad, 71, 72, 229n6
Trotsky, Leon, 48, 62, 65
Truark, Robert, 210

U.S. Bill of Rights, 19
U.S. Constitution, 18, 34–35, 36–37, 38, 43–44
U.S. Declaration of Independence, 3, 18, 19, 23–24, 28–30, 54, 55, 86, 96, 140, 168
U.S. Federal Bureau of Investigation (FBI), 60
Uhuru, 181, 182
Uhuru ceremonies, 147, 151, 171, 178, 180, 182, 183
United Democratic Front, 122
United Kingdom (UK): 18, 84, 88, 89, 156

United Nations (UN): 48, 82–83, 88, 93, 129; Charter, 82, 83, 230n6; Commission on Human Rights (CHR), 81, 82, 83, 84, 88, 89, 120; General Assembly, 77, 84, 85, 87; United Nations Educational, Scientific and Cultural Organization (UNESCO), 88, 89. *See also* Universal Declaration of Human Rights

United States: 82, 84, 92. *See also* American Revolution; U.S. Bill of Rights; U.S. Constitution; U.S. Declaration of Independence; U.S. Federal Bureau of Investigation (FBI)

universal applicability, 83, 85, 105, 120, 134, 137, 202

Universal Declaration of Human Rights: 14, 77, 78, 80, 88, 93, 129, 132–33, 190, 202, 230n6; colonialism, 82, 88, 89, 120; debates over, 83, 85, 86; drafting of, 83, 85, 120, 140; internationalism, 105, 111, 120; pedagogical function, 84, 85, 87, 88; racial exploitation, 82, 88;

Universal Declaration of the Rights of Peoples, 203, 204

universalism/universality: 80, 88, 89, 90, 105, 111, 119–20, 134, 213; abstract universalism, 14, 25, 94, 123, 127; as anti-internationalism, 81, 90, 94, 105, 110, 111. *See also* authority: universal; authorship: universalism; *Cahier d'un retour au pays natal* (Césaire): universality; First World: universalism; human rights: universalism

utopianism: 2, 6, 11, 52, 82, 93, 120, 135–36, 137, 139, 167, 202, 212, 218. *See also* romance

vernacular intellectual, 73
Versailles Treaty, 150
violence: anticolonial warfare, 30, 167; colonial, 7, 17, 19, 27, 33, 94, 97, 152, 167, 210;
founding or revolutionary, 3, 4, 19, 20, 21, 25, 35, 163, 167, 169, 173;
Virgil, 117
Viswanathan, Gauri, 217
Vitoria, Francisco, 10
vodou, 47, 93

Walcott, Derek, 109
Warner, Michael, 35, 36, 44
Wayne, John, 221
we (collective political entity), 37–38, 42, 96, 99–102, 129–30, 132, 139–40, 165–66, 178–79, 181, 183, 202, 205, 222
Weimar Constitution, 150
Wenzel, Jennifer, 6
West Indian Federation, 60, 61
Western intellectual/textual traditions, 18, 49, 50, 54, 55, 56, 59, 74, 153, 173, 185
Westminster constitutional model, 151
White, Hayden, 49
whiteness, 40, 41
Wilder, Gary, 93, 230n4
will to transcendence, 175, 181
Williams, Eric, 60, 229n6
Winkiel, Laura, 54
Wretched of the Earth (Fanon): 14, 26–27, 76, 149, 160, 164, 169–70, 187, 199–200, 234n21; conceptions of the masses, 166, 167; critique of anticolonial creativity, 162, 163; as manifesto, 160–61, 167–68, 169–70, 233n14; as performance of anticolonial resistance, 161, 162; postcolonial political elite, 165–66, 181; spontaneity, 172–73, 174
Wright, Richard, 117

Xuma, Alfred Bitini, 125–26, 131

Young, Robert, 160, 161

www.ingramcontent.com/pod-product-compliance
Lightning Source LLC
Chambersburg PA
CBHW020644230426
43665CB00008B/305